Perspectives on
the Philosophy of Wittgenstein

Edited by IRVING BLOCK

Basil Blackwell · Oxford

© Basil Blackwell Publisher Limited 1981

First published 1981
Basil Blackwell Publisher
108 Cowley Road
Oxford OX4 1JF
England

British Library Cataloguing in Publication Data

Perspectives on the philosophy of Wittgenstein.
  1. Philosophy, English – 20th century – Congresses
  I. Block, Irving
  192   B3376.W564

ISBN 0-631-19550-5

Printed in Great Britain at
The Camelot Press Ltd, Southampton

Contents

Preface

This volume grew out of the Wittgenstein Colloquium held in London, Ontario, Canada commemorating the twenty-fifth anniversary of Wittgenstein's death on 29 April 1951. Some of the papers appear as they were given but others, including those by Dr Blackwell and Professors Cioffi, Stenius and Winch, have been substantially revised or expanded. Professor Kripke has entirely rewritten and expanded the address he originally gave at the Colloquium. It is regretted that, for various reasons, not all the papers given there are included in this volume.

I would like to express my appreciation to my colleague, Bill Demopoulos, who gave me valuable advice on a number of matters and to Connie Varner for her help in editing some of the material. Mr Kai Halweg aided me in taping the sessions of the Colloquium. I owe a debt of gratitude to Penny Lister who industriously typed through various drafts and redrafts.

I take this opportunity to thank the Canada Council for a grant in support of the Colloquium and to thank Dr John Rowe, Dean of the Faculty of Arts at the University of Western Ontario, whose encouragement and support made the Colloquium possible.

Irving Block
London, Ontario

Introduction

IRVING BLOCK

The essays published in this volume range over a wide area of
Wittgenstein's thought. More significantly, they represent divergent interpretations of Wittgenstein's fundamental ideas. It is now over
twenty-five years since Wittgenstein's death and there is still no general
consensus as to how one should understand his philosophy. It is
characteristic of any great philosopher that his work has a certain
subtlety that lends itself to a variety of interpretation. So it is with
Wittgenstein; but his philosophy was, at the time of his writing, so
original and even revolutionary, that it led to quite unusual disparity of
understanding. The purpose of this introduction is to indicate some of
the different perspectives on Wittgenstein's thought found in the essays.

Mr McGuinness takes the apparently realistic metaphysics suggested
in the first paragraphs of the *Tractatus* as a kind of 'myth', or as a heuristic
device to get us to see something about the nature of a proposition.
Wittgenstein never intended these remarks as a piece of traditional
metaphysics. Names do not designate concrete particulars and the formation of elementary sentences from names is not dependent upon
arriving first at the 'meanings' of names through ostension. The
converse was true of Russell's atomism, and thus for Russell there could
be no false atomic propositions. In the *Tractatus*, however, the formation
of elementary propositions was a strictly formal matter involving no
empirical concern for the truth of the proposition. The sense of a proposition is independent of its truth and therefore elementary propositions could be true or false. The 'seeing' of the sense of a proposition
was a matter of 'logic' not science or empirical observation. This is what
is meant by a proposition 'showing' its sense. The objects and substance
of the 1's and 2's of the *Tractatus* are terms that refer to structure or
logical space which is *a priori* or 'unalterable' (2.023). All the interpretations, from Russell onwards, that saw in the *Tractatus* an attempt to

say something about the nature of the world of concrete things have been misguided.

Mr Pears' essay, which attempts to reconstruct the argument that led Wittgenstein in the *Tractatus* to promulgate his doctrine of the logical independence of elementary propositions, gives us just such an interpretation. This doctrine, Mr Pears argues, is the culmination of the demand that the sense of a proposition be determinate and that in the ultimate analysis we have only one name for each simple particular so that there can be no "competition" among names (see p. 84). These simple particulars Wittgenstein called 'objects' and it would seem to be a matter of empirical analysis of language and the world to isolate names and objects, not of formal analysis. The text of the *Tractatus* lends itself to both Mr Pears' and Mr McGuinness' interpretation and therefore provides difficulties for both.

One can see in Miss Ishiguro's essay some affinities with Mr McGuinness' interpretation. Wittgenstein's denial of the possibility of a simple theory of types was based on the doctrine of 'showing' – that one cannot formulate a theory that will tell you when a proposition is well-formed. If it is understood and has a use, it is well-formed. As Miss Ishiguro says, "Understanding what is said by using a sentence, then, is a primitive notion" (p. 44). But if understanding a sentence is a primitive notion, one does not require a theory of types to guide one in the formation of sentences. This understanding is purely 'logical' or formal. The connection between Miss Ishiguro's paper and Mr McGuinness' might be expressed by saying that the formal side of the *Tractatus* expressed in the notion of 'showing' that Mr McGuinness emphasizes, is the source of Wittgenstein's rejection of a theory of types or any kind of meta-language that purports to 'say' when a proposition is well-formed.

The essays by Dr Hacker and Professor Stenius provide different viewpoints on one of Wittgenstein's most enigmatic conceptions, the picture theory of meaning. A question common to both papers is how far Wittgenstein went in rejecting the picture theory of meaning in his later writings. This question is tied to the further issue of how necessary the structure of logical atomism is for the theory. Dr Hacker takes the view that the picture theory is inseparable from the atomism of the *Trac-tatus* and that ". . . without atomism and isomorphism, there is no picture theory of the proposition, but only the phenomenon of the pictoriality of thought and its attendant puzzles" (p. 106). Professor Stenius on the other hand believes that the picture theory, though connected with the atomism of the *Tractatus*, can nevertheless stand on its own as a plausible and workable theory of sentence meaning. Wittgenstein never rejected this theory, though he may have modified it in his later writings. All those passages in the later writings which refer to the 'pictoriality' of the proposition, Professor Stenius sees as a refinement of the picture theory of the *Tractatus*. Professor Stenius' paper is an attempt to work out a more precise formulation of the picture theory without the encumbrance of logical atomism.

Several of the essays deal with the possibility of a theory of language. One of the themes of Mr Dummett's essay is that Wittgenstein's rejection of Frege's assertion sign, whereby an assertion is formed by adding assertoric 'force' to the *Annahme* or unasserted proposition, undercuts all possibility of a systematic theory of language. Mr Dummett thinks that Wittgenstein's intention in the *Philosophical Investigations* is to propound a theory of language, or at least that this is what he should have been trying to do. He believes that Wittgenstein failed in this attempt.

Professor Anscombe in her essay recounts how she once thought that Wittgenstein was propounding a theory of language in the opening paragraphs of the *Philosophical Investigations*. She took the simple language games described there as an attempt by Wittgenstein to show how a sound (uttered by a human being) becomes a word. She believes now that it was a mistake on her part to think that Wittgenstein ever intended this and indeed any such enterprise, as she says, "quickly goes up in smoke" (p. 148). Any such attempt to build up words from sounds is bound to fail because it is impossible to do this without first having a criterion for identifying different sounds as being the same word when they have the same meaning. The truth is that Wittgenstein never intended any such reduction of words to sounds and the example of simplified languages at the beginning of the *Philosophical Investigations* is not an attempt to give us a theory of language showing how this is possible. It is rather an attempt, as is a good part of the rest of the *Philosophical Investigations*, to show how understanding language is understanding its 'grammar', and Professor Anscombe spends the second half of her paper explaining this.

Similarly, Professor Winch denies that Wittgenstein thought a theory of language in the traditional sense was possible. The moral of the title of Professor Winch's essay — Im Anfang war die Tat — is that language has no explanation: one cannot explain how it comes about or what makes it possible. It is a part of human life and action. One starts with language as one starts with intentional action in a novel. There is nothing else to which language can be reduced in terms of which it can be explained or justified. The *Philosophical Investigations* represents a break with the philosophical tradition of attempting to explain the origins of language that was inaugurated by Plato.

Dr Kenny's essay attempts an interesting comparison between the *Tractatus* and the *Philosophical Investigations*. What they have in common is that for both language is inexplicable. As Dr Kenny says on the last page of his essay, ". . . the ultimate criterion of meaning is indescribable (in the *Tractatus*, because it takes place outside the world; in the *Philosophical Investigations*, because all description is within a language game)." This expresses a view that might be said to unite the positions of Mr McGuinness and Miss Ishiguro with that of Professor Winch, in contradistinction to those of Mr Dummett and Professor Anscombe, who interpret Wittgenstein as attempting to formulate a theory of language.

Professor Kripke's essay places Wittgenstein's private language argument within the context of his general discussion of the notion of 'following a rule'. The private language argument as well as many of Wittgenstein's remarks on the philosophy of mathematics can be taken as illustrations of problems involved in understanding what it means to follow a rule. Professor Kripke prefers the examples from mathematics as he thinks this brings out the point Wittgenstein is making more clearly. It is impossible to survey Kripke's rich and provocative paper in a few words, but the purport of what he is saying could be expressed as follows. Wittgenstein in the *Philosophical Investigations* is raising a problem in the tradition of the scepticism of human knowledge that goes much deeper than the scepticism of Hume. Hume's scepticism touched only our empirical knowledge of the world whereas Wittgenstein's touches every facet of human understanding, even logic and mathematics. Essentially there is no difference between the scepticism of the one or the other. Kripke demonstrates that Wittgenstein is arguing that there is no sure ground for my thinking that any given function I use in mathematical calculations as the plus function is the same function I have always used in the past or will use in the future. Wittgenstein's answer to the sceptic which is formulated in terms of his concept of following a rule is very similar to Hume's sceptical solution to his sceptical problem in the *Enquiry*. We simply *do* take these functions for what we understand them to be. This is just the way we think and it is not possible for us to think in any other way. What Wittgenstein calls 'rules' are merely the embodiment of how we do in fact think and the ultimate ground for our knowledge is how we act and live. This recalls the title and some of the ideas expressed in Professor Winch's essay. Professor

Winch, however, would possibly not agree with Professor Kripke's thesis that it is the assertability-conditions, not truth-conditions, that render a sentence meaningful, for the reasons he gives on p. 145 of his essay.

Professor Phillips' discussion of Wittgenstein's remarks on religious belief bears some resemblance to Professor Winch's paper. The validity of religious belief is not to be assessed by some argument that purports to demonstrate, support or even explain it. Religious belief is part of human culture and life and its meaning and validity is bound up with that of the culture of which it is part. There can be no proof of religious belief any more than there is proof of a practice. It is either part of men's lives or it is not. Professor Phillips defends this against the common criticism that it renders religious belief immune to critical evaluation. He attempts an explanation of how, on Wittgenstein's view, religious belief can be criticized and evaluated.

Professors Cioffi and Ziff discuss a similar question. Professor Cioffi discusses Wittgenstein's remarks on Frazer's explanation in *The Golden Bough* of why the Beltane fire-festivals have such a sinister effect upon us. Professor Ziff discusses Wittgenstein's account of how a work of art has a certain effect upon us. In both instances, Wittgenstein denies that causal explanations are relevant. Though the fire-festivals may have evolved from sinister origins such as the ritualistic burning of a man, this is not what gives them their sinister significance today. If they are sinister today, it is because of the meaning they have for us now. Similarly, aesthetic impressions are explained by the web of associations that in our culture surrounds certain objects or situations. This has nothing to do with causal processes in the brain. Or rather causal processes have something to do with the aesthetic impressions in the sense that their existence may be dependent upon them, but their meaning or significance *as aesthetic impressions* does not. Professor Cioffi argues Wittgenstein's position with flair and vigor. Professor Ziff on the other hand counters Wittgenstein's denial of the relevance of causal explanations for aesthetic feelings. He thinks that, if computerized analysis of brain structure becomes sufficiently precise, we will be able to explain why certain visual sensations, for example, give us the aesthetic impressions they do.

Dr Blackwell's essay with which this volume begins is an account of the personal relationship of the early Wittgenstein with Russell. Dr Blackwell attempts to show, primarily from the private letters of Russell to Lady Ottoline Morrell, how light can be thrown on some of the philosophical problems these two men discussed through knowledge of their personal relationship. This approach is seen as particularly fruitful in understanding Wittgenstein's criticisms of Russell's theory of judgment and Russell's reaction to them. Dr Blackwell, who is the Archivist of the Bertrand Russell Archives at McMaster University, utilizes the unpublished papers and letters of Russell to trace this history.

The Early Wittgenstein and the Middle Russell*

KENNETH BLACKWELL

The early relationship of Ludwig Wittgenstein and Bertrand Russell was, perhaps in part because of its intensity, one of the most fruitful in the history of philosophy. To understand the relationship fully requires that attention be paid to both its philosophical and biographical aspects. Yet those who write about a man's philosophy and those who write his life usually fail to integrate the philosophical studies or the life (as the case may be) into their own works. The recent biography of Russell by Ronald W. Clark has, to cite an example on one side, drawn the criticism that its philosophy is there in isolation, "like a remote and un-important country shown in an inset in a map".[1] Perhaps the biographer would answer that philosophical commentators are guilty of a similar fault, namely, that of generally ignoring the life when critical events in a man's philosophical development are under examination. Many books on Wittgenstein, for instance, devote their first chapter to his life and then confine themselves to his philosophy. I have found the biographical

* I am indebted in this essay in various ways to Michael Radner, Evan Simpson, Irving Copi, Albert Shalom (for inviting me to read a draft to his *Tractatus* seminar at McMaster), Stefan Andersson, Nicholas Griffin (for discussions based on his un-published paper, "Russell's Multiple Relation Theory of Judgment"), Elizabeth Ramsden Eames, and John G. Slater. Quotations from unpublished letters and manuscripts by Bertrand Russell are © Res-Lib Ltd., 1981, and are included with the permission of McMaster University and also (in the case of his letters to Lady Ottoline Morrell) the Humanities Research Center, the University of Texas at Austin, and (in the case of manuscripts) the Bertrand Russell Estate. References to Russell's letter to Lady Ottoline are given in the text in the form of a number followed by a date; "p/" before the date stands for "postmarked".

and the philosophical approaches not only inseparable but rewarding.

Much of our knowledge of the personal side of the relationship of Wittgenstein and Russell has only recently come to light, but no treatise has yet been written on the philosophical side. There doubtless will be, for there is room for a substantial volume to trace the interactions in logic and epistemology of these two philosophers of the century. Such a volume would not be grounded in history and biography, but rather in philosophy. Its theme could be the tensions inherent in an epistemology based upon the doctrine of acquaintance. Both Russell and the early Wittgenstein held such an epistemology, and the latter's first work, *Tractatus Logico-Philosophicus*, is (roughly) an account of the world as assumed by this epistemology, but notably lacking in explicit assumptions to that effect. The last book Wittgenstein more or less completed, *Philosophical Investigations*, is an attack on that account and on that epistemology. This is why I think Russell was so notoriously hostile to it, and cast upon the memory of its author the most wounding aspersion he could think of: that in that work Wittgenstein "seems to have grown tired of serious thinking and to have invented a doctrine which would make such an activity unnecessary".[2] Turning to Russell's side of the relationship, we find a history of alterations in his theory of belief due both to Wittgenstein's direct criticisms of it and to various indirect criticisms suggested by Wittgenstein's philosophy of logic (especially with regard to logical constants and forms). In addition, certain technical improvements in *Principia Mathematica* seem due to Wittgenstein, as well as the view that mathematics is wholly tautological (a view which, as Russell put it, "Wittgenstein has sometimes seemed to teach").[3] There is also Russell's own confession – which itself has to be studied and verified – that he "went too far in agreeing with" the early Wittgenstein[4] and that (by implication) his own later work in philosophy repudiates some of the earlier Wittgensteinian influences.

It is insufficiently realized that the personal contacts between Wittgenstein and Russell were not confined to the years up to 1922, when the English translation of the *Tractatus* was published and Russell indicates that Wittgenstein desired to see no more of him.[5] The contacts resumed after Wittgenstein returned to Cambridge in 1929, and seem to have been neither unfriendly nor divest of philosophical discussion. See, for example, Russell's report in 1930 to the Council of Trinity College on *Philosophical Remarks*,[6] or Wittgenstein's letter of (presumably) November 1935, when he wished to attend Russell's paper on "The Limits of Empiricism".[7] As far as I can discover, the personal relationship did not again deteriorate until about the time of Russell's return to Trinity College in 1944. About this time there is the story that "Someone was inclined to defend Russell's writings on marriage, sex, and 'free love': Wittgenstein interposed by saying: 'If a person tells me he has been to the worst of places I have no right to judge him, but if he tells me it was his superior wisdom that enabled him to go there, then I know that he is a fraud.'"[8] Then there are Wittgenstein's remarks that, at a certain meeting of the Moral Sciences Club, Russell was "most disagreeable. Glib and superficial, though, as always, *astonishingly* quick";[9] that "Russell isn't going to kill himself doing philosophy now".[10] There is the incident (which exists in rumour if not in fact) which might be called the "poker–Popper" incident.[11] And after Wittgenstein's death in 1951, there are Russell's diatribes against "the cult of common usage". He even revised the summation of his account of Wittgenstein in the manuscript of his autobiography. As published, it reads: "In spite of such slight foibles, however, he was an impressive human being." In the original version of 1931, which was retained until about 1966, Russell wrote: "In spite of such slight foibles, however, I consider him about the most impressive human being I have ever known."[12] Let us therefore turn from the much less interesting (and less edifying) relationship of the middle and late Wittgenstein and the late and *very* late Russell, to the period in which the middle-aged Russell encountered the youthful Wittgenstein.

The period we are about to examine, namely 1911 to 1914, used to be very little known, even after the publication of Russell's autobiography. I used to think of it principally in terms of his affair with Lady Ottoline Morrell and numerous addresses to the Aristotelian Society. Now, however, with the availability at McMaster University and the University of Texas of the enormous correspondence of Russell with Lady Ottoline, we know much more. Since they could not meet very often, letters were their chief means of communication, and both were indefatigable correspondents. Russell once told Lady Ottoline he could easily write all day long to her (letter #52, p/3 May 1911). His latest biographer devotes 100 pages out of 650 to these years. The image of these years is now somewhat altered. True, there is still the affair with Lady Ottoline, now in daily detail, but the period is also represented in my mind by various writings projects of Russell's which failed, and by the ubiquitous presence of Wittgenstein. From Wittgenstein's side, it is a great help that we now have the *Letters to Russell, Keynes and Moore*, superbly dated, translated and annotated, and we are now much more

certain of the circumstances of the composition of Wittgenstein's first
surviving substantial work, "Notes on Logic", and the order to be
assigned the two surviving versions of the text.[13] There is also a surviving insubstantial work, the review of Peter Coffey's *The Science of
Logic*, which appeared in the *Cambridge Review* for 6 March 1913.[14] And
there are the extracts from David Pinsent's diary, which are available in
Trinity College Library. I have seen only the entries used by von Hayek
in his aborted "Sketch of a Biography of Ludwig Wittgenstein", of
which he sent a carbon copy to Russell. Of a strictly philosophical
nature, the chief document to surface in recent years is Russell's unfinished book on theory of knowledge. This manuscript is a real missing
link. A reviewer of *Notebooks, 1914–1916* remarked that ". . . if
Wittgenstein at this time shared Russell's general conception of the
nature of philosophy, it is also clear that he was reacting sharply to a
number of specific views, either held by Russell at about 1913 or else attributed to him."[15] The implication is that these specific views do not
appear in any of Russell's published writings. The unpublished
manuscript on theory of knowledge was written in 1913, and it provides
a bridge between the views Russell expressed in *The Problems of
Philosophy*, which was written in July 1911, and those in *Our Knowledge
of the External World* (1914) and the lectures on "The Philosophy of
Logical Atomism" (1918). From this plethora of material I shall first
trace the personal relationship which evolved, because it was important
for the philosophy, and then examine a critical event in the
philosophical relationship. I believe the two aspects are inseparable in
understanding Russell's abandonment of the theory of knowledge
manuscript, in particular his "paralysis"[16] over Wittgenstein's
criticism of that work.

Wittgenstein and Russell were twenty-two and thirty-nine, respectively, when they first met. The date was 18 October 1911, and the
Michaelmas term of the second year of Russell's five-year Cambridge
lectureship was a week old. Wittgenstein had apparently been advised
by Frege to study with Russell,[17] though he does not seem to have told
Russell so, and Russell consistently says in his writings on Wittgenstein
that "He asked people at Manchester (so he told me) whether there was
such a subject [as the principles of mathematics], and whether anyone
worked at it. They told him that there was such a subject and that he
could find out more about it by coming to me at Cambridge . . ."[18] It
would be useful for disentangling the separate influences of Frege and
Russell if we knew which came first. Both influences seem to have begun

before the personal relationships developed. Russell, in the article just quoted from, states Wittgenstein "did not, I think, know Frege personally at that time, but he read him and greatly admired him".[19] But although an awareness of the Fregean background is very important to an understanding of the *Tractatus*,[20] the Russellian background seems equally important. Wittgenstein was reading Russell as early as 1909, when he proposed a solution to Russell's contradiction in a letter to Philip Jourdain.[21] The first meeting between Wittgenstein and Russell began auspiciously enough. Russell reported to Lady Ottoline that his new student had "acquired, by himself, a passion for the philosophy of mathematics, and has now come to Cambridge on purpose to hear me" (#225, p/18 Oct. 1911). Wittgenstein refused to speak German on that occasion, although his English was not good. Apparently, the same day, after Russell's lecture, he came back with him to his rooms and "argued till dinner-time". Russell's impression after one day was a definite one: Wittgenstein was "obstinate and perverse, but I think not stupid"; but he threatened to be an infliction (#227, p/19 Oct. 1911).

The memories of this first term remained sharp with Russell, and several of his customary anecdotes about Wittgenstein date from this time. There is the one about Wittgenstein refusing to admit there was not a hippopotamus in the room, in the face of Russell's refutation of his theory that "nothing empirical is knowable" (#241, p/2 Nov. 1911). (In the retelling, forty years later, the non-existent animal became a rhinoceros.[22]) A few days after this incident we get a slight elaboration of Wittgenstein's theory: he "was refusing to admit the existence of anything except asserted propositions" (#247, p/7 Nov. 1911), or maintaining that "there is nothing in the world except asserted propositions" (#254, p/13 Nov. 1911). Can we not see connections between this remark and *Tractatus*, 2.04: "The totality of existent atomic facts is the world"? On the other hand, it contradicts a statement in "Notes on Logic" that "There are only unasserted propositions" (Summary, p. 5). To Russell's discredit as a teacher on this occasion, he told Wittgenstein "it was too large a theme"; his theme remained large and it remained the same. For a short time Russell was disappointed in Wittgenstein: "He is armour-plated against all assaults of reasoning"; "it is really rather a waste of time talking with him" (#259, p/15 ? Nov. 1911). But this impression did not last. By the end of the term Russell reported he was getting to like the man who had turned out to be, as he said, Austrian, literary, pleasant-mannered, and probably very intelligent (#271, p/29 Nov. 1911). The most important of the anecdotes concerns the occasion on which Wittgenstein was hesitating between philosophy and aviation, and asked Russell for advice. The date was 27 November 1911 (#268); Russell later recorded only that this occurred "at the end of his first term".[23] When Wittgenstein brought the piece of writing Russell requested he do over the Christmas vacation, Lady Ottoline was told it was "very good, much better than my English pupils do. I shall certainly encourage him. Perhaps he will do great things." But he had a reservation: "On the other hand I think it very likely he will get tired of philosophy" (#320, p/23 Jan. 1912). The anecdote about Wittgenstein being the only one in Moore's class who looked puzzled dates from Wittgenstein's second term (see #368, p/5 March 1912).

In his obituary notice, Russell recalled that Wittgenstein "made very rapid progress in mathematical logic, and soon knew all that I had to teach".[24] Probably this happened within a year. Indeed, Wittgenstein must already have been advanced in the subject. On 26 January 1912, he proposed to Russell "a definition of logical *form*" (#325). This, unfortunately, is the last time in the letters to Lady Ottoline that Russell identifies Wittgenstein's philosophical views. His explanation of this view is not revealing – he added only that it was "opposed to logical *matter*". I do not know how Russell conceived of "logical form" as distinct from "logical matter" here, unless he regarded the logical constants as the matter of logic. Although Lady Ottoline had studied logic under the neo-Hegelian David G. Ritchie at St Andrews University back in 1897,[25] it would not have been symbolic logic that she studied. It is a pity for our knowledge of this period that she did not have a better grounding. At any rate, Wittgenstein does not seem, by this date, to have developed his fundamental view that "logical form" cannot be described but only shown, or he would not have attempted a definition of "logical form". Subsequent references to philosophy and logic in the correspondence are merely tantalizing. On 27 February 1912, Wittgenstein "brought a very good original suggestion, which I think is right, on an important point in logic" (#360). A few weeks later, Russell and Wittgenstein "had a close equal passionate discussion of the most difficult point in mathematical philosophy . . . He has suggested several new ideas which I think valuable" (#388, p/17 March 1912). A month later, Russell told Lady Ottoline that he had "got a number of new technical ideas from [Wittgenstein] which I think are quite sound and important" (#422, p/23 April 1912). I cannot determine what these "new technical ideas" were, but "the most difficult point in mathematical philosophy" might concern the concept of "logical form", or, as S. T. Sommerville has suggested,[26] the theory of types. Later in the year the point (whatever it was) much exercised Russell in trying to write a paper on "What is Logic?" Near the end of 1912 Wittgenstein was reported to be making "great progress" with what Russell termed "his logical problems" (#615 [Oct. 1912]).

Let us now pay greater attention to the personal relationship, which was developing as fast as Wittgenstein's philosophical ideas. One of the factors in forming the relationship was that Russell saw Wittgenstein as the perfect student. Already by March 1912 Russell had said, "Yes, Wittgenstein has been a great event in my life – whatever may come of him" (#397 [late March 1912]). Yet his impact on Russell had just begun. Russell came to see Wittgenstein as embodying (the Platonic image is appropriate at this stage in Russell's philosophy) the ideal philosophic nature. The qualities of this nature were a strong impulse to analysis, titanic energy, unswerving devotion to work and to truth, contempt for traditional patterns of thought, an ironic wit, utter unconcern with ordinary standards of success (such as getting one's degree), etc. Here are some of Russell's descriptions:

He has the theoretical passion *very* strongly – it is a rare passion and one is glad to find it. He doesn't want to prove this or that, but to find out how things really are . . . something about him makes him a hero. (#373, p/8 March 1912)

No one could be more sincere than Wittgenstein, or more destitute of the false politeness that interferes with truth; but he lets his feelings and affections appear, and it warms one's heart. (#375, p/10 March 1912)

[C. D.] Broad is . . . the most *reliable* pupil I have had – practically certain to do a good deal of useful but not brilliant work; whereas Wittgenstein . . . is full of boiling passion which may drive him anywhere. [Unquestionably a virtue to Russell's romantic mind.] (#384, p/15 March 1912)

He has the intellectual passion in the highest degree; it makes me love him. His disposition is that of an artist, intuitive and moody . . . he has just the sort of rage when he can't understand things that I have. (#385, 16 March 1912)

He is the ideal pupil – he gives passionate admiration with vehement and very intelligent dissent . . . He spoke with intense feeling about the *beauty* of the big book [i.e. *Principia*], said he found it like music. He is not a flatterer, but a man of transparent and absolute sincerity . . . He is far more terrible with Christians than I am. (#388, p/17 March 1912)

I saw a good deal of Wittgenstein this afternoon – he wears well. He is quite as good as I thought. I find him strangely exciting. He lives in the same kind of intense excitement as I do, hardly able to sit still or read a book. He was talking about Beethoven – how a friend described going to Beethoven's door and hearing him "cursing, howling and singing" over his new fugue; after a whole hour Beethoven at last came to the door, looking as if he had been fighting the devil, and having eaten nothing for 36 hours because his cook and parlour-maid had been away from his rage. That's the sort of man to be.

Wittgenstein brought me the most lovely roses today. He is a treasure . . . I shan't feel the subject neglected by my abandoning it, as long as he takes it up. I thought he would have smashed all the furniture in my room today, he got so excited. He asked me how Whitehead and I were going to end our big book, and I said we should have no concluding remarks, but just stop with whatever formula happened to come last. He seemed surprised at first, and then saw that was right. It seems to me the beauty of the book would be spoilt if it contained a single word that could possibly be spared. I argued about Matter with him. He thinks it a trivial problem. He admits that if there is no Matter then no one exists but himself, but he says that doesn't hurt, since physics and astronomy and all the other sciences could still be interpreted so as to be true. – Yes, I think my daily round here *is* useful – Wittgenstein alone would have made it so. (#422, p/23 April 1912)

Wittgenstein's mature philosophic style is recognizable in the early period – just as is his style in domestic furnishings. His style in both these disparate areas has the quality of shunning all ornamentation.[27] Russell tried to change the philosophic style.

I told him he ought not simply to *state* what he thinks true, but to give arguments for it, but he said arguments spoil its beauty, and that he would feel as if he was dirtying a flower with muddy hands. He *does* appeal to me – the artist in intellect is so very rare. I told him I hadn't the heart to say anything against that, and that he had better acquire a slave to state the arguments. (Between #467 and #468 [27 May 1912])

Russell told Wittgenstein that he would not get a degree "unless he learnt to write imperfect things – this all made him more and more furious" (#566 [Sept. 1912]). As for furniture, Wittgenstein lectured Russell on how it should be made: ornamentation should be abolished where it is not part of the construction. Not surprisingly, he had a very difficult time finding anything simple enough either in Cambridge or London.

It was also in mid-1912 that the pair began ethical discussions.

Wittgenstein suddenly said one day how he admired the text "what shall it profit a man if he gain the whole world and lose his own soul", and remarked "how few there are who don't lose their own soul". Russell said "it depended on having a large purpose that one is true to". Wittgenstein replied characteristically that "he thought it depended more on suffering and the power to endure it". Russell was surprised by this discussion (#472, p/30 May 1912). Another ethical discussion drew the comment from Russell that "His outlook is very free; principles and such things seem to him nonsense, because his impulses are strong and never shameful" (#475, p/1 June 1912). Only idealized characters *never* have "shameful" impulses; this was not an occasion on which Russell demonstrated insight into human nature. Wittgenstein, if not before, put him right on this matter in a letter of 3 March 1914, in which he asserted that his life was "*FULL* of the ugliest and pettiest thoughts and acts imaginable".[28] Apparently Russell still had not, at this point, realized Wittgenstein thought this way about himself. In addition to discussions of meta-ethics, they also discussed normative value judgements. I shall come to certain of these soon.

One of the foregoing extracts indicates that Russell was interested at this time (April 1912) in problems connected with knowledge of the material world. In fact, he was committed to delivering a paper on the subject at Cardiff. The paper was duly delivered in May. It was then thoroughly revised (the manuscript is in the Russell Archives), and Russell hoped it would be published in the *Monist*, which had earlier in 1912 published his paper on "The Philosophy of Bergson".[29] Wittgenstein had by now begun making criticisms of Russell's work, but had liked the peroration of the Bergson paper; however, he did not like this sort of thing "unadulterated", as in "The Free Man's Worship" (#387, p/16 March 1912). Then he objected to the last chapter of *The Problems of Philosophy*, on "The Value of Philosophy". One must not *say* that philosophy has value. As Russell reported his view, "people who like philosophy will pursue it, and others won't, and there is an end of it" (#388, p/17 March 1912; see also #387, p/16 March 1912). At first Wittgenstein told Russell that "On Matter" was the best thing he had done – but he had only read the beginning and end. Then he decided he did not like the rest of the paper – "but only", Russell thought, "because of disagreement, not because of its being badly done" (#460, 22 May 1912; 467, 26 May 1912). Yet even after the thorough revisions, Russell did not publish the paper.

This was also for Russell a time of failures in writing projects of a more literary nature. He was always sensitive to criticism from those whose judgment he admired, and because of these failures he was especially susceptible to such criticism. In the summer of 1911, after writing *The Problems of Philosophy*, he had gone on to produce a book-length manuscript on his philosophy of religion, known as "Prisons". Only some outlines and a summary chapter are extant. I shall return to the summary chapter, which was published as "The Essence of Religion". There was also an autobiography, written about April 1912, of which no trace remains. Then came an autobiographical novella, "The Perplexities of John Forstice", written in June 1912 but published posthumously (in Russell's *Collected Stories*) because he was never quite satisfied with it. Only the last could have been influenced by Wittgenstein, and then only with respect to its being withheld from publication; there is, in fact, no evidence that he did influence it. "The Essence of Religion" appeared in the October 1912 issue of the *Hibbert Journal*, and it set out the foundations of Russell's normative ethic. It deals Spinozistically with such concepts as "freedom from the finite self",[30] and Platonistically with three elements in Christianity "which it is desirable to preserve if possible: worship, acquiescence, and love".[31] The language is the language of incarnation. The highest wisdom is to be free of the free man's last prison: "the insistent demand that our ideals shall be already realized in the world". One October afternoon Russell was interrupted in composing a letter to Lady Ottoline: "Here is Wittgenstein just arrived, frightfully pained by my Hibbert article which he evidently *detests*. I must stop because of him" (#597 [Oct. 1912]). A few days later we learn why Wittgenstein detested the article. "He felt I had been a traitor to the gospel of exactness, and wantonly used words vaguely; also that such things are too intimate for print. I minded very much, because I half agree with him" (#600, p/11 Oct. 1912). Two days later, Russell returned to the subject. "Wittgenstein's criticisms disturbed me profoundly. He was so unhappy, so gentle, so wounded in his wish to think well of me" (#602, p/13 Oct. 1912). The same day he told Lady Ottoline that his mind was full of the paper on "What is Logic?". He thought it might be really important. But Wittgenstein had been with him "arguing logic – it *is* difficult, but I feel I must have another go at it". The next day he reported that he could not get on with "What is Logic?" and felt strongly inclined to leave it to Wittgenstein (#603, p/14 Oct. 1912).

Among Russell's papers is a five-page manuscript entitled "What is Logic?" It is not a real paper, only a point-by-point summary of the problems such a paper might discuss. "Logic" is defined as "the study of the forms of complexes". Russell first considers "complex" as a primitive idea, or indefinable. Then he tries "form". He lists the symbols of various atomic forms. He specifically excludes judgment from consideration, and so does not list a form for judgment. He shows that, to avoid an infinite regress, the form of a complex must not be considered a constituent of the complex. (Otherwise a form of the new complex composed of the original constituents plus the original form would be required, and so on.) Wittgenstein's letters to Russell in the next few months show him hard at work on what he calls "the complex problem" and the theory of symbolism. We learn that in December 1912 Wittgenstein discussed with Frege what he called "our Theory of Symbolism" (meaning Russell's and his), and in a letter of January 1913 explained what the theory amounted to. It amounted to the view that "there cannot be different types of things", and that a proper theory of symbolism must render any theory of types "superfluous". In the form of the statement "Socrates is mortal", the variables for "Socrates" and "mortality" must be of different kinds.[32] If they are, they will not be substituted for the wrong way around. It was a letter like this, and the discussions which must have ensued afterwards, which could have led to Russell's statement, in introducing the *Tractatus*, that "In the part of [Wittgenstein's] theory which deals with Symbolism he is concerned with the conditions which would have to be fulfilled by a logically perfect language." We shall see that allegations of imperfect symbolism have been brought against the theory of judgment Russell was soon to develop. It is undeniable, however, that both men were concerned with developing an ideal notation – though that is not to conclude (least of all from the sentence just quoted from the Introduction to the *Tractatus*) that Russell considered that to be Wittgenstein's *only* concern.[33]

By the winter of 1912–13, then, Russell seems to have bequeathed the problems of philosophical logic to Wittgenstein. He more than once remarked to Lady Ottoline that Wittgenstein could soon take his place at Cambridge (#678, p/21 Jan. 1913). Indeed, Wittgenstein was to be a member of a school Russell dreamt of founding, Wittgenstein's qualification being that he was the ideal mathematical philosopher. We find the following reverie in a letter of December 1912:

I believe a certain sort of mathematicians have far more philosophical capacity than most of the people who take up philosophy. Hitherto the people attracted to philosophy have been mostly those who loved the big generalizations, which are all wrong, so that few people with exact minds have taken up the subject. It has long been one of my dreams to found a great school of mathematically-trained philosophers, but I don't know whether I shall ever get it accomplished. I had hopes of [H. T. J.] Norton, but he has not the physique. Broad is all right, but has no fundamental originality. Wittgenstein of course is exactly my dream. But I should like to make mathematics the ordinary training for a philosopher – I am sure it ought to be. That would require a tremendous propaganda of the sort that moves educational bodies; and I am afraid vested interests would always be too strong. However, when I am too old for original work I dare say I shall take it up. (#663, 29 Dec. 1912)

Russell founded no such school, but he never tired of making the point that philosophers ought to come to philosophy with a scientific background. By this time one has the feeling that Russell, while not exactly having surrendered his judgment to Wittgenstein's, had convinced himself that his student was closer to his philosophic ideal than he was himself. Take, for example, the degree of devotion to serious matters. There is the priceless incident of North Whitehead's boat race, which Russell and Wittgenstein went to watch. After the race, Wittgenstein

suddenly stood still and explained that the way we had spent the afternoon was so vile that we ought not to live, or at least he ought not, that nothing is tolerable except producing great works or enjoying those of others, that he has accomplished nothing and never will, etc. – all this with a force that nearly knocks one down. He makes me feel like a bleating lambkin. (#629, p/9 Nov. 1912)

I think Russell had decided by this time that his teaching of Wittgenstein was finished, his main job now being that of guiding Wittgenstein's work and keeping him stable. ("He is a great task but quite worth it," he told Lady Ottoline [#646, p/30 Nov. 1912].) For in logical matters Wittgenstein had now, it appears, learned all that Russell considered he had to teach.

We could expect to hear of criticisms from Wittgenstein of *Principia Mathematica*, and we do catch echoes of discussions on that subject. All three volumes had appeared by April 1913. In the late summer of 1913 Pinsent recorded in his diary that the first volume will have to be rewritten and Wittgenstein will write the first eleven chapters.[34] Russell had already said as much to Lady Ottoline six months before. On 23 February, he told her: "Wittgenstein has persuaded me that the early proofs of Principia Mathematica are very inexact"; adding, "fortunately it is his business to put them right, not mine" (#707). In the same letter Russell mentioned he "could have written a book with the store of ideas I have already, but now I have a higher standard of exactness". The higher standard of exactness was, I infer, due to Wittgenstein's influence. Yet it is worth noting that at this time Wittgenstein published his review of Coffey. The logical points made in the review are not original with Wittgenstein, but rather associated with Russell and the school to which he belonged. Wittgenstein began the points with a complaint indicative of the mathematical logician's concern with clarity:

Mr Coffey, like many logicians, draws a great advantage from an unclear way of expressing himself; for if you cannot tell whether he means to say "Yes" or "No", it is difficult to argue against him. However, even through his foggy expression, many grave mistakes can be recognized clearly enough; and I propose to give a list of some of the most striking ones . . .[35]

I do not mean to deny Wittgenstein's fundamental originality, however. Pinsent, who polished Wittgenstein's own rough translation of this review from the German original, recorded a few days before he worked on the translation that Russell had just acquiesced without a murmur in a new discovery of Wittgenstein's.[36] But it is now time for us to consider the book Russell might have written with the store of ideas he said he already had.

During the Christmas vacation of 1912 Russell had retreated to a small village to work on "matter". Whitehead, he said, was already at work on the mathematical end, and he was working on the psychological end (#662, 28 Dec. 1912). Several brief manuscripts on the subject are extant, and these lines from one of them describe the crux of the problem:

Physics exhibits sensations as functions of physical objects.
But epistemology demands that physical objects should be exhibited as functions of sensations.
Thus we have to solve the equations giving sensations in terms of physical objects, so as to make them give physical objects in terms of sensations.
That is all.[37]

At the same time Russell began to think about the two lecture courses he had agreed to give at Harvard a year hence, and the series of public lectures for the Lowell Institute he was to give at the same time. The public lectures, published as *Our Knowledge of the External World*, were initially planned to cover a very different topic, variously called "the search for wisdom" or "the search for insight" (#737, p/8 April 1913). (This topic was rejected by President Lowell because of the religious implications Russell would draw.[38]) After sketching an outline for the original topic he turned to the course on theory of knowledge. ". . . for a long time", he told Lady Ottoline, "I have planned a book on theory of knowledge, then I thought I could do Matter first, but now I see that even apart from having to lecture, theory of knowledge must come first . . ." (#750, n.d.). Apparently Russell kept the plans for this book from Wittgenstein. By now (April 1913), Russell was writing:

I find I no longer ever talk to him about *my* work, but only about his. When there are no clear arguments, but only inconclusive considerations to be balanced, or unsatisfactory points of view to be set against each other, he is no good; and he treats infant theories with a ferocity which they can only endure when they are grown up. The result is that I become completely reserved, even about work. (#753, p/23 April 1913)

However, if Russell was reserved about philosophical and logical matters, he was not when it came to "improving" Wittgenstein. Here is a report of one struggle to improve him:

I had a terrific contest with Wittgenstein late last night, because I told him it would do him good to read French prose, and that he was in danger of being narrow and uncivilized. He raged and stormed, and I irritated him more and more by merely smiling. We made it up in the end, but he remained quite unconvinced. The things I say to him are just the things you would say to me if you were not afraid of the avalanche they would produce – and his avalanche is just what mine would be! I feel his lack of civilization and suffer from it – it is odd how little music does to civilize people – it is too apart, too passionate, and too remote from words. He has not a sufficiently wide curiosity or a sufficient wish for a broad survey of the world. It won't spoil his work on logic, but it will make him always a very narrow specialist, and rather too much the champion of a party – that is, when judged by the highest standards. (#717, p/6 March 1913)

Whether or not Wittgenstein became, in some sense, too much the champion of a party, the charge of being always a very narrow specialist does not stick. Or perhaps it does, in the sense that *all* his writings are philosophical, whereas Russell wrote on history, science, politics, love, and much else.

I am not going to describe in detail the composition of the unfinished book on theory of knowledge, or the evidence for identifying the missing first six chapters with articles by Russell which appeared quarterly in the *Monist* from 1914 to 1915. A full account, with a reconstruction of the table of contents, has been given elsewhere.[39] The title for this untitled manuscript may as well be "Theory of Knowledge". From a reference within the manuscript, it can be seen that Russell at least placed it within the class of books bearing that name,[40] and he preferred that term to "epistemology". It is the cessation of work on "Theory of Knowledge" which constitutes the critical event in the early philosophical relationship of Russell and Wittgenstein.

"Theory of Knowledge" was to have two major sections, an "analytic" section and a "constructive" section. The analytic section was divided into three parts: acquaintance, judgment, and inference. The latter two parts were also called "atomic propositional thought" and "molecular propositional thought", respectively. Only the first two parts of the analytic section were written. The constructive section, if we have correctly identified the outline of it, was to conclude with "matter". To construct matter logically, Russell planned to move from knowledge of logic to knowledge of sense (including time and space), and thence to knowledge of science. In the final part, the problem was so to state the existence of certain sense-data and certain principles of inference that science would follow. Matter, causality, and induction could all then be dealt with. Clearly Russell had a large book in mind – in fact, his first large book since completing his share of *Principia* three years earlier. We may presume that, after a decade on *Principia*, Russell felt rather disoriented without another large project on hand. So for this reason, and because of the literary and philosophical failures I have mentioned, he became very much involved emotionally when he began "Theory of Knowledge". I believe he hoped (though he did not say so) that it would do for epistemology what *Principia* had done for logic and mathematics. In short, while eschewing axioms and symbolic demonstration, he hoped to erect an unimpeachable system, which would function deductively, demonstrating our knowledge of the external world. It was to be a far grander effort than the book of this title written partly in despair and with drastically pruned ambitions a few months later.[41]

Russell began "Theory of Knowledge" on 7 May 1913. A few days later Wittgenstein appeared on the scene. He gave Russell a climbing rose in a pot (he was fond of giving him flowers), but "was shocked to hear I am writing on Theory of Knowledge – he thinks it will be like the shilling shocker [i.e. *The Problems of Philosophy*], which he hates. *He* is a tyrant if you like" (#775, p/13 May 1913). After the first six chapters were written, Wittgenstein came to Russell "with a refutation of the theory of judgment which I used to hold. He was right, but I think the correction required is not very serious. I shall have to make up my mind within a week, as I shall soon reach judgment" (#782, p/21 May 1913). Russell was now writing on acquaintance with universals – predicates and relations, and logical data such as logical constants and forms ("which is difficult", he confessed [#784, p/23 May 1913]). "I shall come to more interesting things soon, when I get on to judgment" (#783, p/22 May 1913).

When he began judgment, Russell "got a new way of dividing the subject – *quite* new, and much more searching than the traditional divisions . . . any number of really important new ideas came to me" (#785, 24 May 1913). Then, after "trying to understand what is meant by understanding a sentence or statement" (#786, p/25 May 1913), Russell had another visit from Wittgenstein. He was probably half-way into Part II, Chapter II, entitled "Analysis and Synthesis". He had written more than 225 pages. He told Lady Ottoline:

. . . we were both cross from the heat – I showed him a crucial part of what I have been writing. He said it was all wrong, not realizing the difficulties – that he had tried my view and knew it wouldn't work. I couldn't understand his objection – in fact he was very inarticulate – but I feel in my bones that he must be right, and that he has seen something I have missed. If I could see it too I shouldn't mind, but as it is, it is worrying, and has rather destroyed the pleasure in my writing – I can only go on with what I see, and yet I feel it is probably all wrong, and that Wittgenstein will think me a dishonest scoundrel for going on with it. Well well – it is the younger generation knocking at the door – I must make room for him when I can, or I shall become an incubus. (#787, p/28 May 1913)

Russell carried on writing, but without enthusiasm. One difficulty derived from trying to take account of Wittgenstein's criticisms, which had "to do with problems I want to leave to him" (#792, p/28? May 1913). Russell was also worried by "the difficulty of not stealing his ideas – there is really more merit in raising a good problem than in solving it", he said (#793, p/1 June 1913). Wittgenstein chose this susceptible moment to attack Russell personally.

He came analysing all that goes wrong between him and me, and I told him I thought it was only nerves on both sides and everything was all right at bottom. Then he said he never knew whether I was speaking the truth or being polite, so I got vexed and refused to say another word. He went on and on and on. (#798, p/5 June 1913)

After further difficulties, however, the two men were reconciled. Russell finished Part II of Section A on 6 June, and decided to leave Part II and the whole of Section B until later. In thirty-one days – all during the Cambridge Easter term – he had written 350 pages; but as the sheer quantity of output failed to sustain Russell, we need not be overly impressed by it. He judged that "the best thing in my writing on theory of knowledge is the map of the country – that was already partially in the shilling book. It is very new, I think, and much more according to the natural division of the subject." The rest of the book could be corrected at leisure (#806, p/12 June 1913). This was wishful thinking, which Russell must have realized. Indeed, at this point he felt ready for suicide. Wittgenstein wrote to him on 27 July that he was "very sorry to hear that my objection to your theory of judgment paralyzes you. I think it can only be removed by a correct theory of propositions."[42] Russell went on to have a wretched summer. It was compounded by difficulties with Lady Ottoline, and led even to his praying in a cathedral while touring in Italy.[43] Wittgenstein on the other hand, had a productive summer, resulting in his "Notes on Logic".

It is worth noting that Russell's honesty triumphed in the end, since that is what worried him most about the event. It is admirable that his desire for the respect of his philosophic ideal (a mirror-image of his own self-respect) weighed more heavily with him than the investment of energy and several years' thought in "Theory of Knowledge". It reminds one of Frege's admission that Russell's discovery of his contradiction "has shaken the basis on which I intended to build arithmetic". Russell called Frege's dedication to truth on this occasion an act "of integrity and grace". It cannot be said that Russell "responded [like Frege] with intellectual pleasure clearly submerging any feelings of personal disappointment".[44] Nevertheless the fundamental integrity was there. The admission of failure was made only to Lady Ottoline, it appears. He told her Wittgenstein's attack on his work made a large part of the book he intended to write impossible for years to come (#811, p/20 June 1913). Three years later he confessed it was "an event of first-rate importance in my life".[45] Russell did not, however, forgo the opportunity to publish what he still thought correct of the first part of "Theory of Knowledge", and thus we have the six *Monist* articles of 1914–15.[46]

The place of "Theory of Knowledge" in the development of Russell's epistemology raises several historical questions. Wittgenstein knew *The Problems of Philosophy*. In this book Russell had elaborated his theory of knowledge by acquaintance. In it he had also elaborated the theory of judgment published earlier in the Introduction to *Principia Mathematica* and the final essay of *Philosophical Essays* (1910). In *The Problems of Philosophy* he had promoted the concept of the "sense" of the subordinate relation in belief statements to being a characteristic of the multiple judging relation. In this way he had hoped the propositional ordering of the constituents of belief would be less objectionably effected. But Russell was in difficulty in other areas, notably the ontological one. His philosophy at this time was strongly Platonistic: he thought he had to admit that relations have being, and the case for qualities appeared almost as strong.[47] A year of Wittgenstein's impact later, in "What is Logic?", he added the logical form of the proposition believed to the belief complex. In "Theory of Knowledge", as we shall see, he was strongly tempted to say that we have acquaintance with logical forms, as well as with logical constants. The historical questions which puzzle one are these:

(1) what was the "map" of theory of knowledge which Russell said he had acquired while writing *The Problems of Philosophy*?

(2) what could Wittgenstein's "refutation" of Russell's former theory of judgment have been?

(3) what was the non-serious correction Russell thought his new theory of judgment required before he could begin writing it out?

(4) what was the new way of dividing the subject of judgment which he arrived at when he began writing out the new theory?

(5) what was Wittgenstein's criticism of the book, and was it identical with the objection to Russell's theory of judgment which "paralyzed" him when Wittgenstein put it in a letter?

(6) was this objection the only objection Wittgenstein raised to "Theory of Knowledge", and could it have been serious enough to cause Russell the despair which resulted in the abandonment of the

manuscript and the publication of only the first six chapters? (There were three more chapters before the part on judgment – all on acquaintance with universals.)

Answers to the first four questions seem possible from a study of the documents. For instance, the "map" of theory of knowledge may well have been its division into knowledge of things and knowledge of truths, with the subdivision of knowledge of things into knowledge by acquaintance and by description.[48] But it is the last two questions which are by far the most interesting, and they are both philosophical and biographical. We want to know why Russell stopped writing his book, and whether Wittgenstein's criticism, as we have it, was the sole motive force. What exactly was the objection from Wittgenstein? We know what it was verbally – at least we think we do, although it was made in a letter after the second visit, and Russell had already admitted failure in letters to Lady Ottoline. The objection as given in Wittgenstein's letter of *circa* 14 June 1913, is in this passage:

I can now express my objection to your theory of judgment exactly: I believe it is obvious that, from the proposition "A judges that (say) a is in the Relation R to b", if correctly analysed, the proposition "aRb.v.~aRb" must follow directly *without the use of any other premiss*. This condition is not fulfilled by your theory.[49]

One of the chapters Wittgenstein must have seen is Chapter IX of Part I, "Logical Data". This chapter, which is very short, concerns acquaintance with logical constants and logical forms. One commentator has traced Wittgenstein's denial in the *Tractatus* that these phrases denote objects of any kind whatsoever back through the *Notebooks* and to the early letters to Russell. I quote:

The supposed logical constants, then, whose existence Wittgenstein was concerned to deny were not only the supposed references of words like 'and', 'or', 'not', etc.; nor these together with the supposed referents of the words 'some', 'all' and 'is identical with' – though these (truth functions, generality, and identity) did in time become the three ranges of so-called logical constants that he thought he had to deal with. Originally the notion covered much more: all the forms of propositions – the general notion of predicate, the general notion of dual relation, triple relation, and any other forms there might be of whatever complexity and level had been supposed to be logical objects, and Wittgenstein was denying them that status.[50]

This critic goes on to locate the object of Wittgenstein's denial in the chapter on "Logical Data". A second commentator has singled out this chapter, noting that the concept of acquaintance with logical forms and constants does not reappear in "The Philosophy of Logical Atomism" and drawing the inference that Wittgenstein's criticism was the cause.[51] When we examine that chapter, we find that Russell, while still Platonistic, is altogether tentative about the ontological status of logical objects. Although he concludes that "acquaintance with logical form . . . is a primitive constituent of our experience", he adds the rider, "whatever its ultimate analysis be".[52] And earlier in the chapter we can see more clearly that Russell was unsettled about the ultimate analysis. He wrote:

It would seem that logical objects cannot be regarded as "entities", and that, therefore, what we shall call "acquaintance" with them cannot really be a dual relation. The difficulties which result are very formidable, but their solution must be sought in logic. (MS, p. 181)

Russell had temporarily ceased doing fundamental work in logic at this time, and there is here a markedly less confident note than is exhibited in his pre-Wittgenstein article of 1911, "The Philosophical Importance of Mathematical Logic", in the passages dealing with logical objects.[53] Again, later in the chapter, Russell wrote: "'Logical constants', which might seem to be entities occurring in logical propositions, are really concerned with pure *form*, and are not actually constituents of the propositions in the verbal expression of which their names occur" (MS, p. 182). Is this the abolition of "logical matter", about which Russell wrote Lady Ottoline in 1912? And again, "the form is not a 'thing', not another constituent along with the objects that were previously related in that form" (MS, p. 183). There are other, similar reservations. I think it is primarily this topic which comprised the problems Russell wished to leave to Wittgenstein, and on which there was the worry of "the difficulty of not stealing his ideas". It correlates well with a letter of October 1913 to Lady Ottoline. Russell remarked to her that "Theory of Knowledge" ". . . goes to pieces when it touches Wittgenstein's problems . . ." (#900, p/24 Oct. 1913). Indeed, in saying that logical constants are really concerned with pure form, it looks as though Russell was already borrowing from Wittgenstein. For in *Our Knowledge of the External World* he credits the same point to "unpublished work by my friend Ludwig Wittgenstein".[54]

Part II of "Theory of Knowledge" concerns "atomic propositional thought". Part III was to concern "molecular propositional thought", that is, inference. The doctrine of acquaintance with logical data was to be employed in this Part. In an outline Russell wrote:

> Observe. A Judgment requires acquaintance with *one* form of atomic complex. An inferential consciousness requires acquaintance with such terms as *or* and *not*, i.e. with a form of complex in which propositions are constituents.[55]

Thus the inventory of logical forms was to be even further enlarged to include forms of arguments.

What was new in the chapter on "The Understanding of Propositions", to which Wittgenstein surely presented the objection which was called "paralyzing"? (Incidentally, one distinguished critic, in his review of the *Notebooks*, where the letter was first printed, could not take the paralysis seriously. He wrote: "His old teacher must have been teasing him to elicit from Wittgenstein in his letter of 22.7.13 the sober 'I am very sorry to hear that my objection to your theory of judgment paralyzes you'."[56]) What was new in the theory was the introduction of the logical form of propositions expressing attitudes – such as judging or believing, doubting, and understanding – towards other propositions. This development of Russell's theory of judgment from that presented in *The Problems of Philosophy* is just what another distinguished critic had once noted was lacking (in the published accounts, of course). At least this is what I think the following statement means: "Russell's theory would . . . require different relations of judging (differing as to number and the logical types of the terms between which they hold) for every different logical form of sentences expressing judgments."[57] Russell offered the following symbol for the logical form of someone's judgment that A is similar to B:

$$J \, (S, A, B, \text{similarity}, xRy).$$

I have great difficulty in deciding whether Russell originated this analysis. There is nothing, so far as I can see, indicating that credit belongs to Wittgenstein. But on the other hand, Russell twice in the next few years credited him for the discovery of what in 1918 he called "a new beast for our zoo" (adding "nothing that occurs in space is of the same form as belief").[58] In 1914, in the *Monist* version of Chapter IV of "Theory of Knowledge", he put it more fully:

It can be shown that a judgment, and generally all thought whose expression involves *propositions*, must be a fact of a different logical form from any of the series: subject-predicate facts, dual relations, triple relations, etc. In this way, a difficult and interesting problem of pure logic arises, namely a problem of enlarging the inventory of logical forms so as to include forms appropriate to the facts of epistemology.

Russell added in a footnote that he had come to know this through un-published work of his friend Mr Ludwig Wittgenstein.[59] Yet we cannot credit Wittgenstein for the analysis of the form "J (S, A, B, similarity, xRy)", because it was surely just such an analysis that he objected to. Perhaps, then, the credit is for an analysis of judgment into a different form, say the form "J (S, p)", expressing that there is a relation of judgment between a subject S and a proposition p. At least this fits the demand of "Notes on Logic" that "a proposition itself must occur in the statement that it is judged".[60] But to distinguish this form from that of an old theory of Russell's, the concept of the "bipolarity" of "p" must be added.

"Notes on Logic" are the only document we can turn to for an elaboration of Wittgenstein's objection to Russell's theory of judgment. The "Notes" were composed in September and early October 1913. They contain several passages critical of Russell's theory of judgment. I quote from the earlier version:

When we say A judges that etc., then we have to mention a whole proposition which A judges. It will not do either to mention only its constituents, or its constituents and form, but not in the proper order. This shows that a proposition itself must occur in the statement that it is judged . . . (Summary, p. 2)

The proper theory of judgment must make it impossible to judge nonsense. [Repeated at *Tractatus*, 5.5422.] (Summary, p. 5)

Every right theory of judgment must make it impossible for me to judge that this table penholders the book. Russell's theory does not satisfy this requirement. (3rd MS, p. 15)

There is no thing which is the form of a proposition, and no name which is the name of a form. Accordingly we can also not say that a relation which in certain cases holds between things holds sometimes between forms and things. This goes against Russell's theory of judgment. (4th MS, p. 19)

. . . it seems that we shall only be able to express the proposition "A believes p" correctly by the *ab*-notation; say by making "A" having a relation to the poles "a" and "b" of a-p-b. (4th MS, p. 21)

So Wittgenstein thought Russell's analysis of the judging event into constituents and form did not allow for the integrity of the proposition judged; and further, that inappropriate substitutions could be made in Russell's formula. His example, "this table penholders the book", is not, however, a happy one. "Penholders" is not a relation, although Russell's formula calls for a relation between the other two terms in a judgment of the form "aRb". It is a mystery why Wittgenstein thought Russell's formula could yield "this table penholders the book". A superior example of nonsense has been suggested. In this example, a genuine relation is substituted, but a relation which is inappropriate to the objects it purportedly relates. For example, Russell's formula might yield the judgment that "2 loves 7"[61] or "the knife is the square root of the fork".[62] But I do not think that this objection would have been sufficient to "paralyze" Russell. One is not paralyzed until one is unable to move in any direction, and it must first be shown that in Russell's philosophy all avenues were closed. I think we must credit the judging person with a certain amount of selectivity when it comes, under Russell's analysis, to putting terms and relations together. No person would in fact try to make this sort of nonsensical judgment. Yet the crucial chapter does show Russell struggling with other difficulties in forming coherent propositions from his heaps of constituents, all of which leaves me convinced that Russell's philosophical susceptibility to Wittgenstein's paralytic sting lies in this chapter.

In "The Philosophy of Logical Atomism" Russell made much more of the subordinate verb in a judgment. He also made much less of the multiple relation the subject has to the constituents and form of his judgment. It is in this area that Wittgenstein's objection may have had its paralyzing effect. But I put this forward only as a suggestion, for there are passages in "Notes on Logic" which tend to make one think otherwise.

In the passages I quoted from the "Notes", the emphasis is on there being a complete, significant proposition that is judged. Criticism is directed against Russell's analysis into constituents and form, as if from these elements one could never be certain that a powerful multiple judging relation could assemble a significant proposition. This is surely the thrust of Wittgenstein's objection that the proposition "aRb . v . ~aRb" must follow from the proposition "A judges that (say) a is in the Relation R to b". Since 1907 Russell had ceased to believe in propositions as entities.[63] His stock example of a false proposition was: "Charles I died in his bed,"[64] and he refused to admit there was an objective falsehood corresponding to this proposition. The correct explanation of error, he thought, must lie in the judging relation relating the elements of a judgment in a way that they are not, in fact, related – the elements of a judgment being identical with the elements of the fact it is hoped to state. Wittgenstein, in "Notes on Logic", gives ample evidence of believing in the analysis of propositions into constituents and forms. Yet in mid-1913 he was telling Russell that his similar analysis would not put the analysed judgment back together again. In reply, Russell could not revert to his pre-1907 theory that a judgment consists of a person in a judging relation to a complete propositional entity. He could neither opt for his old theory nor see his way to improving the new theory. Thus, I suggest, he was paralyzed. As he told Lady Ottoline: "[Wittgenstein] has seen something I have missed." The chapter on "The Understanding of Propositions", like that on "Logical Data", shows him to be worried by difficulties on all sides; Wittgenstein's criticism, which is admittedly difficult to fathom, seems to have pushed Russell over the brink into rejection of work he was less than confident of even before the criticism. The solution to the problem of Russell's paralysis will, however, not become clear until it is shown how Wittgenstein managed to retain a Russellian analysis of propositions while insisting that only a complete proposition can be the object of judgment.[65]

There is among Russell's papers an undated document, called "Props", which seems to be an attempt to take Wittgenstein's objection into account. The document also grapples with Wittgenstein's new theory of the bipolarity of propositions. This theory was contained in the remark from "Notes on Logic" about "'A' having a relation to the poles 'a' and 'b' of a-p-b." But the document is very obscure, and I shall pass it by with the note that it almost certainly dates from these months, since the first page is written on the verso of a rejected draft of page 197 of "Theory of Knowledge".

By the time of "Notes Dictated to Moore" in April 1914[66] Wittgenstein had another criticism to make of the Russellian theory of judgment. He repeated the criticism in the *Tractatus*. The criticism treats propositions like "A believes that p" as truth-functional, as of the form "'p' says p" (*Tractatus*, 5.542). This analysis dispenses with the subject and correlates the constituents of the proposition with the constituents of the fact it is about. Russell was much attracted to the theory and in 1925 devoted to it Appendix C of the second edition of *Principia Mathematica*; but its attraction was rendered possible for him only by his own abandonment of the subject in 1919.[67] If Wittgenstein had come up with this view in 1913, Russell would not likely have been affected by it. So much for Russell's paralysis.

The story of how "Notes on Logic" came to be written is fairly well known, but I can provide some fresh details of Russell's reaction to Wittgenstein's first substantial piece of work. Russell was happy that at last his star pupil was producing written work. On first hearing of it he told Lady Ottoline: "[Wittgenstein] has done extraordinarily good work, and has I think practically solved the problems he was working at. You can hardly believe what a load this lifts off my spirits – it makes me feel almost young and gay" (#858, p/29 Aug. 1913). A little later, after Wittgenstein had read him bits of the work he had done, Russell remarked that he thought "it is as good as anything that has ever been done on logic" (#883, p/4 Oct. 1913). When it came actually to composing the "Notes", there were great difficulties. ". . . [Wittgenstein's] artistic conscience got in the way, and because he couldn't do it perfectly he couldn't do it at all" (#891, p/9 Oct. 1913); but by trying different methods Russell finally dragged it out of him, as he said, "with pincers". Russell was by now quite over the failure of "Theory of Knowledge", and took pride in making the work of his "ideal pupil" known. "Wittgenstein makes me feel it is worth while I should exist, because no one else could understand him or make the world understand him," he wrote in the letter just cited. Bradley's *Essays in Truth and Reality* appeared in January 1914, and it contained a criticism of Russell's theory of judgment as published in *The Problems of Philosophy* and elsewhere. Russell wrote to Bradley: "Chiefly through the work of an Austrian pupil of mine, I seem now to see answers about unities; but the subject is so difficult and fundamental that I still hesitate."[68] (The term "unities" appears to be synonymous with "complexes" – in this context, "judgments", as the mind was thought to unify the constituents of judgment into a judgment.) The reason we have "Notes on Logic" in the form in which it was published in the *Notebooks* is that Russell wanted to use it, as he said, "for lecturing on logic at Harvard" (#997, p/28 Feb. 1914). Still unable, presumably, to accept Wittgenstein's style of exposition, Russell translated and classified the remarks Wittgenstein had given him. At Harvard Russell was recollected by one observer to have been "enthusiastic" about Wittgenstein, passing around "samples from his papers"[69] and, in the words of a second observer, telling his class about Wittgenstein's genius, and his original ideas".[70] For the next ten years Russell continued the practice of referring, whenever appropriate, to Wittgenstein's unpublished work and, after it was published, to the *Tractatus*.

There is a final episode in the relationship of the early Wittgenstein and the middle Russell – an episode I wish we knew more about. At the beginning of 1914 Wittgenstein wrote Russell at least three letters. The first is full of the usual sort of introspective news and moral advice Russell was accustomed to from that source. The second extant letter refers to a quarrel they had presumably just had. Upon receiving the letter Russell informed Lady Ottoline of Wittgenstein's declaration that

. . . he and I are so dissimilar that it is useless to attempt friendship, and he will never write to me or see me again. I dare say his mood will change after a while. I find I don't care on his account, but only for the sake of logic. And yet I believe I do really care too much to look at it. It is my fault – I have been too sharp with him. (#990, p/19 Feb. 1914)

In the third extant letter Wittgenstein's mood did change. He agreed that they might resume discussing their work, but they must never talk about anything involving their value judgments. That was because neither could ever be honest about his value judgments without hurting the other. There must be a letter missing between the first and second extant letters, and I do not wish to guess at what brought on the crisis, or why Russell might have been "too sharp" with him. The crisis is extraordinary, if we consider it without the benefit of hindsight knowledge of Wittgenstein's character. It is evident that for two full years Russell and Wittgenstein enjoyed a relationship that was extremely fruitful for their shared interests, and it is also evident that there was not only great respect but great affection on both sides. And now Wittgenstein wished to end it because it rankled him that he and Russell could not be perfectly open with another and did not share the same values on all important questions. With hindsight, however, the break is not surprising and indeed seems inevitable.

The early relationship was terminated by the First World War. Russell remained dedicated to getting Wittgenstein's work published, but their relationship was never again a fruitful one. The early relationship saw Wittgenstein learn all that Russell had to teach him in logic and in much of philosophy, and Russell not only kept him fairly stable but encouraged him to communicate his work. It appears that a study of the "Theory of Knowledge" manuscript would show the *Tractatus* to be far more directed against Russell's philosophy than has been supposed.[71] Russell learned – at the peak of his accomplishments in logic – that he must have even higher standards, and that much of what he had derived as philosophically important from mathematical logic was questionable. In particular, the concept of logical form, on which he had worked for many years, turned out to be a very elusive concept indeed. He also found that the work he had set out to do in theory of knowledge was impossible to him for years to come.

In the conflict of these two lives there is much high feeling, mystery and drama. There is much good philosophy. And there are many problems for the philosophical historian and biographer to solve. At one time Wittgenstein gave Russell the lives of several great composers to read, and Russell read them. Wittgenstein was pleased, for, he said, "These are the actual sons of God."[72] It has been a privilege to indulge with you my fascination with the lives and thoughts of two more actual sons of God.

Notes

1. D. F. Pears, "Russell's Life" [review of R. W. Clark, *The Life of Bertrand Russell*], *New Review*, 2 (Dec. 1975), 63–6 (at 65). What Pears actually says is: ". . . the work of a philosopher is too much part of his life to be included in his biography like a remote and unimportant country shown in an inset in a map".

2. *My Philosophical Development* (London: Allen & Unwin, 1959), p. 217.

3. *My Own Philosophy* (Hamilton, Ont.: McMaster University Library Press, 1972), p. 4. Written in 1946. The next year Russell instructed his publisher to alter a statement in the "Introduction to the Second Edition" of *The Principles of Mathematics*, p. ix, line 9. The statement had read: "In order that a proposition may belong to mathematics it must have a further property: according to Wittgenstein it must be 'tautological,' and according to Carnap it must be 'analytic.'" Russell instructed his publisher to alter "Wittgenstein" to "some" (letter to Sir Stanley Unwin, 17 July 1947).

4. *My Philosophical Development*, p. 112.

5. *Autobiography*, II (London: Allen & Unwin, 1968), 100–1.

6. *Autobiography*, II, 199–200.

7. In L. Wittgenstein, *Letters to Russell, Keynes and Moore*, ed. G. H. von Wright (Oxford: Blackwell, 1974). Wittgenstein did attend the paper, and later wrote on its subject. See his "Cause and Effect: Intuitive Awareness", ed. Rush Rhees and trans. Peter Winch, *Philosophia*, 6 (1976), 391–408 (preceded by the German text).

8. M. O'C. Drury, *The Danger of Words* (London: Routledge & Kegan Paul, 1973), p. xiii.

9. *Letters to Russell, Keynes and Moore*, p. 186.

10. Norman Malcolm, *Ludwig Wittgenstein: A Memoir*, 2nd edn (London: Oxford University Press, 1966), p. 68.

11. See Ronald W. Clark, *The Life of Bertrand Russell* (London: Cape/Weidenfeld & Nicolson, 1975), p. 494, and Karl Popper, "Autobiography", *The Philosophy of Karl Popper*, ed. P. A.

Schilpp (La Salle, Ill.: Open Court, 1974), I, 97–8. Peter Geach and Casimer Lewy were at the meeting and deny the incident happened.

12. *Autobiography*, II, 101; "My First Fifty Years", typescript, Bertrand Russell Archives, p. 143, and "printer's copy" (which was withdrawn), p. 502.

13. See B. F. McGuinness, "Bertrand Russell and Ludwig Wittgenstein's 'Notes on Logic'", *Revue Internationale de Philosophie*, 26 (1972), 444–60.

14. Reprinted in Eric Homberger *et al.*, eds., *The Cambridge Mind* (London: Cape, 1970).

15. Max Black, *Mind*, 73 (1964), 134.

16. See Wittgenstein's letter to Russell of 22 July 1913 (*Letters to Russell, Keynes and Moore*, p. 24).

17. According to von Wright's "Biographical Sketch", in Malcolm, p. 5.

18. "Ludwig Wittgenstein", *Mind*, 60 (1951), 297. *Cf. Autobiography*, II, 98; *Portraits from Memory, and Other Essays* (London: Allen and Unwin, 1956), p. 23.

19. *ibid.*, p. 298.

20. Michael Dummett, *Frege: Philosophy of Language* (London: Duckworth, 1973), p. 662.

21. Jourdain noted in his correspondence book on 20 April 1909 that Russell had "said that the views I gave in a reply to Wittgenstein (who had 'solved' Russell's contradiction) agree with his own" (p. 205). Original at Mittag-Leffler Institut, Djursholm, Sweden. I. Grattan-Guinness drew my attention to this. See his *Dear Russell – Dear Jourdain: A Commentary on Russell's Logic, Based on His Correspondence with Philip Jourdain* (London: Duckworth, 1977 [i.e. 1978]), pp. 114–15.

22. *Mind*, 60 (1951), 297. Russell here restated the theory as "that all existential statements are meaningless".

23. *Autobiography*, II, 99.

24. *Mind*, 60 (1951), 298.

25. *The Early Memoirs of Lady Ottoline Morrell*, ed. R. Gathorne-Hardy (London: Faber & Faber, 1963), p. 102. For Ritchie, see David G. Ritchie, *Philosophical Studies*, ed. with a memoir by Robert Latta (London: Macmillan, 1905).

26. In his dissertation, "Types, Categories, and Significance" (unpubl. Ph.D. dissertation, McMaster University, 1979), Appendix A.

27. See Allan Janik and Stephen Toulmin, *Wittgenstein's Vienna* (New York: Simon & Schuster, 1973), pp. 93, 204–5.

28. *Letters to Russell, Keynes and Moore*, p. 53. My quotation contains a correction of the original translation. The correction is the addition of the phrase "and acts" and is due to David Bell in his review of the *Letters* in *Russell: The Journal of the Bertrand Russell Archives*, no. 15 (Autumn 1974), 26–8.

29. Read to The Heretics at Cambridge on 11 March 1912; *Monist*, 22 (July 1912), 321–47.

30. See John King-Farlow, "Self-Enlargement and Union: Neglected Passages of Russell and Famous Ones of Proust", *Theoria to Theory*, 11 (1977), 105–15.

31. "The Essence of Religion", in R. E. Egner and L. E. Denonn, eds., *The Basic Writings of Bertrand Russell* (London: Allen & Unwin, 1961), p. 568. For a discussion – especially of the Platonistic elements – see Ronald Jager, "Russell and Religion", in J. E. Thomas and K. Blackwell, eds., *Russell in Review* (Toronto: Samuel Stevens Hakkert, 1976).

32. For a discussion of this point a couple of years later in Wittgenstein's development, see McGuinness, "The *Grundgedanke* of the *Tractatus*", in Godfrey Vesey, ed., *Understanding Wittgenstein* (London: Macmillan, 1974), p. 56.

33. See M. Teresa Iglesias, "Russell's Introduction to Wittgenstein's *Tractatus*", *Russell*, nos 25–8 (1977), 21–38 (esp. 29, 38).

34. Quoted by von Hayek, p. 18.
35. *The Cambridge Mind*, p. 128.
36. Quoted by von Hayek, pp. 16–17.
37. "Matter" (1913), unpublished manuscript, Russell Archives, p. 9.
38. A. Lawrence Lowell to Russell, 6 June 1913.
39. By Elizabeth Ramsden Eames and myself, "Russell's Unpublished Book on Theory of Knowledge", *Russell*, no. 19 (Autumn 1975), 3–14, 18, and in her Introduction to *Theory of Knowledge: the 1913 Manuscript, The Collected Papers of Bertrand Russell*, vol. VII (London: Allen & Unwin, forthcoming).
40. Blackwell and Eames, p. 4.
41. For a revision of Russell's account of how he wrote this book, see my "Our Knowledge of Our Knowledge", *Russell*, no. 12 (Winter 1973–4), 11–13.
42. *Letters to Russell, Keynes and Moore*, p. 24.
43. See the long letter quoted by Clark, pp. 209–10 (#850, p/19 Aug. 1913).
44. Frege to Russell, 22 June 1902, and Russell to Jean van Heijenoort, 23 November 1962, in van Heijenoort, ed., *From Frege to Gödel* (Cambridge, Mass.: Harvard University Press, 1967), p. 127.
45. *Autobiography*, II, 57 (dated only [1916]).
46. Russell took steps to publish the six chapters within three weeks of putting "Theory of Knowledge" aside. See Blackwell and Eames, pp. 11–12.
47. *The Problems of Philosophy* (London: Williams and Norgate [1912]), ch. 9.
48. ibid., ch. 5, "Knowledge by Acquaintance and Knowledge by Description". I owe this suggestion to John G. Slater.
49. *Letters to Russell, Keynes and Moore*, p. 23.
50. McGuinness, "The *Grundgedanke* of the *Tractatus*", pp. 50–1.
51. Pears, "Russell's Life", p. 65.
52. "Theory of Knowledge", unpublished manuscript, Russell Archives, p. 186.
53. *Revue de Métaphysique et de Morale*, 19 (May 1911), 281–91; trans. into English by P. E. B. Jourdain, *Monist*, 23 (Oct. 1913), 481–93; reprinted (and mistitled) in Russell, *Essays in Analysis*, ed. Douglas Lackey (London: Allen & Unwin, 1973).
54. (London and Chicago: Open Court, 1914), p. 208.
55. "Atomic Propositional Thought", n.d., file 210.06556–F1.
56. Irving Copi, *Journal of Philosophy*, 60 (1963), 766.
57. Peter Geach, *Mental Acts* (London: Routledge & Kegan Paul [1957]), p. 49.
58. "The Philosophy of Logical Atomism", in R. C. Marsh, ed., *Logic and Knowledge* (London: Allen & Unwin, 1956), p. 226.
59. "Definitions and Methodological Principles in Theory of Knowledge", *Monist*, 24 (Oct. 1914), 584.
60. "Notes on Logic", earlier version, Russell Archives, Summary, p. 2. The earlier version has now replaced the later version in Wittgenstein's *Notebooks 1914–1916*, 2nd ed., edited by G. E. M. Anscombe and G. H. von Wright (Oxford: Blackwell, 1979).
61. Black, *A Companion to Wittgenstein's Tractatus* (Ithaca: Cornell University Press, 1964), p. 301.
62. Pears, *Bertrand Russell and the British Tradition in Philosophy*, 2nd edn (London: Collins/Fontana, 1972), p. 217.
63. See Section III of "On the Nature of Truth", *Proceedings of the Aristotelian Society*, n.s. 7 (1907), 44–9. This section was not included when the other sections were reprinted as "The Monistic Theory of Truth" in *Philosophical Essays* (1910).

64. "On the Nature of Truth and Falsehood", *Philosophical Essays* (London: Longmans, Green, 1910), p. 173; "Theory of Knowledge", MS, p. 200.

65. In addition to those already mentioned, there are the following published commentaries on Wittgenstein's criticism of Russell's theory of judgment: G. E. M. Anscombe, *An Introduction to Wittgenstein's Tractatus*, 3rd edn (London: Hutchinson, 1967), pp. 45–6; J. Griffin, *Wittgenstein's Logical Atomism* (Oxford: Blackwell, 1964), pp. 113–14; P. M. S. Hacker, *Insight and Illusion: Wittgenstein on Philosophy and the Metaphysics of Experience* (Oxford: Clarendon Press, 1972), pp. 60–1; A. J. P. Kenny, *Wittgenstein* (London: Allen Lane The Penguin Press, 1973), p. 101; Guy Stock, "Wittgenstein on Russell's Theory of Judgment", in Vesey, ed., *Understanding Wittgenstein*, pp. 62–75. Pears has the benefit of using the manuscript of "Theory of Knowledge" in "The Relation between Wittgenstein's Picture Theory of Propositions and Russell's Theories of Judgment", *Philosophical Review*, 86 (April 1977), 177–96, and in "Wittgenstein's Picture Theory and Russell's *Theory of Knowledge*", in *Wittgenstein and the Vienna Circle and Critical Rationalism: Proceedings of the Third International Wittgenstein Symposium*, ed. H. Berghel, A. Hübner and E. Köhler (Vienna: Hölder-Pichler-Tempsky, 1979), pp. 101–7. See also the bibliography in Nicholas Griffin's unpublished paper (footnote on page 1 above) and Nicholas Griffin, "Russell on the Nature of Logic", *Synthese*, 45 (September 1980), 117–88 (esp. 170–80).

66. Appendix II, *Notebooks, 1914–1916*, p. 118. (Pointed out by Hacker, p 61n.)

67. It should be noted that he did so before receiving the typescript of the *Tractatus* (in June or July 1919). Russell abandoned the subject in "On Propositions: What they Are and How They Mean" (*Aristotelian Society Supp. Vol.*, 2 [1919], 1–43), and he had finished a first draft of this paper by early March 1919 (see Russell to Constance Malleson, 4 March 1919). The paper was not, however, delivered until 11 July 1919.

68. F. H. Bradley, "A Discussion of Some Problems in Connexion with Mr Russell's Doctrine", *Essays in Truth and Reality* (Oxford: Clarendon Press, 1914), pp. 293–309. Russell to Bradley, 30 Jan. 1914, Merton College Library, Oxford (copy at McMaster).

69. Harry T. Costello, "Logic in 1914 and Now", *Journal of Philosophy* 54 (25 April 1957), 246.

70. Victor F. Lenzen, "Bertrand Russell at Harvard, 1914", *Russell*, no. 3 (Autumn 1971), 5.

71. Even the *Tractatus*'s mysticism may be related to Russell's thinking on the subject. For an examination of the affinities, see B. F. McGuinness, "The Mysticism of the *Tractatus*", *Philosophical Review*, 75 (1966), 305–28.

72. Wittgenstein to Russell, 16 Aug. 1912 (*Letters to Russell, Keynes and Moore*, p. 15).

Frege and Wittgenstein

MICHAEL DUMMETT

Everyone knows that Wittgenstein was soaked in Frege's writings and in Frege's thought. Doubtless many philosophers unnamed by Wittgenstein can be shown to have given him ideas. Others, to whom he does refer, provided him with material that he found interesting to reflect or comment on: but Frege is very nearly the only one whom he quotes with approval. It would be an exhausting and a thankless task to cull from Wittgenstein's writings every passage containing an overt or covert reference to Frege, or for the understanding of which it is necessary to know Frege's ideas, and I have not attempted it; I dwell on only a few points that have struck me as of especial interest.

Some of Wittgenstein's work builds on, elaborates or complements that of Frege: and then, I think, Wittgenstein is at his happiest. One example is the famous doctrine of Frege concerning the necessity for criteria of identity (a phrase which Frege introduced into philosophy). It is stated in the *Grundlagen* thus: "If we are to use the sign *a* to designate an object, we must have a criterion for deciding in all cases whether *b* is the same as *a*." The principle here enunciated by Frege is perfectly general, and the idea is fundamental for the first third of the *Philosophical Investigations* (*PI*), and, indeed, throughout that book. Yet Frege himself worked out its implication only to terms for abstract objects, or, to speak more precisely, to terms of such forms as 'the direction of *a*', 'the number of F's', and so on; that is, to terms formed by means of expressions for functions of first or second level which do not, or do not obviously, carry their arguments into objects specifiable without appeal to those functions. It was left to Wittgenstein to apply the principle that the understanding of a singular term involves the apprehension of an appropriate criterion of identity to terms of other sorts, including for what would ordinarily be thought of as concrete objects.

Again, consider Frege's insistence that the sense of an expression is not connected with any psychological process, for instance the evocation of mental images, a principle he expressly associated with the objectivity of sense, with the fact that a thought is communicable without residue from speaker to hearer by means of language. Frege thought it necessary to safeguard the non-psychological character of sense by holding that senses exist timelessly and in independence of whether there is available any means of expressing them. This highly unWittgensteinian thesis he supported by a number of bad arguments, such as that, even before there were men, it was already true that the Earth goes round the Sun, and would have been true even if there had never been any men; and surely what is true is a thought, and a thought is the sense of a sentence. But this did not save Frege from getting into difficulties over the question: Even granted that senses are not mind-dependent, still grasping a sense, or understanding a word or phrase, as expressing a sense, is surely a mental act, something that belongs within the province of psychology. Frege never found a satisfactory answer to this objection: it receives its answer from Wittgenstein's observation (*PI*, §154), "Try not to think of understanding as a 'mentlal process' at all. . . In the sense in which there are processes (including mental processes) which are characteristic of understanding, understanding is not a mental process."

Or, finally, take Frege's views about the relation between sense and reference. Sense determines reference, but reference does not determine sense; nevertheless, when we lay down what the reference of some expression is to be, we thereby provide a sense for it. As I remarked in my book, and as, I understand, Peter Geach has worked out in much more detail, it is difficult to expound this doctrine without inconsistency save by invoking the distinction drawn in the *Tractatus* between *saying* and *showing*. In laying down what an expression is to stand for, we *say* what its reference is, not what its sense is; but, by choosing, as we must, a particular manner of doing this, we *show* what sense it is to have. The distinction between saying and showing is not only consonant with Frege's ideas, but almost required for a coherent statement of them. Indeed, had Frege had this distinction at his command, a great deal of misunderstanding of his doctrine of sense would surely have been avoided. Not only, in laying down the reference of a term, do we not *state*, but only *show*, its sense; but surely, we ought to add, we cannot state the sense of an expression, save as being the same as that of some other expression, something which, within one language, there is no reason to suppose can always be done. That does not mean, in my view, that a theory of sense is mute, that a theory of sense can only be shown, not stated, since while we cannot state the sense of an expression, we can state what it is to grasp that sense and attach it to that expression. Whether or not Frege would have agreed with this last remark, I do not know; but I do feel reasonably certain that, if he had had the distinction between saying and showing to hand, he would not have laid himself open to the charge, which I continue to believe is a misinterpretation, of having held a 'description theory' of proper names.

All these are cases in which Wittgenstein built upon doctrines of Frege to produce what is not only a legitimate, but the only true, development of them. In other cases, Wittgenstein fought against the power of Frege's thought; and in such cases, I believe, he was almost always at his worst. In most of them, in my opinion, Frege was in the right and Wittgenstein in the wrong; but, even when this is not so, Wittgenstein seldom succeeded in framing cogent arguments to show that Frege was wrong. Take, for example, his repeated attacks upon Frege's doctrine of assertion. The first hundred-odd paragraphs of the *Philosophical Investigations* almost all compel assent; although there may be large questions about how one should go on from there, it is almost impossible to read those paragraphs and maintain any reservations about this definitive treatment of the topics with which they deal. But from this classic landscape, paragraph 22 – that in which he attacks Frege's doctrine of assertion – sticks out like a gasometer. To vary the metaphor abruptly, the boxer's punches suddenly become feeble, and miss their mark or are easily blocked.

Or, again, consider the celebrated passage towards the beginning of the *Blue Book* (p. 4) in which Wittgenstein comments on Frege's criticism of the formalist philosophy of mathematics as ignoring the sense, and thus, as Wittgenstein says, the life of the mathematical formulas. He characterizes Frege's conclusion as that ". . . what must be added to the dead signs in order to make a live proposition is something immaterial, with properties different from all mere signs", and reports, "But if we had to name anything which is the life of the sign, we should have to say that it was its *use*." If, as Waismann did, one interprets the 'use' of a mathematical statement as its extra-mathematical application, the idea is very unconvincing. What is the application of the proposition that every number is the sum of four squares? Even if one can think of one, could someone not perfectly well understand this proposition without having the least suspicion of that application? If it is the application of mathematical concepts that ultimately gives them their meaning, then, one must surely say, the injection of meaning may be very remote from the particular proposition considered. One cannot ask for the application proposition by proposition, but, at best, for the applications of the basic concepts; once these are grasped, the mathematical theory takes on a life of its own. But, in this sense, did not Frege do full justice to the relation between a basic mathematical concept and its application? It was not Frege who formulated the Peano axioms or presented number theory as a self-contained axiomatic system; on the contrary, he insisted that the natural numbers could be explained only by reference to their use as cardinal numbers in empirical, and other, propositions; and he thought that the real numbers must, likewise, be explained by reference to the general conception of a conception of a measure of the magnitude of a quantity. In any case, what *is* an application of a mathematical proposition? We are all so used to the fact that there is such a thing as applied mathematics that we do not stop to notice what an odd idea it is that a theory, or a proposition, can be 'applied' to some other subject-matter. I do not mean to deny that mathematics gets applied: I am contending only that an appeal to the application of mathematics cannot help us philosophically until we can say in what such an application consists; and we cannot say this until we have a prior account of the significance of a mathematical statement.

Almost certainly, however, Wittgenstein did not intend to restrict the notion of the 'use' of a mathematical statement to its empirical applications, but had in mind, not only its application within mathematics, but, more generally, its role in the mathematical theory. But what is to show that Frege did not succeed in giving a general account of this? True, Frege took sense to be immaterial and to exist independently of our grasping it; but this does not exhaust his conception of the sense of a sentence: he said a great deal more about that in which such a sense consists, above all, that, in grasping the sense of a sentence, including a mathematical sentence, what we grasp is the condition for that sentence to be true. Perhaps these are not, after all, the right terms in which to explain our understanding of mathematical statements; perhaps it can be shown that the use which we learn to make of such statements is incapable of being explained in this way. But, then, it has to be shown: one cannot simply oppose the notion of use to Frege's notion of sense, as if it were something Frege had obviously left out of account. I am not, of course, here criticizing Wittgenstein's famous conception of meaning as use: I am criticizing only a formulation which makes it appear that, in arriving at this conception, Wittgenstein had discovered something which immediately shows Frege to have been thinking along the wrong lines.

When Wittgenstein is moved to make direct criticisms of Frege, the criticism is usually curiously ineffective, and fails to do justice to Frege's thought. It is one thing to make this observation, however, and quite another to say that, whenever Wittgenstein diverges from Frege on any essential point, he gets on to the wrong track. That would be to make a devastating condemnation of Wittgenstein, if it could be made out; for there is no doubt that the differences between them are not just a matter of style, or of passing remarks, or of disagreements over inessentials: many of Wittgenstein's most fundamental ideas concerning meaning are irreconcilable with those of Frege.

The first attempt to make a radical modification in Frege's conception of how language functions was the picture theory, perhaps, better, the diagram theory, of the *Tractatus*. In Frege, a proper name (singular term) is complete (*selbständig*), and so is a sentence; and the things which they stand for, an object and a truth-value, are likewise complete. But a one- or two-place predicate is incomplete, and so is the concept or relation for which it stands. The incompleteness of the predicate is not a mere semantic property: it does not consist just in its having to be understood as standing for something incomplete, a mapping of objects on to truth-values. Rather, it is itself incomplete: it is not just a string of words that can be extracted from the sentence and stand on its own, not even a dis-connected string; its occurrence in the sentence depends, in general, upon the occurrence in different places in the sentence of the same proper name. It is, thus, not a detachable bit of the sentence, but a feature that the sentence has in common with certain other sentences. The com-pleteness of names and of sentences, conversely, is likewise not a mere semantic property: they are themselves complete – they are objects – in the way that predicates are not.

Now this, notoriously, leads to difficulty. If the fundamental concep-tion of Frege's theory of meaning – that to grasp the sense of a sentence is to know the condition for its truth – is right at all, then surely the iden-tification of the reference of a sentence with its truth-value is correct. Admittedly, this forces us to treat intensional contexts in some special way; but, then, we are already forced to do this by Frege's identification of the semantic values (references) of proper names with their bearers. If the reference of "Napoleon" is a man, and that of "Mont Blanc" a mountain, then we already know that names, at least, cannot have their standard reference when they appear in intensional contexts. But, if the reference of a sentence is its truth-value, we are very easily led into the disastrous step which Frege took of assimilating sentences to proper names: sentences are just complex names of a special kind of object. This step produces intolerable consequences, and so we must seek to undo it: but how? Not, surely by denying that sentences have reference at all. The whole theory of reference is an attempt to give an account of how a sentence is determined as true or false in accordance with its composition: and, if Frege's fundamental conception of the theory of meaning is correct, such an account must be possible, and must underlie any account of sense, which is what determines reference. But sentences can occur as constituent parts of other sentences; and so they must be assigned a reference if the whole theory is to fulfil its appointed task. (If sentences could not occur as parts of other sentences, we should be in no difficulty.) Nor, while sentences are regarded as being complete in the same way that proper names are, does it seem reasonable, in the context of Frege's fundamental conception of a theory of meaning, to deny that what a sentence has as its reference is its truth-value. The only recourse, which I should myself favour, is to deny that truth-values are objects; and this seems a weak response. Of course, we have a strong intuition that sentences are not of the same syntactic or semantic category as proper names, and this implies, at least within a Fregean framework, that the things they stand for will be of different logical types too: but to say that truth-values are not objects hardly illuminates the nature of this type-difference. We can say various things in support. We can, for instance, as Peter Geach has pointed out, say that the principle of the interchangeability of any expression a with ⌜what a stands for⌝ works very badly, if at all, for sentences. Or, again, we can observe that while with names and even with predicates it seems plausible to say that the references of our words are what we talk about, we have not the least inclination to allow that we use a subsentence of a complex sentence to talk about its truth-value. Still, these incongruities seem rather witnesses to the difference between objects and truth-values than explanations of it. If we are going to get such an explanation, it will surely depend upon a much more searching enquiry into what truth-values are.

The picture or diagram theory surely appeared as a brilliant solution of this difficulty. If a predicate is a property, rather than an object, why not take it as a property, not of the sentence, but of the name or names that appear in its argument-places? The predicate will not consist in the property of the atomic sentence that the same proper name occurs in various places between certain other words: rather, (a token of) the predicate will consist in the property of the name that certain tokens of it occur in those places. If we say that, then we can replace the sentence as object – the string of words – by the sentence as fact – the fact that a certain name has a certain property, or that two names stand in a certain relation. And then, abiding by the principle, which is not in Frege, but is partially suggested by his doctrine of predicates and of concepts, that a linguistic ingredient of a given logical type will stand for an entity of the same logical type, we shall arrive at the conclusion that the sentence – considered as fact – must itself stand for or represent a fact, or, rather, since it need not be true, a state of affairs; and now the temptation to think that names and sentences stand for or represent things of the same logical type is totally dissolved.

This would have been a brilliant solution had it worked. Unfortunately, it does not work. A sentence cannot be a fact because it states just one thing; and the hearer, if he understands the language, must know just what it is that it states. A diagram is not a fact, it is an object; and there are many facts about the diagram. If we understand the method of representation, then we shall know which facts about the diagram represent, and which do not: for instance, which lines are drawn in black, and which in red, may or may not be significant; and we may well overlook some of these facts although we see the diagram and understand it. The diagram will show, e.g., that the only man in the village with great-grandchildren has a wife older than himself, and also that only the three oldest men in the village have wives older than themselves, and so on; and what show these different facts are different facts about the diagram, facts not all of which we may notice, and, save with the simplest diagram, some of which we are sure *not* to notice, when we look at the diagram. But a sentence is not like this: though the sentence may imply many things, it *says* just one thing, and, if you understand it at all, you must know what it says; you cannot, just by studying the sentence more closely, elicit new things that it says that you had not noticed before. Well, it may be replied, that is because the diagram is, as you said, not itself a fact but an object: any one fact about the diagram signifies just one fact about what it represents; and the sentence is being claimed to be a fact, not a diagram or picture – hence the inappropriateness of the name 'the picture theory'. But, if a sentence is to represent in the way that a fact about the diagram does, there must be something that plays the role of the diagram, other facts about which will also represent; and what is that? If what represents some state of affairs is a fact about the properties or relations of certain objects, the names or signs, then we must start with some arrangement of these objects in virtue of which that fact obtains, and this arrangement will correspond to the diagram. What can that arrangement be but the sentence, considered, now, not as a fact but as an object with a certain complexity? Thus, if we try to take the picture or diagram theory seriously, we are, after all, forced back on to considering the sentence, once again, as an object; and, since there are not *different* facts about the sentence, as object, which represent different states of affairs, we are forced to conclude that the sentence does not represent as a diagram does, but in a different way altogether.

In his later work, the conception of meaning as use led Wittgenstein into a much more radical divergence from Frege's theory of meaning, although that conception itself owes something to Frege's ideas. For Frege, as I have remarked, it is of the essence of sense that it is communicable. It happens, indeed, that different speakers attach different senses to the same word; but the communicability of sense implies that it must always be objectively discoverable when this is so and objectively discoverable what sense each attaches. But, also, sense is not psychological; it is not because a speaker's utterance of a word occurs in response to some inner mental process, and that utterance triggers off a similar process in the mind of the hearer, and they share a common psychological make-up, that the one understands the other. Their agreement over the sense of the utterance consists in an agreement on the conditions under which it is true. Since sense is objective and communicable, it must be possible to determine from what they say, and how they react to what is said, what truth-conditions they attach to sentences. What makes this possible is that every utterance effects more than just the expression of a thought: the speaker also indicates, tacitly or explicitly, the type of linguistic act that he is performing, e.g. asserting that the thought is true, asking whether it is true, etc.; he thereby attaches one or another type of force to his utterance. Each type of force bears a uniform relation to the sense of the sentence: whether or not it is possible to give a non-circular characterization of the type of linguistic act effected by the utterance of a sentence with this or that variety of force, Frege never said. What is clear, however, is that, on this conception, everything involved in communication, both the sense expressed and the force attached to that expression, is determined by what lies open to view. Since no contact between mind and mind, save that achieved by the medium of linguistic interchange, need be assumed, and since the sense of an utterance and, presumably, the force it carries are objectively determinable, they can only be determined by the observable employment of the language. If a non-circular account of the different varieties of force is attainable, then we may describe how the speakers' use of their sentences determines what they convey by means of them. But, even if such an account is not attainable, that use, and nothing else, determines the content of their utterances: no other supposition would be compatible with the doctrines about language expressly propounded by Frege.

It is easy to see how, when these principles, learned from Frege, had been encapsulated in the slogan, "Meaning is use," Wittgenstein came, in his middle period, to give a verificationist turn to them. There is a tendency to be apologetic about this, as if verificationism were a rather discreditable complaint; but so far as I can see, no discredit attaches to this tendency at all. The cardinal error of logical positivism lay in treating all synthetic propositions as standing on the same level (unless they proved to be pseudo-propositions), that is, in ignoring the articulated structure of language. In the most characteristic forms of positivism, each sentence was treated as if it were in principle intelligible in isolation from the rest of language, being given meaning by some direct association with a set of possible sequences of sense-perceptions, each of which would constitute a verification of it. It was this unnatural picture which led to the complete sundering of analytic or would-be analytic propositions from the main body of language, since they could be established, if at all, only by linguistic operations, and hence had to be regarded as having a meaning of a completely different kind. To obtain a plausible conception of verification, it is necessary to recognize that no sentence can be understood without a mastery of some segment of the language, and that, in establishing a sentence as true, argument, including deductive argument, may always, and often must, play a part. So far as I know, there is no hint in Wittgenstein's writings of the positivists' mistake.

Verificationism naturally first appeared as a sharpening of Frege's conception of sense as given by truth-conditions: someone shows what he takes as the condition for the truth of a sentence by showing what he takes as establishing or excluding the truth. But it appears to me that Wittgenstein came to see it as a rival to Frege's conception. Frege assumed a notion of truth for which the principle of bivalence held good: save for failure of reference, every thought was determinately either true or false. But this means that, when there is no effective means, even in principle, to decide whether a thought is true or false, a knowledge of the condition for it to be true cannot be exhaustively accounted for in terms of a knowledge of those special conditions under which it may be recognized as one or the other. But, then, there seems no other way by which we may account for the supposed knowledge of the truth-condition in terms of actual use, of principles governing the actual employment of the sentence expressing the thought. Hence, if meaning is to be explained solely in terms of use, in such cases we must abandon the idea that a grasp of the sense consists in a knowledge of the condition for the sentence to be true, where the notion of truth is subject to the principle of bivalence, or even the idea that we have any such notion of truth. Rather, the understanding of the sentence consists in an ability to recognize what is taken to establish its truth, and, perhaps, what is taken as ruling it out.

But a much more radical idea superseded this. It is marked, in part, by Wittgenstein's embracing the redundancy theory of truth (of which there is an explicit expression in the *Remarks on the Foundations of Mathematics*, in the Appendix on Gödel's theorem). If an enunciation of the equivalence between a sentence A and the sentence ⌜It is true that A⌝ is the *whole* explanation of the meaning of the word "true", then that word has, as it were, a home only *within* the language, and is of no use in giving an account of the language as from the outside: and this rules out, not only an account of meaning in terms of truth-conditions, but, equally, one in terms of verification. Passages like *PI*, §304 and §317 and, particularly, the middle paragraph of §363 are the expression of a total rejection of Frege's approach to language. For Frege, an utterance is an assertion, a question, a command, a request, a piece of advice, an instruction, an expression of a wish, or one of some small and determinate number of other things. What the particular content of the utterance is, is a matter of its sense; what type of utterance it is, is a matter of the force attached to it. So, as I remarked, there must be a uniform explanation, or at least way of grasping, the significance of each type of utterance, the nature of each type of force, and, in particular, of assertoric force: uniform, that is, over all the possible particular contents, the senses, of utterances of that type. "What is the language-game of telling?" *That* is the question that must have an answer if Frege's approach to language is at all correct: and here the difference between an account of sense in terms of truth-conditions and in terms of verification is quite beside the point; neither is workable unless we can distinguish sense from force. *PI,*

§363 is an overt repudiation of the possibility of such a distinction, or, at least, of any uniform account of what it is to make an assertion. And this, of course, explains Wittgenstein's hostility to Frege's doctrine of assertion. The confused objection of *PI*, §22 is not the point. *PI*, §23 is more to the point: if no definitive list of types of force can be made, then no complete account of a language can be arrived at by Frege's strategy. Even that is not the real point, however; we might be content to let some of the minor cases take care of themselves, if only we could deal with the most prominent uses of language. The real point is to deny that there is any 'language-game' of such generality as that of assertion; and, if there is not, then, it seems to me, there is no general distinction between sense and force.

What is the ground for this denial? That is something I have never been able to understand. Perhaps it is just that it seems so difficult to achieve a general account of assertoric force, of the language-game of assertion. Perhaps some watertight formulation can be arrived at along Gricean lines; but then to invoke the concept, not only of intention, but of belief, appears to be begging the question, since most of the beliefs formed on the testimony of others could not be intelligibly ascribed to anyone who had not the command of a language. If we forswear all appeal to propositional attitudes, however, we hardly know how to begin. But, now, what is supposed to be the alternative? Is it just that a systematic account of how a language functions, or of what we know when we know a language, is impossible? But, then, how can this be? It is something that we do, something that we learn to do: how can it be impossible to say what it is that we do, what it is that we learn? Of course, in one sense, we already know what we do: but we do not know how to *say* what it is we do. The simple language-games described by Wittgenstein, like the one about people going into a shop and saying things like, "Five red apples", are supposed to be some kind of model. But these tiny languages are ones the practice of speaking which *can* be systematically described: so, if they are really a model, such descriptions can be given also for larger and larger fragments of language, and eventually the whole of it. Yet, as soon as one starts to think how one might set about doing this for even some quite restricted language that still permits anything resembling the discourse of every day, rather than the employment of language as an adjunct to one specific activity, one's first thought is the necessity of some distinction between sense and force. Or, if one imagines a language with only assertions, what seems to be needed is an account of the particular content of each utterance in terms of some central notion such as truth or verification, set against the background of some uniform explanation of the significance of an utterance with some arbitrary given content, so determined. It is not that I think this would be easy to do: my difficulty, as I said, is to understand what alternative it was that Wittgenstein had in mind, something that I have never learned either from his writings or from those of philosophers who acknowledge him as their master.

Wittgenstein and the Theory of Types[1]

HIDÉ ISHIGURO

> The reason why a function cannot be its own argument is that the sign for a function already contains the prototype of its argument, and it cannot contain itself.
>
> For let us suppose that the function $F(fx)$ could be its own argument: in that case there would be a proposition '$F(F(fx))$' in which the outer function F and the inner function F must have different meanings, since the inner one has the form $\varphi(fx)$ and the outer one has the form $\psi(\varphi(fx))$. Only the letter 'F' is common to the two functions, but the letter by itself signifies nothing.
>
> This immediately becomes clear if instead of '$F(Fu)$' we write '$(\exists\varphi):F(\varphi u).\varphi u = Fu$'.
>
> That disposes of Russell's paradox.
>
> (Tractatus, 3.333)

We all know that in the *Tractatus* Wittgenstein does not as a rule attempt to explain his own doctrines or discuss their background or sources. Aphorism is his habitual form, both for challenging the doctrines of his contemporaries and for expressing agreement with them. There are a fair number of exceptions to this, however: passages where he refers to the views with which he disagrees and states his own doctrine as an explicit improvement. One case of this is his brief comment on the theory of types, which I believe reveals many interesting insights. If we follow the *Tractatus* view of how propositional functions are identified within a proposition and constitute themselves into types, I think Russell's paradox can be avoided. It can be avoided so long as one makes two further assumptions. The first is one which Russell himself made in *Principia*, that classes are logical fictions, and that talk about membership in classes is only a *façon de parler*. The second assumption is disjunctive and it requires one *either* to hold, as Wittgenstein did, that formal concepts (e.g. *being an object* or *being a property*) cannot be expressed by propositional functions, *or* to make a distinction between a meta-language and object language, and rule that some predicates of the metalanguage cannot be predicates of the object language.

Wittgenstein's interest in the theory of types did not come from a concern to provide a coherent foundation of mathematics. Wittgenstein did not believe that mathematics could be or need be given a foundation. ("Theory of classes is superfluous in mathematics", 6.031.) His claim that mathematics is a method of logic (6.234) appears to be based on his belief that reiterable operations which form the basis of mathematics are already part of any logic.[2] Natural numbers at least were identified not with sets of any kind, but with exponents of operations (6.021). (I take this as implying that the understanding of *how often* an operation is reiterated is more primitive than the understanding of *how many* objects there are.) Nevertheless, Wittgenstein thought that the logical paradoxes arose from a misunderstanding about how propositional functions could be individuated. The need to clarify this was extremely important for logic, he thought, and for the understanding of the nature of symbolism and language. He never uses talk about sets in his discussion of the paradoxes, but expresses the problem in terms of propositional functions. Wittgenstein's approach was somewhat different from those of Frege and Russell, however. They had said that certain kinds of sentences or expressions were not legitimately constructed according to their theory, and *therefore* 'senseless'. Whereas Wittgenstein would say that *if* we do not understand a seeming sentence made up of words which we know, *then* it is not well formed. *If* we do understand a proposition on the other hand and see it as saying something, i.e. as expressing a truth-condition, *then* the proposition is well-formed (5.4733). Understanding what is said by using a sentence, then, is a primitive notion.

Russell had said that '$\varphi(\varphi\hat{x})$' (where '$\varphi\hat{x}$' is supposed to express the propositional function itself) does not express anything – it is not significant. This was for two different reasons. First, because of the vicious circle principle, Russell thought it impossible to understand what the propositional function $\varphi\hat{x}$ is, except by a prior understanding of the domain of its variable. It followed that the domain could not include the propositional function itself.[3] The point can be reproduced for natural language. "Being blue is blue" does not say something false. It does not say anything at all. The predicate " – is blue" can be understood as ascribing something only when the domain of its application is already determined. It follows that the feature of being blue that it ascribes cannot be among the members of its domain. Russell also has a second and different reason. He claimed that a propositional function is not a definitive object, and so not the kind of thing that satisfies any first-order function.[4] This would render meaningless any subject-predicate statement with a propositional function in subject-place. Thus not only is "Being blue is blue" meaningless, but "Being blue is a man" is also meaningless, rather than false.

Wittgenstein agreed with Russell that a propositional function cannot be its own argument (3.333). We will see that Wittgenstein's cursorily expressed thoughts link up the two reasons which Russell gave and joins them in ways in which Russell himself did not. But why did Wittgenstein criticize Russell's formulation of the theory of types? All that the *Tractatus* says is that Russell's formulation of the theory of types must be wrong because he has to mention the references of the signs whose types he is discussing. By this cryptic remark, I take Wittgenstein to be referring to the fact that Russell had to say things like "A function is not a definite object which could or could not be a man – it is a mere ambiguity awaiting determination."[5] Further, in explaining what a first-order propositional function was, Russell had to write, "This function presupposes the totality of individuals."[6] What all this suggested was that we can look and find that some entities are ambiguous and others not, or that we can look for objects or individuals without looking for objects of any particular kind. However, for Wittgenstein, being a propositional function or being an object are correlates of certain logical categories of our language. Propositional functions and objects are not different kinds of things, as tables and animals are different kinds. Thus he wrote to Russell in 1913: "All theories of types must be done away with by a theory of symbolism showing that what seem to be *different kinds* of things are symbolized by different kinds of symbols, which *cannot* possibly be substituted in one another's places." (*Notebooks 1914–1916* [NB], p. 121) Notice here that the right theory is supposed to *show* rather than *say* what we are to understand about symbolism.

Wittgenstein's view about symbolism is closely linked with his views about how we express higher order propositional functions. The values of higher order propositional functions are always identical with the value of some truth-function of elementary propositions, and our symbolism must show what kinds of propositional functions they are. The sense of a propositional function sign depends on what kind of generalization on propositions or sets of propositions it corresponds to.

The sign for the propositional function must show the generalization procedure. Ramsey said that propositional functions have an identity independent of the "manner of their construction". The *Tractatus* view is different. The only propositional functions we can understand are those that are expressible in our language, i.e. those which we use or can construct, and the complexity of construction should show itself in the symbols. That is why he believed that there must be a hierarchy of propositional functions, and not of propositions. *Tractatus* says "We can foresee (*voraussehen*) only what we ourselves construct" (5.556).

Many have thought that Wittgenstein's comments on the theory of types show Wittgenstein at his most dogmatic. Wittgenstein seems to dismiss in half a page the difficulties which led to the theory of types. The last line of 3.333 which said, "that disposes of Russell's paradox" seems philistine and arrogant. Others have suggested that it is one of the passages of the *Tractatus* which is most clearly dated. (The work by Church and Scott on the λ-calculus, they say, has clearly shown that Wittgenstein is simply wrong in thinking that a function cannot be its own argument.)

Now I believe that Wittgenstein's attitude to the theory of types and the cluster of his views related to it should be taken more seriously, and for two reasons. The first is that they were taken very seriously by Russell himself, who, in his second edition to the *Principia Mathematica* of 1927, added an introductory chapter of 46 pages as well as three appendices to accommodate Wittgenstein's criticism.[7] Wittgenstein wrote that the Axiom of Reducibility is not a logical proposition. Even if the Axiom of Reducibility were true, he says, this could only be a fortunate accident. (*Tractatus*, 6.1232) (He believed that apart from truth-functional tautologies and certain identities, no sentence could express a necessary truth.) In the added chapters of the second edition, Russell attempts to work out a new ramified theory of types without the Axiom of Reducibility.[8] The axiom became redundant in many areas if one took the *Tractatus* view about functions, operations and types. Commenting on the views of the *Tractatus*, Russell writes in his new introduction, "We are not prepared to assert that this theory is certainly right, but it has seemed worthwhile to work out its consequences in the following pages."

The *Tractatus* view was also taken very seriously by Ramsey, who thought that he could reinterpret Russell's simple theory of types in the light of Wittgenstein's doctrines.[9] Whether Ramsey's view is based on a correct understanding of the *Tractatus* is far from certain. I myself believe that Ramsey misinterprets the *Tractatus* in many aspects. His interpretation involves a Platonistic view much stronger than anything stated in the *Tractatus*. Certainly the Platonism diverges from anything that Wittgenstein was to express later in *Remarks on the Foundation of Mathematics*, or *Philosophical Grammar*. But those who take seriously Ramsey's 1926 papers collected in *Foundations of Mathematics* cannot ignore the *Tractatus* doctrines from which Ramsey claims his views were derived.

The second and most important reason why I think one should understand and take seriously Wittgenstein's briefly expressed view on the theory of types[10] is that these are not unimportant digressions on Wittgenstein's part. He thought they were part of his central and most important theses about propositions, symbolism and facts. They are all of a piece with the view that logical forms of propositions, the very structure which makes us understand propositions as pieces of language, cannot be expressed in language. His often quoted dictum is "What is shown cannot be said". Spelled out, this dictum says that the logical form of a proposition is something we must grasp in order for us to understand that the words in the proposition say anything at all. A proposition cannot say what its own logical form is. In the *Tractatus* Wittgenstein also (mistakenly) believed that there is something that could be called the general logical form of a proposition which is common to all propositions. Thus, we cannot informatively be *told* what this general logical form is in words.

But if Wittgenstein believed in logical types, what exactly is a logical type for him, or for anyone for that matter? In *Philosophische Bemerkungen*, 1.6 (1930) Wittgenstein writes that philosophical grammar or logical syntax is a theory of logical types. For Wittgenstein, a theory of types was a necessary truth about symbolism and language: something which could be grasped as evident, if we correctly understand the nature of symbolism. It was not a philosophical position which we can argue for or against in a non-circular manner. Nor on the other hand is it something we are free to decide by stipulation. But surely, people would say, the existence of logical types cannot be such an evident truth. For Frege believed his symbolism was as impeccable as his thinking was rigorous. Yet he landed himself in an unexpected paradox. To this it must be replied that Wittgenstein's theory of types (which avoids the paradox) is very close to what was already in Frege, for Frege stratified propositional functions (at least up to the third order). He stratified, by finding the type of expression that was needed to fill in the gaps in order to make up a complete proposition.[11] If one gets a proposition by filling the gaps in the sign for a propositional function, e.g. "——— is tall", with a name of an object, e.g. "John", or names of objects, then it is a first-order function. If one fills the gap with a sign for a first-order function, then it is a sign of a second-order function. "There is something which ———" is an expression for a second-order function, because the gap can be filled by a sign for a propositional function like "is tall". People have often expressed doubt how the theory of types could be just a theory of symbolism, implying that they had intuitions about logical types, which did not depend on the way the properties of the entities were expressed. As I have no such intuition, the direction which Wittgenstein took seems more plausible to me.

What is important is to resist the temptation to think of the theory of types as a general classification of kinds of things. A theory which tells one the relationship between elementary particles and atoms, or between molecules and cells, may be a theory of certain kinds of entities and their interrelation. There may well be predicates that can sensibly be ascribed to elementary particles but not to atoms, or predicates which it makes sense to ascribe to cells but not to molecules. But even philosophers cannot make *a priori* legislation about the inappropriateness of the ascription of certain predicates to one kind of entity rather than to another if the inappropriateness comes from the property of the entities in question, which property one can inspect by looking at the world. They may see with the rest of humanity that certain predicates are false of certain things, but this is different from saying that they cannot meaningfully be ascribed to them. After all many predicates apply both to classes of things and to their members (e.g. 'having few members' applies to species and to classes of species). We do not decide what kind of logical type an entity is by inspecting the non linguistic part of the world. Thus the *Tractatus* says, "Hierarchies are and must be independent of reality." (5.5561)

Wittgenstein thought that the theory of types gives us two theses:

(1) that a proposition cannot make a statement about itself;
(2) that a propositional function cannot take itself as an argument.

These two theses were seen by him as truths about symbolism or language. They tell us what can and what cannot be expressed. They are more like the truth that in a map one cannot express at the same time that Paris is north of Rome *and* that it is to the south of it. It is not as though a map shows that Rome is both south and north of Paris and it be for us to decide whether what the map says is false or nonsense. No map can ever express such a fact. Similarly, according to Wittgenstein, "no proposition can make a statement about itself, because a propositional sign cannot be contained in itself" (3.332). I think it is wrong for Wittgenstein to reject outright the possibility of any self-reference by a proposition. Thus what I will have to say here about the theory of types will be a defence of the second thesis which is about propositional functions, but not of the first thesis which is about propositions.

However, before I proceed further we should just recall briefly what a proposition was for Wittgenstein, and why he thought that the first and second thesis were connected. A proposition (*Satz*) for him is not a thought or mental entity expressed by a sentence (propositional sign: *Satzzeichen*). Nor is it an abstract entity denoted by the sentence. It is the sentence itself in its projective relation to the world. Thus a proposition can be printed (3.4), set out on a page (4.011), and we may perceive it by our senses as an expression of our thought. In addition, Wittgenstein believes that a sentence is a fact (3.143), and a fact can never be named, but only stated. The fact in question is a fact about the signs that make up the sentence, i.e. the fact that certain expressions stand to other expressions in a certain relation. By virtue of perceiving this fact, people who know the expressions understand what the proposition says. They see that it presents a different state of affairs, i.e. another possible fact.

I disagree with Wittgenstein's view that a propositional sign – *Satzzeichen* – (sentence) is a fact, and think that it is a complex sign about which certain facts hold. Thus one can name it or number it, and reference can be made to the propositional sign without having to reproduce it. I nevertheless think that there is a deep insight in what Wittgenstein says, and that it leads to his second thesis about the theory of types concerning propositional functions, with which this paper is concerned. This is the relationship between logical forms of propositions, the identity of propositional functions and facts about signs.[12] It is important to remind ourselves here that for both Russell and Wittgenstein the value of a propositional function is not a truth-value but a proposition, and that the arguments for first-order propositional functions are individuals for Russell whereas for Wittgenstein they are names (4.24). Thus for Russell a predicate expresses a function which maps individuals into propositions, and for Wittgenstein a predicate expresses a function which maps names into propositions.

The first point I would like to discuss, then, is the question of the identity of propositional functions. We often talk about *the* logical form of a proposition, but it seems that one and the same proposition can be seen as exhibiting different logical forms. For example "Harold loves Mary" can be of the form 'f(Harold, Mary))' where 'fxy' means 'x loves y' or of the form 'g(Mary)' where 'gx' means 'x is loved by Harold' or of the form 'h(Harold)' where 'hx' means 'x loves Mary'. These different propositional functions give us different logical forms. We grasp a logical form of a proposition by grasping the form represented by the propositional function of which it is a value, and we identify the propositional function, e.g. fx̂, by grasping a fact which is common to a number of propositional signs, e.g. 'fa' 'fb' 'fc'. It is the structure of the sign of the propositional function which indicates the logical form of the proposition to us.

My view is closely connected with Wittgenstein's conviction that function signs and names play their roles in quite different ways. What identifies a function sign is not merely the letters or expressions. It is the fact that the letters (e.g. 'f') or expressions (e.g. 'is blue') stand in a certain relation to names (which are their arguments) which makes the letters or expressions function signs.[13] Thus if 'x' and 'y' are variables, then 'f(x)' and 'f(xy)' are different function signs, as are, for example, the predicate 'x runs' and the relational expression 'x runs y'. As Wittgenstein says in 3.333, where he discusses the theory of types and propositional functions, "a function sign already contains the prototype of its own argument". Thus, a function sign which has one argument place, and one which has two argument places, are different function signs, corresponding to different propositional functions. In contrast to this, a name is identified by its designating a particular object. Whether a name occurs as the subject or as a direct object, it is the same name.

In "Notes Dictated to Moore in 1914" (*NB*, p. 116) Wittgenstein discusses whether a predicate which ascribes properties to objects could take another predicate as an argument, and he writes that "φ cannot possible stand to the left of (or in any other relation to) the symbol of a property. For the symbol of a property, e.g. ψx, is *that* ψ stands to the left of a name form, and another symbol φ cannot possibly stand to the left of such a fact." The *Tractatus* view is basically the same. A part of what makes an expression a predicate is *the fact of its standing in a certain relation to* a subject expression. A word cannot be a predicate by itself. 'f' cannot be a function sign by itself, but we can say that in 'fa', 'f' is a predicate by virtue of its standing to the left of 'a'.

This particular way of identifying propositional functions via the arrangement of the signs in relation to names in a given sentence can be traced back to Frege. Frege had claimed that a concept (or a propositional function) is the reference of a concept word, and that a first-level concept word is made by removing a singular term (*Eigenname*) from a sentence. Frege and Russell maintained theories which made a fundamental distinction between properties or references of predicates, and objects or references of names corresponding to the different syntactic roles played by predicates and names. But they supported their views with the obscure claim that the references of names and references of predicates are different kinds of entities, the latter being something unsaturated (Frege) or indefinite (Russell). Frege made it impossible for a property (or what he calls a 'concept' [*Begriff*] to occur as a subject of any proposition (i.e. what a proposition is about), by ruling that the reference of a proper name or noun phrase was *eo ipso* not a property. Thus, he said the concept 'horse' is not a concept. As I mentioned before, Russell also comments in *Principia Mathematica* (p. 48) that a propositional function is indefinite and cannot be used as a subject. This is his second justification for the theory of types.

In contrast to this Wittgenstein offers no theory whatsoever about the kind of entity which a propositional function is. It is not a prior theory about types of entities which make the formula '$\varphi(\varphi)$' ill formed for us. How are we to read '$\varphi(\varphi)$'? Is (φ) a name? If it were, '$\varphi(\varphi)$' would be a concatenation of two names and in English that is not a sentence. Now, according to the *Tractatus*, we can in principle always express an elementary proposition by a mere pattern of the names of objects the proposition is about. Thus if 'φ' is a name, by writing '$\varphi\varphi$' we could read it as stating that, e.g. φ hits φ, or φ hits itself. But then the propositional function which occurs in this proposition is not 'φ'. 'φ' is an argument of another propositional function, which is here expressed by the concatenation of the two 'φ's. Could the 'φ' on the left side then be a predicate? For Wittgenstein suggests that when the sign 'φ' appears to the left of a name, the fact of its doing so expresses that the thing named has a certain property. But then, "φ" on the right hand side ceases to be a sign for a propositional function. Thus, '$\varphi(\varphi)$' is no more well-formed than "Is blue is blue".

I believe that there is much truth in what Wittgenstein says here. For, although both names and predicates occur in sentences, it is the predicate which carries the logical form with it. A predicate is not so much a constituent of a sentence but, as Dummett has said,[14] something which corresponds to a feature of a sentence. Similarly *Tractatus*[15] suggests that every propositional function corresponds to a class of propositions which have a common characteristic. Propositional functions show us the logical form of propositions in ways that names do not. However, just as the distinction between concept and object did not by itself check the generation of Russell-type paradoxes, so the distinction between propositional functions and arguments in a sentence does not, by itself, check the paradoxes.

The second point I come to is the distinction of predicates of different orders (or types). A sign for a propositional function which takes names in the argument place cannot take a sign for a propositional function as argument. (The result being a non-well-formed sequence of signs and not a proposition.) This, however, does not lead to the conclusion that there can be no propositional functions which take predicates as their arguments. Nothing that Wittgenstein says goes against the possibility of there being propositional functions which take predicates as arguments and give propositions as values – i.e. what we call 'second-order predicates, or in Russellian language, "second-level" functions'. (The second half of 3.333 presupposes that there are such second-order predicates or propositional functions which take predicate expressions, or function signs as their arguments. It describes $F(fx)$ as a function. I take 'fx' here is a predicate variable, and the arguments that occupy its place should be particular first-order propositional function signs.[16])

For both Frege and Russell, quantifiers were such second-level functions which took first-order functions as their arguments.[17] Such functions cannot take themselves as arguments either. '$(x)(x)fx$' or '$(\exists x)(\exists x)fx$' are simply ill-formed and are not propositions. (Contrast some modern presentations where quantifiers are introduced as operators on formulae and, thus '$(x)(x)fx$' becomes well formed.) If 'is blue' is a first-order predicate, then an example of a second-order predicate which takes 'is blue' as argument is not 'is a colour'. For 'Is blue is a colour' is not a well-formed sentence.[18] Wittgenstein does not spell out what he thinks about sentences of the form '$(y)(\exists x)fxy$', which obviously makes sense and which would have to be considered well-formed. He would probably have treated '$(\exists x)fx-.$' as a first-order predicate like 'fa–'.

Tractatus 3.333 goes on to say that if a (second-order) function *could* be its own argument, then there would be a proposition '$F(F(fx))$'. But then, Wittgenstein says, the outer 'F' and the inner 'F' must have different references (*Bedeutungen*). The inner 'F' would have the form '$\varphi(fx)$' (where 'fx' is a variable) – namely 'F–' takes first-order predicates as arguments. The outer 'F' would have the form '$\psi(\varphi(fx))$'

(where '$\varphi(fx)$' would be variable). In other words, it has to be a function which takes second-order function signs – such as signs for the quantifiers – as arguments, and gives propositions as values. The non-identity of these functions shows itself by the different position the function sign occupies in an arrangement of different complexity. As Wittgenstein says, "Only the letter 'F' is common to the two functions but the letter by itself signifies nothing."

This means that even if we were to use the same expression to express a second-order propositional function and a third-order propositional function, we should already be identifying them as different propositional functions. For the kind of expressions that fill in the blank places and which will give us a complete proposition are different. Thus, one and the same propositional function *cannot* occur twice in the same proposition once as a second-order function and once as a third-order function. Propositional functions of different order are *eo ipso* different propositional functions. Self-predication therefore becomes an impossibility. If '$(\exists x)(\exists x)\, fx$' is meaningless for us, this is because we have not assigned a way of reading $(\exists x)$ as a third-order propositional function. However, if propositions of the form $(F(F(fx))$ are meaningful to us, then we are already interpreting the outer 'F' as a third-order predicate and therefore different from the inner 'F'.

Someone may object and say, surely the property of being a property is also a property. Thus, the very same predicate "is a property" can be a second-order predicate as well as a third-order predicate. The answer to this is no, and the reason why this is not so is very important for Wittgenstein. This brings me to the third point I would like to raise. For Wittgenstein being an object, or being a property (Frege's "*Begriff*" or concept) is a formal concept. They are not attributes which can be ascribed to objects. They are shown by the kind of signs which we use to refer to them. We cannot in our language have propositions like 'Ox' or 'Px' where 'O—' means '—is an object' or 'P—' means '— is a property'. We express them by the choice of letters we use to express the variables (4.126). We do in English have the words "property" or "object". However, we do not use these words to indicate basic categories. We say for example, "That is a beautiful object" or "That's a property I admire", not "Is it a property or an object?". If we allow a metalanguage, as Wittgenstein did not, we can say that an object is a reference of a possible name, and a first-order property is what is ascribed to objects by possible constructible predicates. However, these are not properties that are expressible in the object language. "Formal concepts cannot, in fact, be represented by means of a propositional function as concepts proper can." (4.126) The 'meta' property of being a referent of a predicate in the object language, is not a referent of a predicate in the object language. Thus, for a person who distinguishes object language and metalanguage, the statement, "The property of being a property is a property" is a confused one which has the appearance of being a self-predication when it is not. It is simply false.

As Wittgenstein was not thinking of an artificial formal language, but of our ordinary language, he did not think there could be a metalanguage which stands above all of our language. Yet, he thought it extremely important to distinguish between what we say or express by means of our language, and the categorial understanding we have. This understanding reflects our grasp of logical syntax. This is the grasp of the logical form of our language. That we understand a sequence of signs as a piece of language – i.e. as a propositional sign – means that we already see its logical form or forms. We see one sign, for instance, as the symbol for an object, and another as a sign which, by standing to the previous symbol in a certain relation, says what property or relation holds of the object.

Someone may say in 'F(F(u))' the outer and inner 'F' can express identical functions if what they express are truth-functions. It is true that if the two occurrences of 'F—' express the same truth function and if 'u' expresses a propositional variable, then this will not be ill-formed. However, if 'F—' expresses a truth-function, then the problem of types does not arise. The reason is that unlike second-order functions which take first-order function signs (i.e. predicates) as arguments, truth-functions take propositions as arguments and they are all of the same type for the *Tractatus*.

Let us here remind ourselves of the fact that neither *Principia Mathematica* nor *Tractatus* take sentences as names of truth-values. Frege's theory is that by using sentences one refers to truth-values. A truth-function is a mapping of truth-values. The arguments are truth-values and the values are truth-values. This is not the case for Russell or Wittgenstein, who both thought that a meaningful sentence or proposition does not refer to a truth-value but *has* a truth-value. According to *Principia Mathematica*, a truth-function is a function from propositions to propositions. A proposition p is a truth-function of q and r (the value of a truth-function which take q and r as arguments) if the truth-value of p is a function of the truth-values of q and r.[19] Further, there is no reason why one cannot get as value of a truth-function what we then make into the argument of the same truth-function.

However, this is not an example of a function being its own argument. For a value of a function to be its own argument, is not for the function itself to be its own argument. There is nothing strange about the domain and range of a function being overlapping or even coinciding so that the value of the function for a particular argument can be the argument of the very same function. Thus *Tractatus*, 5.25–5.251 says, "Operations and function must not be confused. A function cannot be its own argument, but the result of an operation can be the base of that very operation." An operation defines a function, and what Wittgenstein calls truth-operations on propositions define truth-functions. A propositional function is, however, not defined by an operation. It is quite different from truth-functions. The arguments and values are quite distinct kinds of linguistic entities, so that the domain and range do not overlap. However even when operations define functions they are not for Wittgenstein identical with functions. One would never make the mistake of asking whether an operation can operate on itself, because operation·is not the kind of thing that has the substantive status. One would just say that the result of an operation could be the base of the very same operation. In the case of functions, people have been tempted to ask not merely of a value of the function whether it can be an argument of the very same function, but whether a function can by itself be an argument of itself. The fact that a function and certain classes (say a particular class of ordered pairs) can be uniquely matched, has tempted us to identify the two. (Even if there were a one-to-one correlation between a person and his fingerprints, we would not identify them.)

Truth-functions then, for Russell and Wittgenstein, are entirely different from propositional functions. The values for both are propositions; but the arguments in the case of truth-functions are propositions while the arguments of propositional functions (of whatever order) are never propositions. For Russell they are either individuals or propositional functions of an order lower than the function of which they are arguments. For Wittgenstein the arguments are expressions which are constituents of propositions but are never propositions themselves. Furthermore, since for Wittgenstein all propositions are of the same logical type, the theory of types does not apply to truth-functions. The problems of non-self-application and of logical types thus comes back to propositional functions. It is propositional functions which have logical form.

We said that it is impossible for the very same symbol to be both subject and predicate, or first-order predicate, and second-order predicate within the same sentence. Self-predication (as well as any predication which is not well-founded) was ruled out. However, there is no reason why the same name referring to the same object occurs more than once in the same sentence. Wittgenstein cannot possibly say that sentences of the form 'aRa' are ill-formed.[20] I can say, "John loves John" or "I hit myself". So how can the ruling out of self-predication prohibit propositions of the form 'x∈x' and 'x ϕx', which is used in Russell's formulation of the paradoxes?

Here we must make a fourth point in order to complete our interpretation of his theory. This is that Wittgenstein obviously would agree with Russell that sets were logical fictions, and that talk of membership in sets was only another way of talking about the state of affairs we describe by using names and propositional functions. In *Principia Mathematica*, expressions denoting classes are contextually defined, and sentences containing them can be translated into one in which propositional functions occur instead. Russell defined 'x∈ϕẑ' or x is a member of class ϕ, as 'ϕ!x' (p. 188). '∈' is not a primitive sign, and it is not an independent relational sign, which whenever it occurs between names says that a relation holds between two objects. If we can introduce '∈' only as contextually defined, then the ascription of every seeming relation of self-membership will become nothing more than the problem of self-predication, which we have been discussing before. Thus, if one accepts Russell's no-class theory, then Wittgenstein's syntactic version of the theory of types tells us how the paradoxes cannot arise.

I now come to the last point which I want to make. I said that Russell gave two independent reasons for his theory of types: the vicious circle principle and a doctrine about the ambiguous nature of propositional functions which blocked them from being subjects of propositions. These separate reasons become linked in Wittgenstein's theory. Wittgenstein's *Tractatus* seems to assume, as Frege did, that understanding a propositional function involves understanding the domain over which the variables range. A propositional function, he says, contains a prototype of its argument. By this he seems to mean not only that it shows how many argument places it contains, but also that it shows the categories of the expressions that can become arguments. However, can the range of possible arguments for a first-level propositional function, say, be delimited only by the requirement that these be names or singular terms? This was Frege's view. For Frege, if the 'concept' or the propositional function takes objects (the references of names) as arguments, it must range over *every* object. "Mary Smith has many members" is as well-formed as "The class of all integers is blue". These are false but not ill-formed. For every first-order predicate one has to be able to ask for *any* object, whether the predicate applies to it or not. These include objects denoted by definite descriptions using the very first-order predicate itself. We know that we will derive paradoxes if we take such a position.

On Wittgenstein's theory, as on Russell's, this cannot be the case. We have seen that the arguments of a propositional function were expressions and that the values were propositions. If a first-order propositional function takes names or singular terms as arguments, there are certain restrictions among the names or singular terms that it can take. The very rough remark in 3.333: ". . . that the sign for a function already contains the prototype of its argument, and it cannot contain itself", suggests that no singular term which is formed by using the propositional function f$\hat{x}$, can occur as an argument of f$\hat{x}$. This, we know, is too strong a claim. What Wittgenstein wants to say must be rather that a propositional function cannot take as arguments any expression that involves quantification over the whole of its domain because "the function already contains the prototype of its argument". Wittgenstein's view interpreted in the way I have done excludes the formation of singular terms like "the class of all the singular terms which can become arguments of this propositional function". We must assume that the new term which involves quantification over the whole domain has a reference different from that of any of the original singular terms, which was a member of the domain of the propositional function. Therefore, we cannot assume that the reference of this new term belongs already to the original domain. The two separate reasons which Russell gave for his theory of types becomes related in Wittgenstein's view.

To summarize: I have said that the way in which predicates are identified in the *Tractatus* makes it impossible for the same word to function both as a subject and a predicate in the same sentence, or as predicates of different orders in the same sentence. This combines with the view that logical categories or logical forms cannot be described by predicates of our language, and with the view that 'ϵ' does not express a relation proper but is to be contextually eliminated. These points, together, block the formation of Russell's paradox.

One last comment. Wittgenstein later explicitly rejected some *Tractatus* doctrines which both Ramsey, in his own way, and Russell in the second edition of the *Principia Mathematica* adopted, in building an amended theory of types. For example, Wittgenstein came to think that it was a mistake to identify general propositions like '$(x)fx$', or '$(\exists x)fx$' with logical sums or logical products, if the domain of 'fx' was infinite. This would damage fundamentally both Ramsey's and Russell's efforts to provide a foundation of mathematics by means of an amended theory of types without the axiom of reducibility. However, as I said in the very beginning of this paper, Wittgenstein was not trying to provide a foundation of mathematics in the *Tractatus*. Even if the views about symbolism which enabled him to avoid the paradoxes, together with his later rejection for infinite domains of the doctrine of general propositions as logical sums and logical products, make it impossible for him to reconstruct some important parts of classical mathematics, this need not have worried him. He had no desire to reduce the number concept. What was important for him was to make clear what it is to understand predicates or propositional functions.

Granted his views of what propositional functions were and how they were identified, perhaps it is no wonder that later, when Wittgenstein did write about the foundation of mathematics, he took an extremely constructivist position. Whether he is right or wrong about that, however, is a separate question which was not the topic of this paper.

Notes

1. In writing this paper I profited very much from discussions with or comments by Paul Benacerraf, Cora Diamond, Verena Dyson, Bill Hart, Charles Parsons, Bas van Fraassen, Hao Wang, and by the editor, Irving Block.

2. Those who think of Wittgenstein as a Platonist who was subsequently converted by Brouwer ought to find this surprising. But the common Kantian formation of their beliefs should be self-evident.

3. *Principia Mathematica*, p. 39.

4. *ibid.*, p. 48.

5. *ibid.*, Introduction Ch. II, §IV, p. 48.

6. *ibid.*, Introduction Ch. II, §II, p. 54.

7. In the first edition of *Principia Mathematica*, Russell had developed a ramified theory of types as distinct from his simple theory of types and other ways of avoiding the paradoxes discussed in the *Principles of Mathematics*. In order to justify induction, to retain the theorem

asserting the existence of the least upper bound of a bounded set of real numbers, and to give a general definition of identity (which the ramified theory made impossible), he was obliged to introduce the Axiom of Reducibility, although he was in great doubt about the status of this.

8. *Principia Mathematica*, Introduction §XXXV, §XXXVII.

9. He describes his own views as "natural consequences of the logical theories of Mr Wittgenstein's". *Foundations of Mathematics*, p. 33.

10. See *Tractatus*, 3.331, 3.332, 3.333, 5.25, 5.251.

11. In Frege's case it might be better to render *Satz* as "sentence" rather than "proposition".

12. I have discussed in "Representation, a discussion of a passage in the *Tractatus*" that a proposition is a propositional sign, although the ways in which we individuate them are different. I suggest that the "is" here is not an "is" of identity but like the "is" in "A dollar bill is a dollar". A dollar bill does not express or name a dollar, but to present a dollar bill just *is* to present a dollar. *Forms of Representation*, ed. Bruce Freed *et al*. (Amsterdam: North-Holland, 1975), pp. 189–202.

13. In principle we do not need function signs in order to express a function. We can express the function by the arrangement of the variables. However, as we have limited ways of arranging the variables in patterns, we use function signs as well.

14. Frege, *Philosophy of Language* (London: Duckworth), p. 49.

15. *Tractatus*, 3.315, 3.317.

16. The way in which Wittgenstein reformulates his problem in the latter half of 3.333 is misleading. He writes that the reason why in 'F(Fu)' the outer 'F' and the inner 'F' cannot be the same becomes clear if we try to rewrite it as '($\exists\phi$): F(ϕu), ϕu=Fu'. This is drawing attention to someone confusing first-order and second-order predicates, whereas the original example 'F(F(fx))' was based on a confusion between second- and third-order predicates.

17. For Wittgenstein '($\exists$x)—x' or '(x)—x' should express functions, which take first-order predicate *expressions* (first-order function signs) as arguments and give propositions as values.

18. Another kind of second-order function in *Principia Mathematica* is one whose values are formulae (what Russell calls matrices: formulae containing predicates of individuals or signs of functions of individuals as well as name variables). By putting both predicates and names as arguments in their respective places, one obtains a molecular proposition as a value of the function. In the *Tractatus*, as a matter of fact, every general proposition is equivalent to a molecular proposition. Nevertheless, a quantifier differs from a second-order function which gives a matrix of first-order functions because a quantifier takes first-order predicates as arguments and gives propositions as values, whereas the latter kind of second-order function gives a proposition only when both predicates *and names* are supplied as arguments.

19. Thus, the fact that a proposition p is a truth-function of the propositions q and r does not necessarily mean that p is a function of q and r, unless there is a one-to-one or many-one correspondence between truth-values and propositions. If every time propositions stand in truth-functional relation to each other, they also stand in a functional relation to each other as well, then this has to be argued for. For example, that in a certain country one can determine a person's title just by knowing the title of his parents does not entail that a person stands in a functional relation to his parents. Since the same parents can have many children, one cannot determine the identity of a person by knowing the identity of his parents.

20. In 5.531 he gives us examples of propositions 'f(a.a)', 'f(b.b)'.

The So-called Realism of *Wittgenstein's* Tractatus

BRIAN McGUINNESS

On the face of it we have in Wittgenstein's *Tractatus* the classic statement of a realist semantics. In his picture theory an explanation is given of how propositions have sense, i.e. are true or false, which immediately invokes ontological categories. He tells us:

The possibility of propositions is based on the principle that objects have signs as their representatives. (4.0312)

and further,

One name stands for one thing, another for another thing, and they are combined with one another. In this way the whole group – like a *tableau vivant* – presents a state of affairs. (4.0311)

A proposition or a picture is the fact that its elements are combined in a certain way: it says something because those elements are correlated with objects in the world.

These correlations are, as it were, the feelers of the picture's elements, with which the picture touches reality. (2.1515)

In a proposition, in the ideal case, the elements are of course names. Their meaning (*Bedeutung*) is identical with the objects they stand for (*vertreten*). There is no trace here, for these names, of the distinction that Wittgenstein was later to draw between *Träger* and *Bedeutung*, according to which one could say that Herr Schmidt was the *Träger* of the name Schmidt, but not, I think, that he was its *Bedeutung*.

We are naturally inclined to attribute to Wittgenstein, therefore, a theory on the following lines. Propositions have sense, i.e. are either true or false, because the following is a conceivable series of events for every one of them: first, a set of names or simple signs (that is to say signs no parts of which function as signs) is correlated with a set of objects by ostensive definition. Second, some of these names are put into a relation which is possible for them. It happens that any relation which is possible for the names is possible also for the objects with which the names have been correlated. The fact that the names stand in the relation in question will then be a proposition to the effect that the objects also stand in that relation. Now, one of two states of affairs holds, either the objects are so related or they are not. Whichever of these two is the fact must be compared with the proposition, and if it corresponds, the proposition will be true. However, it will be seen that it can only be either true or false. Thus given that every proposition could in theory be constructed in the way described, it will be seen that every proposition will be either true or false and what its being true or false consists in. It is this that a semantic theory should establish for us.

Now many features of this account are not in Wittgenstein at all. He does not mention ostensive definition – he was to say later that its nature was unclear to him at the time of the *Tractatus*. Nor does he talk as if names just happened to permit of precisely those combinations that were possible for the objects they represented, as it were by some lucky power of our minds. This Hertz seems to suggest when he says:

We make for ourselves inner pictures or symbols of outer objects, and we make them in such a way that the consequences of the pictures that are necessary for our thought are also at the same time pictures of the consequences that are naturally necessary for the objects depicted. In order that this requirement should be capable of being fulfilled, there must be certain correspondences already in existence between nature and our mind.[1]

Wittgenstein took much of his notion of picturing from Hertz, but not, so far as I can see, this part. Ostensive definitions and a coincidence in the capacity to form relations are introduced into Wittgenstein's account only by interpretation, and should be viewed critically.

What he certainly seems to assume, and what this account of his views is right in presupposing, is a magazine of objects which form, in one sense, the realm of *Bedeutung*. The objects assumed are simple in a much stricter sense than that given above for the simplicity of signs, and one consequence of their simplicity is that they are common to all possible worlds. They form the substance of the world or the form of the world. They are what is unalterable and persistent (*bestehend*), while the configuration of objects, the states of affairs, are what varies from one possible world to another. These configurations of objects, these states of affairs, give objects what material or external properties they have. Naturally, there is only one set of configurations that is actually realized, and this is what we call reality or the world. The internal properties of objects are their possibilities of combination with one another, and the possession of these properties is necessary, not a mere matter of fact.

What is meant by assuming a magazine of objects of this kind? Clearly not that something *exists* which might not exist. All unrealized possibilities are simply dispositions of objects different from that which actually obtains. To put the same matter in another way, all questions of existence are questions about what configurations of objects actually obtain. Thus we might say that all existence is a matter of fact, a matter of what is *in* the world. This corresponds to an early statement in the *Tractatus*:

The world is a totality of facts, not of things. (1.1)

This seems to yield a moderately complicated ontology: the world or reality consists of facts, that is to say in the *Bestehen* (in one sense), the obtaining, of states of affairs. States of affairs themselves, on the other hand, are combinations of objects, which *bestehen* or exist (subsist) in another sense. Existence as normally spoken of is equivalent to the *Bestehen* in the first sense of a certain state of affairs. Professor Black suggests that this ontology was suggested to Wittgenstein by his views about language.[2]

Now, to be sure, the attraction of the opening pages of the *Tractatus* is that they seem to derive substantial and metaphysical results like those long hoped-for from philosophy, all on the basis of some quite natural assumptions about propositions being true or false. However, I agree with Mr Rhees[3] that it is important not to be misled by these opening pages. It was not Wittgenstein's intention to base a metaphysics upon logic or the nature of our language. He was not saying that there is something by which our grammar is determined, and therefore he did not try to infer features of the world from our language. It may seem, indeed, that he argues that propositions with sense are possible only because some more primitive operations are possible – notably the correlation of names with objects, and it may seem that he goes on to argue that these more primitive operations are possible only because the world possesses certain characteristics. However, it will be clear on reflection that such arguments would be the sort of metaphysics that he condemns.

How then are we to account for the ontological parts of the *Tractatus*? This is a larger form of our earlier question, what is it for objects to subsist (*bestehen*) as this is understood in the *Tractatus*? Still more generally the question might take the form, what is Wittgenstein doing in the *Tractatus*? I have so far been saying merely what he is *not* doing. Some interpretation is clearly needed. The answer here is that he is doing logic and basing philosophy on it. He thinks and says that philosophy is not a science alongside the others, but is something over or beneath them. Yet occasionally he speaks of philosophy or logic as if it were a science with its own range of data or facts. Thus, for example, in the middle of 2.0121 he says:

Logic deals with every possibility and all possibilities are its facts.

I want to say that there we have a transferred and strictly illegitimate use of the word "fact", and that similarly the whole ontology is a transferred and illegitimate use of words like *bestehen*. It is a kind of ontological myth that he wants to give us to show us the nature of language. As is well-known, one of the chief results of the view of language so attained is the rejection of all such myths.

I say that Wittgenstein is doing logic and basing philosophy on it. It is important to see what this means. When Russell wrote to him with some questions about the *Tractatus*, then a mere typescript newly arrived in England, Wittgenstein wrote:

I'm afraid you haven't got hold of my main contention to which the whole business of logical propositions is only a corollary. The main point is the theory of what can be expressed (*gesagt*) by propositions – i.e. by language – (and which comes to the same thing what can be *thought*) and what cannot be expressed by propositions, but only shown (*gezeigt*); which, I believe, is the cardinal problem of philosophy.[4]

Philosophy, it will be remembered, is thought of as a critique of language – it is the activity of making clear the limits of language, which are identical with the limits of thought. It is a pointing to, or an attempt to make clear, something that cannot be stated directly, since it is not one half of a contradiction, not one of two mutually exclusive alternatives. What philosophy tries to make clear is not sayable, but it is shown by ordinary propositions that can be true or false. Conversely, a mistaken philosophy will be the attempt to say these things. Logic comes in, in the first place, because it was Wittgenstein's starting-point: its propositions were the first that he discovered to say nothing but to show something — to show:

> . . . the formal — logical — properties of language and the world. (6.12)

He wants to bring out in the *Tractatus* that philosophy and logic have to do not with a special realm of objects but with the necessary features of language — that is to say of any language whatsoever. This happens most clearly in the case of logic. The propositions of logic, the tautologies, are by various devices shown to be inevitable offshoots or by-products of the activity of saying anything true or false. As such they show us something about what it is to say something true or false.

It is in order to reach this result that Wittgenstein must say what it is for a proposition to be true or false in the ordinary way, and in the course of doing that he gives the semantic theory we described at the beginning. There can be propositions which are always true or always false — i.e. tautologies and contradictions, because there are propositions which *may* be true and *may* be false, and this is so because it is possible for a proposition to exist which may be false, but which, if not false, is true. I will not argue that connexion here. For our present purposes — which is the derivation of objects — I wish to take it as a premiss. Wittgenstein's thought is that in order for there to be propositions that may be either true or false, but must be one of the two, there will have to be a possibility of expressing those propositions by means of signs which of themselves will serve to express a proposition independently of what is the case. A state of affairs cannot be designated independently of whether it exists or not unless signs can be used whose significance could be given and understood and determined without reference to the obtaining or non-obtaining of that state of affairs. This can be done only if, in order to say that a state of affairs exists, it would be possible to produce a complex of signs. A simple sign could be correlated with a state of affairs only by revealing or assuming the existence of the state of affairs. It follows that in order to make a statement which would have sense, i.e. be either true or false, whatever the case in the world was, it would be necessary to suppose that in principle that statement could be made by the use of signs which could function in a proposition whatever the case in the world was.

Now Wittgenstein believed (and I think there are good grounds for thinking him correct, though it is not my purpose to argue it here) that we could make statements knowing them to be either true or false whatever the case in the world was. He therefore thought that we were committed to the possibility of those propositions being expressed in such a form that all the constituent signs used could function in that particular combination whatever the case in the world was. They would therefore (those supposedly possible signs) be possible constituents in propositions or possible contributors to producing a true or false proposition, regardless of what was the case in the world. He did not necessarily suppose us to have produced signs with these characteristics, as our actual signs may depend for their meaning on all sorts of accidental circumstances, but he thought we are committed to the possibility of rephrasing all that we want to say with the use of such signs alone.

Such signs, I believe, were Wittgenstein's names, and you will notice that in sketching an argument for their possibility I have made no reference to the complexity of a state of affairs or to the fact that "objects" figure in a state of affairs. Wittgenstein does indeed mention that states of affairs are combinations of objects and introduces objects themselves into his *Tractatus* before he says anything about the necessity for a proposition to be articulated and to consist of simple signs, but I believe that the order of his exposition reverses the order of his thinking.

It will be evident to those who have read Professor Tugendhat's article on Frege in *Analysis* (1970) or Mr Dummett's criticisms of it in his book on *Frege*,[5] that I am suggesting an interpretation of Wittgenstein rather like Tugendhat's of Frege. An object in the *Tractatus* which is the reference of a name or simple sign can be viewed as simply the truth-value potential of a certain expression. The semantic role of the supposedly possible simple sign or name is that of being combined with other simple signs or names to produce a proposition having a truth-value. Any sign which in the same combinations will produce exactly the same truth-values is the same sign or has the same reference. Another parallel with the view I am advocating is the conclusion reached by Miss Ishiguro in her article on "Use and Reference of Names"[6] when she says that *Bedeutung* is an intensional notion in the *Tractatus*. In her view the existence of objects adds no extra content to the logical theory.

I shall have occasion shortly to disagree with some points she makes, but one powerful argument she uses I can adopt. She points to Wittgenstein's repeated use of the Fregean slogan – "only in the context of a proposition does a name have a reference" – and interprets this as meaning that reference cannot be determined independently of how we settle or understand sense. To understand the reference of a name is to know something about the truth-conditions of some propositions. By this Miss Ishiguro does not merely mean (like Miss Anscombe in her *Introduction*) that there is no point in attaching a reference to a name unless you are going to go on to use that name in a proposition. She means rather that it is a fundamental idea of the *Tractatus* that there is no securing of reference prior to occurrence in a proposition. To show this she points out, quite correctly, that objects as spoken of in the *Tractatus* cannot be identified by a definite description or picked out by pointing, since their *Bestehen* (existence or subsistence) is supposed to be independent of what is the case. (She goes on to give an account of how reference can be secured – an account of Wittgenstein's notion of *Erläuterung* – with which I disagree.) The chief result of Miss Ishiguro's discussions – and a result that I think valid in any case – is that we ought not to contrast the *Tractatus* with its notion of *Bedeutung* and the *Philosophical Investigations* with its notion that the naming is the use. Use determines reference in the *Tractatus* also – though to be sure it is only "use for the purpose of saying something true or false" as other forms of use are not there considered.

Now, can Tugendhat's account of *Bedeutung* (whether true or false of Frege) be applied to Wittgenstein's *Tractatus*? To see this I will consider some objections brought by Dummett against Tugendhat considered as an interpreter of Frege, and see whether they would hold against Tugendhat considered as an interpreter of Wittgenstein. First, however, I will indicate one point – curiously enough a linguistic point about German – in respect of which Tugendhat does not fit Wittgenstein. Tugendhat says that the rendering of *Bedeutung* by "reference", "denotation" and "nominatum" suggests, what is false, that Frege meant by the *Bedeutung* of an expression the object which the expression names. Now I believe it is very clear in Wittgenstein's *Tractatus* that the *Bedeutung* of a name *is* meant to be identical with the object named. Indeed translating "*Bedeutung*" as "meaning", for which I am partly responsible, could be criticized on this ground alone. At the same time it is true that in the long run I wish to explain the object as an entity definable in terms of semantic equivalence.

I will discuss Dummett's criticisms of Tugendhat because disposing of the minor ones throws some light on what Wittgenstein is doing, as opposed to Frege, while the major one raises the whole issue of this paper. The minor criticisms are first that the identification of *Bedeutung* with truth-value potential (that is to say with the semantic role alone) does not at first sight allow us to distinguish between intensional and extensional contexts, or between contexts in which the name is used to refer to its indirect reference (its sense) and those in which it is used to refer to its real reference (its bearer). ". . . there would be a natural presumption", Dummett says, "in favour of a uniform semantic treatment for all contexts".[7] That is, however, precisely what Wittgenstein wants, and he does indeed allow no distinction between intensional and extensional contexts. The reason for this can be seen by considering another form of Dummett's objection to Tugendhat. (It will be remembered that we are here by no means criticizing Dummett's argument in itself, but only as applied to a supposed interpretation of Wittgenstein.) The second minor objection is that if reference is defined solely in terms of semantic role, or if having the same reference (*Bedeutung*) is defined in terms of interchangeability in all contexts without change of truth-value, then the use of an expression without a reference would be its use in a sentence which failed to say anything at all and failed to perform a linguistic act. What we wish to be able to say, however, is that there may perfectly well be intelligible utterances of sentences containing expressions which lack a *bearer*. These will differ (on Dummett's and Frege's view) from other sentences all of whose expressions of the same kind have bearers, in that the others will be and they will not be either true or false. The conception of reference as semantic role pays no attention to whether there is a bearer or not and does not allow us to call these sentences devoid of truth-value. This last is most easily done by identifying the reference with the bearer and saying that an expression may lack reference but still have sense. In virtue of its sense, a sentence in which it occurs is intelligible; in virtue of its lack of reference (bearer), a sentence in which it occurs lacks truth-value.

This may be a reason for saying that Tugendhat's account will not fit Frege, but it serves here to bring out that Wittgenstein, like Tugendhat, rejects the notion that names have both a reference and a sense. He does indeed think that the use of a name without reference results in saying nothing whatsoever. The only case parallel to those mentioned by Dummett that Wittgenstein mentions is the sentence about a *complex* that does not exist. Such a sentence does not indeed become nonsense, but simply false (3.24). As Wittgenstein said to Russell early in the development of the thoughts published in the *Tractatus*:

Your theory of descriptions is quite certainly right, even though the objects are quite other than you imagined.[8]

The fact is that the objects he has in mind are quite different from any Russell talked of, for the same reason that the notion of 'bearer' is an odd one when applied to his names. It is inconceivable that anything which can function as a name at all should lack a bearer, just because its bearer is given with its semantic role. All that can go wrong with a name is that it may be used, or an attempt may be made to use it, otherwise than in its proper semantic role. The examples that Wittgenstein gives of this are the nonsensical propositions, "Socrates Plato"[9] and "Socrates is identical".[10] They only show the *sort* of thing that might go wrong: "Socrates" and "Plato" are not real names in Wittgenstein's sense, they *might* lack bearers. (The case about "identical" is more complicated than we need discuss here.) Miss Ishiguro gives a good example of the sort of name that could not lack a bearer: "Let *a* be the centre of a circle . . .". In the discussion that follows, the question whether *a exists* cannot be raised. That is the sort of impossibility Wittgenstein has in mind. Of course it is true, as regards the actual example, that it may be part of an activity parasitic upon the identification of drawn figures and marked points on a sheet of paper. We have to consider what it would be like for names of this sort to form the whole substructure of language.

This brings us to the main difference between Frege in Dummett's account and Tugendhat's interpretation of Frege. Frege, Dummett says, surely with some justice, took the relation of name and bearer as the prototype of a semantic role. He assumed "that the semantic role of every expression which is a semantically significant unit can always be construed as consisting in its relation to something in the real world".[11] This amounts to saying that Frege makes use in his account of how our sentences have sense and reference of a number of intuitive pre-systematic notions, among them that of the relation of a name to a bearer. This comes, Dummett says, from our practice of ostension, "from our possession, in the use of a demonstrative accompanied by a pointing gesture, of another means than the employment of a name (the text has: as a name) for picking out a concrete object".[12] Dummett points out, surely correctly, that the notion of reference supplies us with a definite and readily acceptable picture of the semantical roles of the simplest types of expressions just because it is associated with this fundamental practice of identifying an object as the bearer of a name, and also with a fundamental practice of ostensive predication – of applying predicates to objects picked out ostensively. Now we have already seen that Wittgenstein wishes to assume no such fundamental practice, and we have claimed that he talks in the language of reference and bearer because of its attractiveness, but does not rely on the network of assumptions that make it so attractive. What we have to ask therefore is what contribution *Wittgenstein's* notion of reference makes in clarifying both what it is for us to utter sentences which are either true or false and how it is we come to do so.

We have already seen that every proposition we utter is true or false whatever is the case in the world. This demands that every proposition be capable of a full analysis in just one form, whether or not such analysis has ever been reached. If we imagine the totality of all propositions, true and false, in their fully articulated form (which form we know to be possible in principle), then we know that every element in this articulation has meaning in the sense that it contributes to the truth-value (whatever it is) of any proposition in which it occurs. However, this is all we are saying when we say that objects form the substance of the world. Understanding those elements or becoming acquainted with those objects (the two processes are identical) does not demand any experience of what is the case, since by definition the proposition is fully analysed and hence the objects have *Bestehen* (existence or subsistence) independently of what is the case. How then *do* we understand a proposition? What does it require? It is interesting that the question never appears in quite this form in Wittgenstein. I believe there is a good reason for this. It is not a *feat*, not an achievement, to understand a proposition. To have in the mind a conformation or structure corresponding to that of a possible state of affairs *is* to understand a proposition. It will be seen at once that this amounts to saying that there is no proposition to be understood *until* there is an understanding of a proposition. Thus the question is transferred to that of how we come to understand a propositional sign. How do we think a sense into a set of words? Wittgenstein tells us:

We use the perceptible sign of a proposition (spoken or written, etc.) as a projection of a possible situation.
Thinking the sense of the proposition is the method of projection. (3.11)[13]

Thinking the sense into the proposition is nothing other than so using the words of the sentence that their logical behaviour *is* that of the desired proposition. Or, to look at the matter in another way, whatever logical properties we give to the words we use will determine which proposition (if any) it is that we assert by means of them. Thus we must not think of the realm of reference as a mysterious, infinitely extended magazine of things, as if they were concrete objects, with which we might or might not be lucky enough in a full life to have acquaintance by, so to speak, coming across them in a street. There is already contained in language and thought the possibility of all objects that are possible. All logical forms are logically possible *within* language, *within* thought. No separate investigation or exploration of 'reality' is conceivable.

When I say we can do anything we like with language, I mean the triviality that whatever we do with the elements of language or thought will have the logical consequences that it actually has. However, there is of course also the question how I learn *a* language, an existing language, a particular language. On this issue we have a much discussed pronouncement by Wittgenstein:

The meanings of primitive signs can be explained by means of elucidations. Elucidations are propositions that contain the primitive signs. So they can only be understood if the meanings of those signs are already known. (3.263)

Miss Ishiguro thinks that elucidations will be propositions in which the internal properties that objects possess are ascribed to them. I do not believe it is necessary to assume this. The internal properties of an object are its possibilities of combination with other objects, and these properties are shown by any ordinary proposition about that object, be it true or false. I conclude that Wittgenstein is pointing out that teaching can be carried out only by means of complete propositions or complete thoughts. The learner has to grasp these as a whole, and, when he has done that, he will have an understanding of the primitive signs contained in that proposition. I am not reverting here to the use of ostensive definitions. Propositions used in teaching meaning need not be true or concerned with the immediate environment, any more than we can claim these properties for '*Balbus aedificat murum*'.

However, whether I am right and elucidations are quite ordinary propositions, or Miss Ishiguro is right and they are more like logical propositions, the reader may wish to ask me or her: How do I know *which* object is meant by a particular sign, or *which* fact or state of affairs is stated by a particular proposition used in teaching? Surely there can be more than one object with the same logical form? With questions like this, we are in constant danger of supposing that there is some particular mental act of meaning or intending a particular thing which has to be explained. However, if I suppose two objects of the same logical form and call them "a" and "b", and if I suppose that "a" has one set of material properties and "b" another, there is really no sense to the question whether perhaps in reality "b" has the set of properties I have assigned to "a", and conversely. Miss Ishiguro puts this well by saying that names are in effect dummy names and can be interchanged (within the same logical form) if one does so consistently. To some extent, therefore, the question which object is meant is empty of content. In so far as it does make sense it must mean, How do I indicate to myself or to others, that I mean just the F that has G? To this question the answer is clearly that to mean this I must say it, or in other words my statement must have the appropriate overt or concealed logical multiplicity.

Perhaps Wittgenstein's fundamental point about semantics can be put by saying that only structure can represent (*darstellen*).

Only facts can express a sense, a set of names cannot. (3.142)

The problem of language is the problem of the false proposition. The false proposition is possible only because it is possible for one to form a structure which will serve to express just that situation which (in saying that the proposition is false) we are supposing not to exist, and no other. It need not, and we need not judge whether it can, do this in virtue of its visible or audible form alone. However, the use of the elements of the structure must be such that only the situation in question could correspond to it. This I take to be one of the main points in the picture theory of propositional meaning. It rests on a certain insight which is compatible with some aspects of what Dummett calls realism. For Wittgenstein, as for Frege,

. . . a sentence is determined as true under certain conditions, which conditions are derivable from the way in which the sentence is constructed out of its constituent words.[14]

However, the processes of explaining the truth-conditions of a proposition and of determining the truth-value of a proposition cannot be broken down into any simpler operations than that of grasping or expressing the. proposition. All these operations possess the same multiplicity. Wittgenstein was to urge this point as a justification of his picture theory in the early 1930s, and it obviously also underlies the development from the *Tractatus* to the dictum that the sense of a proposition is the method of its verification.

However, if, after all, objects are required by Wittgenstein's theory of language, then why should we not call him a realist in respect of them? The answer is that Wittgenstein's objects are not concrete objects which may sensibly be said to exist or not. Nor are they properties of concrete objects, since that makes the self-contradictory assumption that there is something simpler than the simplest thing that can be referred to. Miss Ishiguro makes them 'like' instantiations of simple properties, and that is certainly the model that Wittgenstein himself used in the *Philosophical Investigations*. Relative to the language there described those instantiations are simple, but it is easily seen that an example of an absolutely simple object cannot be given. We cannot grasp anything other than a concatenation of objects.

The answer to the question about realism then, is: Wittgenstein does indeed subscribe to the view Dummett attributes to Frege:

... the thoughts we express are true or false objectively, in virtue of how things stand in the real world – the realm of reference – and independently of whether we know them to be true or false (of whether we exist or can think at all);[15]

however, from Wittgenstein's point of view the words "the realm of reference" are a misnomer here. I have previously called it a myth, but I might equally call it rhetoric, to say as Dummett does:

... we do actually succeed in speaking about the actual objects, in the real world, which are the referents of the names we use, and not about any intermediate surrogates for or representations of them.[16]

Certainly, our propositions in the last analysis are not about the workings of our own minds: what Wittgenstein is trying to convey is a point of view according to which what they are about is not *in* the world any more than it is *in* thought or *in* language. Objects are the form of all these realms, and our acquaintance with objects (our contact with them, to borrow a metaphor from Aristotle) is not an experience or knowledge of something over against which we stand. Thus it is not properly experience or knowledge at all. Objects are *eti epekeina tēs ousias* (beyond being), and it is therefore misleading to regard Wittgenstein as a realist in respect of them. His position is one, as indeed he tells us, from which realism, idealism and solipsism can all be seen as one. However, it would require at least another lecture to explore that remark.

Notes

1. Heinrich R. Hertz, *Die Prinzipien der Mechanik, Gesammelte Werke*, vol. 13, ed. Philip Lenard (Leipzig, 1894), p. 1. English translation supplied by Mr McGuinness.
2. Max Black, *A Companion to Wittgenstein's Tractatus* (Ithaca: Cornell University Press, 1966), p. 8.
3. Rush Rhees, *Discussions of Wittgenstein* (London: Routledge & Kegan Paul, 1970), pp. 24–5.
4. *Letters to Russell, Keynes and Moore*, ed. G. H. von Wright (Oxford: Blackwell, 1974), R. 37.
5. Michael Dummett, *Frege* (London: Duckworth, 1973), pp. 199–203.
6. *Studies in the Philosophy of Wittgenstein*, ed. Peter Winch (London: Routledge & Kegan Paul, 1969, pp. 20–50.
7. *op. cit.*, p. 401.
8. *op. cit.*, R. 23.
9. "Notes Dictated to G. E. Moore in Norway", in *Notebooks 1914–1916*, p. 115.
10. *Tractatus*, 5.4733.
11. Cf. Dummett, p. 405.
12. Cf. *ibid.*, p. 406.
13. This translation differs in the last line from the rendering in the translation of the *Tractatus* (Pears and McGuinness), which was justly criticized by Rush Rhees. Cf. *Discussions of Wittgenstein*, p. 39.
14. Cf. Dummett, p. 194.
15. *ibid.*, p. 198.
16. *ibid.*, p. 196.

The Logical Independence of Elementary Propositions

DAVID PEARS

"It is a sign of a proposition's being elementary that there can be no elementary proposition contradicting it." (*Tractatus*, 4.211) Why did Wittgenstein require the elementary propositions of the *Tractatus* to pass this difficult test? Later, he admitted that he had been mistaken and conceded that there might be some kind of *a priori* incompatibility between elementary propositions. Commentators have written much about this change of mind, the first to occur after the publication of the *Tractatus*, but little about the reasons for the original view. In this paper I shall make an attempt to explain why he ever adopted it.

An explanation is needed, because the original specification of elementary propositions is so extreme and implausible. Wittgenstein probably knew that Russell was inclined to take the more moderate view, that there might be *a priori* incompatibilities between atomic propositions, which were the counterpart in his system of the elementary propositions of the *Tractatus*.[1] Later, when Wittgenstein retreated to a very similar moderate view, what he said was closely related to something that he had put into the *Tractatus*: "A speck in the visual field, though it need not be red, must have some colour: it is, so to speak, surrounded by colour-space." (2.0131) This almost anticipates one of the ideas that went into his recantation in 1929: ". . . when I say: such and such a point in the visual field is blue, I know not only that, but also that the point is not green, not red, not yellow and so on". (*Wittgenstein und der Wiener Kreis* [*WWK*], ed. F. Waismann, p. 64) So when a colour is ascribed to a point, it is not the single proposition that is "laid against reality like a ruler" (as he said in the *Tractatus* [2.1512]), but the whole system of colour-propositions, only one of which will be commensurate. When he had developed this theory, he took the decisive step that he had been prevented from taking in the *Tractatus*: he applied it to elementary propositions, and it then became possible to maintain that colour-propositions are elementary. This is not only a plausible result, but also one that could have been reached very naturally along one of the main lines of thought of the *Tractatus*, namely its holism. So what prevented him from taking the decisive step sooner?

It is circular to answer this question by pointing out that the idea that elementary propositions are logically independent of one another fits other features of the system of the *Tractatus* which are consequences of it. It certainly fits the theory that there are no *de re* necessities governing specific types of things, and the related claim that the truth-table of the logical product of two elementary propositions can always be completed. But that is only because these are among its consequences. What is needed is an explanation that will show what led Wittgenstein to adopt the idea in the first place.

There are two lines of inquiry which might lead to such an explanation. First, we can examine his reasons for believing that ordinary factual propositions can be analysed into elementary propositions that are logically independent of one another. Secondly, we can sift his later recantation for clues to his earlier thoughts.

Before I attempt these two tasks, there are three preliminary points that need to be made.

First, the inquiry will not be concerned with the question whether elementary propositions are immune from error. It is true that this question can be connected with the question of their logical independence, and Russell did make the connection. But in the *Tractatus* the question, whether elementary propositions would be immune from error, is not raised.

The second point is a similar one. The inquiry will not be concerned with the question, how the meanings of simple words are learned. Russell's interest in *a priori* connections between atomic propositions was connected with his interest in that question, and it was his view that, in spite of the *a priori* connections that he allowed between atomic propositions, the meanings of simple words could be learned only through acquaintance with the things that they signified. Those things, according to him, were their meanings. But very little is said in the *Tractatus* about learning the meanings of simple words, and what is said is none too clear (3.263). So the best policy is to investigate the theory of elementary propositions without getting entangled in the question how their vocabulary would be learned.

The third preliminary point has a different character. It might be objected at the start that the project is a hopeless one. For the aim is to discover how Wittgenstein came to overlook the contribution made by general words to the senses of the elementary propositions in which they occurred, but he himself later expressed complete agnosticism about the precise nature of elementary propositions, and pointed out that they might turn out to be quite unlike ordinary propositions which mention monadic and polyadic relations (*WWK*, p. 42). So there is really no hope of a detailed answer to the question why he overlooked the contribution made by words signifying such relations. The only possible answer is the disappointing one, that he did not find it necessary to consider the matter.

There is some truth in this. He certainly believed that he could prove the existence of elementary propositions, as specified in the *Tractatus*, starting from general premisses about the nature of factual language, and that it was neither necessary nor possible for him to specify them in more detail − that was something that would require further empirical investigation. Later, looking back on this combination of dogmatism and agnosticism, he found it unacceptable (see *WWK*, p. 182 and Norman Malcolm's *Memoir*, p. 86). But while he adhered to it he left unanswered all questions about any contribution that might be made by general words to the senses of elementary propositions. Nevertheless, the ordinary factual propositions which he supposed to be analysable into elementary propositions certainly contained general words, and so there ought to be some clues to his analysis of them, especially in his later recantation. Also it really ought to be possible to see why his argument for the existence of elementary propositions required them to be logically independent of one another.

The argument is the natural place to start. There is a brief statement of it near the beginning of the *Tractatus*:

If the world had no substance, then whether a proposition had sense would depend on whether another proposition was true.

In that case we could not produce any picture of the world (true or false). (2.0211−12)

Later, this argument is connected with the requirement that sense must be determinate:

The requirement that simple signs be possible is the requirement that sense be determinate. (3.23)

A proposition about a complex stands in an internal relation to a proposition about a constituent of the complex.
A complex can be given only by its description, which will be right or wrong. A proposition that mentions a complex will not be nonsensical, if the complex does not exist, but simply false.
When a propositional element signifies a complex, this can be seen from an indeterminateness in the propositions in which it occurs. In such cases we *know* that the proposition leaves something undetermined. (In fact the notation for generality *contains* a prototype.) (3.24)

The argument of 2.0211 is reductive, and one of its premises is the assumption that at some stage in the analysis of any factual proposition all non-logical words will represent (*vertreten*) existing things (*Tractatus*, 4.03 – 4.0312). What is being rejected is the hypothesis that the analysis can be regarded as complete at a stage at which these things are still complex. The first step towards the rejection of the hypothesis is the contention that, if it were correct, the sense of the original proposition would depend on the truth of another proposition. The second step is the contention that in that case factual language would be impossible.

At least, that is how the argument was interpreted by Russell in his Introduction to the *Tractatus* (p. xiii), and he has been followed by most subsequent commentators. But Hidé Ishiguro has argued that this interpretation cannot be reconciled with the evident fact that Wittgenstein accepted Rusell's theory of definite descriptions.[2] In order to appreciate her argument, we must assume that the further proposition 'q' which would have to be true, if the original proposition 'p' was to have a sense, is the proposition that the complex exists – or better, the more informative proposition that the constituents of the complex are arranged in the way that is required for its existence. If we use Wittgenstein's later illustration of an analysis, our assumption will be that 'q' is the proposition that the brush is attached to the broomstick, because the truth of this proposition is required for the existence of the broom (*Philosophical Investigations* [*PI*], §60). But then, Ishiguro argues, given Wittgenstein's acceptance of Russell's theory of definite descriptions, the falsity of 'q' would make 'p' false rather than senseless.

But this objection to Russell's interpretation of the argument is not unanswerable. Certainly, Wittgenstein would argue that the falsity of 'q' would make 'p' false rather than senseless. But that is because he would include 'q' in the analysis of 'p'. However, in 2.0211 he is arguing against the rival hypothesis that the analysis of 'p' is complete at a stage at which it does not yet include 'q'. That hypothesis gives 'q' a different role to play: it is not a part of the analysis of 'p', but a contingent condition of the possession of sense by 'p'. For the hypothesis is that the sense of 'p' requires that one of its non-logical words should represent a complex, and that requires that the complex should exist. Against this hypothesis, he argues that 'q' cannot play this role, and since his argument is reductive, his use of it is consistent with his own view that the role of 'q' is really a different one.

It is not enough to defend Russell's interpretation against this criticism. It is also necessary to explain how Wittgenstein's argument, interpreted in this way, applies to qualities and relations. For even if qualities and relations are not mentioned in elementary propositions, they are mentioned in the ordinary factual propositions that are supposed to be analysable into elementary propositions. However, that explanation is still a rather remote goal, which cannot be approached until two further questions about the argument have been answered. Why cannot 'q' play the role assigned to it by the hypothesis that Wittgenstein rejects? And what exactly is the connection with determinateness of sense? These are both difficult questions. It really is not clear why the sense of 'p' should not depend on the truth of another proposition, 'q', or how this veto is connected with determinateness of sense.

Perhaps the best way to approach the first problem would be to consider the whole range of interesting instantiations of 'q'. Just now it was assumed that 'q' would be a proposition about a complex 'C' mentioned in 'p', and it was pointed out that there are really two possibilities here: either 'q' might be the proposition that the so and so exists, where 'C' is identical with the so and so, or it might be the proposition that the constituents of 'C' are arranged in the way required for the existence of 'C'. If Wittgenstein was interested in one of these two instantiations of 'q', it was almost certainly the second one, because he was concerned with the kind of analysis that breaks down complexes into their constituents rather than with the kind that merely gives them definite descriptions.[3] Incidentally, the same is true of Russell.

But these are not the only interesting instantiations of 'q'. For 'q' might not be a proposition about a complex mentioned in 'p'. It might be the proposition that the form of 'p' exists. Or it might be the even more general proposition that something exists.

These two possibilities may seem very remote. But Wittgenstein gives us a clear statement of his view about the second one, that 'q' might be the proposition that something exists: it is not a genuine proposition, because it is not an experience (*Tractatus*, 5.552, cf. *WWK*, p. 77). But this is really directed against the more general theory that we need to experience some fact in order to understand logic, rather than in order to understand a particular proposition. However, the particular target is included in the general target, which is, in fact, an unpublished chapter of Russell's *Theory of Knowledge*. The chapter contains the following claim, ". . . there certainly is such a thing as 'logical experience', by which I mean that kind of immediate knowledge, other than judgement, which enables us to understand logical terms." (pt I "On the Nature of Acquaintance", ch. 9)

It is more worthwhile considering the possibility that 'q' is the proposition that the form of 'p' exists, because Wittgenstein was once attracted by a theory of this kind, and Russell developed a version of it in the same unpublished work. Russell argued that, in order to understand the proposition "Socrates precedes Plato", I must be acquainted with the form $x \zeta y$ (*loc. cit.*, pt I, ch. 9), and he was inclined to think that this acquaintance presupposes knowledge of the completely general fact that something stands in some dyadic relation to something else (*loc. cit.*, pt II, ch. 3). Now Wittgenstein never regarded the form of a proposition as a possible object of acquaintance. But he does say in *Notebooks 1914–1916* [*NB*] that he once thought that the sense of a proposition, such as 'φa' was connected with the entirely general fact $(\exists x)(\exists \varphi)(\varphi x)$. However, he rejects this theory, because ". . . it is impossible to see why 'φa' should be possible only if there is another proposition of the same form." He must mean "only if there is another true proposition of the same form", because he continues, "'φa' surely does not need any precedent. (For suppose that there existed only the two elementary propositions 'φa' and 'ψa' and that 'φa' were false: why should this proposition make sense only if ψa is true?)" [*NB*, 21/10/14: cf. *Tractatus*, 5.55–5.555]. Apart from the question of acquaintance with forms, the two theories are strikingly similar. In Russell's version understanding of the sense of a proposition presupposes knowledge of the completely general fact, while in the version that Wittgenstein rejects the existence of the sense presupposes the existence of the fact.

These completely general propositions are interesting instantiations of 'q'. For the main point of the picture theory is that a proposition acquires its sense without any outside help merely through the correlation of its words with objects (*NB*, 5/11/14: cf. *Tractatus*, 4.03ff. and 5.525), and this would not be the case if the sense of 'p' depended on the truth of its complete generalization, 'q'.

Part of the answer to the first question why Wittgenstein vetoed the dependence of the sense of *p* on the truth of *q* must be that he believed that it would lead to an infinite regress of sense and truth. But there is also something else than can be added to this answer. However, before that can be done, it is necessary to trace the connection with determinateness of sense.

Whatever instantiation of 'q', 'q' is a contingent proposition. So the sense of 'p' would be precarious if it did depend on the truth of 'q'. Or, as Wittgenstein puts it later, I could never be sure that 'p' had a sense, because I could never be sure that the word in it that was supposed to signify an existing complex really did signify an existing complex. Worse, the task of removing this doubt would be infinite if I could never reach elementary propositions (*WWK*, pp. 252–3). A. Kenny rightly emphasizes this aspect of Wittgenstein's argument,[4] and there is no doubt that part of the meaning of the postulate, that sense be determinate, is that there must not be anything contingent in its foundations (see *NB*, 17/6/16 and *Tractatus*, 2.02ff.).

But there is more in the postulate than this. If 'q' is a proposition about a complex constituent of 'p', then Wittgenstein's view was that 'q' should be included in the sense of 'p'. This gives special importance to the version of his veto that envisages this particular instantiation of 'q': "The question whether a proposition has sense (*Sinn*) can never depend on the truth of another proposition about a constituent of the first" ("Notes dictated to G. E. Moore", *NB*, p. 116). For the rationale of this version of the veto is that the infinite regress would involve an infinite expansion of the sense of 'p'. So in *Notebooks 1914–1916* he says:

We might demand determinateness [*sc.* of sense] in this way too: if a proposition is to make sense, then the syntactical employment of each of its parts must be settled in advance – It is, for example, not possible *only subsequently to come upon* the fact that a proposition follows from it. But, for example, what propositions follow from a proposition must be completely settled before the proposition can have a sense. (18/6/15: cf. *Prototractatus*, 3.20102–3)

This version of the veto is evidently connected with Frege's idea that the sense of a proposition must be absolutely precise.

Wittgenstein's argument for the existence of elementary propositions is deployed on a wide front, and it supports the central contention of the picture theory. But the search for the explanation of the logical independence of elementary propositions ought to concentrate on the particular sector in which he opposes the idea that the sense of 'p' depends on the truth of another proposition, 'q', about a constituent of 'p'. For it is here, if anywhere, that a reason might be found for the restriction that he imposes on the constituents of elementary propositions – that they must not produce any *a priori* incompatibilities between one elementary proposition and another.

The first thing that needs to be established is the way in which this restriction affects particulars. The most interesting case is, as Wittgenstein's choice of an illustration in *Philosophical Investigations* implies, the case in which 'p' mentions a complex, 'C', which is analysed into its constituents at the next level down (henceforth assumed to be the ultimate level, for the sake of brevity). Let C be the broom, and let 'q' be the proposition, that the brush is attached to the stick, $\alpha R \beta$. Of course, 'q' has now been accepted as part of the sense of 'p', in the spirit of Russell's theory of definite descriptions. Then the word 'C' may produce an *a priori* incompatibility between the proposition 'φC' and some other proposition of the same level, say 'φD'. For the specifications of the composition of C and D may both include the same part, α, and in such a case 'φC' and 'φD' cannot both be true. But neither α nor β can produce *a priori* incompatibilities between any proposition in which one of them is mentioned and any other proposition of the same level. For *ex hypothesi* α and β have no parts. Admittedly, '$\alpha R \beta$' is *a priori* compatible with '$\alpha R \gamma$', but perhaps the relation R, attachment, can take the blame for that.

This way of proving the innocence of certain particulars, the simple ones, may seem to make it all the more necessary to do the same of universals. But here we have to allow for Wittgenstein's agnosticism about the nature of elementary propositions. We do not have to show that he believed that general words occur in them. For we did not have to show that he believed that singular referring expressions occur in them. All that had to be shown was that he believed that, when singular referring expressions occurred at the penultimate level, they could be analysed in some way that would not produce *a priori* incompatibilities between the resulting elementary propositions. So the question is not, "What was his actual analysis of general words occurring at the penultimate level?" but rather, "What possibilities did he think that he saw?"

This is, of course, a question about all general words occurring at the penultimate level, and not only about monadic predicates, such as colour words. It is essentially important to remember polyadic predicates, because, as already noted, the attempt to find innocent particulars seems to succeed only when use is made of culpable universals. There may be an *a priori* incompatibility between '$aR\beta$' and '$aR\gamma$', and this is just as important as the possibility that there may be one between '$aR\beta$' and '$aS\beta$'.

In any case the brief discussion of "the logical structure of colour" in the *Tractatus* mentions the velocities of particles and their spatial and temporal relations:

> For example, the simultaneous presence of two colours at the same place in the visual field is impossible, in fact logically impossible, since it is ruled out by the logical structure of colour.
>
> Let us think how this contradiction appears in physics: more or less as follows – a particle cannot have two velocities at the same time; that is to say, it cannot be in two places at the same time, that is to say, particles that are in different places at the same time cannot be identical.
>
> It is clear that the logical product of two elementary propositions can neither be a tautology nor a contradiction. The statement that a point in the visual field has two different colours at the same time is a contradiction. (*Tractatus*, 6.3751: cf. *NB*, 16/8/16 and 11/9/16)

The main emphasis here is on the fact that colours have some logical structure, and he does not pronounce on its precise character. However, he does make a suggestion which is clearly intended as a step towards achieving for complex universals what he thought that he could achieve for complex particulars. The difficulty is that the analysis cannot be complete so long as it mentions velocities or locations, because specific velocities are *a priori* incompatible with one another, and so too are specific locations. So he suggests that, instead of ascribing a series of different positions to a particle at a series of different times we should regard this history as constitutive of its identity. But this can only be a temporary expedient in the system of the *Tractatus*. For if the word signifying the particle includes all this information, it will not be a simple word.

He does not mention this line of thought in his most detailed recantation of his requirement that elementary propositions must be logically independent of one another.[5] Instead, he says that he had assumed that the proposition that a thing has a certain degree of a quality could be analysed as a conjunction of propositions each ascribing to it a unit on the appropriate scale of degrees. For example, the proposition that E has two degrees of brightness, 'E2b' would be analysed as the conjunction 'Eb. Eb'. This analysis would then need what he calls "a completing supplementary statement": i.e. it is necessary to add ". . . and those are all the degrees that it possesses". Otherwise, the analysis would mean only that E had not less than 2 degrees of brightness.[6]

The criticism of this assumption is interesting.[7] Wittgenstein observes that 'Eb. Eb' says no more than "Eb": ". . . if, on the other hand, we try to distinguish between the units and consequently write $E(2b) = E(b') \& E(b'')$, we assume two different units of brightness; and then, if an entity possesses one unit, the question could arise, which of the two $-b'$ or $b''-$ it is; which is obviously absurd."

This throws some light on his earlier ideas. Evidently he had assumed that in the ultimate analysis it would be possible to eliminate all *a priori* incompatibilities produced by the ranges of determinable properties that are indispensable to ordinary factual discourse. In particular, he had assumed that the word signifying the unit of degree, "b", would not produce any *a priori* incompatibilities between any proposition in which it occurred and any other proposition belonging to the same level. His criticism is that this innocence is secured in a way that makes the suggested analysis inadequate. For the reason why there are no *a priori* incompatibilities between 'Eb' and any other elementary proposition concerned with the same property, brightness, is only that there are no others. But this makes it impossible at the ultimate level to build up to the proposition 'E2b'. That could be done only if each unit in the progression were distinguished by its position, or, to make the difference clearer, by a superscript. But it is of the essence of units that they are not distinguished in this way or in any other way. So these would not really be units. In any case, whatever method is used to indicate the number of degrees of brightness, the completing supplementary statement has to be added, and *a priori* incompatibilities are then inevitable.

The criticism implies that, when Wittgenstein thought about objects, his model was always a simple particular. This is confirmed by many of his later comments on the logical atomism of the *Tractatus*. Of course, it does not follow that he believed objects to be simple particulars, but only that they seemed to him to be suitable candidates because their innocence could be demonstrated. The implication of his later criticism is that the attempt to treat 'b' like a word signifying a simple particular had been a failure. It ensured the innocence of 'b', but only in a way that prevented it from doing what he wanted it to do. He therefore abandoned the requirement that there must be no *a priori* incompatibilities between elementary propositions.

This explanation of his long adherence to it in spite of its implausibility may be summed up in the following way. If logical analysis is conceived as a kind of taking to pieces, it will seem that words signifying particulars will produce *a priori* incompatibilities between the propositions in which they occur only because there is competition for the pieces of the particulars. So when a word signifies a simple particular, there will be no *a priori* incompatibilities, because there are no pieces, and, therefore, no competition. The meaning of the word is the simple particular it is entirely self-contained, and so it cannot produce any *a priori* incompatibilities. The next step is to take the analysis of singular referring expressions as a model, and to assume that complex universals can be taken to pieces in a way that will yield the same result. There would then be no residual source of *a priori* incompatibilities between elementary propositions. But universals are more intractable.

Notes

1. In *Our Knowledge of the External World* he says, "Perhaps one atomic fact may sometimes be capable of being inferred from another, though this is very doubtful." (p. 62) This sounds like a cautious expression of the extreme view. But the context makes it clear that what he is doubting is whether an atomic proposition about one particular can ever be inferred from an atomic proposition about another particular. He felt quite certain that there was an *a priori* incompatibility between two atomic propositions about the same particular – e.g. "This sense-datum is red" and "This sense-datum is green." (See *Principles of Mathematics*, 2nd edn, p. 467, and *The Philosophy of Logical Atomism*, in *Essays in Logic and Knowledge*, ed. R. C. Marsh (London: Allen & Unwin, 1956), pp. 194–5). Of course, Wittgenstein too felt certain of the *a priori* incompatibility of these two propositions. The difference between the two philosophers' views comes out in Wittgenstein's inference that therefore these two cannot be elementary. (*Tractatus*, 6.3751).

2. "Use and Reference of Names" in *Studies in the Philosophy of Wittgenstein*, ed. Peter Winch (London: Routledge & Kegan Paul, 1969), pp. 41–3.

3. See J. Griffin, *Wittgenstein's Logical Atomism* (Oxford: Blackwell, 1964), pp. 47–52.

4. A. Kenny, *Wittgenstein* (London: Allen Lane The Penguin Press, 1973), p. 78.

5. "Some Remarks on Logical Form", *Proceedings of the Aristotelian Society*, *1929*: reprinted in *Essays on Wittgenstein's Tractatus*, ed. I. M. Copi and R. W. Beard (New York: Macmillan, 1966).

6. *ibid.*, p. 35.

7. See J. Griffin, *Wittgenstein's Logical Atomism*, pp. 79–85 for a detailed discussion of this part of "Some Remarks on Logical Form".

The Rise and Fall of the Picture Theory*

P. M. S. HACKER

---

1 Preliminaries

Philosophy, as practised in the *Tractatus*, has one overarching goal – to render an account of the essence of the world. This can be done by giving an analysis of the essence of all description, for our knowledge of the world is expressed in our description of it, and whatever is essential to our description must be, so Wittgenstein thought, essential to reality in general. To give the essence of all description is to give the essence of a proposition (*Tractatus*, 5.471 – 5.4711). So the overarching goal is pursued by searching for the essential nature of the proposition. Once this is revealed, all lesser philosophical problems will solve themselves. The key to the search is the notion of depiction (*Tractatus*, 4.016). The Picture Theory of the Proposition[1] contains Wittgenstein's answer. In this paper I wish to examine the structure of the picture theory, and by so doing throw some light upon the question of its continuity in Wittgenstein's post-1929 philosophy. The sketch of the structure of the picture theory of the proposition that follows is not the only way to display Wittgenstein's early account of propositional representation. All I wish to claim is that it is one legitimate way of so doing, which will serve the purpose at hand. The immediate purpose is to elaborate the logical or methodological *Weltanschauung* that informs the *Tractatus*, to

* I am most grateful to Dr Kit Fine and Dr Anthony Kenny for their generous comments on, and criticisms of, earlier drafts of this paper. My greatest debt, as always, is to my colleague, Dr Gordon Baker.

investigate the relationship between the logical atomism of the *Tractatus* and the picture theory, and to determine what can legitimately be said to constitute the 'logical part' of the picture theory of meaning. The ultimate purpose of the exercise is to contrast the picture theory with Wittgenstein's later remarks on the pictoriality of the proposition in order to show that these observations on pictoriality do not indicate that the logical core of the picture theory remains intact throughout Wittgenstein's work.

The conception of a picture as the key to the essence of the proposition did not emerge until 29 September 1914.[2] It is noteworthy that many of the elements of the picture theory had occurred to Wittgenstein before this date. The conception of the proposition as a picture of reality enabled him to draw together disparate elements into a unified account. His objection to Russell's Theory of Types, and his own view that what the Theory of Types attempts incoherently to say is shown by the symbolism, occurred to him well before September 1914. So too did the analysis of tautologies and contradictions as senseless propositions. Both these insights yielded the distinction between showing and saying which was to be enshrined in the picture theory. Likewise his apprehension that truth-functions are not material functions and that there are no logical objects antedates the picture theory.

Any philosophical 'theory' of the proposition is designed to meet certain requirements. The adequacy of the account will be partly determined by the extent to which and method by which the requirements are met. The requirements can be seen as insights into the essence of the proposition. There is no reason to suppose that their specification will be 'flat'; if they are not hierarchically ordered at any rate some degree of interdependency may be expected. The requirements are enshrined in the theory, but they are not part of the theory in the sense that acceptance of the requirements necessitates acceptance of the theory (although if the theory is accepted, so too are the requirements).

The theory itself must be distinguished from the requirements. It consists of a set of essential contentions which, *inter alia* meet (or are alleged to meet) the requirements. The essential contentions are distinguishable from the consequences of the theory. The consequences follow from the essential propositions, but, of course, one may accept the consequences without accepting the theory; for one may derive them in other ways, or include them in the requirements.

I do not want to make this division between requirements, essential propositions and consequences seem sharper than it is. But I think the crude distinction can shed light upon the picture theory and its aftermath.

2 The Requirements

R-1. The first fundamental requirement stems from Wittgenstein's insight that, *contra* Frege and Russell, ordinary language is in order as it is.[3] The real structure of language is in good logical order, although philosophical analysis is necessary to reveal it. This means that no truth-value gaps occur, for a language in which well-formed sentences can lack a truth-value is not in good logical order since the laws of logic would not apply to it. The requirement that emerges from this preconception is that the essence of the proposition must conform to the Principle of Bivalency (*Notebooks, 1914–1916* [*NB*], pp. 97, 112; cf. pp. 23, 64).

Since the existence of (apparent) truth-value gaps is attributable to the occurrence of vacuous proper names and apparent vagueness, Wittgenstein's requirement of bivalency seemed to necessitate acceptance of the Russellian Theory of Descriptions and the Fregean requirement of determinacy of sense. Both these consequential demands should be viewed as ways of amplifying the insight that ordinary language is in order. Hence they should not appear on the fundamental list.

R-2. A second requirement is that the sense of a proposition does not in general determine its truth-value. Therefore grasping its sense does not entail knowing its truth-value. We must, in general, be able to understand a proposition without knowing if it is true or false (*NB*, p. 93).

R-3. The first and second requirements carry in their wake a third, crucial requirement: it must be possible to say something meaningful but false. That things are *not* as the proposition says they are does no imply that it has said nothing, i.e. a proposition must be capable of saying something false. It has a sense even when false. It follows from this, *inter alia*, that what makes a proposition with sense true cannot be identical with what gives it sense.

R-4. A fourth requirement consists of the apprehension of the generative powers of language, now a well-known thesis due to Chomsky, but clearly enunciated by Wittgenstein in 1913 (*NB*, p. 98) and hammered home repeatedly in the *Tractatus* (4.02, 4.027).

R-5.   The final fundamental insight constituting a requirement is that the proposition must be composite. An essential feature for any proposition to say what it does, indeed to say anything at all, is that it be articulated. For only if the proposition is articulated can it be meaningful but false. And only if it is composed of elements, put together in rule-governed ways, can the generative requirement be met without postulating an infinite number of simple signs.

Before examining the methodological dogmas underlying the *Tractatus'* semantics there is a further point. It is less a requirement than a fundamental principle of semantic analysis. The keystone of the conception of meaning which dominates the *Tractatus* is the notion of truth-conditions. The sense of any sentence consists in the conditions under which it is true and the conditions under which it is false. "The expression of agreement and disagreement with the truth-possibilities of elementary propositions expresses the truth-conditions of a proposition" (*Tractatus*, 4.431). In the case of the fully analysed elementary proposition, its sense is a function of its constituent expressions, i.e. their meanings and logico-syntactical arrangement determine the conditions under which the atomic sentence is true. This conception of the sense of a sentence, coupled with the conception of logical connectives as operators (rather than 'representatives' of literal functions) is the basis for a radical explanation of logical necessity in terms of tautologousness. The notion of truth-conditions is interpreted in Realist terms, i.e. it is not demanded that the truth-conditions we assign to our sentences be limited to conditions we can verify. Sense may, apparently, transcend conditions of possible knowledge.

Wittgenstein's methodological dogmas were a Fregean legacy. They stem from Frege's Principle of Purity in semantics: "Always to separate sharply the psychological from the logical, the subjective from the objective."[4] In Wittgenstein's hands, too, this principle has crucial corollaries.

Firstly, psychological considerations pertaining to the study of thought processes are logically irrelevant (*Tractatus*, 4.1121). Sense is independent of ideas, association of ideas and mental representations.

Secondly, the point of a proposition, the purposes to which it is put are of no logical significance. "What interests logic are only the unasserted propositions" (*NB*, p. 96). Judgment, command, question all stand on the same level – the only feature of logical import is the common propositional form.

Thirdly, *pari passu*, the assertion sign is without logical significance

(*NB*, p. 96); it is an external feature of a proposition. The assertion sign belongs to the proposition no more than a number arbitrarily assigned to it in an ordering.

Fourthly, judgment, and presumably grounds of judgment, are irrelevant to the theory of the proposition. Grounds of judgment, e.g. grounds for inductive reasoning, have no logical but only psychological justification (*Tractatus*, 6.3631). The avowed aim of the *Tractatus* is to set a limit to thought (p. 3). But the limits of thought may well transcend the limits of possible cognition. Indeed, we can think of the future, but can have no knowledge of it (*Tractatus*, 6.36311). Nevertheless propositions about the future have a sense. Sense is independent of possible cognition.

Hence, fifthly, how we come to know whether a proposition is true or false, and whether we can know it, is irrelevant to specification of the sense of the proposition. We grasp the sense of a proposition when we know what must be the case if it is true, and what must be the case if it is false. To know whether it is true or false, we must compare the proposition with reality. What makes it true or false is something objective, existing independently of cognition. Whether we "mere mortals" with our "medical limitations" *can* compare the proposition with the relevant reality is an empirical question. Sense is given independently of any means of recognition of truth.

With these five, strikingly Realist, methodological dogmas, five fundamental requirements and one strategic principle, we can now turn to the picture theory to see how its essential theses meet the requirements in conformity with the methodological principles.

3 The Picture Theory of Representation

The picture theory of the proposition is an application of a general theory of representation to the special case of the proposition.[5] How is representation possible? The key to the answer, Wittgenstein believed, lies in the notion of isomorphism. If we make a model of a state of affairs, the model represents in virtue of being isomorphic with what it represents. Wittgenstein's general theory of representation is displayable by six theses and three corollaries. I shall call the conjunction of the theses "The Doctrine of Isomorphism".

1. *Compositeness*
    (*a*) A model must be composite, must consist of different elements.

(*b*) The elements of the model stand for the elements of what it represents. This relation between the elements of the model and the elements of what it represents is the "pictorial relation".

2. *Form and structure.* A model must have both form and structure. The form of a model is the possibility of its structure. The structure of a model is the (conventionally determined) way in which the elements of the model are arranged in order for it to be a model. Different models in various representational "media" (dioramas, paintings, music) will have different representational forms (3 dimensionality, 2 dimensionality, linear ordering, etc.) but will, if they represent the same state of affairs, have the same logical form, i.e. identical multiplicity and conventionally determined possibilities of arrangement.

3. *Common structure.* Any model represents a state of affairs. The structure of the state of affairs represented by a model consists of the way the elements of the state of affairs are connected with each other (*Tractatus*, 2.032). For a model to represent a given state of affairs the elements of the model must be arranged isomorphically with the elements of what it represents, given the appropriate method of projection (*Tractatus*, 2.15).

4. *Models are facts.* The model *qua* representation is a fact. It is *the fact* that the elements are arranged thus and so that represents what is represented (*Tractatus*, 2.141 − 2.15). Only in a fact are elements knit together to make representation possible.

5. *Truth.* A model is true if it agrees with reality, if things are as the model represents them as being; otherwise it is false.

6. *Cognition.* To know whether a model is true or false, it must be compared with reality.

Three consequences flow from this general theory:

A. No model can be true *a priori*. This follows from the sixth thesis.

B. There must be an internal relation between a model and what it represents, no matter whether it represents truly or falsely. For structural isomorphism to be possible, model and what it represents must have identical logical form, i.e. multiplicity and combinatorial possibility. That a model M which represents μ has the form it does is essential to its identity as a model of μ. That μ has the same form is essential to its identity as μ. This relation of M to μ which is essential for M to be capable of representing μ is internal rather than contingent.

C.   No model can represent its own (internal) relation to what it is a model of. "A picture cannot depict its pictorial form, it displays it" (*Tractatus*, 2.172). This is intuitively plausible. But it also follows from 6 (or A). For if a model could represent its pictorial form, then it could lack the pictorial form which is essential to its own identity.

We can now turn to "propositional representation" as a special case. Wittgenstein's purpose is to produce a general account of the proposition which will explain the nature and limits of propositional representation. "The proposition", Wittgenstein contends, "only says something in so far as it is a picture" (*NB*, p. 8). As such it must share the essential features of all pictures or models:

1a.   *Qua* picture the proposition must be composite: "A proposition is a picture of a situation only in so far as it is logically articulated," Wittgenstein wrote (*NB*, p. 8); "A simple – non-articulated – sign can be neither true nor false."

1b.   The elements of the proposition must go proxy for the elements of what the proposition represents (*Tractatus*, 3.22).

2.   The proposition must have a form and a structure. Its logical form consists of the combinatorial possibilities of its elements according to rules of logical syntax. Its structure is the determinate relation between its elements (*Tractatus*, 3.14).

3.   The structure of the proposition is isomorphic with the logical structure of what it represents. "The configuration of objects in a situation corresponds to the configuration of simple signs in the propositional sign" (*Tractatus*, 3.21).

4.   "A propositional sign is a fact" (*Tractatus*, 3.14). As with a model, it is the fact that the elemnts (signs) are arranged as they are (according to logical syntax) that syas what the proposition says, given the pictorial relation.

5.   A proposition is true if it agrees with reality, otherwise it is false. Truth consists in the correspondence between proposition and fact.

6. To know whether a proposition is true it must be compared with reality.

These theses are not yet a statement of the picture theory of the proposition. They are only the first stage in applying the general theory of representation to the proposition. But they contribute to meeting the five requirements. Compositeness (R-5) is met by a proposition's being a depicting fact. Bivalency and the Excluded Middle are partially satisfied by 1a and 5. The materials for satisfying requirements 2–4 are at hand. Different combinatorial possibilities of elements will explain the generative power of language. Understanding elements and knowledge of forms will satisfy the requirement of understanding independently of knowledge of truth-value, and that of the possibility of false assertion. Moreover, the consequences of the general theory of representation (A, B and C) look as though they can be given obvious application to sustain Wittgenstein's antecedent repudiation of the Theory of Types, his conception of logical propositions, and his distinction between showing and saying. So; looked at from the genetic–analytic point of view, the strategy appears fruitful.

But much yet remains to be done to yield a theory of the proposition. First, the elements of the picturing fact, i.e. the proposition, must be characterized formally. Secondly, the nature of the objects for which the elements of the proposition go proxy must be specified. Thirdly, the nature of the logical form which picture and pictured have in common must be clarified. This must be done so as to satisfy the requirements completely (in particular, determinacy of sense must be secured and the impossibility of reference failure ensured). Moreover it must be done for every kind of proposition *if* a general theory is to be produced. For thus far we have no account of the sense of a proposition, no account of the way in which the elements of a proposition contribute to its sense, no criterion of identity for sense, no analysis of logical operations, and no account of the various forms of compound propositions.

To the Doctrine of Isomorphism we must add the Doctrine of Atomism as a second step in applying the general theory of representation to the proposition in order to generate the picture theory of the proposition.

4   The Doctrine of Atomism

The Doctrine of Atomism is designed to supplement the foregoing fragmentary theory of propositional representation. This supplementation yields a special theory of the proposition – the theory of the elementary proposition. The particular requirements which the Doctrine of Atomism is designed to meet are determinacy of sense and absence of reference failure; these conditions must be met in order to satisfy the Law of Excluded Middle. In so doing the radical thesis of bipolarity for atomic propositions emerges. In the course of meeting these requirements, however, a substantial contribution is made to fulfilling the other requirements. I shall present the Doctrine of Atomism by means of two distinct groups of theses: the Theses of Logical Atomism, and the Theses of Metaphysical Atomism. The latter are, as one would expect from a philosopher who thought that logic was prior to metaphysics, an outgrowth of the former. Metaphysical Atomism is rationally required in order to sustain the theses of Logical Atomism.

The Theses of Logical Atomism are three:

(1)   The Thesis of Terminable Analysis: A fully analysed proposition consists only of simple names (so simple names are unanalysable).

(2)   The Thesis of Senseless Names: Simple names have no sense but necessarily have a reference. They refer to the same object (entity), come what may.

(3)   The Holistic Thesis: The sense of an elementary proposition is a function of (the reference of) its constituent expressions. A sense is produced by combining names according to logico-syntactical rules.

How do these claims emerge? A proposition is composed of expressions. An expression may be complex or simple. A complex expression is analysable. Thus a complex concept-word is, following Frege, replaceable by its characteristic marks (*Merkmale*).[6] A sentence containing a singular definite description is translatable, following Russell, into a conjunction of sentences which do not. Thus the truth of a proposition containing a complex expression will depend upon the truth of the propositions into which it is analysable. *But analysis must come to an end.* Why?

For two reasons: first, because of the Realist conception of truth. Truth is objective, dependent upon objectively existing realities. The truth of propositions containing complex expressions is dependent upon the truth of simpler propositions from which those expressions have been eliminated. But if truth is to be objective, and – in conformity with Thesis 6 of the Doctrine of Isomorphism – ascertainable by comparison with reality, then analysis must come to an end with propositions whose truth depends only upon agreement with reality. Secondly, because of the requirement that sense be independent of the facts, in particular of existence and inexistence. Whether a proposition has sense cannot depend upon whether some other proposition is true (*Tractatus*, 2.0211). The Russellian theory of descriptions meets this requirement, but only on the condition that the names which represent the values of the bound variables in the analysans are assured of reference. If they are themselves complex, they must be subjected to further analysis.

That complex names be analysable into simple names, however, is only the first move. The next move is the requirement that such simple names denote simple things. If names denoted complexes, then the complex which they denote might cease to exist. So analysis must yield simple names denoting simple objects. Such names, Wittgenstein argues, do not have a sense, but only a reference. They always denote the same object, and the object they denote is a necessary existent.

The logical demand for simple names is imposed not only by the requirement that truth-value gaps be impossible, but also by the requirement that sense be determinate, that every function be defined for every possible argument (within its range). If to have a sense is to be true-or-false, as Wittgenstein claims, then there can be no propositions without a determinate truth-value, and if the identity of sense is to be determined by truth-conditions (in the case of molecular propositions by entailments) then "it cannot occur to one only subsequently that a certain proposition follows from it [a given proposition with sense]. Before a proposition can have a sense, it must be completely settled what propositions follow from it" (*Prototractatus*, 3.20103). Why does this require the existence of senseless names? Because the occurrence of expressions denoting complexes in a proposition is eliminable by Russellian analysis into quantified propositions. But a variable is only a place-holder for a range of values with a common form. So any quantified proposition must itself be analysable into a logical sum or product containing no variables but only names. If these are not simple, they must be further analysable (otherwise not all entailments will have been settled in advance). Only propositions that are analysable into simple names will ensure that the Law of Excluded Middle is preserved, that propositions correspond (or fail to correspond) with reality in a wholly determinate manner. Once logically proper names have been reached then we have reached, as we shall see in a moment, logically independent propositions. So determinacy of sense thus interpreted requires logically proper names.

The third thesis is that the sense of an elementary proposition is a function of its constituent expressions. This thesis is Fregean in spirit if not in letter. The arrangement of the constituent names according to the rules of logical syntax constitutes a logical picture of a possible state of affairs. The sense of a proposition is its truth conditions. The names in an elementary proposition, together with its logico-syntactical form, determine what must be the case for the proposition to be true, i.e. that such-and-such objects are thus concatenated. One understands the sense of an elementary proposition if one understands its constituents and knows its form — then one knows what is the case if it is true.

It follows (or Wittgenstein thought it followed) from the three theses that the elementary proposition is logically independent. For at the time of the *Tractatus* Wittgenstein took it that the existence of a logical dependence between propositions was a mark of internal complexity. If 'p' entails 'q' then some constituent of 'p' must be complex, for that the sense of 'q' is contained in the sense of 'p' is explained by the fact that some component of 'q' is a characteristic mark of some component of 'p'. When all complexity is eliminated the resultant elementary propositions are logically independent.

The three logical theses of atomism require a metaphysical substructure. Three notions must be introduced: an object is a metaphysical atom i.e. an indestructible, simple, entity. The form of an object consists of the conjunction of its combinatorial possibilities (with other objects). A state of affairs is a (possible) complete combination of objects. The salient theses of Metaphysical Atomism are then:

(1)   Simple objects make up the substance of the world.

(2)   The limits of the world are determined by the forms of all objects, or, what comes to the same thing, by the range of (possible) states of affairs.

(3)   The existence or non-existence of a given state of affairs is logically independent of the existence or non-existence of any other state of affairs.

That the world should have a substance is a requirement forced by the theses of logical atomism. It is a condition of the possibility of representation (*Tractatus*, 2.0212), for only thus, Wittgenstein thought, could logic itself be possible. Unless there were subsistent objects, then whether a proposition had sense or not would depend upon the facts.

What are the consequences of these metaphysical doctrines? First, the limits of all possible worlds are absolutely determinate. Secondly, the limits of possible worlds are wholly independent of language. *Pari passu*, what is necessary and what is possible is determined (extralinguistically) by metaphysics. These necessities are ineffable.

A difficult problem is to unravel the rationale for the radical thesis of bipolarity. Frege's concept of a thought (*Gedanke*) required only that a thought be *capable* of bearing a truth-value. Thus in his analysis of ordinary language he countenanced truth-value gaps. Russell, however, adopted a more stringent standard for propositionhood, namely Bivalence. Although Wittgenstein's preconception that ordinary language is in good logical order committed him to the requirement of bivalence and applicability of the Law of Excluded Middle, he adopted, in the course of his atomism, the much more radical position of Bipolarity for elementary propositions. This of course satisfies bivalency, but it goes much further, for it commits him to the unique position of denying that there are any necessary elementary propositions. Any proposition that has a sense must not just be capable of being true or false, it must be capable of being true and also capable of being false. Of course molecular propositions need not be bipolar; if they are tautologies or contradictions then they have only one 'pole'. But then they are degenerate, senseless, propositions.

What, in this context, does bipolarity achieve? It ensures the possibility of understanding a proposition independently of knowing its truth-value. It ensures that what makes a proposition true is not identical with what gives it its sense. So it also explains how a proposition can be false but meaningful; and it explains the nature of logical propositions.

But how is bipolarity derived? Certainly one can view bipolarity as part of the wider claim that each fact "can be the case or not the case while everything else remains the same" i.e. bipolarity for atomic propositions follows from the independence postulate. But this does not really advance things. Similarly one might want to claim that simple objects cannot enter into necessary configurations, for then one of the simples would necessarily have the property of entering into that particular configuration. But the internal properties of objects are inexpressible – they are *shown* by features of the symbolism, and represented not by names but by variables i.e. formal concepts. So a *Satzzeichen* together with its lines of projection must pick out a possible state of affairs which may either be instantiated or not. Hence the sense expressed must have 'two poles' i.e. must be capable of being true and also capable of being false.

Now we may conjoin the doctrines of Isomorphism and Atomism to see what results can be obtained by way of meeting the fundamental requirements.

An elementary proposition, Wittgenstein argues, is a fact – the fact that the names in it are combined, according to syntactical rules, in the way in which they are. It represents, by means of constituting a logical picture, a possible state of affairs – namely that state of affairs which consists of the objects named by its constituent names being concatenated as it says they are. It is true if those objects are thus concatenated. Otherwise it is false. The picture theory of the atomic proposition meets the requirement of the Law of Excluded Middle by the stringent doctrine of bipolarity. One can understand a proposition independently of its truth-value, knowing the sense of a proposition is knowing what must be the case if it is true (and what must be the case if it is false). False propositions have a sense no less than true ones. The creative powers of language are explained by reference to knowledge of names and forms. The compositeness requirement is met by the Doctrine of Isomorphism and filled in by the Doctrine of Atomism. Determinacy of sense is met by the claim that analysis terminates in simple names designating metaphysical simples.

A host of further logical and metaphysical claims can be extracted from the conjunction of the two doctrines. The second corollary of the general theory of representation (B) can now be applied to the proposition: the internal relation between proposition and the state of affairs it depicts consists of possession of identical logical multiplicity and form (*Tractatus*, 4.04). It is crucial to note that the logical multiplicity of states of affairs is transcendent. The first and third corollaries evidently apply too. Much else that is of no direct concern to us can be milked out of the special theory of the elementary proposition.[7]

5   The Doctrine of Truth-Functional Composition

We still do not have a complete theory of the proposition. To produce *the* picture theory of the proposition we must add one further doctrine: the Doctrine of Truth-Functional Composition. This consists of two essential theses:

First, the logical connectives are not names. (*Tractatus*, 4.0312; 5.4)

Secondly, all propositions are truth-functions of elementary propositions (*Tractatus*, 5.3), i.e. result from truth-operations on them.

The elaboration of these two theses enables Wittgenstein to generalize the special theory of the proposition to capture within his net everything which he is willing to call a genuine proposition.[8] The fundamental insight is expressed at *Tractatus*, 4.411:

It immediately strikes one as probable that the introduction of elementary propositions provides the basis for understanding all other kinds of proposition. Indeed the understanding of general propositions *palpably* depends on the understanding of elementary propositions.

The first thesis was of course one of Wittgenstein's very first insights (*vide* Russell correspondence), and it sharply differentiated his conception of the logical connectives from Frege's.

From the point of view of our concern with the general theory of the proposition the important results are: (1) that the sense of any compound proposition (with sense) is a function of its component elementary propositions; (2) the sense of a compound (as of a simple) proposition is constituted by its truth-conditions, i.e. what must be the case for it to be true, i.e. its entailments. The criterion for the identity of two propositions is given by their having identical entailments; (3) tautologies and contradictions are senseless; (4) apparently non-extensional contexts are eliminable.

Now, and only now, do we have the picture theory of the proposition which, by conjoining the doctrines of isomorphism, atomism and truth-functional composition, provides a general account of the scope and limits of possible representation. Although metaphysical necessities are swept under the carpet as ineffabilia, logical necessity is triumphantly explained in conventionalist, linguistic terms.

6 The Problem of the Continuity of the Picture Theory

In recent years there has been a justifiable reaction to the initial conception of the relationship between Wittgenstein's two masterpieces. To be sure there is profound change in his philosophy, but there is also profound continuity. But exactly what changes and what continues is no easy matter to discern. This is not surprising, for if what Wittgenstein has done is to rotate the axis of reference of his investigation 180 degrees (*Philosophical Investigations* [*PI*], §108), then the difference of the sameness, as it were, will be difficult to perceive.

It has been argued, most elegantly and persuasively by Dr Anthony Kenny,[9] that the picture theory of meaning, though transformed, survives the abandonment of the atomism of the *Tractatus*, that one can isolate a 'logical aspect' of the picture theory which is never repudiated. Certainly many claims made in the *Tractatus* are retained in the later philosophy. One might single out the salient contentions about the nature of philosophy; or – in a more logical vein – the bipolarity of the proposition[10] with the attendant rejection of *a priori* propositions[11] and insistence that what makes a proposition true cannot be identical with what gives it sense. On the negative, critical, side, Wittgenstein continues to object to any theory of types, for grammar cannot be justified (although in the *Tractatus* grammar was, *ineffably*, justified by the language-independent structure of reality); similarly he never relinquishes his *Grundgedanke* that there are no logical objects. But despite these, and many other, threads of continuity, I think that it is most misleading to talk of the continuity of the picture theory of the proposition.

As we have seen, the picture theory is what it purports to be – a theory of propositional representation. It is intended as a quite general theory which will provide an analysis of *any* type of proposition. It gives us an account of the internal structure of the elementary proposition, and so of names, forms and operations. It is, therefore, doubtful whether one can isolate a "logical aspect of the picture theory" from the doctrines of atomism and truth-functional composition, since without these we do not have a theory of the *proposition*, whether general or atomic, nor of the internal structure and constituents of the proposition. Whatever the "logical aspects" of an account of the essence of the proposition are, they must surely encompass the specification of the way in which the elements of a proposition contribute to its sense, of what the sense of a proposition consists in, of the criteria of identity for sense. They must include a specification of the nature of truth, and perhaps also indicate what relation, if any, obtained between the limits of sense and the limits of possible knowledge. But if the previous discussion of the structure of the picture theory is correct in its broad outlines, then it is evident that one cannot shear off the doctrines of atomism, logical and metaphysical alike, without destroying the picture theory as a theory of the proposition.[12] Indeed, even the General Theory of Representation out of which the picture theory of the proposition grows, cannot survive the transformation of Wittgenstein's philosophy, for it requires a full-blooded doctrine of isomorphism (i.e. a model (language)-independent structure of what is represented; a representation of facts by facts; a correlation of elements of model with independent elements of reality; a strong correspondence theory of truth).

Of course, there are many features of continuity. The five requirements, with some minor modifications and qualifications remain intact. But they are not part of the picture theory, merely requirements to be met by it. The later account of the proposition attempts to meet them, and other novel requirements, but in a totally different way. Likewise the three consequences (A, B, C) of the general theory of representation, though dramatically transformed by repudiation of the doctrine of isomorphism, are retained. But to show that this indicates a continuity of the picture theory requires one to show that they are derived in the same way from its essential components. The same goes for the consequences of the doctrines of atomism which survive.

To trace in detail the fall of the picture theory in the early 1930s is not possible here. Space will not allow me to examine Wittgenstein's arguments which, beginning with the independence postulate, rapidly eroded the foundations of the doctrines of isomorphism, repudiated the transcendence of logical possibility, rejected the correspondence theory of truth and brought about the collapse of the main struts of the picture theory. Instead of retelling this well-known story, I shall briefly survey the change in Wittgenstein's strategy and methodological principles in order to highlight the transformation that occurred. Subsequently I shall explore his later discussion of pictoriality.

7   The Transformation of the Methodological Principles

Wittgenstein continued to think that psychological features of thought processes are logically irrelevant. In the *Philosophical Investigations* he insists repeatedly that mental representations and accompanying experiences are irrelevant to sense and understanding. The doctrine of avowals underlines the principle that it must always be possible to distinguish being true from being believed to be true, and the private language argument emphasizes the necessity of the distinction between being right and believing oneself to be right. So here we find an anti-psychologism, an affinity with Realism, which, because of the criterial link neither involves the Realist disregard for the conditions of possible knowledge as determining the bounds of sense, nor slips into the typical reductionism of Anti-realism.

Despite this affinity, however, even the anti-psychologism is transformed. In the first place, it is no longer wedded to Realist dogmas

— in particular the transcendence (as opposed to the independence) of truth. In the second, the boundary between philosophy and psychology has shifted dramatically. The *Tractatus* was tacitly or explicitly committed to a host of psychological hypotheses about arcane mental processes whose relation to reality was mediated by language. Thought, understanding and belief, although they had a logical structure similar to the proposition, and contained unknown psychic constituents, were of no philosophical consequence (except in so far as sentences like "A believes p" threaten the thesis of extensionality). The assignment of meaning to indefinables, the forging of links between language and reality, applying the method of projection are all mental processes. How they are done is a matter for psychology; all that concerns logic is that they are done. In the later work this is repudiated. The subjects of meaning, understanding and thinking are essential to a proper grasp of the nature of language. For the relations between meaning that p, understanding 'p' and the sense of 'p' are internal. Therefore no psychological explanation or hypothesis can replace a philosophical account of these relations.

The second Fregean dogma that the point and purpose of a proposition is irrelevant to its sense is repudiated. The slogan "The meaning is the use" is vague, and might seem, out of context, to legitimate both the *Tractatus'* and *Philosophical Investigations'* semantics. But one aspect of use which concerned Wittgenstein after 1929 was the point of an utterance (*Philosophische Bemerkungen* [PB], p. 59; *Philosophical Grammar* [PG], p. 87; *Remarks on the Foundations of Mathematics* [RFM], p. 49; *PI*, §6) as an essential element of its sense. In particular, fundamental (logical) distinctions between kinds of sentence are given by ordinary grammatical form *only to the extent* that a given grammatical form is canonically used for a kind of purpose. Logical form is determined by kind of use and standard purpose (and one can give orders with declarative sentences, make statements with interrogative ones, and ask questions with imperatives). Consequently it is nonsense to suggest that differences in force are logically irrelevant to sense or meaning.

The third dogma is likewise transformed. Wittgenstein continues to insist that the assertion *sign* is logically irrelevant. It does not mark an internal act of judgment, nor does it contribute to the sense of what is asserted. The most it can do is to function as a mark of a complete 'move in a language-game'. But the rationale for this is now reversed — it is just because the relation between sense and force is internal that the assertion sign, for Frege externally related to the proposition, is logically irrelevant. If difference in use, function or purpose of sentences constitutes a difference in sense, then the force of a sentence must affect its sense. Hence the relation of assertibility to the sense of a declarative sentence (*Behauptungsatz*) is an essential feature of it (*RFM*, p. 49).

This clearly leads to the total repudiation of the fourth Realist dogma, namely the irrelevance to logic of the grounds of judgment. The grounds of judgment, being what justify assertion, constitute, at least in certain cases, the sense of a proposition. The grounds are grammatically related to the proposition and tell us what proposition it is (*Zettel*, §437).

This in turn involves rejection of the Realist dismissal of the relevance of the conditions of possible cognition to the determination of the limits of sense. In *Zettel* he remarks, "It is only apparently possible 'to transcend any possible experience', even these words only seem to make sense, because they are arranged on the analogy of significant expressions" (*Zettel*, §260). Elsewhere, arguing against scepticism, he writes "How can I even make the hypothesis [that anyone else has experiences] if it transcends any possible experience? How could such an hypothesis be backed by meaning?" (*Blue and Brown Books* [*BB*], p. 48). Finally, in the *Philosophical Investigations* he stresses: "Asking for the way and possibility of verifying a proposition is only a special form of the question 'How do you mean that?'. The answer is a contribution to the grammar of the proposition" (*PI*, §353).[13]

In short, the later philosophy replaces the Realist methodological principles by diametrically opposed principles. The bounds of sense and the limits of possible knowledge must coincide. We can squeeze no more sense out of a proposition than we can put into one. We can assign sense to a proposition only in so far as we can stipulate the conditions which would justify its employment. Consequently the crucial strategic principle that sense is given by truth-conditions independently of means of recognition of truth, which dominates the *Tractatus* semantics, is now rejected. Sense of at least some kinds of *Behauptungsätze* is given by assertion conditions: the sense of an assertion is given by what circumstances justify asserting it (*PG*, p. 81). The grounds for an assertion are part of its grammar, and tell us what proposition it is. To specify the grounds for an assertion is to explain its sense; sense is given by explanations of sense. Explanations of sense function as justifications and are internally, grammatically, related to their explananda. Four cardinal principles of explanation of sense dominate Wittgenstein's later philosophy: explanations must be (1) *general*, (2) *public*, (3) *non-trivial*, and (4) *language-immanent*. The contrast with the picture theory of meaning here runs deep. For the picture theory of the atomic proposition explicitly violates the principles of immanence, tacitly infringes the publicity principles, and is arguably implicitly committed to defying the non-triviality principle.

Space will not permit me to explore the way which these novel methodological principles and different strategic principle are wedded to an enlarged range of fundamental requirements to produce a dramatically different account of language in Wittgenstein's later philosophy. But I hope that the foregoing sketch suffices to cast doubt upon the continuity of the picture theory. Nevertheless, nothing thus far said is intended to deny that Wittgenstein continued to believe in the *pictoriality* of the proposition. The moot question, however, is – what is the "pictoriality" of the proposition?

8   The Pictoriality of the Proposition

In his later work Wittgenstein frequently talks of the pictoriality of the proposition – and it might be thought that this refutes the contention that the essentials of the picture theory die with the demise of the doctrines of isomorphism and atomism. To show that this is mistaken we must examine what features are intended, in the later writings, to be captured by the term 'pictoriality'.

1.   A variety of analogies are drawn: understanding a proposition is akin to understanding a picture (*PG*, p. 42); the difference between a proposition of fiction and a non-fictional proposition is akin to the difference between a genre picture and an historical picture (*PG*, p. 164); a picture can be substituted for an expression in a sentence without changing its sense (*Wittgenstein und der Wiener Kreis* [*WWK*], p. 185); one can use a picture in the same way one uses a sentence – what makes this possible is their common pictoriality (*WWK*, p. 185); what is meant by 'the pictoriality of the proposition' is that one acts in accordance with a proposition in the same way one acts in accordance with a picture (*PG*, p. 163). These are, however, mere analogies, no matter how illuminating. They do not point in the direction of any particular account of the sense of a proposition.

2.   In *WWK* (p. 90) Wittgenstein remarks "Das Wesentliche am Satz ist aber, dass er *ein Bild* ist und Zusammensetzung hat." His point is that a proposition must be composite, composed of function and argument.

Moreover the two must be independent of each other if the proposition is to say anything. If "This is yellow" is to express a proposition then it must be possible for *this* not to be yellow, but green or blue, etc. This is important, and continues to be important subsequently, since it is an essential element in the private language argument.[14] But that compositeness is thus constant does not show a continuity of the picture theory. Compositeness was a requirement which the picture theory had to meet. It continues, *qua* requirement, but only in a modified form. For in the *Philosophical Investigations* Wittgenstein envisages language-games with non-composite signs which lack combinatorial possibilities but are used as degenrate (but not elliptical) sentences. Likewise he contemplates the use of simple signs, which *do* have combinatorial possibilities, in non-composite descriptions (*PI*, §49). So it is not argued that anything we might call a proposition must be composite, but rather that the function and argument of any composite proposition must be independent. The compositeness requirement in the *Tractatus* semantics was *met* by three features: (a) that the proposition is a picture, and all pictures (models) represent via their complexity, (b) that the proposition is a fact; it says what it says because it is a fact – its factuality is essential to its representative capacity, and a fact is necessarily complex, (c) that the proposition consists of names and forms, i.e. the elements that constitute the composite proposition are simple names in concatenation. Since the latter two claims are obviously repudiated, and the first is just what is at stake, the issue of compositeness does not support the continuity thesis.

3.   The third element captured by the notion of pictoriality in the 1930s is implicit in the foregoing discussion. A proposition must have the same logical multiplicity as what makes it true or satisfies it. An order or instruction to make a model must have the same multiplicity as the movements which comply with it. A negative proposition has the multiplicity of the proposition it negates not of those propositions which are true in its stead (*WWK*, p. 84; *PB*, p. 57). Given the collapse of the doctrines of isomorphism and the notion of reality possessing a language-independent logical structure, then the logical multiplicity of compliance with a command *is* the logical multiplicity of the description of the compliance. So the feature of identical multiplicity is that of the harmony between thought and reality for composite propositions. This I shall discuss shortly.

4.   The fourth feature of pictoriality is presaged in the third. Just as

pictures have a two-way fit with respect to reality, *qua* drawings and *qua* blueprints, so too does language. Descriptions stand to reality as drawings do, commands, wishes and intentions stand to reality as do blueprints. Thus stated this feature is merely an analogy. But it leads to the final and most important element of pictoriality, the harmony between thought and reality.

5. Expectations, commands, wishes, intentions contain a picture of what satisfies them (*PB*, pp. 63, 66, 69, 71; *PG*, pp. 136ff.; cf. *BB*, pp. 31ff.). The expectation that *p* will occur is satisfied by the occurrence of *p*. The expectation that A will come is satisfied by just *A* just *coming*. This raises a host of problems and confusions. How can I will the very thing I will not be doing until five minutes hence? How can I expect an event when it is not yet there, and, indeed, may never be? How can expectation thus anticipate the future, and, in a sense, already contain it? The pictoriality of expectation is merely another form of one of the key problems of the *Tractatus* – a point Wittgenstein makes explicitly.

Here we have the old problem [he writes *a propos* intention, wishing and expectation], which we would like to express in the following way: 'the thought that p is the case doesn't presuppose that it is the case; yet on the other hand there must be something in the fact that is a presupposition even of having the thought (I can't think something is red, if the colour red does not exist)'. It is the problem of the harmony between world and thought. (*PG*, p. 142)

'The pictoriality of the proposition', in the later work, is the name of a feature of language which presents a philosophical problem. The *Tractatus'* picture theory of meaning was, with respect to the requirement that it be possible to say something false but yet meaningful, the answer to that problem. The *Tractatus* provided a complex and non-trivial logico-metaphysical *explanation* of the pictoriality of thought by way of the doctrines of isomorphism and atomism. Agreement between thought and reality was held to be agreement in form, and an elaborate atomist logic and metaphysics was delineated to *explain* isomorphism. But Wittgenstein's later philosophy adamantly rejects the atomist realist conception of a language-independent *form* of reality. All that remains of *that* explanation is that every projection must have something in common with what is projected, no matter what the method (*PG*, p. 163). But all that amounts to is extending the concept of 'having in common' to the point of equating it to that of projection, i.e. every projection must be projectible! So without the atomism and isomorphism there is no picture theory of the proposition, but only the phenomenon of the pictoriality of thought and its attendant puzzles.

The harmony between thought and reality, Wittgenstein now argues, lies not in isomorphism between picture and reality, but, like everything metaphysical, in the grammar of language (*PG*, p. 162; *Zettel*, § 55). The expectation that A should come seems so intimately connected with its satisfaction, with A's coming, as to almost merge with it. We expect just A (and no one else) to do the coming (and not another thing) – but then that is just what the expectation was *said* to be (*BB*, p. 37). The 'link' is via the explanations that by "A" I mean *him*, and by 'coming', doing *this* (*PG*, p. 143), and these, far from having to wait upon the future, are grammatical, intralinguistic, connections: "It is *in language* that it is all done."[15]

Yet surely an order anticipates its execution, and expectation its fulfilment? – by ordering and expecting just that which later happens? But, of course, *it may not happen*. So all we can say is that an order anticipates the future by ordering that which later happens or does not happen.[16] And that is no contribution to futurology. To the question "How can an expectation anticipate the future?" there is only one answer. If, e.g., A promised to come, and he is generally reliable, then my expectation that he will come will probably anticipate the future. On the other hand, if he is held up in a traffic jam, it will not. In an early draft of the *Philosophical Investigations* (in a different context) Wittgenstein remarked, "this is what the solutions to all philosophical difficulties look like. Our answers, if they are correct, must be ordinary and trivial. For these answers, as it were, make fun of the questions."

But at least the expression of expectation determines in advance what will satisfy it or fail to satisfy it, as the proposition determines in advance what will make it true or false. However, this merely amounts to saying that the proposition 'p' determines that p must be the case for it to be true. This plumbs no metaphysical depths concerning the structure of reality – it merely indicates an articulation of grammar: that "the proposition 'p'" has the same sense as "the proposition that the fact that p makes true". Similarly the problem of the pictoriality of intention or expectation, the deep problem of how it is possible to expect now what will satisfy the expectation in the future, is trivially dissolved. "The statement that the wish for it to be the case that p is satisfied by the event p, merely enunciates a rule for signs: (the wish for it to be the case that

p) = (the wish that is satisfied by the event p)" (*PG*, pp. 161f.). This truism, and not the picture theory of the proposition, resolves – or dissolves – the confusions generated by pictoriality, not by constructing elaborate metaphysical *explanations*, but by describing the internal structure of language which we all know.

To be sure, this answer to the great problem of the harmony between language and reality seems, by comparison with the picture theory of meaning and its exciting logico-metaphysical atomism, trivial, even uninteresting. Madness is more interesting than sanity. But it is much better to be sane than to be mad.

Notes

1. Two caveats are in order. "*Bild*" means both "picture" and "model". In English these two terms lack etymological association, and the translation of the *Tractatus* cannot capitalize upon the tacit association in "*Bild*" between picture and model. The picture theory is in many ways less misleadingly thought of if conceived under the appellation "The Model Theory of the Proposition". Secondly, the term "theory" is used loosely here. The picture theory is not a theory about the nature of the proposition on a par with a scientific theory about the nature of e.g. gravitation. Although Wittgenstein uses the term "theory" quite freely in the *Notebooks 1914–1916* (e.g. *NB*, p. 17: "My theory of logical portrayal") his animus against the Russellian conception of philosophy as a very general theory which may approximate more or less closely to the facts (and which is so popular in USA today) constitutes a thread of continuity running through all his philosophy.

2. The occurrence of the notion of "giving us pictures of reality" in the "Notes on Logic" of 1913 does not disprove this contention. "Philosophy", Wittgenstein wrote (*NB*, p. 93), "gives us no pictures of reality, and can neither confirm nor confute scientific investigations." This remark does not indicate the emergence of the picture theory. Wittgenstein was drawing the anti-Russellian contrast between philosophy and science mentioned in the previous note. He had learnt from Hertz that the method of science is theory construction, and that theory construction consists of forming pictures (*Scheinbilder*) or models which must be logically isomorphic with what they portray. Philosophy, Witgenstein was convinced, does not consist of theory construction, and is not subject to empirical confirmation. It was only much later that the idea of drastically generalizing and modifying Hertz's conception of scientific models to language in general occurred to him.

3. To be sure, Wittgenstein did not think ordinary language lacked defects – on the contrary, surface grammar conceals logical form; much that is essential to sense depends on complicated tacit conventions; there is enormously much added in thought to each sentence and not said; apparent vagueness and ambiguity are rampant; ordinary language permits the formation of nonsensical strings of words which appear well-formed (such as the sentences of the *Tractatus*). But these defects merely highlight the gap between the appearance and reality of language. Anything in ordinary language which genuinely expresses a sense, is, just as it stands, in good logical order.

4. Frege, *The Foundations of Arithmetic*, p. x.

5. cf. A. J. P. Kenny, *Wittgenstein* (London: Allen Lane The Penguin Press, 1973), p. 54.

6. Wittgenstein does not explicitly say this. But his deliberate use of *"Merkmale"* (cf. *Letters to C. K. Ogden*, ed. G. H. von Wright (Oxford: Blackwell, 1973), pp. 28f.) in 4.126 and his argument that formal concepts cannot be represented by means of functions (so 'A is an object' is ill-formed *because* their characteristics (*Merkmale*) are not expressible by means of functions, suggests that he thought that ordinary definable concept words are typically definable by *Merkmale*.

7. e.g. the logical theses of the indefinability of simple names, and the consequent introduction of the notion of an elucidation (*Erläuterung*); the allocation to the rules of syntax of the misguided role of the Russellian Theory of Types, together with the conception of the variable as representing logico-syntactical form mirroring metaphysical essence, and the consequent ineffability of essences.

8. Although his views on general *a priori* propositions of science are most obscure. Are they senseless, like tautologies, or nonsensical, like philosophical propositions?

9. Kenny, *Wittgenstein*, ch. 12.

10. With some qualms about propositions which belong to the *Weltbild*.

11. Although he now rejects any 'ineffable' necessities of the kind the *Tractatus* indicated, and no longer argues that sentences such as "Red is a colour" are ill-formed. They are senseless, but not nonsense.

12. In this respect the picture theory is unlike Russell's Theory of Descriptions, for the Theory of Descriptions can be severed from Russell's atomism. But that is just because the Theory of Descriptions *does give a contextual definition* of the singular definite article quite independently of atomism. The picture theory, by contrast, gives no account of the sense of any expression once shorn of the doctrine of atomism and truth-functional composition.

13. It has been suggested that §353 marks the *loss* of importance of verification to the *Philosophical Investigations*. This is wrong. The section, like *Zettel*, §437 ("The causes of our belief in a proposition are indeed irrelevant to the question what we believe. Not so the grounds, which are grammatically related to the proposition, and tell us what proposition it is.") comes from the Big Typescript, §60 entitled *"Sage mir, was Du mit einem Satz anfängst, wie Du ihn verifizierst, etc, und ich werde ihn verstehen."* It is quite clear from the context that there is no diminution of the importance of verification to the determination of sense (although the reductivism, the hypothesis-relation, and the primacy of experiential propositions in the earlier work are all repudiated). To specify the verification of a sentence, he stresses, is a *contribution* to its grammar. Language cannot go beyond the possibility of evidence. It is a mistake to think that one can even believe a sentence which no conceivable evidence supports, for the sentence "I believe that what such & such sentence says is the case" has no sense if the 'believed' sentence has no sense, since we can give no explanation of what it is to believe thus in as much as we cannot explain what the sentence says. Belief cannot outstrip the possibility of evidence.

The origin of *PI*, §353 had *"andere"* instead of *"besondere"*, and an alternative to *"wie meinst Du das"* was *"Was tut man mit diesem Satz"*. Of course, verification is only a contribution to the grammar of a sentence, and it is *not* being claimed that *every* significant sentence has its sense explained by specification of its verification conditions.

14. cf. Kenny, *Wittgenstein*, p. 196.

15. This remarkable shift in Wittgenstein's conception of the relation between thought and reality is indeed associated with the notion of *pictoriality*, which no longer intimates isomorphism, but the autonomy of language. In a forerunner of the Big Typescript Wittgenstein wrote:

Das Charackteristische an der Sprache ist, dass alle Erklärungen zum Voraus gegeben werden können. D.h., das mann sie alle müsste voraussehen können und keine erst ad hoc gegeben werden muss. (Und das ist es, was die Bildhaftigkeit auszumachen scheint.) (TS 211, p. 7)

16. Comparable to the joke: "I have a well-trained dog – whenever I order him 'Rex will you come here this minute or not' he always obeys."

The Picture Theory and Wittgenstein's Later Attitude to it

ERIK STENIUS

1. In the Preface of the *Philosophical Investigations* Wittgenstein says that his new thoughts can be understood only by contrast with the thoughts of the *Tractatus*, and that the *Tractatus* contains many grave mistakes. But he does not tell us in what way his new thoughts should be contrasted with his old thoughts, nor what the grave mistakes in the latter were.

Many commentators have thought that they were able to fill in this gap with the guidance of the hints given in the *Investigations* and elsewhere in Wittgenstein's later writings. And most of these commentators have thought that among the mistakes was the picture theory of sentence meaning. Some of them have even contended that Wittgenstein's "rejection" of the picture theory forms the demarcation line between Wittgenstein's later and earlier philosophy.

That Wittgenstein rejected the picture theory was claimed by George Pitcher, whose book on Wittgenstein was announced as the first joint treatment of the *Tractatus* and the *Investigations*. Pitcher says that as a result of certain of Wittgenstein's later criticisms "the picture theory is dissolved into nothingness. It vanishes without a trace" (p. 183). Peter Hacker and James Bogen, who have published two of the most recent books on the subject, argue in a similar way.

But did Wittgenstein reject the picture theory? For one thing, none of the adherents of the rejection thesis has been able to quote any statement of Wittgenstein's in which he says in so many words that the picture theory is to be rejected. Secondly, Anthony Kenny has listed a great number of statements which suggest that this was not so (pp. 224–7).

The latest of statements of this kind is §522 in the *Investigations* (not mentioned by Kenny), where Wittgenstein says that the "comparison" of a sentence to a picture "has point".

Now it goes without saying that Wittgenstein later thought that the *Tractatus* was wrong in giving the picture theory a too central position in the explanation of how language works. His negative attitude to the picture theory in *this* respect was partly founded on a sound criticism of the *Tractatus* position – above all his criticism of the *Tractatus* characterization of "the general form of a proposition". But it was also founded on a rather surprising lack of interest in those problems concerning sentence meaning which gave the picture theory philosophical significance (cf. below, §13 and §28).

Further it is true that Wittgenstein's explicit later remarks on the picture theory suggest that he found it problematic in many respects. One might state that Wittgenstein later became *dissatisfied* with the picture theory as it was presented in the *Tractatus*. But this does not mean that he rejected it or considered it as one of the fundamental errors in this book. Like his attitude to many other problems he discussed, Wittgenstein's attitude to the picture theory remained inconclusive.

2. When first planning this paper I thought I could discuss Wittgenstein's later attitude to the picture theory much more thoroughly than I am really able to do. For several reasons I have to restrict myself to a few observations. One reason is this. In my book on the *Tractatus* I give the picture theory of sentence meaning a *precise* formulation. However, books on Wittgenstein written after my book show that their authors do not know what my version of the picture theory is. Either they leave it out of consideration or state it wrongly on crucial points. So I have to start with a statement of this version of the picture theory, emphasizing some of its essential points and its philosophical relevance. But after that is done, there will be little time left for comments on Wittgenstein's later attitude to it. Hence I must restrict myself to a few observations on that topic.

When preparing the paper for print I have been able to include in it several points that were left out from the oral version. But even then a really thorough discussion of Wittgenstein's later attitude to the picture theory – with all its ramifications concerning, among other things, Wittgenstein's varying conceptions of what he in different contexts calls "elementary sentences" – falls outside its scope. A main concern of this paper is what *justified* criticisms against the picture theory one can find in Wittgenstein's later writings.[1] Only on the basis of some clarity about this, can the part played by the picture theory in Wittgenstein's later philosophy be discussed in a balanced way.

3.   I shall now proceed to an attempt to give an account of my version of the picture theory. Not that I really believe this will be of any use. There is a strong resistance against even *understanding* my version of the picture theory, a resistance which may have different psychological roots.

I shall take my starting point in *Tractatus*, 4.012:

It is obvious that a sentence of the form '*aRb*' strikes us as a picture. In this case the sign is obviously a likeness of what is signified.

This statement has been ignored by philosophers who, like Irving Copi, think that a sentence of the form '*aRb*' cannot be an elementary sentence according to the *Tractatus*. Anthony Kenny, again, thinks that Wittgenstein tacitly assumes that '*aRb*' here refers to a sentence which says that *a* is to the left of *b*.[2] But I cannot take this suggestion seriously. Nowhere in the *Tractatus* or the writings prior to it Wittgenstein makes such an assumption. The "obvious likeness" cannot be due to giving the relation sign a spatial interpretation. The point of 4.012 must be this. According to the *Tractatus* all sentences are pictures in a *wide* sense, since they "show" their truth-conditions. But some sentences — of which '*aRb*' is an instance — are pictures in a more narrow and proper sense, in that there is an obvious *likeness* between such sentences and what they signify. That this is so can be called the picture theory in the *narrow* sense — which applies to elementary sentences. Like other commentators I shall here restrict myself to the picture theory in the narrow sense. What is, for instance, the "likeness" between '*aRb*' and what it signifies?

4.   In his book on Wittgenstein David Pears seems to assume that the picture theory of sentence meaning must be rejected as soon as logical atomism is rejected.[3] But this is certainly not so and was certainly not the view of the later Wittgenstein. Most of what was said in the *Tractatus* or earlier on a sentence as a picture has good sense even if logical atomism is dropped. In my book on the *Tractatus* the picture theory was applied to certain kinds of quite ordinary sentences, which I called "semantic elementary sentences". As an example of semantic elementary sentences we may take the sentence

Alan is the father of Brian   (1)

or

aRb (2)

understood as a formalization of (1).

What are the truth-conditions of (1) or (2)? Common sense says:

(1) is true if and only if the person called Alan is the father of the   (3)
person called Brian

Sentence (2) has of course the same truth-conditions, but I shall formulate them like this:

(2) is true if and only if the person which 'a' stands for is the father   (4)
of the person which 'b' stands for.

Logical atomism implies that this common sense view is false. In order to state the truth-conditions of (1) we must, according to logical atomism, among other things pay attention to the fact that the person called Alan is a complex, and describe the complex in terms of logically "atomic" objects, qualities and relations. But if we reject logical atomism we can take (3) and (4) to be the truth-conditions of (1) and (2). And then, according to the picture theory, we can say that there is a "likeness" between these sentences and what they signify, though − as we shall see − we had better express ourselves somewhat more carefully when giving the picture theory a more explicit formulation.

5.   I shall restrict myself to sentence (2). In what way what is said about (2) also applies to (1) is easy to see.

According to the picture theory of sentence meaning, sentence (2) show its truth-conditions by showing what is to be the case for it to be true. It shows that for it to be true Alan must be the father of Brian − this is something we *read off* from the sentence.

But how can (2) show this? In order to give an answer to this question I employed in *WT* (chs VI–VII) the idea of "isomorphic representation". Consider the diagram

                                                                               (5)

which is to be interpreted by means of the following key of interpretation:

'*a*'——Alan   (*Read: Letter 'a' stands for the person called*
               "*Alan*";
               and similarly for the rest of the table.)
'*b*'—— Brian
'*c*' —— Christopher   (6)
'*d*' —— David
'*e*' —— Edward

The arrow-from-
to relation   —— the father–son relation

Here the "arrow-from-to relation" is the relation which obtains between two letters if and only if there is an *arrow* going *from* the one *to* the other. (Note that the element standing for the father–son relation is this *relation* and not, for instance, an arrow.)

Now, given key (6), diagram (5) shows what is to be the case for it to be correct in the following way:

The *fact* that in the diagram there is an arrow going from letter '*a*' to letter '*b*' shows that for the diagram to be correct Alan must be the father of Brian, etc.

The fact that in the diagram no arrow goes from letter '*b*' to letter '*d*' shows that for the picture to be correct Alan must not be the father of David, etc.

This kind of showing means that provided that the diagram is correct we can – by means of the key – *read off* from it what is the case about our family.

6. Of course diagram (5) shows what ought to be the case for it to be correct irrespective of whether it is really correct or not. Suppose that (5) *is* correct, and let us apply key (6) to the diagram

(7)

Then this diagram shows, for instance, that in order for it to be correct, Brian must be the father of David, in spite of the fact that this is not really the case.

The difference between the correct diagram and the incorrect one is that, whereas there is a "likeness", that is a specific *structural similarity* between the former and the family group it refers to, there is a specific structural *dissimilarity* between the latter and this family group.

Now it is in full accordance with the use of the words *Bild* and *Abbildung* in German mathematical texts to call a diagram like (5) a *Bild* or *Abbildung* of the family group. And when we speak of "pictures" or "representations" in our present context we must take these words to refer to pictures or representations of this schematic kind.[4]

7.   The fact that – given the key, i.e. (6) – diagrams (5) and (7) *show* what is to be the case for them to be correct entails that – again *given the* (same) *key* – the same is true of the partial "diagrams"

$$a \longrightarrow b \tag{8}$$

and

$$b \longrightarrow d. \tag{9}$$

But now the sentences

$$aRb \tag{10}$$

and

$$bRd \tag{11}$$

can be regarded as diagrams, which in the same way *show* what is to be the case for them to be true, the only difference being that the arrow-from-to relation is replaced by the relation which holds between two letters, if the one is to the left and the other to the right of a letter of the type 'R'. Since we read (10) from left to right I shall call it the "R-from-to relation". Thus sentences (10) and (11) show what is to be the case for them to be true *in respect of the following key*:

$$\begin{array}{ll} \text{'}a\text{'} \longrightarrow \text{Alan} & \\ \text{'}b\text{'} \longrightarrow \text{Brian} & (12) \\ \text{'}d\text{'} \longrightarrow \text{David} & \end{array}$$

The 'R'-from-to relation ——the father–son relation,

where

> The '*R*'-from-to relation = the relation which holds between two   (13)
> letters, if the one is to the left, the other to the right of an '*R*'.

The fact that what I call semantic elementary sentences are "pictures" *in the precise sense* exemplified by diagrams (5) and (7) and sentences (10) and (11) is the fundamental point stated by my version of the picture theory of sentence meaning. I said that this is a *fact* and I *mean* it. It is what can be called a kind of mathematical fact that cannot be disputed – whatever alleged objections to it based on misstatements of the theory have been raised. *This* cannot be disputed. If anything might be disputed it concerns the *relevance* of this fact for the understanding of how language works – or more precisely of this fact alone or in combination with the assumption that when we understand sentences of the above kind we construe them as pictures in this sense.

8.   I shall now list some of the ways in which realizing the pictorial nature of semantic elementary sentences may be of relevance for understanding how language works.

8.1   Since what stands for an element of the fact described by sentence '*aRb*' is the '*R*'-from-to relation and not the letter '*R*', we may say that the *symbols* (the symbolizing elements) occurring in sentence '*aRb*' are '*a*', '*b*' and the '*R*'-from-to relation. Using the word "symbol" in such a way we may state that the *symbols* in a sentence are not always linguistic *objects* like words or letters but may also be "*universals*"[5] like the '*R*'-from-to relation in (10) and (11).[6] This means among other things that the "symbols" in a sentence are not always *parts* of the sentence.

Compare this with Wittgenstein's formulation: "E.g. in '*aRb*', '*R*' is *not* a symbol but that '*R*' is between one name and another symbolizes" (*Notebooks – NB*, p. 108). This is obviously also what is meant in *Tractatus*, 3.1432. (Cf. Stenius, *WT*, ch. VII, §5 and §7.)

8.2   The articulation of diagram (5) or (7) in terms of the elements listed to the left of (6) can be made without having yet correlated these elements with any elements of reality. (Cf. Stenius, *WT*, ch. VII, §6 and ch. X, §4.)

The same is of course true of sentences (10) and (11). These sentences can be articulated in terms of the elements occurring to the left of key (12) without being yet correlated with any elements of reality. This articulation can be said to be a matter of syntax, and in this sense the syntactical articulation of a sentence is a matter of perception, not of interpretation. A sentence must be *perceived* in such a way that its *symbols* stand out.[7]

Compare this with Wittgenstein's dictum that we *see* the type of the symbol when we know "*what* symbolizes" (*NB*, p. 109).

8.3   According to the *Tractatus* the sentential sign is a fact. This has been contested, since, for instance, the expressions (10) and (11) are naturally conceived of as complex objects. But if such objects are called "sentential signs", then a sentential sign is not a *symbol* in the above sense. The sentential symbol is a fact – in (10) it is the fact that there is an '*R*' going from letter '*a*' to letter '*b*'. This fact is the sentential symbol, since it is from *it* that we read off what is the case if the sentence is true. (Cf. Stenius, *WT*, ch. vii, §6.)

Seeing the sentential symbol as a fact is, irrespective of the interpretation of the sentence, something that in itself gives the sentence "life". (Cf. *Blue Book [BB]*, p. 4, *PI*, §432.)

8.4   There is a *structural* similarity between the sentential symbol of a true pictorial sentence and the fact it describes, but any other kind of similarity is redundant. Thus any similarity between the subordinate symbols in a sentence and the entities they correspond to – except an ontological one – is also redundant.

8.5   It is, however, an essential prerequisite for the formation of a pictorial sentence in the sense indicated above that its symbols be of the same ontological category as the entities in reality they correspond to according to the key.

8.6   The structural similarity between the sentential symbol of a true pictorial sentence and the fact described by the symbol allows us to *read off* what is the case *from* the sentence by means of the key.[8]

8.7   The picture theory gives an elegant account of the correspondence theory of truth.

8.8   The picture theory solves what could be called the problems of (1) the thing-quality nexus – or the things-relation nexus – and of (2) the sentential nexus. It solves it by showing that each nexus is of the same kind.

The nexus is in both cases simply that the *thing* and its *quality* (or the things and the relation between them) *form* a *fact*.[9]

8.9   We tend unconsciously to assume an ontological similarity between symbols and what they correspond to. This explains the difficulty in stating the difference between ontological categories like objects ("particulars"), qualities or relations ("universals") and facts. So, for instance, the last statement in 8.8 is difficult to understand, because it is grammatically misleading, that is, the words "quality", "relation" and "fact" occur in this (non-pictorial) sentence as syntactical *objects* and therefore seem parodoxically to refer to *objects*. There is *some* truth in the *Tractatus* view that such categorical distinctions can only be shown but not stated.[10]

8.10   The picture theory solves the problem of the *false* and the *new* sentence.

8.11   The picture theory explains the function of *names* in language – and thus of what is nowadays called semantic reference.[11]

8.12   The picture theory suggests a connection between the human capacity of understanding sentences and the human capacity of understanding other pictorial representation. This observation may account for the fact that, whereas "the meanings of simple signs (words) must be explained to us if we are to understand them" (*Tractatus*, 4.026), "we understand the sense of the sentential sign without its having been explained to us" (*Tractatus*, 4.02).

8.13   A good understanding of the picture theory is the only basis for an account of the important ways in which sentences may differ from pictures in the above sense. (Hints about this are given in Stenius, *WT*, pp. 142 ff., ch. IX, pp. 211–13 and *passim*.)

9.   I shall not go into more detail about these points except for those features which have played an important part in the discussion of the tenability of the picture theory and Wittgenstein's later attitude to it.

First it should be stressed that there is no doubt that the picture theory in my version solves the "nexus" problem of 8.8. Irving Copi's contention, accepted by others, that it does not, appears to be founded on a lack of understanding of how this theory works.[12] Copi should be given due credit for having seen and stressed the relevance of the nexus problem as a moving force behind the picture theory (see OPR, pp. 179ff.). Unfor-

tunately, however, he connected this idea with a very artificial interpretation of the *Tractatus*, which prevented him from seeing that there is
a much simpler interpretation which does the same service in respect of
the nexus problem, and which *works* – whereas Copi's version of the
picture theory actually does not work (cf. below, §11).

10. Features 8.6 and 8.7 should not be confused. Peter Hacker argues
(*Insight and Illusion*, p. 53) in the following way:

Agreement of picture and pictured, as a paradigm of cognition, presupposes
what it is meant to explain. In order that I be able to judge that the model is accurate, . . . I must already be able to judge how the facts which it models are. I
can 'compare' a musical score with a tune only if I can both pick out the notes I
hear and bring them under concepts, and if I am able to read and understand the
score.

What is to be said about this? Well, it is true that in order to *compare*
two entities we must know both entities. But this certainly does not
mean that the picture theory is circular. With a sentence as a picture one
can perform, for instance, the following "language games":
  (1) Person *A* produces a sentence. Person *B* perceives the sentential
sign, possesses the key for its interpretation and can take for granted that
what *A* says is true. Then *B* can "read off" from the sentence what is the
case, and will be informed about a fact that he did not know in advance.
(This is an application of 8.6.)
  (2) Person *A* produces a sentence. Person *B* perceives the sentential
sign and possesses the key for its interpretation, but cannot take for
granted that what *A* says is true but regards it as a hypothesis which he
has to confirm or reject by observation. Then the key informs him about
what fact to look for (cf. *BB*, p. 31), and by comparing the sentence with
the fact he can decide whether it is structurally similar or structurally
dissimilar with this fact (true or false). (This is an application of 8.7.)
  Hacker confuses these two games. Further it is to be noted that the
normal use of a score is not to compare it with the tune but either to
produce the tune by reading it off from the score by means of the known
key for interpreting musical notation or to produce the score from the
tune in the inverse way. One can, of course, play "games" corresponding to these uses with a sentence. If we are able to *produce* a fact
described by a sentence we can do so using the sentence and the key for
its interpretation as a blueprint; and given a fact we can use the key
backwards in order to produce the sentence from the fact.

It is noteworthy that Hacker uses an argument which, if it were correct, would show that the conception of a "model" of any kind is circular. According to him we cannot, for instance, interpret a score without knowing the tune in advance. Hacker is of course not alone in trying to back up a philosophical conviction by arguments which are obviously irrelevant because they prove too much.

Hacker is, moreover, not the only commentator on Wittgenstein who regards the idea of a comparison as a point at which the picture theory could be assaulted. Such an approach is also adopted by Norman Malcolm in his review of *Philosophische Bemerkungen* (*PB*), though Malcolm's argument is very different from Hacker's. If one realizes that the picture theory need not be rejected just because logical atomism in itself is rejected, one might try to argue that it must be rejected as soon as the *Tractatus* view that elementary sentences can be mutually logically independent is rejected. This seems to be Malcolm's idea. He argues in the following way. In the *Tractatus*, 2.1512 Wittgenstein says that a picture is "laid against reality like a ruler". As a comment to his later view that there must be systems of elementary sentences which in my terminology belong to the same dimension (cf. *WT*, ch. IV, §1), i.e. systems of mutually incompatible elementary sentences, Wittgenstein says: "I do not lay a sentence against reality like a ruler but a *system* of sentences" (*PB*, p. 110). Malcolm quotes this on p. 221 of his review. On p. 222 he takes this passage as an argument against the picture theory, supporting his view with an additional reference to a passage from *PB*, p. 111, where, according to Malcolm, Wittgenstein says that the sentences in a system of sentences of the kind mentioned "form *one* picture". "Perhaps this", he says "is a tenable position," and adds: "But surely the picture conception is losing its charm." How could one compare a whole system, which one cannot "even *look at*", with reality? So a system "cannot literally serve me as a picture".

This argument contains many mistakes. Malcolm's statement of what is said on *PB*, p. 111, is incorrect. The context of *PB*, p. 111, is a discussion of the conception of an elementary sentence and of logical connectives in the *Tractatus*. What is to "form *one* picture" is not a system of the kind mentioned but the *conjunction* of elementary sentences. Now the idea that a conjunction of two or more elementary sentences form *one* picture is in itself quite in accordance with the picture theory (in a wider sense) of the *Tractatus*. What is a change of the *Tractatus* view is that we cannot take for granted that the members of such a conjunction are compatible. Now, if they are incompatible they form an "impossible picture" (cf. Stenius *WT*, pp. 103ff. and 201), and it does not make sense to compare an impossible picture with reality. So the comparison of a system of sentences with reality cannot mean anything like this (and is certainly not said to mean anything like this in the *PB*). Such an idea would certainly not be "tenable". What a comparison of a system of elementary sentences with reality means here is obvious from Wittgenstein's subsequent text. He thinks in this context that elementary sentences were, say, of the form "*a* has the quality Q to the degree *d*" (cf. *PB*, p. 111, §83 (4)), and of a "language game" in which we are comparing different sentences of this form, which have a common *a* and Q, but a varying *d*, with reality until we find that value of *d* for which such a sentence turns out to be true. This (or at least something very near this) is meant by "laying a system of sentences against reality like a ruler".

Thus a necessary condition for the comparison of a "system" of elementary sentences with reality is that we can compare each individual sentence of this system with reality, which in its turn presupposes that the elementary sentences themselves are "pictures". Now sentences of the form "*a* has the quality Q to the degree *d*" are not "semantic elementary sentences" in the sense discussed above. But there is nothing to prevent them from being regarded as pictures — though the key of interpretation differs from the simple kind of key exemplified by key (12). It would, however, take us too far to discuss this matter here.

Certainly taking sentences of this form as pictures does not prevent one from also regarding semantical elementary sentences as pictures. Wittgenstein's hunch that elementary sentences should have this "new" form has certainly nothing to do with their having an eminent "pictorial character" but with ideas more akin to logical atomism. Malcolm's idea that the picture theory was still accepted in the beginning of *PB* but rejected later in this book has no foundation. Wittgenstein was quite aware of the problem of gradable qualities from the very beginning of the *PB*.

11.   Finally a comment on the problem of the false and the new sentence (8.10).

The problem of the false sentence is an ancient problem arising from the tendency to accept what can be called the Name Theory of Linguistic Meaning. According to this theory, for a linguistic expression to have "meaning" or "sense" there must be an entity which it means, and to know the meaning or sense of an expression is to know *what* entity it means. Now we might possibly say that a true sentence "means" the fact that it describes. But what is then the meaning of a false sentence? The answer to this question given by the picture theory is that for a (semantic elementary) sentence to have a sense it suffices that its *elements* have meanings in the sense required by the Name Theory: as soon as the "meaning" of the elements, i.e. the key of interpretation, is given, the sentence *shows* what is to be the case for it to be true: we can read off this from the sentential sign by means of the key. This is so, irrespective of whether the sentence is true or false, so we need in neither case introduce an entity called the "meaning" or the "sense" of a sentence with which the sentential sign is correlated like a name with its denominatum.

Wittgenstein does not in the *Tractatus* state the problem of the false sentence in so many words, though it is inherent in much that is said in this book. The "problem of the new sentence" is, however, explicitly stated in the *Tractatus* (4.027, 4.03). And in fact this problem is essentially the same as the problem of the false sentence. The Name Theory cannot even explain how we understand a true sentence, if this sentence describes a new fact which is not known in advance. For then we do not know the fact which it is required to "mean" and thus do not know its meaning. The solution of both problems is the same.

In the *Blue Book* (pp. 31–7) Wittgenstein discusses the problem of the false sentence. The discussion is rather confusing because it involves a great number of different problems more or less intimately connected with this one. But among other things, Wittgenstein asks whether the sense of a (true or false) sentence, since it cannot be a fact, can be "a shadow of a fact" (p. 32), and ends up with saying that a sentence is a picture "which hasn't the slightest similarity with what it represents", and that since this is so the "interpolation of a shadow between the sentence and what it represents loses all point" for "now the sentence itself can serve as such a shadow" (p. 37).[13] This is nothing but an attempt to give an explanation in non-technical terms of a basic problem underlying the picture theory of the *Tractatus*. It is to be noted that Wittgenstein adds to the statement just quoted that what we do if we want to explain the meaning of a sentence is simply that we correlate the elements of the sentence with the elements of the reality they describe.[14]

To be sure, according to the *Tractatus* even a false sentence has a kind of similarity with the fact of which it is a (false) picture, since its elements are of the same category as the elements of reality they stand for, so the expression "which hasn't the slightest similarity" suggests a deviation from the *Tractatus* view (see above §8.5). Moreover the existence of such a similarity Wittgenstein seems to have regarded as doubtful at the time when he wrote the *Blue Book*.[15] But this difference is irrelevant in the context. For what is essential in the argument is not that a sentence *qua* (true or false) picture does not have any kind of similarity with what it represents. What is essential is only that for something to be a picture there is *not* required any kind of similarity with what it represents, which would *prevent* a sentence from being *itself* a picture and a "shadow of a fact".[16] Of course this is not a rejection of the picture theory, rather it is a defence of it.

In the *Investigations* the problem of the false and the new sentence is not mentioned, but there is a mention of a problem which is essentially the same, namely the problem about how we understand what action a command describes (§519). And again Wittgenstein appeals to the picture theory.

James Bogen maintains that the picture theory does not solve the problem of the false sentence. His counter-arguments are very confused. But they seem in part to rely on an acceptance of a Copian interpretation of the *Tractatus*.[17] And it is true that this account does not solve our problems. In order for a sentence to show what is to be the case for it to be true it is essential that the key gives an interpretation not only of the 'names' in an ordinary sense – as for instance, letters '*a*' and '*b*' in (10) – but also to the "universal" symbol – that is in respect of (10) the '*R*'-from-to relation. And since the Copian account eliminates the correlation between the universal symbol and what it corresponds to from the key of interpretation it fails to account for the problem of the false sentence.

12.   Before going further I must clarify in *what* sense my version of the picture theory can be regarded as an interpretation of the picture theory of the *Tractatus*. It is to be noted that Wittgenstein never worked out the picture theory explicitly or even consistently. So one cannot say that Wittgenstein's picture theory is identical with my version of the picture theory. As I pointed out in *WT*, the *Tractatus* contains statements which suggest that Wittgenstein had incorrect views about the way in which a sentence really is a picture (see *WT*, ch. vii, §5). But all these statements are vague, so though one cannot say that the picture theory of the *Tractatus* is identical with the picture theory in my version one cannot either

say that the picture theory in the *Tractatus* really differs from my version of the theory. The picture theory of the *Tractatus* has the form of an *image*. Now it is clear that this image is much more like my version of the picture theory than any other version offered in the literature – indeed this version can be characterized as just a somewhat more exact and consistent reconstruction of the picture theory of the *Tractatus*. But nevertheless it must be remembered that this image *was* more or less obscure and that the statement of it was not free from inconsistencies.

The vagueness of the *Tractatus* image of the picture theory may, of course, have been a reason for the later Wittgenstein mistakenly to reject the picture theory once for all. But it is not *this* that most adherents of the rejection thesis maintain. They maintain that the idea that sentences like (10) can be conceived of as pictures is *in itself* untenable and therefore *must* be rejected, and that this was what Wittgenstein later realized. This argument is certainly mistaken. And since, as a rule, this argument is the main basis of the convictions held by the adherents of the rejection thesis, their convictions have a weak foundation. What is true, however, is that the vagueness of the statement of the picture theory in the *Tractatus* may have been one of the reasons why Wittgenstein later lost his interest in the picture theory and showed dissatisfaction with it.[18] But is this the whole story?

13.   If one asks why Wittgenstein lost most of his interest in the picture theory one must notice that – as I stated earlier – he lost most of his interest in the problems connected with it listed above in §8. Whereas all these problems are present and central in the *Tractatus* or the writings before the *Tractatus* they are almost completely absent in the *Investigations*. The only exception is the problem of the false and the new sentence, which, as we saw, in a way is present in the *Investigations* and felt to require a picture theory of sentence meaning, but certainly it has by no means a central position in the *Investigations* as Bogen believes (Bogen, p. 5 and *passim*). The rest of the problems have almost completely disappeared, and when a related problem sporadically turns up Wittgenstein does not refer to what he had said about the problem in the *Tractatus*. (Cf. below, §28.)

Why did Wittgenstein lose his interest in these problems? This is a difficult question, the answer of which falls outside the scope of this paper. Only one thing should be mentioned in this context. This is that, as all know, Wittgenstein was not a systematic philosopher. Having discovered great mistakes in the *Tractatus* he did not undertake a careful revision of the thoughts in this book. Such a thing would have been outside the capacity of Wittgenstein as a thinker. What he did was that to a considerable extent he gradually turned his back to the problems underlying this book. In view of this general trend it is almost surprising to note how often he later touched on the picture theory itself.

14. But, as I said, Wittgenstein did not only lose most of his interest in the picture theory and the philosophical points connected with it. He certainly also was really dissatisfied with it in certain respects. So what were the sources of this dissatisfaction?

One source of dissatisfaction was the vocabulary in which the picture theory was presented in the *Tractatus*. An example of this kind of dissatisfaction concerned the use of the word "*Gegenstand*" in this context. The key of interpretation of a sentence like (10) is, according to the *Tractatus*, the correlation of names to *Gegenstände*. Many commentators have thought that the *Gegenstände* of the *Tractatus* comprise only individual things and not, as I said in *WT*, both individual things and universals. That I was right on this *ought* to be established by now. But, as I also pointed out in *WT*, Wittgenstein's terminology in this respect was misleading. About this terminology Wittgenstein himself says in a notebook from 1943 (after having quoted *Tractatus*, 4.22, 3.21, 3.22, 3.14, 2.03, 2.72 and 2.01):

What a linguistic misuse (*die sprachwidrige Verwendung*) of the word '*Gegenstand + Konfiguration*'. A configuration can be made up by balls which are spatially related in a certain way; but not of the balls *and* their spatial relations. And if I say 'I see here three *Gegenstände*' I do not mean: two balls + their mutual position.[19]

That the *Tractatus* use of the word *Gegenstand* is a linguistic misuse is a point which Wittgenstein makes in different places. But as a matter of fact what is to be criticized is not only a misuse of language. I shall return to this point later on.

15. Another source of Wittgenstein's dissatisfaction might be the "epistemological turn" of Wittgenstein's semantics, that is, his adherence to what has been called the "verification theory of meaning". Some philosophers have maintained that the truth-conditional semantics of the *Tractatus* was itself an expression of the verification theory of meaning. This is not so – rather the two theories stand in a certain contrast to each

other. According to the picture theory we know the meaning of the sentence

Plato was taller than Socrates   (14)

if we know that it is true if and only if the person denoted by 'Plato' was taller than the person denoted by 'Socrates'. According to the semantics of the verification theory we know the meaning of (14) only if we know how (today) we can verify or falsify this sentence – thus including into semantic analysis all the epistemological difficulties about how we can *know* whether a statement is true or false. And though it sometimes is of advantage for a semantic analysis to ask how we could verify or falsify a sentence, I think that the epistemological turn of semantics is the source of more confusion than clarity. Now during Wittgenstein's period of rather strong verificationism he did not seem to be aware of the contrast between this conception and truth-conditional semantics, and this period was rather short. But something of this view seems to have remained throughout his life. I shall, however, not try to penetrate this possible source of dissatisfaction with the picture theory, since I think it is in any case unjustified and of minor interest.

16.   A source of dissatisfaction with the picture theory which is more justified and interesting is Wittgenstein's criticism of truth-conditional semantics in general. According to the *Tractatus*, to understand a sentence is to know its truth-conditions. This is certainly not true. Not all sentences have truth-conditions, and even in respect of those that have, to understand them often means both more and less than knowing their truth-conditions. In our present context it is to be noted that, as Wittgenstein says, the conception of a sentence as a picture cannot give a sentence a greater significance than pictures have. Showing a picture can mean different things, and thus the showing of a picture cannot in itself have the same function as *asserting* a sentence. For giving a semantic account of "assertion" the picture theory does not suffice, but must be supplemented by a reference to "language games" or something of the kind, as I have stressed in my book on the *Tractatus* and elsewhere (*WT*, ch. IX and *MLG*). I shall not go into this here.

17.   Another source of dissatisfaction with the picture theory is that in its *Tractatus* version it applies only to sentences which give a true or false

description of *facts*. But what about sentences in, for instance, fiction? If understanding (semantic elementary) sentences means construing them as pictures, the same ought to be true of sentences in fiction. Sentences as pictures may be true or false representations of facts, but they ought also possibly be what Wittgenstein calls "genre pictures", as for instance sentences in fiction. (Cf. *PI*, §522, *PG*, §114. I have touched on this problem in *WT*, ch. VI, §11 and ch. VII, §9.) I do not think that this is a serious difficulty for the picture theory of sentence meaning, and there is no sign that Wittgenstein himself thought so.

18.   Are there other justified reasons for a dissatisfaction with the picture theory? I think there are. Understanding a semantic elementary sentence requires according to the picture theory that we interpret it by means of a *key of interpretation*. Thus in order to understand a sentence we must in some way *know* what key to use. And what I consider the most important of the reasons for a dissatisfaction with the picture theory can be centred around one single question, that is:

How is the key of interpretation given to us?   (15)

A diagram like diagram (5) cannot be understood unless we add to it the key of interpretation. But when we utter or write sentences we do not provide them with a particular key for each context. So how then is the key of interpretation given for pictorial sentences?

I shall now turn to this question.

19.   The *Tractatus* does not contain any explicit answer to this question. But from the general outlook of the *Tractatus* we may extract a position which can be divided into two aspects:

(i)   We do not need a separate key of interpretation for each context, for the key of interpretation is given to us by learning the *language* in which sentences are formulated. If we know a language we know the "meanings" of its words and thereby the meanings of the elements of pictorial sentences. Thus the key of interpretation for pictorial sentences is given by the correlation of the elements of sentences with their linguistic meanings.

(ii)   As Russell rightly points out in his introduction to the *Tractatus* (p. xix, cf. Hacker, p. 38), the semantics of the *Tractatus* is a-psychological. The author of the *Tractatus* seems to think that the question about how the meanings of the elements of sentences are given to us is a matter of psychology and does not concern him as a philosopher and logician.

20.   In respect of aspect (i) a very important objection can be extracted from the *Investigations*, §40 and §55. This is the distinction between the *meaning* of a linguistic symbol and the *bearer of a name*. The distinction resembles Alan Gardiner's earlier distinction between "language meaning" and "the thing meant" in a certain context. One may put it like this. Knowing a language we know the meaning of the symbols, but knowing the "things meant" by such symbols in a certain context is *not* just a matter of knowing a language but is based on knowledge of a different kind. Knowing the language "meaning" of the phrase "The president of the United States" does not entail knowing what object this phrase refers to. And something similar seems to apply even to proper names. So aspect (i) of the *Tractatus* view is rather unsatisfactory.

21.   If one feels inclined to criticize aspect (ii) one must bear in mind that such an attitude is not peculiar to the *Tractatus* but is shared by trends having a quite different background, i.e. certain trends among linguists to separate theoretical linguistics from psychology. For my part I have sympathy with such trends. If linguistic theory is not kept apart from all kinds of psychological problems it will be suffocated.

But I admit that linguistic theory *cannot* be entirely separated from psychology – or at least from some kind of psychological models concerning users of language. So aspect (ii) of the *Tractatus* is also rather unsatisfactory. This seems also to have been the final view of the later Wittgenstein.

22.   Since both the aspects of the *Tractatus* view on question (15) are unsatisfactory, how is the question to be answered? This problem may be divided into two partial problems:

> How is the key of interpretation for names of individual objects   (16)
> given to us?

and

> How is the key of interpretation for symbols standing for qualities   (17)
> or relations given to us?

23.   Questions (16) and (17) are of quite different kinds. I shall start with the latter question. Consider the sentence

$$a \text{ is red,} \tag{18}$$

where '*a*' is introduced to denote a certain flower. The key of interpretation for (18) is

'*a*'——the flower spoken of   (19)
left-of-
'is red'——the quality of redness

How is the second part of this key given to us?

In the *Investigations* sections 28–36 Wittgenstein discusses the possibility of defining words by ostension, and among other things argues that we cannot indicate the reference of a colour word by ostension. For if a teacher points to something red saying, for instance, "this is red", the learner cannot understand what is meant unless he knows in advance that what the teacher is pointing at is the colour of an object and not, for instance, its shape (§33). Now one might take this argument as intended to show that we cannot define a colour word by correlating it with a colour. And from this conclusion one might draw the further conclusion that question (17) is illegitimate, and that in order to show the fly the way out of the fly-bottle (*PI*, §309) we have to realize that the picture theory on which it is based is to be rejected.

This argument differs from most alleged Wittgensteinian arguments against the picture theory in being concise and having at least some real support in Wittgenstein's text.

24.   However, if one attributes an argument of this kind to Wittgenstein one must realize that it is fallacious. The fact that Wittgenstein in the *Tractatus* called both particulars and universals *Gegenstände* suggests that he tended to conceive of qualities as more like objects and of objects as more like qualities than they really are.[20] I now want to add that in spite of Wittgenstein's later criticisms of his use of the word *Gegenstand*, he *still* tended to conceive of qualities (or relations) as something more like objects than they really are – and this is also what most of his commentators do.

A quality is indeed not an "object" to which one can point. One cannot point to the quality of redness, one can only point to objects that possess (or do not possess) this quality. A quality is a *distinctive* feature. So in order to teach a person to what quality the word "red" refers, one has to teach him the *difference* between objects called "red" and objects not so called. For this purpose it is not enough to point to *one* object which is called "red"; one must rather indicate a sufficient number of objects called "red", and a sufficient number of objects not called "red", that is, a sufficient number of both kinds for the learner to be able to discover by *what* feature objects called "red" *differ* from objects not called "red". For this purpose a previous knowledge of this difference being a difference in *colour* is certainly not required.

In this context it must be stressed that if in a teaching situation we say "this is red" and accompany it with a pointing gesture, the word "this" refers to an *object* pointed at, not to the colour of it. Wittgenstein seems often to take the word "is" in the phrase "this is red" used in a teaching situation as an identity sign. But in an actual teaching situation this is certainly not so, and if the word "is" is used at all it is used as a copula.[21] If it were an identity sign we may have at least some of the difficulties which Hacker sees in ostensive explanation.

Wittgenstein stresses that learning to know the use of certain words requires a *training (PI, §§5–6)*. Here we have an example of what kind such a training may be. That it works has been confirmed by experiments with very small children.

So we certainly can teach the "meaning" of colour words (or more exactly "symbols for colours") by correlating them with the colours they refer to. We must only realize that this correlation is a correlation between *distinctions* – the distinction between being called "red" and not being called "red" is correlated with the distinction between being red and not being red.

The way of the fly out of this bottle is not a rejection of the picture theory but a more appropriate way of conceiving of qualities and relations. However, against conceiving of qualities and relations in this appropriate way most philosophers react vehemently.

25. The fact that philosophers for the most part do not see that a quality is a distinctive feature is often connected with the obscure idea that a colour word 'C' cannot have a determinate sense unless it refers to a quite determinate shade of colour, so that two objects which have the colour C must have exactly the same colour. This is of course not true. Colour words in ordinary language do not refer to exact shades. And this does not *in itself* mean that colour words have not a determinate

sense. The fact that there are different shades of red does not mean that this word has not a determinate sense. For a colour word to have an absolutely determined sense it is not required that it refer to a single shade of colour; what is required is at most that the *borderline* between shades falling under it, and shades not falling under it, be sharp. Now, as a matter of fact, this borderline is as a rule *not* sharp. *This* fact means that the sense of, for instance, the word "red" is vague to a certain degree, but that this is so does not follow from the mere fact that there is a wide range of colours called "shades of red".

The idea that the sense of a colour word is indeterminate unless it refers to a single shade of colour may lead one to think that *not* having the colour C is not a colour quality. But there is no reason for thinking so. It is true that the range of shades of colour corresponding to "red" appears to us as more restricted than the range of shades corresponding to "not red", and the same is true of other colour words. This fact may make those colour words which we possess more useful. But it does not entail that there is an ontological difference between "positive" and "negative" colours. Even determinate shades of red are distinctive features and thus presuppose their negatives.

Wittgenstein seems to have shared misconceptions of the kind mentioned in his later philosophy as well as in his earlier. However, though these misconceptions are of relevance for logical atomism, they are of no relevance for the picture theory proper. There is, by the way, a notable passage in *WWK* (p. 89) where he argues for a correct view in this respect.

26.   The answer to question (16) may seem simpler than the answer to question (17), for here simple ostension may seem to work. At some places in the *Investigations* Wittgenstein seems to take this attitude to the problem. In §15 he ends the discussion by saying: "It is in this and more or less similar ways that a name means and is given to a thing.—It will often prove useful in philosophy to say to ourselves: naming something is like attaching a label to a thing."

But in fact the answer to question (16) is much more complicated than the answer to question (17) – and certainly Wittgenstein in other places is aware of the difficulties, as is shown for instance in §79, in which he discusses, among other things, what is meant by understanding the name "Moses". And his discussion of what it means to "mean" somebody may also be related to this problem.

It is in this context – and only in this context – that the distinction between the meaning of a symbol and the bearer of a name, between language meaning and the thing meant in a given situation, is important.

For my part I think the solution of this problem is along the following lines.

All of us possess what might be called an internal map of the world. By a "map" I do not here mean a geographical map, though some kind of geographical map is a part of it. The internal map of a person comprises all facts he knows about the world and all states of affairs which he believes to obtain (though possibly mistakenly). Now everybody has *himself* a position on his internal map – thus the map comprises all his real or believed relations to his environment, including other persons. Thus a person's internal map is an important basis for his actions. And though the internal map of a person is his private map, the internal maps of different persons have that in common that they are maps of the external world, the common world of human interaction.

Now knowing what is the thing meant by a name is mainly being able to *localize* this thing on one's internal map. If we ask "Who is 'Ronald Reagan?'" and get the answer "He is the president of the United States" we have got an answer which makes it possible to localize the denominatum of the name "Ronald Reagan" on our internal map. If we ask: "Who is the president of the United States?" and get the answer "Ronald Reagan", this answer gives us real information about who is the president of the United States only if we have localized the denominatum of the name "Ronald Reagan" in advance. Otherwise the only information given by the answer is that the name of the president of the United States is "Ronald Reagan", and therefore the answer "Ronald Reagan" on this question is in fact a more appropriate answer to the question "What is the name of the president of the United States?"

As our example shows the key of interpretation of names of individual objects is given to us as localizations of the denominata of such names on our internal map. This observation should not be misunderstood to mean that what such names stand for *are* objects belonging to our internal map. Our internal map is private, and this means that the *way* in which the key of interpretation for names of individual object is given to us is "private" in the trivial sense that *my* "knowing" the denominatum of a name is different from any other person's knowing this denominatum. But the *denominatum* itself is public, and thus the key of interpretation correlates names with public objects as the picture theory requires.

All this means that knowing the denominatum of a name of an individual is by no means just a "knowledge of a language" but involves situational factors which vary from speaker to speaker and listener to listener. In respect of such names as "the flower" the language meaning of the word "flower" just forms a clue for finding the denominatum of this expression in a given context. (Cf. *WT*, pp. 140 and 196.)

Thus question (16) can be answered, and so need not be a source of further dissatisfaction with the picture theory. Further it should be emphasized that this answer is needed only to eliminate a source of *dissatisfaction* with the picture theory – for in respect of the *tenability* of the theory it is rather irrelevant. For certainly there are names of individual objects, and the question how the names become correlated with their denominata is therefore not a problem of the picture theory as distinct from other theories of language.

27. To sum up: Though I think that the problem (15) about how the key of interpretation is given to us, and the rejection of what may be taken as the *Tractatus* attitude to it, is a justified reason for dissatisfaction with the picture theory, I consider the assumption of its being "unsolvable" an *unjustified* criticism of this theory. Though one can with justification say that the picture theory is in need of supplementing, there is no justification for saying that it is false. (Cf. Kenny, p. 226.) So if one attributes to the later Wittgenstein a rejection of the picture theory on these grounds, one attributes to him a philosophical error. And this is not what adherents of the rejection thesis want to do.

Further, one must remember that the arguments against the picture theory produced above in connection with question (15) are *extrapolations* from arguments really found in Wittgenstein's writings. It is even an extrapolation to assume that Wittgenstein was concerned with these questions at all. Since he did not explicitly raise these questions, he possibly was not consciously aware of them.

28. It is to be noted that in his discussion of "names" in the *Investigations*, Wittgenstein does not make any clear distinction between names of individual things and "names" of "universals" – like the generic name "slab" or colour names. The idea that giving names is like attaching labels to their denominata is in the *Investigations*, §26 applied not only to ordinary *Gegenstände* as men, but also to shapes, colours, pains and so on. This is confused: what could one mean by attaching a label to the colour red or to pain? Thus he uses the word *Gegenstand* in

this context as well as in other contexts in the *Investigations* in the very same objectionable way as he condemned in respect of the *Tractatus*.

It is further an astounding fact about the discussion of names and their functions in the beginning of the *Investigations* that Wittgenstein does not even *mention* the function of names in sentences as described in the *Tractatus*, that is, their standing proxy for their denominata. Naming things, Wittgenstein says in §26 "is preparatory for the use of a word". And he adds the question:: "But *what* is it a preparation for?" But how can he raise this question without further comment? Why does he not state his attitude to the idea in the *Tractatus* that the correlation between names and their denominata forms a key for interpreting pictorial sentences? Well, of course, names may have different functions as well – for instance the function they have when we call a person (§27). But this is no reason for discarding their function in sentences like (1), (10) and (11). And when Wittgenstein points out that the mere act of naming does not show how to use names in talk he does not even discuss the concern in the *Tractatus* with the sentential nexus. How is this to be explained?

One possibility is that Wittgenstein found it tiresome to stress such points which he had already made in the *Tractatus* and which he still thought to be correct but which nobody had understood.

Another possibility is that in this context the pictorial conception of sentences was not present to Wittgenstein's mind. In fact one has often the impression that when he later speaks of themes related to the picture theory he, as it were, asks himself "What did I really mean?" and does not find an answer to this question. And such a reaction to one's earlier thought is by no means improbable if the earlier thought was indeed vague and in addition was produced in a climate of thought to which one has become more or less alien.[22]

I think that the truth lies somewhere between these two possibilities.

This means that Wittgenstein's idea that his later thoughts should be understood by *contrasting* them to the views of the *Tractatus* is grossly exaggerated. Actually the very fact that this idea, as he says, occurred to him *suddenly* makes the truth of it very improbable.

This means also that what the thoughts expressed in the *Investigations* should be contrasted with is not always Wittgenstein's own earlier thoughts but the thoughts of other people. And in so far they should be contrasted with Wittgenstein's own earlier thoughts they should not only be contrasted with the thoughts of the *Tractatus* but also with the thoughts of what has been called the "transition" period. And, finally, the thoughts expressed in the *Investigations* should be contrasted with other thoughts in the very same book.[23]

This means that interpreters of Wittgenstein often base their interpretations on a false image, that is, the image that Wittgenstein abruptly or gradually moved from the *Tractatus* "position" to the "position" of the *Investigations*. There was no real development from one position to another position, at most there was a development of interests and attitude. This is so, for the simple reason that there is nothing that might appropriately be called *the position* of the *Investigations*. The views expressed in the *Investigations* are by no means consistent. From one angle things looked one way, from another angle they looked differently. The fly never escaped from the fly bottle.

The idea that Wittgenstein rejected the picture theory is founded on a dogmatism, which at least in this respect was alien to Wittgenstein. As far as Wittgenstein remembered the picture theory it remained throughout his life one aspect of how language works, it was how things looked from one angle. And he could not make up his mind as to how far this aspect was reconcilable with the aspects he arrived at by looking at things from another angle.

The fact that Wittgenstein never tried systematically to reconcile the different aspects of his philosophical problems – or even to work out the different aspects systematically – I consider a severe weakness in his later philosophy. This weakness was inseparably connected with his genius as a philosopher. Many of Wittgenstein's commentators seem to have inherited his weakness – but not his genius.

Notes

1. The fact that a main concern of this paper is the one stated in the text does not in itself form a difference between this paper and most other writings on the subject. Commentators on Wittgenstein who state that Wittgenstein rejected the picture theory certainly assume that he did so on grounds which were justified – for the most part relying on reasons which they have themselves constructed and then attributed to Wittgenstein. However, their arguments are for the most part based on a superficial knowledge of what is really said in the *Tractatus* and of what a picture theory of sentence meaning can amount to. This kind of argument is moreover hampered by the fact that many commentators are not aware of the difference between, on the one hand, interpreting Wittgenstein and, on the other hand, attributing to him their own thoughts or trying to make his thought palatable to people with an ordinary philosophical training.

2. Cf. Kenny, p. 5. This slip of Kenny's thought does not agree with the general and, on the main, sound trend of his book. Kenny stresses on p. 227 the highly abstract character of the similarity between the sentence and the fact according to the *Tractatus*.

3. See pp. 65f.

4. It might be fortunate to follow Michael Dummett in speaking of the "diagram theory of sentence meaning" rather than the "picture theory of sentence meaning".

5. I have put the word "universals" in quotation marks, because I do not really like this word as a name of qualities and relations. The difference between individual objects, on the one hand, and qualities or relations, on the other, is not a difference in quantity, as would be suggested by the terms "particular" and "universal"; it is of a quite different kind.

6. This observation not only applies to symbols for qualities or relations but also has a much wider application. Cf. Stenius, SSL.

7. Cf. Stenius, SSL.

8. The structural similarity spoken of here, on which we rely when we read off what is the case from a true sentence, should not be confused with the ontological similarity between corresponding elements spoken of in §8.5.

9. The nexus between Alan, Brian and the father–son relation, which is that these entities form a fact, is mirrored by the same nexus holding between the letters 'a' and 'b' and the 'R'-from-to relation. That is, the linguistic entities form a linguistic *fact*, which is the sentential symbol in 'aRb'. (Regarding this problem see *WT*, pp. 128, 182 and *passim*. In this work I used the word "connection" for what I here call "nexus". Cf. also Stenius *BS*, §17–§22 and *SFW*, §11–§18.)

10. See Stenius *WT*, ch. X, §2 and §3. Cf. also Wittgenstein's formulations in *NB*, p. 109. It is noteworthy that the distinction between what according to the *Tractatus* is shown *and* said and what can be *shown* and "therefore" *cannot* be said is passed over in silence by almost all commentators on the *Tractatus*. This omission has given rise to much confusion.

11. See Stenius, *WT*, ch. VII, §7. Even recent writers on what is called "referring" take this as some kind of basic concept in linguistics, without asking themselves what is the *function* of referring in linguistic description.

12. In *RWS*, p. 386, Copi says that I am "missing the point, the brilliant point, of Wittgenstein's 2.03", i.e. the point that the *Tractatus* "*does provide* an answer to Bradley's arguments against relations", i.e., what has been called "Bradley's infinite regress". This is the paradox we arrive at by thinking that the thing-relation nexus is again a *relation*, so that if it is the case that aRb we must not only ask what is the nexus between the relation R and the individuals a and b, but also ask what is the second-order nexus between this nexus, the relation R and the individuals a and b, and so on *ad infinitum*.

13. The reader should keep in mind that the similarity spoken of here is a similarity which would obtain *irrespectively* of whether the picture is true or false, and does not concern the "likeness" mentioned in *Tractatus*, 4.012. (Cf. above, §§3 and 8.6, and n. 8. Cf. also Stenius *WT*, ch. VI. Moreover, what Wittgenstein means by "shadow of a fact" must be a "shadow fact" (*Schattentatsache*).

14. These elements are, however, given in a wrong way, since Wittgenstein here takes "words" as elements, and not what according to the picture theory are symbols (see above §8.1). This mistake can be due to corresponding obscurities in the *Tractatus*, but they can also be due to the fact that Wittgenstein seems to have "popularized" his views when writing the *Blue Book*. Wittgenstein's tendency to "popularize" should be taken into account when one interprets the *Blue Book*, and it is unfortunate that so many philosophers have built their understanding of Wittgenstein on this book (and the *Brown Book*).

15. In *PG*, §113, Wittgenstein says that the *Tractatus* is misleading in maintaining that *Bildhaftigkeit* means any kind of agreement (*Übereinstimmung*). This suggests that he doubts not only

that there is a similarity between every picture – true or false – and its prototype but also that there must be an agreement between a *true* picture and its prototype. The argument is that anything can be a picture of anything if we extend the concept of a picture in a corresponding way. What is essential, Wittgenstein continues, is only that if I say that a sentence is a picture I mean that it must be a picture in order to *show* what I shall do; in order that I can be guided by it. (Wittgenstein is obviously here thinking of a command which I may obey. Cf. below p. 123). If the passage is interpreted in this way, it may be taken as a criticism of the picture theory of the *Tractatus*. But one must note that Wittgenstein here certainly does not restrict the pictorial character of sentences to elementary sentences but takes the picture theory in a *wide* sense – so that truth-functional compounds of elementary sentences are also regarded as pictures. And it is indeed misleading to say that every true truth-functional compound of pictorial sentences has a common form with reality. (Cf. in respect of the semantics of truth-functional compounds Stenius *WT*, ch. VIII.) What one can say about the whole discussion in this context is that it shows how vague the picture theory had become when Wittgenstein wrote the *PG*. The discussion remains inconclusive and certainly cannot be regarded as a justified criticism of the picture theory of semantic elementary sentences.

16. If there is a more than ontological similarity between the elements of the picture and the elements they stand for I have called the picture "naturalistic". (See *WT*, ch. VI, §9.)

17. See Bogen, p. 26. In this context may be mentioned that Bogen (p. 22) refers to a passage in an unpublished notebook of Wittgenstein's (from about 1931), in which Wittgenstein sketches what Bogen calls a "Stenius-like" account of a feature of the picture theory and – according to Bogen – rejects it. But it is not true that Wittgenstein rejects this account. He just elaborates it to a certain extent. Bogen's mistake in this respect is presumably mainly due to the fact that he translates the German word *Zimmer* as "space" and thinks that what Wittgenstein refers to is a logical space. Bogen's (correct) characterization of the Wittgensteinian sketch as "Stenius-like" does not square with his statement that my account fails to provide a false sentence with a clear prototype (pp. 22 and 27).

18. During the discussion of this paper at the Colloquium one speaker said that Wittgenstein could not reject the picture theory in my version because he did not know it; thus presumably implying that this theory is irrelevant for a discussion of Wittgenstein's philosophy. What does such a formulation really amount to? Perhaps this: There is indeed a "picture theory" of sentence meaning which works and gives a solution to many philosophical problems. Unfortunately Wittgenstein did not know this theory. Thus he arrived at the false conclusion that any such theory is fundamentally wrong.

This is *prima facie* a plausible suggestion (though it is certainly not what the rejectionists want to say). But how shall one explain that the *Tractatus* came so near to such a theory, and that Wittgenstein did not later say explicitly that the picture theory was fundamentally wrong? Moreover, to substantiate such a suggestion, one ought to know what a working picture theory states. (In order to know this it is not enough just to have "read" an exposition of it, as the one given above, in an ordinary way – one must in addition have *rethought* what one is reading.) It is tempting to say, that according to this speaker, what Wittgenstein could not do, his commentators can – that is, reject the picture theory in the version given above without knowing it.

19. I am indebted to Mr André Maury for spotting this and other relevant passages from Wittgenstein's unpublished manuscripts.

20. Cf. Stenius, *WT*, p. 63.

21. That "is" is used as a copula means that what is correlated with redness is the symbol of

standing to the left of the words "is red". If we just say "red" and point to an object, the pointing gesture becomes an element of the symbol correlated with redness.

22. That the *Tractatus* did not remain present in Wittgenstein's mind is shown by the fact that criticisms of the use in *Tractatus* of *Gegenstände* of the same kind as the one quoted in §14 above are made many times earlier, and that then the *Tractatus* is accused of speaking of facts as complexes. (Cf. *PG*, pp. 199–201, *PI*, §47 (4).) However, in no place in the *Tractatus* are facts called "complexes". This kind of terminology is due to Russell, and is echoed in letters from Wittgenstein to Russell (*NB*, p. 120), but it is not in the *Tractatus*.

23. Bogen's idea that Wittgenstein's concern with the false sentence forms a demarcation line between his earlier and later philosophy is probably founded on the mistake of taking for granted that what Wittgenstein said in his later philosophy – in this instance in the *Blue Book* – must be directed against the *Tractatus*. (Cf. above §11.)

References

Bogen, James, *Wittgenstein's Philosophy of Language*, London: Routledge & Kegan Paul, 1972

Copi, Irving M., (OPR) "Objects, Properties and Relations in the Tractatus", *Mind* (1958). Reprinted in Copi & Beard, pp. 167–86

(RSW) Review of Stenius, *WT*, *Philosophical Review*, 72 (1963), pp. 382–90

Copi, Irving M. & Beard, Robert W. (eds), *Essays on Wittgenstein's Tractatus*, New York: Macmillan, 1966

Hacker, P. M. S., *Insight and Illusion*, Oxford: Clarendon Press, 1972

Kenny, Anthony, *Wittgenstein*, London: Allen Lane The Penguin Press, 1973

Malcolm, Norman, "Wittgenstein's *Philosophische Bemerkungen*", *Philosophical Review*, 76 (1967), pp. 220–29

Pears, David, *Wittgenstein*, London: Fontana/Collins, 1971

Pitcher, George, *The Philosophy of Wittgenstein*, Englewood Cliffs, New Jersey: Prentice-Hall Inc., 1964

Stenius, Erik, (*WT*) *Wittgenstein's Tractatus. A Critical Exposition*, Oxford: Blackwell, and Ithaca: Cornell University Press, 1960; 2nd ed. 1964

(MLG) "Mood and Language-Game", (*Synthese*, 1967). Reprinted in *CE*, pp. 182–202

(SSL) "Syntax of Symbolic Logic and Transformational Grammar", *Synthese*, 26 (1973/74), pp. 57–80

(CE) *Critical Essays* (Acta Philosophica Fennica, Fasc. xxv), Amsterdam: North-Holland, 1972

(BS) "Die Bildtheorie des Satzes", *Erkenntnis*, 9 (1975), pp. 35–45

(SFW) "The Sentence as a Function of its Constituents in Frege and Wittgenstein", *Essays on Wittgenstein in Honour of G. H. von Wright* (Acta Philosophica Fennica 28), Amsterdam: North-Holland, 1976, pp. 71–84

Waismann, Friedrich, (*WWK*) *Wittgenstein und der Wiener Kreis*, Oxford: Blackwell, 1967

Wittgenstein, Ludwig, *Tractatus Logico-Philosophicus*, London: Routledge & Kegan Paul, 1922

(PI) *Philosophical Investigations*, Oxford: Blackwell, 1953

(BB) *The Blue and Brown Books*, Oxford: Blackwell, 1958
(NB) *Notebooks 1914–1916*, Oxford: Blackwell, 1961
(PB) *Philosophische Bemerkungen*, Oxford: Blackwell, 1964
(PG) *Philosophische Grammatik*, Oxford: Blackwell, 1969
(WWK), *see* Waismann.

Wittgenstein's Early Philosophy of Mind

ANTHONY KENNY

"Theory of knowledge", said Wittgenstein in the *Tractatus* (4.1121), "is the philosophy of psychology." The context makes clear that *Erkenntnistheorie* does not mean epistemology, if epistemology is an inquiry into the justification of beliefs, the possibility of knowledge, and the tenability or refutability of scepticism. Rather, it means what is nowadays called "philosophy of mind" – an analysis of sentences reporting beliefs, judgments, perception and the like (cf. 5.541). Psychology is one of the natural sciences: the philosophy of psychology will do for it what philosophy, according to the *Tractatus*, is to do for each of the sciences; it will clarify its thought and draw limits to its competence (4.112; 4.113).

Two sections of the *Tractatus* are devoted to this enterprise. The passages in *Tractatus*, 3–3.5, linking Wittgenstein's general theory of representation to his theory that a proposition is a picture, tell us much about the nature of thoughts and thinking (*Gedanke* and *denken*). *Tractatus*, 5.541–5.5423 discusses the analysis of such propositions as "A believes that *p*", "A has the thought that *p*", "A judges that *p*", "A perceives *p*", with the immediate purpose of showing how these propositions are not exceptions to the rule that propositions can occur in other propositions only as bases of truth operations.

It has been the custom of commentators to discuss these passages in comparative isolation from each other. It may even be questioned whether they do deal with the same topic at all. Is the *Gedanke* of the 3s a psychological matter at all? May it not have more in common with

Frege's Platonic entity than with the topic of Russell's theory of judgment? The clearest evidence that a *Gedanke* is psychological comes in a letter from Wittgenstein to Russell in 1919. "What are the constituents of a *Gedanke*?" Russell had asked. "I don't know what the constituents of a thought are but I know *that* it must have such constituents which correspond to the words of Language. Again the kind of relation of the constituents of the thought and the pictured fact is irrelevant, it would be a matter of psychology to find out." A *Gedanke* did not consist of words, but "of psychical constituents that have the same sort of relation to reality as words". This is unequivocal: but one might wish it did not follow an exegesis of the meaning of "*Sachverhalt*" and "*Tatsache*" which is notoriously difficult to reconcile with the actual text of the *Tractatus*. Direct evidence from the text of the 2s and 3s is not so explicit: still, a thought is a picture, and pictures are things which *we* make (3.2); thinking is something that *we* do (3.03); and a thought is something which unless expressed in a propositional sign is imperceptible by the senses (3.1). Clearly, then, it is neither a Platonic proposition nor a perceptible sentence: a psychological fact, the holding of a relation between psychic elements, as described by Wittgenstein to Russell, would certainly fit these requirements. I shall therefore assume that the thinking discussed in the 3s and early 4s is the same as the thinking discussed in 5.541ff.

The first thing that we are told about a thought is that it is a logical picture of facts; a logical picture, we have already been told, is a picture whose pictorial form is logical form (2.181), and pictorial form is what a picture must have in common with the reality it depicts (2.17). Pictures may have more than logical form in common with what they depict – a spatial picture, for instance, has spatial form in common with what it depicts – but every picture must have at least logical form in common (2.18). In this sense every picture is a logical picture: what then are we to make of the statement that a thought is a logical picture? There seem to be two ways in which we could take it: either as meaning that every picture is a thought, or as meaning that a thought was a picture whose pictorial form was *only* logical form. Against the former interpretation we must count the fact that thought seems to be related so closely to a proposition as to be capable of being identified with it (4); and whereas all propositions are pictures, there is no reason to think that the *Tractatus* regards all pictures as propositions. In favour of the latter is the fact that it is quite natural, and was long traditional, to regard the mental and the physical as distinct realms whose inhabitants had no properties in common: so that a psychic fact and the physical fact it depicted could have nothing in common beyond the bare logical form.[1]

The relation between thought and proposition is variously described by Wittgenstein: in 3.1 the proposition *expresses* the thought; in 4 the proposition *is* the thought. There is no contradiction here, only a verbal carelessness: like every great philosopher Wittgenstein was inconsistent in his use of his own technical terms. In 3.12 Wittgenstein introduced the term *"Satzzeichen"* ("propositional sign") for the perceptible state of affairs – the holding of a relation between written or spoken words or code-signs in more substantial hardware (3.1433) – which expresses the thought. So far as it expresses a thought, the propositional sign is a projection of a possible state of affairs (3.11–12). Just as a propositional sign can only be a proposition if projected by a thought on to the world, so a relationship holding between psychic elements can only be a thought if it is a projection, an application, of a propositional sign (3.5). This last sentence, in Wittgenstein's thought, is formally analogous to: Just as a man can only be a husband if married to a wife, so a woman can only be a wife if married to a man. The propositional sign, plus the thought, is the proposition; the thought is what gives the proposition its sense; a little loosely, we can say that thought *is* the sense-full proposition (*sinn-volle Satz*: proposition with its sense; not sensible as opposed to senseless proposition, for strictly speaking there is no such thing as a proposition without sense).

3.11, 3.12 and the 3.14s discuss various features of the *Satzzeichen* or propositional sign. 3.13 does not mention the propositional sign, but makes various remarks about the proposition (*Satz*). In the *Prototractatus* this passage occurred in a different, later, context. The fact that Wittgenstein moved it here suggests that he realized that what it contained illuminated the notion of *Satzzeichen* more than it illuminated that of *Satz*. He did not, however, make the changes in vocabulary that would have rendered it totally appropriate to its new context. A reading of it, however, suggests that it makes much better sense if we distinguish within it between *Satz* and *Satzzeichen*. The passage – difficult to understand on any interpretation – runs as follows.

Zum Satz gehört alles, was zur Projektion gehört; aber nicht das Projizierte.	A proposition includes all that the projection includes, but not what is projected.
Also die Möglichkeit des Projizierten, aber nicht dieses selbst.	Therefore, though what is projected is not itself included, its possibility is.

Im Satz ist also sein Sinn noch nicht enthalten, wohl aber die Möglichkeit ihn auszudrücken.	A proposition, therefore, does not actually contain its sense, but does contain the possibility of expressing it.
("Der Inhalt des Satzes" heisst der Inhalt des sinnvollen Satzes.)	('The content of a proposition' means the content of a proposition that has sense.)
Im Satz ist die Form seine Sinnes enthalten, aber nicht dessen Inhalt.	A proposition contains the form, but not the content of its sense.

The first two sentences are intelligible enough with "*Satz*" taken as "proposition"; their relevance to their new context is clear. The proposition includes not only the propositional sign, but also the projecting thought; it does not include the state of affairs which is projected (if the proposition is false there is no such state of affairs for it to include) but it includes the possibility of that state of affairs (because of its pictorial form, which is the possibility that things are related to one another in the same way as the elements of the picture, 2.151). But the next sentence is hard to make sense of if "*Satz*" means proposition: commentators have tended to ignore the "*ihn auszudrücken*" at the end and taken it as if, like the previous sentence, it was saying that a proposition contained the possibility of its sense's *being the case*. But that is not at all the same as the possibility of its *expressing* its sense. But is there not something very odd about saying that a proposition contains *the possibility of* expressing its sense, when what it does is *actually to express* its sense? Everything at once becomes clear if we read "*Satz*" here as "*Satzzeichen*": a propositional sign, without the projecting thought, will not have a sense; but, being capable of being projected, it will be capable of expressing that sense. This reading also makes it possible to make sense of the puzzling parenthesis which follows. The content of the propositional sign, *when it becomes a proposition*, is its sense; the content of the sense of the proposition are the objects of the possible state of affairs which the proposition depicts; the proposition as a whole – the proposition which is propositional sign plus thought sense – contains the form but not the content of its sense: it is made up of objects which are not identical with, but formally congruent with, the objects in the possible state of affairs.

"In a proposition", Wittgenstein says at 3.2, "a thought can be expressed in such a way that elements of the propositional sign correspond to the objects of the thought." The expression "the objects of the thought" is ambiguous. Does it mean: the objects which constitute the thought; or does it mean: the objects which the thought is about? One might be inclined to think the latter if one did not consult the corresponding passage in the *Prototractatus*. Between the *Prototractatus* and the *Tractatus* a passage which clearly meant the latter has been altered into one which more naturally means the former. "The objects of the thought" will be the psychic elements whose relation to each other constitutes the thought. A proposition is fully analysed when the elements of the propositional sign correspond to the elements of the thought. An unanalysed proposition of ordinary language does not bear this relation to the thought: on the contrary, it disguises the thought; and we can understand ordinary language, we can grasp the thought beneath the folds of language, only because of enormously complicated tacit conventions (4.002). Bits of ordinary language – signs – such as the word "is" may signify in many different ways: they belong to different symbols (3.323). What makes the difference between sign and symbol is the significant use of the sign. This goes for propositional signs too: it is the use, the application, which makes the propositional sign into the symbol, the proposition (3.326–7). The physical features of the propositional sign are those which enable it to express its sense (3.34). The most important of these is the mathematical multiplicity which is in common with the situation depicted (4.04). Normally, the propositional sign, in itself, will not have this multiplicity: if it did, it could not be said to "disguise thought". The multiplicity is therefore given by the tacit conventions which relate the sign and the symbol, the tacit conventions which are tantamount to the rules of logical syntax (3.334).

We may now turn to the second part of the *Tractatus* philosophy of mind: the analysis of propositions reporting belief, thought and judgment. "It is clear", says Wittgenstein, "that 'A believes that p', 'A has the thought p' and 'A says p' are of the form ' "p" says p': and this does not involve a correlation of a fact with an object, but rather the correlation of facts by means of the correlation of their objects" (5.542). This comes in a passage where Wittgenstein is explaining how such propositions are not exceptions to the rule that propositions can be constructed out of other propositions only truth-functionally.

Professor Anscombe, in her *Introduction to Wittgenstein's Tractatus*, explains this passage as follows:

... for anything to be capable of representing the fact that p, it must be as complex as the fact that p; but a thought that p, or a belief or statement that p, must be potentially a representation of the fact that p (and of course actually a representation of it, if it *is* a fact that p). It is perhaps not quite right to say that 'A judges p' is of the form ' "p" says that p'; what he should have said was that the business part of 'A judges that p', the part that relates to something having as its content a potential representation of the fact that p, was of the form ' "p" says that p': 'A believes p' or 'conceives p' or 'says p' must mean 'There occurs in A or is produced by A something which is (capable of being) a picture of p'.[2]

This seems correct. But Professor Anscombe goes on to say that " 'p' says that p" is offered by Wittgenstein as a possible form of proposition, with true–false poles. She quotes 3.1432 ("The complex sign 'aRb' says that a stands in the relation R to b". No, not that but rather "*That* 'a' stands to 'b' in a certain relation says *that aRb*.") and gives as an instance of the kind of thing that Wittgenstein meant "it is . . . the fact that 'a' stands to the left, and 'b' to the right of 'R', that says that aRb".[3]

To me it seems, on the contrary, that Wittgenstein regarded " 'p' says that p" as a pseudo-proposition.[4] It is false that it is the fact that, say, in "London is bigger than Paris" "London" is to the left of "is bigger than" and "Paris" is to the right of "is bigger than" that *says* that London is bigger than Paris. It is only this fact *plus the conventions of the English language* that says any such thing. The description of any fact, such as Professor Anscombe mentions, which falls short of specifying those conventions in full would at best be a description of accidental features of the *Satzzeichen*. What does the saying in that sentence is what the propositional sign has in common with all other propositional signs which could achieve the same purpose; and what *this* is could only be described by – *per impossible* – specifying and making explicit the tacit conventions of English.

" 'p' says that p" does not have true–false poles. For what appears within the nested quotation marks is either – as Anscombe understands it – a description of accidental features of the propositional sign, in which case the proposition is always false; or it is a description which identifies 'p' precisely as the proposition which says that p; in which case the proposition is necessarily true (and therefore, for Wittgenstein, a pseudo-proposition). But even if Anscombe were correct in thinking that " 'p' says that p" were a genuine proposition, it is difficult to see how, on her account, 'p' does not occur non-truth-functionally in it. Whereas if " 'p' says that p" is only a pseudo-proposition, and "A believes that 'p' " is of that form, it is easy to see how propositions reporting beliefs are no exception to the rule that propositions can only occur in other genuine propositions as the bases of truth-functional operations.

" 'p' says that p", though a pseudo-proposition, is of course a *correct* pseudo-proposition: it is a thesis of the *Tractatus*. It is shown by the proposition 'p': (4.022; 4.462). This alone suffices to show that it cannot be *said* for what can be shown cannot be said; and anything that attempts to say what can only be shown is a pseudo-proposition (4.1212).

We are now in a better position to see in what way the philosophy of psychology clarifies psychological propositions. Suppose that I think a certain thought: my thinking that thought will consist in certain psychic elements – mental images or internal impressions, perhaps – standing in a relation to each other. That these elements stand in such and such a relation will be a psychological fact; a fact in the world, within the purview of the natural sciences; just as the fact that the penholder is on the table is a physical fact within the purview of the natural sciences. But the fact that these mental elements have the meaning they have will not be a fact of science, any more than the fact (if it is a fact) that the penholder's being on the table says that the cat is on the mat (if the appropriate code is in force).

Meaning is conferred on signs by *us*, by our conventions (3.3; 3.322; 3.342; 4.026; 6.53, etc.). But where are the acts of the will that confer the meaning, that set up the conventions? They cannot be in the empirical soul studied by superficial psychology: any relation between *that* will and any pair of objects would be a fact in the world, capable of study by natural science, and therefore incapable of the ineffable activity of conferring meaning. When I confer meaning on the symbols I use, the I that does so must be the metaphysical I, not the self that is studied by psychology (5.631ff.).

There is a tension between the 5.541s as I have explained them and the 3s as Wittgenstein explained them to Russell. From the 5.541s it seems as if what gives meaning to the perceptible signs of language cannot be anything psychic. From the 3s it seems as though the projection lines between the propositional sign and the world are drawn in the realm of psychology: it is thinking which constructs the sense of the proposition. But perhaps the *Tractatus* philosophy of mind is easy to make consistent: we need only to draw in the 3s a distinction suggested by our reflections on the 5.54s. In the thought itself, perhaps, we can distinguish between the particular mental configuration, studiable by psychology, and the significance or intentionality of that configuration, conferred by the metaphysical self. Thought, unlike language, will have the right mathematical multiplicity to depict the facts; but its multiplicity gives it only the *possibility* of depicting; that it actually does depict depends on the meaning of its elements, and that is given by the extra-psychological will giving those elements a use, an application.

The later Wittgenstein came to believe that it was absurd to look for a multiplicity of mental items in independence from the multiplicity of their expression. For this reason he could jeer at the idea that things were possible in the mysterious medium of the mind which were impossible in the public light of day. The *Tractatus* may perhaps have conceived thought as a gaseous medium: but if I am right it did *not* think that thought — the realm of introspectionist psychology — could confer meaning. The constant later polemic against the imagist theory of meaning goes further than the *Tractatus* in that it argued that even images are only identifiable as the images they are in virtue of the meaning we attach to them. But the *Tractatus* itself did not think, as the British empiricists did, that impressions and ideas could themselves confer meaning unaided. In the *Tractatus* meaning is conferred by pure will, the pure will of the extra-mundane solipsistic metaphysical self; in the *Philosophical Investigations* it is conferred by the active participation of the human being in the social community in the empirical world. From one point of view the two conceptions could hardly be further apart. But common to both are two theses of fundamental importance: first, that introspectionist psychology can never explain meaning; secondly, that the ultimate creation of meaning is indescribable (in the *Tractatus*, because it takes place outside the world; in the *Philosophical Investigations*, because all description is within a language-game). And common to both are the tasks and method of philosophy of mind: to clarify psychological statements by separating out the logical and intentional from the contingent and empirical.

Notes

1. But would they not have temporality in common? And what of thoughts about thoughts? The first question is not answered either in the *Tractatus* or this paper: the second is answered at 5.541 and below.
2. G. E. M. Anscombe, *An Introduction to Wittgenstein's Tractatus* (London, 1959), p. 88.
3. *ibid.*, p. 89.
4. Cf. A. Kenny, *Wittgenstein* (London: Allen Lane The Penguin Press, 1973), p. 101.

A Theory of Language?

G. E. M. ANSCOMBE

"But such a sound is an expression only in a particular language-game, which now has to be described" (*Philosophical Investigations* [*PI*], §261). I take this sentence out of context and I will leave out the first two and last six words. I derive a possible basic statement of a theory of language:

A sound is an expression only in a particular language-game.

This will be a basic statement of a theory of language only if we regard the task of 'describing the language-game' as one whose point is to show how noises are significant speech. The idea has quite a lot of attraction and it attracted me for a long time. Indeed, I once thought that that was the main thing, or the most fundamental thing, that was going on in Wittgenstein. Now I believe that the idea of such an enterprise is one which quite quickly goes up in smoke.

All the same it is worth shewing this, because it will give us some clues to better understanding.

If one pursues that conception, one at once feels constrained to distinguish between 'primitive' and 'non-primitive' language-games, because one can't describe many without presupposing others. And so one starts something like this:

A primitive language-game is an action or procedure into which words, or perhaps we should rather say, sounds (e.g.) are interwoven. Just their role in the procedure makes them to be words or signs. In describing this role one makes no assumption about the occurrence of the same sounds in other procedures. Naturally, one thinks there are very few primitive language-games that determine sounds to be the signs they become. Greeting would be an example.

"A great deal of stage-setting in the language is presupposed to any act of naming" (*PI*, §257). If that is so, then "naming" couldn't be the name of a primitive language-game. Or, better: naming couldn't be accomplished in a primitive language-game. "Naming" there of course meant *conferring* a name. But we could say the same of using a word to name something, i.e. as a name of something.

A *non-primitive* language-game will be a procedure using what are already words. And here there will be two cases. In one, nothing but what are already words will be used in the new procedure. In the other – and this one is nearer to the 'primitive games' – there will be some old words and some new sounds together woven into, i.e. given a role in the new procedure. An obvious example is given by Wittgenstein's builders, who are first described as using just four words "Slab", "Block", etc. (which was to be conceived as "a complete primitive language") and then as having the extra words "a", "b", "c", etc. together with "this" and "over there". These appear in utterances like "d-slab-over there" by A, accompanied by a pointing gesture, in response to which B carries four slabs to the place indicated.

If it is the use of a word that constitutes it as a name, but the use of a word as a name cannot be said to occur in any primitive language-game, then in what sort of non-primitive language-games do we get it? For the word doesn't occur as a new sign (it isn't a new sound) like "d" and "there".

Is it like this: there are *several* primitive *and* near-primitive language-games played with the four original sounds "Slab" etc., and it takes occurrences in several games to constitute "Slab" as a name? That "Slab" is a *name* of a certain shape of building stone isn't established just because language-game (2) is played. Consider Wittgenstein's discussion of whether "Slab!" in (2) means "Bring me a slab" or just means "slab"; and of whether it is a sentence or a word. "In fact, it *is* our 'elliptical' sentence." This he says in spite of obvious objections (which he considers). The point is: "When I call 'Slab!' what I want is *that he should bring me a slab*!" – and that was what "Slab!" amounted to in (2). Wanting that doesn't consist in thinking (in some form or other) a *different* sentence from the one you utter. This raises the question whether "Bring me a slab" might be meant as one long word corresponding to "Slab!"

We should not be put off by the extreme simplicity of the example. Language and human capacity are so complex that e.g. different words can come to be counted as in some way the same word. Cf. different *in-*

flections, as we call them. Or it might be that one used a different sound the next time: "Slab", "Tink", "Noffle" might all be the 'same word' – you say "Tink" if *last* time you said "Slab" etc. but otherwise the role is the same. I don't know of any language in which that happens, but it *might*. That people master different inflections is itself impressive. "Romam" is after all quite as different from "Roma" as "broken" is from "broker". But let us forget these possible complications in order to see the difficulty even in very simple cases. The 'theory' before us is that a sufficient number of different language-games with the same word can make that word into a name. It will occur in combination with other words. First we have a mere sound, say "Slab", whose use has a certain point in an activity; no more reason to call it a name than the shout "Bingo!" *in* the game of that name. Then we have it fitted together with other sounds, e.g. 'Slab there', 'Four slabs' – but *what is the identity?* We have the same sound, equally fitted together with others, in "This lab work." And, of course the sound "Slab" itself was already a conjunction of sounds.

Our attention is now called to the question: What is the difference between a 'mere' phonemic combination and a morphemic or verbal one? Many philosophers of otherwise diverse tendency (e.g. Aristotle, Russell) have explained a simple sign as one which has no parts which are signs; or, more strictly, no parts which function as signs within the sign in which they occur. Only for a crossword-puzzle man does "Churchill" contain "Church" and "hill" and "ill".

But how can we pretend to that account from the position that we have taken up? We are trying to say *what* about the occurrence of a sound constitutes it as a sign, and in particular as a name. So the idea of a part's not being a sign can't be used to discriminate between what occurs as a sign and what occurs as a 'mere' phoneme or 'mere' syllable.

"The sound which is a sign has a certain role as part of a procedure" – but isn't that *also* true of the mere phoneme? We are accustomed to think that Plato in the Cratylus was extraordinarily blind in assuming that phonemes have meaning-roles. But this, as often, may be a failure on our part to see a problem.

We may be inclined to say: the most elementary sounds usually form clusters, and it is certain clusters that can be recognized as having what we've called "a role" in an activity and so as being signs. In the limiting case, as with "I", "a", etc. the elementary sound *itself* has a 'role' and is a sign. In all other cases the most elementary sounds themselves have what we are calling a "role" merely *as* parts of a cluster which has one.

The latter expression demands explanation. Shall we say: By itself the phoneme S does not have the kind of role we mean, the role of the sound in the language-game, but only when combined with other phonemes to make the sound 'slab'? Only the sequence has that role, and the single phoneme's contribution is that it is part of that sequence. To be sure the individual phoneme matters, witness the difference between 'slab' and 'slat'; we can't deny that it 'matters for the meaning'; Plato was wrong only in thinking it mattered by making a *meaning-contribution*.

We are talking ourselves into greater difficulty, not reducing it. *What* is the difference between 'mattering for the meaning' and 'making a meaning-contribution'?

We may say: Very well, the mere phoneme does make a meaning-contribution, but not in the way Plato thought. A cluster of phonemes plays a role in a language-game and its elements play the role collectively. There is a difference between phonemic and morphemic concatenation. It is when you have morphemic concatenations that you have the same sign, the same *word*, occurring in a new combination with other signs. Whatever 'language-game' you may introduce "This lab work" into, if this is the familiar phrase, the concatenation of the S phoneme with the cluster of l-a-b isn't morphemic. − But now, of course, we want to know the criterion for morphemic as opposed to phonemic concatenation. − Someone may wish to introduce pronunciation, thus retreating to the acoustic qualities of what is said; but the suggestion that the actual stretch of sounds s-l-a is regularly different according to whether a word beginning 'sla' is occurring or not, is not one I'm willing to buy.

If Zellig Harris is right (and I am willing to believe that it is often so), there is a way of generally ascertaining the morphemes of a language without making any more appeal to meaning than is made in an assumed preliminary process of ascertaining its phonemes. Starting with any old phoneme of the language, you put another possible one after it (i.e. one that does occur after it) and ask how wide open the possibilities are now, for the next place. The morphemic divisions of sample sequences of phonemes generated in this way will be at the peaks of possibility for the next phoneme. (If in doubt, try it backwards!) Of course in giving examples one relies on grasp of the possibilities for the language, but if the 'possibilities' were established just as a matter of frequencies for a language that was not understood, the method would work − if Harris is right − as long as the acoustic identifications of the phonemes was reasonably reliable. Now in telling us this method for determining what are the morphemes of language, Harris does not suggest that it is a criterion: the method can be investigated for its success in identifying morphemes or in morphemic segmentation. So it doesn't tell us what we are to *call* correct morphemic division but assumes we already have a fair idea of that. Now Harris's actual explanation of morphemic segmentation seems not to be successful.[1] One cannot help suspecting a covert reliance on etymological knowledge, which nevertheless is also scouted; cf. his observation that 'ice' is no morpheme in 'notice': but, after all, the "ice" in "notice" also occurs in "service", if etymology is relevant; and if it not, one feels grave doubts whether the concept of a morpheme has any validity. (Cf. Chomsky's bogus treatment of "eous" in "righteous". The matter is of some importance vis-a-vis post-Harris linguistics, especially when there are claims to base something about *the mind* on the 'transformations'.) I have turned to Harris because he is noticeably conscious of the question I have raised, and also because he attempted a theory which is 'micro-reductionist' in spirit; such a theory is also what I tried to read into Wittgenstein. Harris is of course correct in observing that "the morphemic boundaries in an utterance are determined, not on the basis of considerations interior to the utterance, but on the basis of comparison with other utterances." Now this is equally true of the break-up of utterances into 'words'. Cf. Wittgenstein's observation:

But now it looks as if when someone says "Bring me a slab" he could mean this as one long word corresponding to the single word 'Slab!' . . . We mean the sentence as four words when we use it in contrast with other sentences such as "*Hand* me a slab," "Bring *him* a slab," "Bring two slabs" etc.; . . . that is, in contrast with other sentences containing the words of our order in other combinations – But what does using one sentence in contrast with others consist in? . . . We say we use the order in contrast with other sentences because *our language* contains the possibility of those other sentences . . . a foreigner might believe the whole series of sounds was one word.

In fact the concept of 'an individual word' is so familiar to us largely because of the division into 'separate words' by printers. Printers' divisions, and lack of them, are in part purely conventional. Without the familiarity engendered by the printed word, the concept of an individual word is a product of rather sophisticated reflection. The more primitive idea is that still retained in such a phrase as "a word in your ear", or "word came to me that . . ."

I once had the following dialogue with a four-year-old who had a piece of paper in her hand:

I: Give me that.
C: Whose is it? (Hands it over)
I: How many words did I say?
C: When?
I: When I asked you to give it to me.
C. One.
I: What was that one word?
C: "Can I have the paper, please."

The last utterance of the child is in quotation marks because it was quite clearly an answer — which came quite pat — to my last question; she did not want the paper back. This story is no very weighty support for, but is an excellent illustration of, my contention: the division of utterances into distinct words is a sophisticated proceeding. Not just the historically but the psychologically and epistemologically primitive sense of "word" is "thing said". If this is right, then either Wittgenstein is wrong to say "We mean the sentence as four words . . . because *our language* contains the possibility of those other sentences," or "meaning the sentence as four words" does not involve having the idea of four distinct words. The latter is the correct interpretation.

Harris's effort was an unsuccessful enterprise of micro-reduction, and if we conceive Wittgenstein as also engaged in such an enterprise we must equally say that he fails. Indeed the pretended attempt would be positively fraudulent. He deliberately constructs a very small number of proceedings with a very small number of noises, each of which is a cluster of phonemes, and invites us to consider the very first type of pro-ceeding as a "complete primitive language". When the additions are given, we are presumably to consider the whole set of procedures of the builders as now constituting their 'complete language'. Certainly, as it happens, the problem of reidentification does not arise, that is to say, as the thing was set up, there was no possibility of the occurrence within a 'game' of any of the sound-clusters that are designated as words, without their being *those* words. Thus no problem is presented such as appears when we say we are quite sure that the word "red" doesn't occur in "Get it ready," "He's read it," "Don't tread there," "Better edit it," "Have you any bread?," "It's easy to shred," "It's predatory," etc., etc. If what we have at the beginning of *Philosophical Investigations* is an embryonic micro-reductionist theory of language such as we envisaged, and we are given those 'objects of comparison' the 'clear and simple language-games', to illustrate the theory by presenting it in a simple model – then the presentation is fraudulent. The difficulties of identification would be supposed to be overcome by a wave of the hand and muttering about 'complexity'.

When Wittgenstein adds the new words and introduces "d-slab-there", the question "What determines that 'slab' is the same word as in the first language-game?" has the same answer as the question: "What determines that 'Horatio' is the name of Hamlet's friend?" The author determines it: explicitly or implicitly, he tells us it is so.

We could formulate an exercise: Assume that the builders proceed as described, except that the vocal part of their activity is only described as their making those noises at these points. Now construct further developments such that when we consider the whole, the sound-cluster "s-l-a-b" occurring in "deeslabthere" was not after all a word, or not the same word as at its first appearance. Or again, the sound-clusters "Slab" etc., though identifiable as repetition of the same morphemes, turn out not to be names of shapes of building stone.

The main purpose of the opening of the *Investigations* is to persuade us not to look at the connection between a word and its meaning either as set up or as explained (a) by ostensive definition, or (b) by association, or (c) by mental pictures, or (d) by experiences characteristic of meaning one thing rather than another, or (e) by a general relation of reference or naming or designation or signifying which has (logically) different kinds of objects as its terms in different cases. The "clear and simple language-games" are offered as objects of comparison, not models – to give us the idea of the possible functioning of a word in use, without even invoking that of meaning. For it "surrounds our consideration with a fog".

This was an enormously difficult trick to pull off, because there is an internal relation between a word and its meaning such that under some circumstances we would so use the expression "that word" that 'it' wouldn't 'be the same word' if it hadn't the same meaning.

The question then arises: was Wittgenstein trying to break the 'internal relation' – to set up external relations instead? To speak of words without faces, offering them to us without their peculiar physiognomy? That would be a misunderstanding, as comes out if we reflect (a) on his free assumption of authority to identify words and (b) on his claims about grammar. (a) alone might betoken blindness, but (b) rules out that possibility. We must therefore turn our attention to (b).

Surgeons may order the manufacture of instruments adapted to catch hold of different items. Catching-hold-of is in every case the same kind of thing, but the objects caught hold of vary in shape and so they may need instruments the business parts of which are differently shaped. Consider now the difference between naming a number, naming a particular man, and naming a kind of fruit. We might conceive it on the analogy of the surgeon's instruments, and, while this would suggest that naming, or "using a word for a ———" was always the same kind of thing, still it would also give us the idea of the analogue of a "difference of shape" in the catching-hold part of the instrument. But what is in question is a difference of *logical* shape. I speak in metaphors: what I thereby seek to express is what according to Wittgenstein belongs to the grammatical characterization of words. If I am right, it would for example be perfectly correct according to his thinking to call "numeral" the name of a grammatical part of speech. I know of no place where he did say this, but unless I misunderstand the matter, he must have assented to it. No doubt it makes too little contribution to solving the problems about the foundations of mathematics that interested him, for him ever to have said it.

His use of the word "grammatical" has of course been noticed, and it has been widely supposed that he had an odd taste for using "grammatical" where others would use "logical". He himself claimed that when he said "grammar" he meant grammar – more of the sort of stuff one learns at school when one learns grammar. People have found it very hard to believe this. But we ought to remember that there can be a difference of opinion *about* grammar, even though "grammar" is the word for what the disagreement is about – just as there can be different beliefs about God, though the word is not the wrong one to use for the topic of disagreement.

Strange to say, Wittgenstein's conception of the grammatical is far closer to the Platonic–Aristotelian tradition than that of the linguistics which seems to hold the field at the present day. It is strange, because Wittgenstein is always inveighing against the influence of "Aristotelian" logic in causing people to force uses of language all into one mould; and here "Aristotelian" logic is to be understood so broadly that Frege and Russell are examples of it too. In this tradition Plato initiated the distinction between name and verb, or subject and predicate. This division is so generic that it covers an immense variety of diverse structures. But a man who complains of the forcing of diverse things into one generic mould may be doing so because he wants many more specific patterns described: not because he wants to change the direction of interest of the enquiry. Plato saw the *grammatical* difference between "Theaetetus" and "walks", Wittgenstein, the *grammatical* difference between "Theaetetus" and "two". If "proper name" is a grammatical category, then so in his conception is "numeral" and so is "colour-name" and so is "psychological verb". But by Wittgensteinian considerations even all of these turn out to be somewhat generic: that is, there are "categorial" differences within each kind.

Now "numerals" would often be a special chapter in the grammar of a particular language. This is, however, largely because numerals affect cases and constructions of sentences in peculiar ways. Colour-words do not in the languages I know. If there are languages in which they do, then the treatment of those languages by grammarians will equally include separate chapters for them.

The difference of opinion about what belongs to grammar arises from belief in and practice of a 'formal' science of grammar on the one hand, and a study of what a given use of words amounts to or achieves or tells us on the other. The former belief leads to an examination of the ways that words occur together and an attempt to formulate rules and explanations of this, always in terms of purely linguistic structures. The latter leads to consideration of contrasts between say "For how long did you forget that?" and "For how long did you reflect on that?" or between intermission of intention and intermission of attention. There is nothing obscure about calling "grammatical" the observation of the different temporalities involved in these cases. But it is not a kind of observation that we expect from the formal grammarians. Plato's distinction at the beginning of our tradition might seem to belong to either conception of the grammatical; but his interest in making it (the problem of falsehood and negation) put it in the philosophical class of grammatical investigations: the 'formal' grammarian is interested in the structures of language for their own sake.

See how close Wittgenstein is to Plato just here.

Wittgenstein:

The agreement, the harmony, between language and reality consists in this: if I say falsely that something is red, then, after all, it isn't *red*. And if I want to explain "red" to someone in the statement that this is not red I do it by pointing to something red. (*PI*, §420)

The harmony between language and reality is found in the false statement no less than the true. This false statement says (of what is) something that (it) is not – but *something* nevertheless, which is. Here we can point to that which the thing is not.

Plato:

A statement does not consist of names spoken in succession or verbs apart from names . . . it does not merely name something, but gets you somewhere by weaving together verbs with names . . . those that fit together make a statement . . . stating something *of* something (of you, say) . . . the false statement stating of you, as being, things which are different from the things that *are* of you, and so things which are not, but all the same things which do exist. (*Sophist*, 262–3B)

(Suppose the question arises: would the two part company about empty predicates? – Well, whatever way there is of explaining a predicate when used positively, just that way explains it too when it is used negatively.)

"If I say falsely that something is red, then all the same it isn't *red*." – the mere truism suddenly looks astonishing. If I can change a false statement to a true by negating it or cancelling a negation this is possible because of the distinction of the different kinds of words which fit together to make descriptions. The grammar of "red" is not determined by mere experience of the colour.

If you trained someone to emit a particular sound at the sight of something red, another at the sight of something yellow, and so on for other colours, still he would not yet be describing objects by their colours. Though he might be a help to us in giving a description. A description is a representation of a distribution in a space (in that of time, for instance).

If I let my gaze wander round a room and suddenly it lights on an object of a striking red colour, and I say "Red!" – that is not a description. (*PI*, II, ix)

Whereas, had I said *of* the object that *it* was red, or had I said that my visual field was not suffused with (or that it did contain) red, here there would be "a representation of a distribution in a space".

It is thus not the case at all that Wittgenstein means anything but "grammatical" when he says "grammatical". What is contentious is his claim that a vast number of philosophical and metaphysical statements are disguised statements of grammar – and *that*, of course, is his interest in grammar. So far as I can see each such claim has to be examined separately, and when he says that something, "like everything metaphysical", is rooted in the grammar of our language, it is difficult to form a judgment on the general claim.

I conclude, then, that there is after all no theory of language in Wittgenstein. It may be worthwhile to end with a warning. What he calls "a grammatical proposition" is of course a proposition *of* grammar. But his references to "grammar" and his occasional statements of the form "That is not how the language-game is played" may have played some part in leading 'formal' grammarians to try to characterize as 'ungrammatical' various forms of statement, such as "I mean to punish the mountain," or "The mountain devoured the boy" where there is for example an inappropriate object for a verb or the like. In view of the pictoriality of our use of language, the endless possibilities of a metaphor and picturesque new applications of words, such attempts on the part of formal grammarians are bound to fail. If they have been at all influenced by Wittgenstein in taking this direction that can only have been through a misunderstanding.

Notes

1. See Zellig Harris, *Methods in Structural Linguistics* (Chicago: University of Chicago Press, 1951), pp. 160–2, including the footnote.

Im Anfang war die Tat

PETER WINCH

I

Philosophers these days distinguish between the truth-conditions of a proposition and the conditions for asserting that proposition. It is often said that, whereas in the *Tractatus* Wittgenstein stressed the first of these notions, the later development of his thought involved emphasis rather on the second. I do not think that this states the important changes in Wittgenstein's thought at all clearly and should like to consider why.

In *Tractatus*, 4.0312 Wittgenstein says that his fundamental thought is that "the 'logical constants' do not represent". This reflects his concern to give an account of logical inference such that the validity of an inference should not be made to look as though it depended on an appeal to something's "being the case". His account was couched in terms of a system of truth-functions generated by repeated applications of the operation of negation on elementary propositions the essence of which was that they could be either true or false. The account therefore seemed to need a demonstration that there could and must be such elementary propositions. The idea of elementary propositions as pictures (*Bilder*) of possible states of affairs belongs to this demonstration. This idea has many ramifications which I must ignore, but one of its essential aspects is the thought that elementary propositions must be logically independent of each other: and this is important to the case I want to develop.

If elementary propositions were not logically independent there would be relations of logical dependence between propositions, not captured by the *Tractatus* account of truth-functions. (In his post-*Tractatus* writings, of course, Wittgenstein very soon recognized that there are indeed such relations.)[1] Furthermore, it might seem that, without logically independent elementary propositions, we should be unable ever to assert anything at all. For if we are *ever* to be in a position to say that any proposition is true (or false) there must obviously be some propositions the truth (or falsity) of which we can determine without first determining the truth (or falsity) of some other.

But this leads to the doctrine of logically independent elementary propositions only because the *Tractatus* so austerely excludes those epistemological considerations which Wittgenstein later came to see as central to the discussion of such questions. That I can determine the truth or falsity of p independently of the truth or falsity of q does not require that p and q should be logically independent. I can see that this coat is blue (p) without questions about the truth or falsity of its being yellow (q) or red (r) entering into my reflections at all. Nevertheless p *can* only be true if q and r are both false.

The difficulty is dealt with (for instance in *Philosophical Remarks* and *Philosophical Grammar*) by substituting for the *Tractatus* view, that what we "lay against reality" are individual elementary propositions, the view that what we lay against reality are *systems* of propositions. This move goes along with recognizing that there are countless different such systems, involving different understandings of what it is for a proposition to "correspond with reality"; and hence with abandoning the attempt to give a single general account of what determining the truth or falsity of a proposition consists in. "A proposition is everything that can be true or false" *looks* as though it determines what a proposition is, only because we mistakenly think we have some independent grasp of truth and falsity enabling us to determine what is and is not a proposition. Whereas all we can say is "that we only predicate 'true' and 'false' of what we call a proposition".[2] Our understanding of how these terms are to be applied varies *pari passu* with our understanding of the propositions to which we apply them, and they cannot be used as points of reference for fixing the sense of the propositions.

The *Tractatus* had compared *Bilder* (and hence propositions) with measuring rods which we "apply to reality" (2.1512). Wittgenstein's later emphasis on diversity of course robs this comparison of its central place. But the comparison itself was insufficiently thought through, as is brought out in a difficult and important discussion in *Philosophical Grammar*, Part I, Sect. VI, §79, which is worth looking at closely for the light it throws on confusions which seem to me still endemic in treatments of our topic. The passage raises the question whether we should write:

"p" is true (as in the *Tractatus*)

or rather

p is true.

Shouldn't it be the latter? "The ink mark is after all not *true*; in the way it's black and curved." If we say that a *Satz* "agrees with reality", *of what* are we saying this? Let us say

p = This object is one metre long

and

"p" is true = This object has the length of this metre rule.

The second equation makes explicit the comparison of one thing with another which is supposed to be involved in the use of "true". The ruler must be taken here as standing in for the *Satz* "p"; it "agrees with reality" if its ends coincide with those of the object. To operate the analogy we should have to say the ruler "says" that this object is one metre long; and that the correspondence of the ends of the ruler with those of the object "says" that it is true that the object is one metre long. It's important that we're already in trouble here in trying to make the ruler and the correspondence of the ends "say" anything. We have to imagine perhaps that I simply produce the ruler and approach the object with it; and perhaps to interpret *this* as my saying that the object is one metre long. But it is apparent that this interpretation already presupposes a background of technique and standards; and this is what Wittgenstein is getting at when he says the whole comparison is wrong because the phrase "this metre rule" is *a description* and the phrase "metre rule" *the determination of a concept*. In other words my laying this piece of metal against this object is no more than just that, not a case of *measuring* the object, except in so far as the piece of metal is being *seen as* a metre rule, which is possible only within the whole context of the practice of metric measurement. This context determines the concept, *metre rule*, and thus provides the possibility of describing the piece of metal as "a metre rule".

I put the ruler and the object together and their ends coincide. That is (within the context of metric measurement) I can say that the object is as long as the metre rule; which, in terms of the comparison under examination, corresponds to the proposition " 'This object is one metre long' is true." Wittgenstein's comment is:

in " 'p' is true" the ruler enters immediately into the proposition. "p" represents here simply the length and not the metre rule.

In other words, the piece of metal (which I describe as a metre rule) belongs to the method of applying the concept *one metre long*; it enters the picture simply as a *standard* of length. The ruler – Wittgenstein says – is here "a purely geometrical appendage of the measured line". We might say that I am measuring the object against the concept *one metre long*, not against the piece of metal, though the latter plays a role, as "a purely geometrical appendage", in this application of the concept.

Wittgenstein's conclusion is:

It can also be put thus: The proposition " 'p' is true" can only be understood if one understands the grammar of the sign "p" as a propositional sign; not if "p" is simply the name of the shape of a particular ink mark. In the end one can only say that the quotation marks in the sentence " 'p' is true" are simply superfluous.

We can now expand the equivalence of "p is true" and "p" in the following way. "This object is as long as this metre rule" says the same as "This object is one metre long," while emphasizing that the result has been arrived at in a way appropriate for reaching such results. Analogously "p is true" says the same as "p", while emphasizing that "p" is being asserted on appropriate grounds; that is, it insists that I am justified in asserting p. And to say "p corresponds with reality" is just another way of insisting that we are justified (on appropriate grounds) in asserting p.

II

In the light of the foregoing, I want next to look at some things Bernard Williams and Michael Dummett have said about Wittgenstein.

Bernard Williams claims in his "Wittgenstein and Idealism"[3] that Wittgenstein's view of the relation between truth and warranted assertion is either "a triviality" or must have "quite amazing consequences". The amazing consequences are generated by the following argument-scheme:

(i) "S" has the meaning we give it.
(ii) A necessary condition of our giving "S" a meaning is Q.
ergo
(iii) Unless Q, "S" would not have a meaning.
(iv) If "S" did not have a meaning, "S" would not be true.
ergo
(v) Unless Q, "S" would not be true.

Williams comments:

Since any number of substitutions for Q in (ii) which relate to human existence, language use, etc. make it true for any "S" one likes, and since (i) is supposedly true for any "S", and (iv) for any true "S", we can get the truth of any true "S" dependent on human existence, etc.; that is, prove unrestricted idealism.

As he concedes, the argument is unworrying if (v) is taken to mean "Unless Q, 'S' would not express a truth," since that does not entail "Unless Q, not-S." He thinks, though, that Wittgenstein's so-called "theory of justified assertion" may prevent one from distinguishing "between the sentence 'S' expressing the truth, and what is the case if S".

But Williams's phrase "the sentence 'S' expressing the truth" is confusing here. (He slides from "expresses *a* truth" to "expresses *the* truth".) "'S' expresses the truth" *sounds* like another way of saying "S is true". But in the context of Williams's argument it telescopes two expressions:

(a) "'S' expresses a proposition"

and

(b) "S is true".

Given (a), quotation marks round "S" are not necessary in (b), and if (a) does not hold then (b) is as senseless as "S" itself. But if "S" is senseless so, obviously, is the expression "what is the case if S". Williams is quite wrong in supposing that Wittgenstein's position allows us to "get the *truth* [my italics] of any true 'S' dependent on human existence, language, use etc." If we *do* (with Williams) express Wittgenstein's thought as being "that the determinacy of reality comes from what we have decided or are prepared to count as determinate", it is imperative to remember that the "determinacy" in question is one of *sense* not of *truth*. Whether this reduces Wittgenstein's position to "a triviality" must be judged in the light of its role in his discussions of related questions.

This issue is quite central to any understanding of Wittgenstein's work, and I shall now pursue it further by discussing Michael Dummett's treatment of the dispute between "realist" and "anti-realist" conceptions of truth in chapter 13 of his *Frege, Philosophy of Language.*[4] As Wittgenstein is the only alleged[5] anti-realist named, I shall treat the anti-realist arguments advanced in Dummett's discussion as intended to apply to Wittgenstein, even when this is not explicitly stated.

Let me start by considering Dummett's explicit attribution of certain positions to Wittgenstein. He refers to *Remarks on the Foundations of Mathematics*, Part I, Appendix I,[6] part of which runs as follows:

So what does it mean to say a proposition '*is true*'? '*p*'*is true* $=p$. (This is the answer).

Presumably it is the remark in parentheses that leads Dummett to characterize Wittgenstein's view as being "that the sole explanation that can be given of the notion of truth consists precisely in the direct stipulation of the equivalence thesis".[7] However, the way Wittgenstein continues this passage makes it clear this is *not* what he is saying. His point is in fact very like that which Dummett himself makes earlier in the chapter when he comments on the unjustified optimism of those who think that the notions of truth and falsity will by themselves provide a sufficient basis for a theory of meaning. When Wittgenstein says: "So perhaps what is being asked is: under what circumstances does one assert a proposition?" he cannot be taken as *contrasting* the question with: "Under what circumstances is a proposition true?" For he has said that to call a proposition "true" *comes to* asserting that proposition. His point is even clearer in *Philosophical Investigations* (*PI*) where he says that in one sense what a proposition is, is determined "by the use of the sign in the language-game. And the use of the words 'true' and 'false' may be among the constituent parts of this game; and if so it belongs to our concept 'proposition' but does not '*fit*' it."[8] *On Certainty*, §200 reads:

Really "the proposition is true or false" only means that it must be possible to decide for or against it. But this does not say what such a decision is like.

So far from claiming, as Dummett says, that "the *whole* explanation of the word 'true'" as applied to a given *Satz* is given by the equivalence thesis, Wittgenstein is explicitly denying this. The equivalence thesis gives us all we can say *in general* about "true", but the real work is done by a detailed examination of how it is applied in particular cases, and such an examination yields different results in different cases. In the examinations which Wittgenstein undertakes he places at least as much emphasis as does Dummett on what the latter calls the "consequences" of accepting p (= accepting that p is true); and he *includes* in those consequences the possibility of applying the truth-functional calculus to it:

And to say that a proposition is whatever can be true or false amounts to saying: we call something a proposition when *in our language* we apply the calculus of truth-functions to it. (*PI*, §136)

Wittgenstein is emphasizing the dangers of looking at the matter the other way round; i.e. of starting with the calculus of truth-functions, supposing that our ability to construct this calculus rests on an intuitive idea of what it is for a proposition to be true or false. We then come across various expressions which look like propositions and assume that they can be slotted without more ado into the calculus. We suppose that *therefore* we understand what it is to specify truth-conditions for the putative proposition. Then, because our attention has been distracted from the actual circumstances (if any) in which we regard someone as entitled to assert p, we are tempted into a mythological account of p's truth-conditions. We find ourselves obsessed with a certain picture, but have no clear idea of what we are talking about when we speak of "the truth-conditions of p".

Dummett's realist plunges straight into such a mythology with his thesis "that a thought can be true only if there is something in virtue of which it is true", a thesis which he thinks requires an "ontological realm of facts to constitute that in virtue of which thoughts may be true".[9]

Read in one way the "realist thesis" is perfectly in order: namely, if it means that we cannot simply assert anything at will. – In what sense "cannot"? – Of course I can perfectly well arbitrarily utter certain words which, uttered in other circumstances, would constitute an assertion. But to the same extent as you thought I *had* uttered them arbitrarily, you would be disinclined to think I had made any assertion. Discussing a different, but closely related issue, Wittgenstein wrote:

"*Can* that happen?" – Certainly. Just describe it in detail and you will then see that the procedure you describe can perfectly well be imagined, although you will clearly not apply such and such expressions to it.[10]

Suppose I am walking with you down a familiar street and, out of the blue, point and say "That house is made of *papier maché*." Asked to explain, I offer nothing that you (or anybody else) would for a moment accept as a reason for thinking the house is made of *papier maché*. Being patient and concerned, you take me into the house and we feel the (perfectly normal) walls, doors, etc. I continue to utter my original words in the manner of one making an assertion. You wouldn't know *what* to make of my behaviour.

But was I not asserting something false? The question is whether I'm to be described as having "asserted something" at all. Someone will object at this point that you must have understood my words as an assertion, since you took me into the house and did the things appropriate to testing such an assertion. But it isn't of course denied that my behaviour was in many ways like that of one making an assertion. Still, you could equally well, better, be interpreted as testing whether I really was making the assertion which in *some* ways I seemed to be making.

The point becomes clearer if we imagine a society in which people are constantly doing that sort of thing, though they *also* "make genuine assertions" (i.e. speak in circumstances similar to those in which we do normally take people to be making assertions). Could the members of such a society treat the cases which strike us as anomalies in the same way as they treat the "genuine" cases? "Could they?" That means, can we imagine their doing things which we should be willing to *count* as "treating these cases in the same way", in respects relevant to what we understand by "assertions"? For instance, when someone says of a perfectly ordinary house that it's made of *papier maché*, they methodically demolish it, looking hard at the pieces of rubble and putting them alongside pieces of *papier maché*; and at the end of all this they say, "perhaps all the same it's made of *papier maché*". Would *we* say they were "investigating whether . . . etc.", and that they regarded the results as "inconclusive". Everybody must answer this for himself. My answer is that I shouldn't say this.

So the "realist's" thesis that a thought can be true only if there is something in virtue of which it is true can be given a perfectly acceptable interpretation. It has to be remembered that, on this interpretation, what this "something" is has to be understood in the context of what we are willing to count as a case of exhibiting it, and that this will vary enormously for different kinds of case. The trouble with the "realist", as is shown by his gesture towards an "ontological realm of facts to constitute that in virtue of which thoughts may be true", is that he has a vague picture of an interpretation of quite a different sort – which does have an obvious application to some kinds of case, but not to problematic ones. What distinguishes him from his opponent is not, as Dummett claims, that *he* makes truth-conditions fundamental to meaning whilst his opponent doesn't, but rather that he tries to interpret "truth-conditions" according to a certain model which he takes to be "the most elementary level": that of "observation-sentences".[11] He wants to apply this picture across the board because he mistakenly thinks there is a certain kind of systematic connection between the various cases exhibited by the calculus of truth-functions: overlooking the fact that there are *other* systems of operations which the truth-functional calculus does not capture, and which have to be presupposed before we can ever arrive at the necessary "elementary" bases on which the truth-functional operations can be performed.[12]

Dummett himself thinks that "our original grasp of there being something that makes a statement true derives from our use of basic forms of statement as reports of observation", and this provides us with "a model for what it would be to recognize the sentences as true by the most direct means". The "realist" believes that a sentence the truth of which is recognizable, if at all, only "indirectly" is one which "contains expressions whose sense is given in terms of perceptual or mental operations which go beyond our capacities", e.g. one involving quantification over an infinite domain. We can understand such a sentence "by analogy with the finite case, even though we are subject to the limitation of only being able to carry out finitely many observations or tests within a finite time".[13] Such an analogy can be developed via the postulation of "some suitably placed hypothetical being with sufficiently extended powers".[14]

This calls for several comments. In the first place, the contention that our original grasp of what it is for something to make a statement true derives from basic observation statements seems little more than an empiricist prejudice. "Realism without empiricism in philosophy, that's what is most difficult."[15] In any case, the passage from *Philosophical Grammar* (*PG*), I, VI, §79, which I discussed earlier, shows the complexity involved even in cases which we might be most inclined to call "basic reports of observation". And if the example of measuring length is considered insufficiently "basic", it has to be remembered that to report anything at all we have to apply a concept which has been determined in some way,[16] namely, as Wittgenstein repeatedly argues, by a system of *practices*.

As to the idea that, where quantification over an infinite domain is involved, we can grasp the truth of what is said "only indirectly", consider the following passage from *Philosophical Grammar*, II, ii, § 10:

> But what makes a sign an expression of infinity? What gives the peculiar character that belongs to what we call infinite? I believe that it is like the case of a sign for an enormous number. For the characteristic of the infinite, conceived in this way, is its enormous size.
>
> But there isn't anything that is an enumeration and yet not an enumeration; a generality that enumerates in a cloudy kind of way without really enumerating or enumerating to a determinate limit.
>
> The dots in "1 = 1 = 1 = 1. . . ." are just the four dots: a sign for which it must be possible to give certain rules. (The same rules, in fact, as for the sign "and so on ad inf.".) This sign does in a manner ape enumeration, but it isn't an enumeration. And that means that the rules governing it don't totally agree with those which govern an enumeration; they agree only up to a point.
>
> There is no third thing between the particular enumeration and the general sign.

Wittgenstein's point would be missed by anyone who took him to be simply contradicting Dummett's realist. He is of course attacking the whole distinction between "direct" and "indirect" needed for expressing the "realist's" case. The "realist" thinks that "1 + 1 + 1 + 1 . . ." is related to "1 + 1 + 1 + 1" as is, say "1 + 1 + 1 + 1 + 1 + 1 + 1 + 1", only, as it were, enormously more so – so much more so that it is (literally) beyond us to say how much more so. Whereas, though the expressions are indeed related, they are not related like that. The way in which we come to grasp the sense of the expression involving infinity is indeed difficult to describe (the difficulty springing from our not realizing when we should stop and simply say: that *is* the description): it is what Wittgenstein is describing in his discussions of *following a rule* and of the kind of training on which this rests. The response to the training *is* the grasping of the sense and not the taking of a hint about something that lies beyond.

Or let me put it this way: the response to the training is indeed a response – a movement beyond the training itself.[17] It consists in the adoption of a new concept, manifested in grammatical differences in the way the trainee talks. But the way he now talks is perfectly describable – differently of course from what fits the more "primitive" way of talking out of which the new concept developed: but *completely* describable nonetheless. The appearance of incompleteness comes only from a faulty grasp of the relation between the new and the old way of speaking in which the new is seen as simply a fresh application of an existing concept instead of the expression of a *different* concept.

The attempt by Dummett's realist to make his point by postulating "some suitably placed hypothetical being with sufficiently extended powers" is bound to fail. For this being is conceived *entirely* in terms of his "suitable placing" and "sufficiently extended powers": and *the whole trouble* right from the start was that we were supposed not to be able to describe these. Postulating a being able to make infinitely many observations in a finite time is not like postulating, on a much larger scale, a being who lives long enough to experience the whole life-cycle of a redwood tree, from its germination to its withering. We can describe what it would be to make the latter observations, not the former: hence we cannot describe a being who can make the former. If we could, we should never have experienced our original difficulty.

I think the preceding discussion provides the means of answering the final objection offered by Dummett's realist:

Replacement of the notions of truth and falsity, as the central notions for the theory of meaning, by those of verification and falsification must result in a different logic, that is, in the rejection of certain forms of argument which are valid on a classical, i.e., two-valued interpretation of the logical constants. In this respect, the linguistic practice which we actually learn is in conformity with the realist's conception of meaning: repudiation of realism as a philosophical doctrine entails revisionism about certain features of actual use.[18]

Dummett illustrates this objection with statements in the past tense. If such a statement is made, e.g. from memory, then the present memory "constitutes the verification of the assertion". This, he says, makes the past-tense sentence "undecidable", since what could decide it would only be a past observation of the event asserted to have occurred, and "a verification cannot precede the making of the assertion verified."[19]

However, "the linguistic practice which we actually learn" *does* involve our saying in certain cases that we do *know* (from memory) that such and such a past event occurred. We do not look for further verification; or, in cases where we do, "verification comes to an end" and at the end we say that the occurrence has been established. (Or, of course, that it has not: but it is not in dispute that we are often *in fact* unable to establish the truth about many matters.) Our linguistic practice does not consist in our saying that the past-tense statement *means the same* as the description of those present circumstances which we take as warranting us in making the statement. Rather *in* the present circumstances (which can of course be described) we do confidently make the past-tense statement and, beyond a certain point, we attach no sense to apparent "expressions of doubt" as to whether it is true or not. Misled by a certain picture we may, when philosophizing, find it strange that we should have such a practice, and this appearance of strangeness can only be dissipated by closer attention to what the practice is. This is the very reverse of "revisionism".

Dummett's realist is particularly concerned about those cases in which someone remembers "that either A or B without remembering whether A or not or whether B or not", concluding that such a disjunction cannot be interpreted "in terms of a notion of truth for such sentences which coincides with the existence of a warrant for asserting them".[20] Now Wittgenstein does not say that these "coincide". As we have noted, he says (amongst other things):

(1) p is true=p
(2) to understand the use of "true" and "false" in connection with a given "p", we should ask in what circumstances "p" is asserted.
(3) *One* feature of this use is the application to "p" of the truth-functional calculus.

Applying this to Dummett's case we have:

(1) "p or q is true"="p or q"
(2) "p or q" can be asserted when we can't assert "p" or assert "q"
(3) The truth-functional calculus has *already* been applied in the construction of "p or q".

If someone convinces me that not p and that not q, then I withdraw my original assertion. If he confirms that p (and/or that q) he confirms my original assertion. This is, as it were, part of the logical space to which my assertion belongs; there is certainly no departure from classical logic, no rejection of forms of argument "valid on a . . . two-valued interpretation of the logical constants".

Nor is there any revision of our actual use. It is a certain picture of the relation of that use to the truth-functional calculus which leads to "revisionism". Led by that picture to think that "elementary" propositions must occupy a special place in our language, we may come to think that no one has a right to insist on the truth of p or q unless he has a right to insist either on the truth of p or on the truth of q. As Dummett is himself pointing out, the truth of p or q may stand firmer for someone than that of either of its disjuncts; and it may be added that in asserting p or q he need have absolutely no interest in *which* of the disjuncts is true.

"Truth-conditions" is a logician's term of art. Its use may already presuppose an approach to questions about meaning which Wittgenstein is rejecting. This does not imply that he is denying that the words "true" and "false" play an important role in our understanding of propositions. To say that he *replaced* "truth-conditions" by "assertion-conditions" (another term of art) in the "theory of meaning" is misleading in its suggestion that he was offering an alternative theory of meaning. Wheareas his point was that the notion of meaning and its connection with truth and falsity is not to be elucidated in terms of a general theory at all.

III

Close to the surface of all the issues I have been discussing lies the question of the kind of "relation of language to the world" which is needed if we are to be able to *say* anything which is grounded in something independent. In the *Tractatus* the point of contact is located in the possibility of a direct "comparison" between an elementary proposition and a *Sachverhalt*; and this possibility in its turn depends on the role of "names" in the proposition whose meanings *are* their bearers: "objects" which constitute "the substance of the world". Names and objects, however, are presented as a purely logical requirement, something which just has to be accepted. We cannot ask any questions about them, since to do so we should have to use those very names in our questions and presuppose that they do have meaning. Compare *Tractatus*, 3.263 which speaks of explaining primitive signs by means of elucidatory propositions containing those very signs, the meanings of which must therefore already be known before the "elucidations" can be understood. Although Wittgenstein of course subsequently abandoned the misleading imagery associated with "names" and "objects", his insistence that "the harmony of thought and reality is to be found in the grammar of our language" and on the "arbitrariness" of grammar,[21] expresses an unremitting opposition to the idea that our ways of speaking can receive any justification from some sort of extra-linguistic insight into the relation between words and things.

Many philosophers have, however, thought they could offer such a justification. Russell tried to do so in "The Limits of Empiricism",[22] an article which stimulated Wittgenstein to develop, around 1937, some of his most thought-provoking ideas – ideas which prefigure much of what is central to his last writings, *On Certainty*.[23]

Russell argued that our words are causally connected with what we perceive and that this causal connection can itself be directly perceived, i.e. it is not inferred from repeated past experience, even though it may be set up by the development of habits involving previous experience.

But when I know that I said "cat" because there was a cat, I am not knowing that, in large numbers of similar instances, similar visual appearances have been followed by similar utterances . . . I am asserting something which I can know without going outside what is now happening. This is essential, since the knowledge is required for the connection of sensible occurrences with the verbal assertion of them.[24]

I think Russell's thought here is: if I had to "go outside" what is now happening, the evidence might show that there is, after all, no causal connection between my words and the sensible occurrences. That would mean I was mistaken in what I thought I meant, perhaps even in supposing that I meant anything at all. And if I can't ever be sure beyond the possibility of refutation that I mean something, how can I ever be sure that I mean anything at all. Perhaps all my utterances would turn out to be meaningless noises. So Russell's position is that our use of language must be based on an ultimate certainty, a knowledge *that something is so*, which is invulnerable to further falsification.

Wittgenstein agrees with Russell that we do often speak of one thing's being the cause of another without first establishing some general law by repeated observations or experiments. For instance, if I feel a tug on a cord which I am holding, look along it, and see someone pulling at the other end of it, I do not normally need further evidence to convince me that he caused the tug which I felt. This case is contrasted with that of a goat-farmer who experiments with various kinds of fodder to determine which is the cause of his goats' varying milk yield.[25]

On the other hand, our application of the word "cause" in the first kind of case (and in Russell's examples) is not itself based simply on our immediate experience of the moment ("without going outside what is now happening"). Wittgenstein wrote in a pocket note-book (in about 1937):

"I am immediately aware that my exclamation is caused by something." – So I'm immediately aware that the word "cause" fits this case? But remember that *words* are public property . . .

What if I said: The word "cause" fits my impression privately? – But "to fit" is a public word.

Ask yourself: What do we make this noise of words for?[26]

These remarks are very damaging to Russell's position, the heart of which is that we understand what our words mean only because we see them to be caused by something extra-linguistic; if this "perception of the cause" is itself conceivable only *within* an established use of language, the foundation for language, which Russell thought he had provided, collapses. He is simply going round in a circle – *within* language.

The point might be put like this: *Given* an established use of the word "cause", it is certainly possible to use it in cases where we have not conducted repeated observations and experiments to "establish the causal connection". Still, in calling A the cause of B we may be right or wrong and our judgment is vulnerable to further evidence. (This does not mean that we cannot be completely – and justifiably – certain that our judgment will *not* be overturned. That our judgment is immediate and confident doesn't make it *infallible*.)

It is just as if somebody claimed to have knowledge of human anatomy by intuition; and we say: "We don't doubt it; but if you want to be a doctor, you must pass all the examinations like anybody else."[27]

So Wittgenstein's first point in response to Russell is this: there is such a thing as "recognizing the cause of something immediately", but this is not an infallible, self-authenticating "knowing". At the same time, however, he recognizes that Russell is close to something important in believing that our use of language fundamentally involves an unhesitating response to situations on our part concerning which it cannot intelligibly be supposed that we "might be wrong": not because we are infallibly *right*, but because "the point is that there is no *right* (or wrong) about it. (And of course no one would say: 'I'm sure I'm right that I have pain.')"[28] I shall return to this later, but first I want to explore Wittgenstein's reasons for agreeing that an unhesitating "certainty" is fundamental to language.

The *basic form* of our game must be one in which there is no such thing as doubt. – What makes us sure of this? It can't surely be a matter of historical certainty.

"The basic form of the game can't include doubt." What we are doing here above all is to *imagine* a basic form: a possibility, indeed a *very important* possibility. (We often confuse what is an important possibility with historical reality.)[29]

So Wittgenstein describes various possible ways in which people might act and speak, where it might seem possible to say that hesitation, or doubt as to whether something is or is not the case, is, as it were, their point of departure. For instance:

So imagine a mother whose child is crying and holding his cheek. *One* kind of reaction to this is for the mother to try and comfort her child and to nurse him in some way or other. In this case there is nothing corresponding to a doubt whether the child is really in pain. Another case would be this: The usual reaction to the child's complaints is as just described, but under some circumstances the mother behaves sceptically. Perhaps she shakes her head suspiciously, stops comforting and nursing her child – even expresses annoyance and lack of sympathy. But now imagine a mother who is sceptical right from the very beginning: If her child cries, she shrugs her shoulders and shakes her head; sometimes she looks at him inquiringly, examines him; on exceptional occasions she also makes vague attempts to comfort and nurse him. – Were we to encounter such behaviour, we definitely wouldn't call it scepticism; it would strike us as queer and crazy. – "The game can't begin with doubting" means: we shouldn't call it "doubting" if the game began with it.[30]

To say, of the first of the cases described, that "there is nothing corresponding to a doubt", is to warn us against the temptation to think the mother is making an "unquestioning assumption" or "knows something intuitively". There is no question of her assuming or knowing anything; she just unhesitatingly *acts* in certain ways. *Given* such a background of unhesitating reactions, we can *then* imagine, as in the second case, forms of behaviour which we could regard as expressing doubt. But if she were to exhibit that sort of behaviour *without* such a background, as in the third case, we should not want to call it "the expression of doubt": "As things are, the *reasons* for doubting are reasons for leaving a familiar track," and "Doubt is a moment of hesitation and is, *essentially*, an exception to the rule."[31]

How is this discussion related to the issues raised earlier in this paper concerning the true–false "bipolarity" which belongs to our idea of a proposition? We *use* the terms "true" and "false" in contexts, for instance, where we are wondering or investigating whether something is so or not, hesitating whether we should accept that something is so, manifesting doubt as to whether something is so, or insisting that something is so in the face of scepticism: contexts involving the contemplation of two mutually exclusive possibilities. Without these human phenomena the words "true" and "false" would not have the sense they do have for us. That these phenomena are fundamental to the lives we lead has much to do with our preoccupation with "exploring the nature of things" or "finding out how things are". Hence it is very natural – and perfectly proper – that we should want to make the distinction between truth and falsity central in trying to account for the kind of harmony that obtains between our thought (and our language) and the world. Carefully investigating what is true and what false *is* the process of, as it were, achieving a close fit between our thoughts, beliefs and the way things actually are. But although the distinction between truth and falsity is indeed, in this sense, fundamental to the link between what we say and the way things are, it is not *the* 'primitive' link. Wittgenstein's discussions show this by demonstrating that the phenomena of human behaviour to which the use of "true" and "false" belongs would not have the sense they do have – would not be regarded as manifestations of doubt and questioning – without the background of a pattern of unquestioning responses: responses which are "unquestioning" in the sense that the contexts in which they occur do not make any room for the idea of a question's being asked. As Wittgenstein puts it, within the practice of investigating something (e.g. the cause of something):

something that we call doubt and uncertainty plays a role, but this is a second-order feature. In an analogous way it is characteristic of how a sewing machine functions that its parts may wear out and get bent, and its axles may wobble in their bearings, but still this is a second-order characteristic compared with the normal working of the machine.[32]

And again:

Language – I want to say – is a refinement, *im Anfang war die Tat* ('in the beginning was the deed').
First there must be firm, hard stone for building and the blocks are laid rough-hewn one on another. *Afterwards* it's certainly important that the stone can be trimmed, that it's not *too* hard.[33]

Goethe's "*Im Anfang war die Tat*" of course has considerable resonances. On the whole, the best thing to do with resonances is to leave them alone to resonate. However, Wittgenstein's quotation of the line reverberates through many different corners of his philosophy, and I should like to conclude by just gesturing in the direction of some of them. Goethe was drawing attention to the *creative* role of "the deed", and in Wittgenstein this is expressed in the importance ascribed to certain primitive human actions and reactions for *concept-formation*. This gets its most general form of treatment in the pervasive discussions of what is involved in learning and following a rule. Again, in his discussion of the role of ostensive definition in the conferring of names on objects, he draws attention to the fact that when I see someone point with his finger, I characteristically don't look *at* his finger, but *away* from it in what I call "the direction in which he is pointing" – and I *have* this latter concept only by virtue of the fact that I *do* naturally, along with everyone else, react to his outstretched arm and finger in that way. In the 1937 notes to which I have been referring Wittgenstein emphasizes the importance for our concept of causality of a certain typical reaction of people towards states of affairs they want to get rid of.

> *We react to the cause.*
> Calling something 'the cause' is like pointing and saying: "He's to blame!"
> We instinctively get rid of the cause if we don't want the effect. We instinctively look from what has been hit to what has hit it. (I am assuming that we do this.)[34]

Simone Weil makes a closely analogous point in the emphasis she places on *methodical ways of working* in our dealings with nature, as what brings to birth the concept of natural necessities. – If, for instance, we want to lift a stone that is too heavy for us, we, as it may seem paradoxically, direct our immediate attention away from the stone and look for something we can use as a lever. Simone Weil also speaks of the relation men have to physical objects, which makes it possible for them to distinguish their various properties, as a sort of "dance":[35] and she means, quite literally, a pattern of movements of people's *bodies*, involved, for example in distinguishing an object's weight, shape, texture, flexibility and so on. These patterns of movement don't *follow* a prior recognition of such properties, they belong to the formation and application of the concepts of the properties in question. The point Simone Weil is making here is closely akin to Wittgenstein's. Something similar is involved in the way Wittgenstein treats our reaction to a man's groans and writhings in relation to the concept of pain and even to the concept of a human being:

How am I filled with pity *for this man*? How does it come out what the object of my pity is? (Pity, one may say, is a form of conviction that someone else is in pain.)[36]

— It is instructive to reflect on the contrast between Wittgenstein's treatment of this subject and Strawson's.[37] Strawson's starting point is the *statement* in which a predicate is ascribed to an identified subject; Wittgenstein's is the primitive *reaction*. Not, of course, that Wittgenstein denies that we can make true and false assertions about persons: his point is that these assertions make use of a concept which is the creation of a mode of acting to which the true–false bipolarity does not apply. "The deed" now fills the role taken in the *Tractatus* by the relation of "name" to "object". One important difference is that deeds, unlike "objects" can be described; another is that emphasis on the deed opens the door to an understanding of how *new* concepts can be created and to a way of grasping concepts and ways of thinking very different from our own. And just because there is no application for the true–false polarity at the level of the deed, this is *not* to open the door to "idealism" or "relativism".

Notes

1. Cf. for example, *Philosophical Remarks* (*PR*), VIII; *Philosophical Grammar* (*PG*), Part I, Appendix 4.
2. *Philosophical Investigations* (*PI*), §136.
3. In *Understanding Wittgenstein*, Royal Institute of Philosophy Lectures, vol. 7, 1972/3 (London: Macmillan, 1974), pp. 93–4.
4. Michael Dummett, *Frege, Philosophy of Language* (London: Duckworth, 1973).
5. Cf. *Bemerkungen über die Grundlagen der Mathematik* (*BGM*), (Berlin: Suhrkamp, 1974), VI, §23: "Nicht Empirie und doch Realismus in der Philosophie, das ist das schwerste." I quote from this 1974 German edition as it includes material which I wish to cite and which is not in the Blackwell edition of 1956.
6. Teil I, Anhang III in the 1974 Suhrkamp edition of *BGM*.
7. *Frege*, p. 458.
8. *PI*, I, §136.
9. *Frege*, p. 464.
10. L. Wittgenstein, "Ursache und Wirkung: Intuitives Erfassen", edited with supplementary notes by Rush Rhees, and with a translation by Peter Winch: "Cause and Effect: Intuitive Awareness", *Philosophia*, vol. 6, nos 3–4 (Sept.–Dec. 1976), p. 415.

11. *Frege*, pp. 466–7.
12. Cf. *PR*, VIII, especially §76.
13. *Frege*, p. 465.
14. *ibid.*, p. 467.
15. *BGM*, VI, §23.
16. Cf. the discussion of "seeing an aspect" in *PI*, II, xi.
17. Cf. *BGM*, VI, §10:

    "You extract a theorem (eine Lehre) from the proof. So the sense of the theorem must be independent of the proof; for otherwise it could never have been separated from the proof.

    Analogously I can remove the lines of construction from a drawing and leave the rest there.

    So it is as if the proof did not determine the sense of the proposition proved; and yet again as if it did.

    But isn't it like that with every verification of every proposition?"
18. *Frege*, p. 468.
19. *ibid.*, p. 469. For further discussion of this issue see *PR*, V.
20. p. 469. The discussion in *PR*, IX, is very relevant to the issue; but I cannot go into it here.
21. *Zettel*, §320.
22. *Proceedings of the Aristotelian Society*, 1935–6.
23. See note 10 above.
24. *op. cit.*, p. 136.
25. "Cause and Effect: Intuitive Awareness", pp. 416–17.
26. *ibid.*, pp. 429–30.
27. *ibid.*, p. 419.
28. *ibid.*, p. 430.
29. *ibid.*, p. 411.
30. *ibid.*, p. 414.
31. *ibid.*, p. 412.
32. *ibid.*, p. 420.
33. *ibid.*, p. 420.
34. *ibid.*, p. 410.
35. Simone Weil, *Leçons de philosophie* (from the notes of Anne Reynaud) (Paris: Plon 1959); translated by Hugh Price as *Lectures on Philosophy*, with an introduction by Peter Winch (Cambridge: Cambridge University Press, 1978).
36. *PI*, I, §287. For further discussion see Peter Winch, "Eine Einstellung zur Seele", *Proceedings of the Aristotelian Society*, 1980–1.
37. P. F. Strawson, *Individuals* (London: Methuen 1964) (chapter on "Persons") – though his essay "Freedom and Resentment" contains suggestions of a position closer to Wittgenstein's.

Wittgenstein's Full Stop

D. Z. PHILLIPS

In *Zettel*, §314, Wittgenstein describes what he calls

a remarkable and characteristic phenomenon in philosophical investigation:
the difficulty – I might say – is not that of finding the solution but rather of
recognizing as the solution something that looks as if it were only a preliminary
to it. 'We have already said everything. – Not anything that follows from this,
no *this* itself is the solution!'

This is connected, I believe, with our wrongly expecting an explanation,
whereas the solution of the difficulty is a description, if we give it the right
place in our considerations. If we dwell upon it, and do not try to get beyond
it.

The difficulty here is: to stop.

In Wittgenstein's work the difficulty of stopping, the urge to go beyond
a certain point in a search for explanations, justifications and foundations
is explored in a variety of contexts. The nature of the difficulties and
temptations varies and does not form a neat unity. Nevertheless, the
difficulties and temptations all involve in some way or other a failure to
stop when one should stop.

We want to ask how we know that we are seeing a tree when we are
directly confronting it, how we know we are in pain while we are
experiencing it, how we know that others are happy when we see them
smile and laugh, how we know that a certain number will not occur in a
mathematical progression, how we know that we are justified in
drawing a statistical curve, how we know that the colour we see is red,
and so on. Many commentators on Wittgenstein's work have written
penetratingly on these various topics. It is an interesting fact, however,
that some of them are strangely silent regarding Wittgenstein's remarks

on ethics and religion. Of course, there is no guarantee that what a philosopher says on various topics is equally worthwhile, and these commentators may feel that there were blind-spots in his work. When they themselves write on such topics they certainly do so as if Wittgenstein had never said a word on such matters. Yet I believe that there is a more adequate explanation of their silence, one that is philosophical in character. It has to do with Wittgenstein's insistence on the hold which certain philosophical tendencies have on us, tendencies to say what cannot be said. The hold of these tendencies is stronger than we realize. Thinking we are free of them we turn to some new field, in which philosophical difficulties arise, only to find that they reassert their hold on us with all their old force. Thus we may be prepared to say with Wittgenstein in *On Certainty* that to question certain propositions which are held fast by all that surrounds them is senseless. If our trust in these propositions were undermined, if we could not show in our actions that we took these things for granted, we would not say that we were mistaken, since we would not know any more what it would mean to speak of knowing, not knowing, believing, not believing, being right or being mistaken, about such things. At certain points we say, "But this is what I mean by saying it's a tree, a person, or a certain colour." Or in physics we say, "This is what I mean when I say that the conclusion is justified." Wittgenstein asks, "Is it wrong for me to be guided in my actions by the propositions of physics? Am I to say that I have no good ground for doing so? Isn't precisely this what we call a 'good ground'?" (*On Certainty*, §608) Our request for justifications in our talk about physical objects, persons, colours and physics, comes to an end. Our assurance is shown in the way we do go on, in the way we act with respect to these things. But just as we are about to accept these conclusions Wittgenstein juxtaposes the following example which illustrates how deep are the tendencies to resist them:

Supposing we met people who did not regard that as a telling reason. Now, how do we imagine this? Instead of the physicist, they consult an oracle. (And for that we consider them primitive.) Is it wrong for them to consult an oracle and be guided by it? – If we call this 'wrong' aren't we using our language-game as a base from which to *combat* theirs? (*On Certainty*, §609)

This resistance, Wittgenstein claims, is due to a misunderstanding of the nature of our language-games. There is a continuity between the questions raised in *On Certainty* and what Wittgenstein called "the great question" in the *Philosophical Investigations* (*PI*) (§65), namely, the question of whether one ought, having noted the multiplicity of language-games, go on to search for something in common to them, some essence, which would make them all language. It is our desire to look beyond the language-games involved in religious beliefs and rituals which makes it difficult for us to see how Wittgenstein's full stop has any application here. We may be unable to see its application even when we can see its application elsewhere clearly.

It may be that Wittgenstein's influence on the philosophy of religion has aroused more hostility recently than any other aspect of his work. It has been said that "the years since the Second World War have been a sorry time for the philosophy of religion in English-speaking countries", and that this is due, not least, to the disastrous influence of Wittgenstein.[1] The blame is not attributed so much to Wittgenstein himself as to his influence, and we have seen the growth of a philosophy by innuendo by which it is hinted that what Wittgenstein is said to have said about religion and rituals is not related closely to the rest of his work, cannot be found in his work, or is an aberration on the part of some of those influenced by him. Complaints such as these have been heard for more than a decade.[2] Their essential content can be summed up in terms of a recent version:

The idea of autonomous language games, each of which can be understood only from within, by those who actually play the game in question, and which is therefore immune to all external criticism, seems to me open to objection . . . If it is carried to a point at which any fruitful dialogue between religious belief and critical philosophy is excluded, theology retreats into a kind of ghetto, cut off from the cultural life of which philosophy is one expression.[3]

Kenny quotes these remarks with approval. Clearly it is thought that to speak of Wittgenstein's full stop here puts a stop to many commendable activities, understanding, dialogue, criticism. Philosophical attempts at throwing light on the nature of religious beliefs or rituals have been seen as attempts to shield them against criticism. This alleged anti-intellectualism and conservatism has been given the name 'fideism', a term which, unfortunately, seems here to stay.[4] In this paper, I want to show how these misgivings are unjustified, do not follow from a proper reading of Wittgenstein's remarks, and take us away from the central questions which Wittgenstein was raising.

Language-Games and Wittgenstein's Full Stop

First, I shall try to show how Wittgenstein's remarks on language-games give rise to some of the misgivings I have mentioned. Given Wittgenstein's use of the term, it makes no sense to speak of a confused language-game. H. O. Mounce reminds us that one of Wittgenstein's reasons for introducing the notion of a language-game,

> was to free us from the idea that logic constitutes what he called 'the *a priori* order of the world', the idea that logic is, as it were, 'prior to all experience'. He wished us to see rather, that logic – the difference between sense and nonsense – is learnt, when, through taking part in a social life, we come to speak a language. Logic is to be found not 'outside' language but only within the various language games themselves.

This implies ". . . that the sense of any language game cannot itself be questioned; for one could do so only on the assumption which Wittgenstein rejects, that logic does lie 'outside' it".[5] In a footnote to the phrase "the sense of any language game cannot itself be questioned", Mounce adds, "the 'cannot', of course, is logical. I do not mean that if one tried one would fail, but that it would be senseless to try" (p. 349). Now, if one argues that there are distinctive language-games involved in rituals or religious beliefs it follows that it makes no sense to question their sense. But, surely, people do respond to religious beliefs by saying, "That belief makes no sense" or "I no longer see anything in that belief." So it seems that if one does say that there are distinctive language-games associated with rituals and religion, one at the same time protects those rituals and that religion from criticism. But religious practices and rituals *are* criticized, so it seems that to interpret Wittgenstein in this way is to indulge in conservatism and protectionism. Kenny says, "The concept of language-games is an obscure and ambiguous one in Wittgenstein's own writings: in the hands of some of his religious admirers it has become a stone-wall defence against any demand for a justification of belief in God" (p. 145).

At this point, it is tempting to take a short-way-out of these difficulties. One could do so by suggesting that one must make a distinction between the notion of a language-game on the one hand, and the notion of modes of discourse or a practice on the other. By contrasting language-games with modes of discourse one might approach a normative view of language-games. Modes of discourse could be criticized because they might distort language-games in some way or other. Thus it would not be sufficient to appeal to the fact that these are moral or religious modes of discourse to avoid the charge of senselessness. Thus one might say that "Language has a variety of uses, and people who speak a language frequently use that language for religious purposes."[6] But what does it mean to speak of language being used for religious purposes? Is it like saying that an argument is being used for political or prudential purposes, where the status of the argument is quite distinct from the purposes for which it is employed?

Consider another contrast. Could we say that the only difference between moral and prudential commendation is in the different purposes for which the concept of commendation is employed? Wittgenstein would not have agreed with this way of putting the matter. In his "Lecture on Ethics"[7] Wittgenstein wants to distinguish between what he calls absolute and relative uses of 'ought'. So if we compare "You ought to keep your matches dry" and "You ought to treat her decently" are we to say that we have here two instances of doing the same thing – of commending? The moral context makes a difference to what the commending comes to. Bell wants to say of religion, what he would probably say of ethics also, namely, that

uses of language . . . do not convert the status of 'utterances', 'assertions' or 'expressions' to a different level of linguistic understanding . . . Thus when 'religious' is used with 'language' it should draw our attention to the fact that certain concepts are being used for religious purposes, and not that some kind of semantic or substantive shift has been made to a new type of discourse. (p. 6)

But this cannot be said of the moral use of 'ought'. One cannot say that the concept is used for moral purposes, since it is these so-called purposes which give the concept its distinctive grammatical status. One cannot distinguish between the language-game and the moral issues about which commendations are made, since it is precisely the character of the issues which affect the character of the commendation. But do religious beliefs have a distinctive grammatical status? In fact Bell's article contains an admission of such grammatical distinctions, but he does not seem to realize its significance for his more general comments: "'Asking, thanking, cursing, greeting, praying': In theological and religious behaviour these language-games usually have liturgical functions which only partially parallel their ordinary use" (p. 13). So this short-way with our difficulties does not succeed.

Another, more subtle, but equally unsatisfactory attempt at a short-way with our difficulties can be found in H. O. Mounce's attempt to distinguish between language-games and practices. This does not involve a normative view of language-games. It is not denied that distinctive language-games may be involved in modes of discourse or practices, but simply that one cannot identify every practice with a language-game. To do so would preclude the possibility of speaking of confused practices. However pervasive a practice, it may nevertheless be confused. The suggestion advanced is that Wittgenstein usually meant by language-games, not a practice, but a set of concepts which run through almost any conceivable practice:

When we speak of our certainty that another person is in pain, for example, we play a different game from when we speak of our certainty that there is a table in the next room. Now . . . it would be difficult to suppose that what Wittgenstein here means by a language game is anything like a practice such as conducting scientific experiments or worshipping in church. For example, one may speak of people coming together to conduct a scientific experiment but hardly of their coming together to exercise the concept of pain; one may speak of a person giving up religious worship but not of his giving up the use of the notion of an object. What we here mean by a language game is not a practice or set of practices but a set of concepts which may enter into almost any practice we can imagine.[8]

There are difficulties, as we shall see, in Mounce's attempt to distinguish between language-games and practices in Wittgenstein, but in any case, how general a phenomenon is the distinction he draws of the examples Wittgenstein provides? Mounce suggests it is general:

For example, one instance of a language game is giving an order. Now if a person gives an order one may say that he is performing an action but hardly that he is engaged in an activity or practice. One may say, it is true, that an order can be given in the *course* of an activity. The point is, however, that in saying this, one does not have any particular activity in mind. Almost any activity can be the occasion for giving an order. Similar remarks apply to most of Wittgenstein's other examples.[9]

This is an overstatement and oversimplification of Wittgenstein's notion of language-games. That it is an overstatement can be seen from the examples of language-games Wittgenstein provides in *PI*, §23. While one has examples such as "Giving orders and obeying them", "Asking", "Thanking", etc., one also has examples such as "Presenting the results of an experiment in tables and diagrams" and "Solving a problem in practical arithmetic." Wittgenstein says that the instances are countless and extremely varied. Nor will it do to say that what giving an order amounts to always comes to the same thing. "What the general commands," "What the gods command" and "What the state commands" are importantly different. I mean that the grammar of "command" is importantly different. This can be illustrated by Wittgenstein's own examples of language-games. He gives the following list: "Asking, thanking, cursing, greeting, praying" (*PI*, §23). Clearly, praying, worshipping, is an example of an activity which is also called a language-game. It makes sense to speak of people coming together for this purpose, and of their giving up praying. But, more importantly, we cannot say without qualification of asking, thanking and cursing that whereas they can occur in the course of a wider activity one need not have any particular activity in mind. Failure to keep in mind the activity in question may lead to the ignoring of important conceptual differences. For example, it is obvious that one asks and thanks for things in prayer. It is also the case that people have cursed God. If the activity of praying made no conceptual difference to what asking and thanking amount to, its inclusion in the list of language-games would be superfluous. It cannot be said that the difference between asking God for something and asking another human being for something resides in the resources of him to whom the request is made, since this would not introduce any conceptual change into the nature of the asking. The presence of prayer in the list of language-games means that Wittgenstein thought that some conceptual distinction is involved. I cannot explore this conceptual difference here, but I have suggested elsewhere that asking and thanking in prayer is to come to a certain kind of understanding of those features of our lives which prompt our gratitude and ingratitude and occasion our desires.[10] Similarly, conceptual differences would emerge from a comparison of cursing God with cursing another human being. Just as we can say, "My friend forgives me, but I cannot forgive myself," but not, "God forgives me, but I cannot forgive myself," so, in one context at least, one can curse another person and still find life meaningful, whereas to curse God is to curse the day that one was born.

For the above reasons I think Mounce's distinction between language-games and practices will not do. More importantly it obscures the importance of the notion of a practice in Wittgenstein. One cannot speak of conceptual distinctions as though they were logically or temporally prior to practices since, for Wittgenstein, the language-game is rooted in practice, in how we take things, in what we do. For example, we cannot separate the conceptual distinctions involved in the language-games we play with colours and pains from the ways in which we react and respond since the concepts are themselves rooted in these common reactions and responses, by these practices. Without the common practices, there would be no concepts concerning colours or pains.

So it seems as though our problem still remains. If we cannot seek short-cuts to our difficulties by distinguishing between language-games on the one hand and modes of discourse on the other, and if we say that rituals and religious beliefs are rooted in certain practices, does it follow that Wittgenstein has left no room for criticism of these practices? The difficulty remains.

Rituals, Beliefs and Applications in Human Life

Let us now try to approach the difficulty from another direction. Wittgenstein insisted that each language-game is complete. It is not a partial or confused attempt to indicate something else to which it approximates. But this very claim of completeness with respect to language-games involved with rituals or religion has again led people to feel that this puts a full stop to any interaction between religious practices and other features of human life. These practices begin to look more like esoteric games, just as, if one thought of building activity as similarly cut off from all that surrounds it it begins to look more like a game with building blocks.[11] Here the analogy between language and games begins to limp, since although we do not say that all games make one big game, we do say that people engaged in the various language-games are engaged in the same language. It would be misleading to ask how many language-games need to be played in order to describe what is going on as language, but, clearly, it is a fact that many of the language-games we do play would not make sense were there not language-games independent of them. This applies to rituals and religious practices. One could not have songs and dances concerning the harvest unless independently of such songs and dances one had activities concerning the harvest, sowing and reaping and notions concerning what constitutes a good or bad harvest, and so on. Similarly, there would be little point in prayers of thanks, confession and petition, if independently of them there were not purposive activities, successes and failures, hopes and frustrations, good acts and evil acts. Otherwise, what would be brought to God in prayer? The prayer would have no substance.

If, however, we admit all this, must we not also admit that there is two-way traffic involved? Just as various events and activities in human life can be celebrated in ritual or brought before God under the aspect of prayer, may not the aspects of rituals and prayers themselves be changed by these various events and activities? And if this is admitted, may not their aspect change for the worse, sometimes, may not confusion and distortion set in? May they not cease to be distinctive language-games? These questions must be answered in the affirmative, but there is no reason to think that Wittgenstein cannot allow such an answer. On the contrary, one cannot ascribe to Wittgenstein the view that anything that is called religious or ritualistic is free from confusion.[12] That much is clear from the following passage from "Remarks on Frazer's *Golden Bough*" (RF):

We should distinguish between magical operations and those operations which rest on a false, oversimplified notion of things and processes. For instance, if someone says that the illness is moving from one part of the body into another, or if he takes measures to draw off the illness as though it were a liquid or a temperature. He is then using a false picture, a picture that doesn't fit. (p. 31)

Wittgenstein, apparently, had in mind here quack doctors and certain kinds of faith-healing. But he *also* thought that confusion could be found in practices which did not purport to be substitutes for science. In a remark to Drury Wittgenstein said that myths and rites were closer to metaphysical than to scientific errors. To illustrate what Wittgenstein may have had in mind contrast acupuncture with sticking pins in an effigy. Acupuncture may have various consequences, some good, some bad. But whatever one's view of its status, it clearly aims at achieving ends similar to those of other medical methods. But sticking pins in an effigy may not have an aim in that sense, any more than a war dance in conducting a war. How, then, does a ritual tell us something? Here the distinction between a language-game and a form of life is important for Wittgenstein. How the language-game, certain ritualistic songs and dances, say, is taken, depends on its connection with other things. It does not convey its meaning in itself, any more than the act of pointing does. To think otherwise is to adopt what Wittgenstein would call a magical view of meaning. This larger context of human life in which we see how a language-game is taken Wittgenstein calls a form of life. The notion of a form of life is essential in seeing in what sense a ritual can say something.

The ritual may contain words and gestures peculiar to the ritual, but it will also contain words and gestures which have an application in the non-ritualistic contexts of life. Without this application the ritual could not have its power and its force. Without it, as we have seen, it becomes an esoteric game. And yet this notion of the power of the ritual may breed confusion: the idea that the power resides in the words themselves, a common idea where magic is concerned. The confusion involved may be akin to metaphysical confusion. Consider the following example:

I point with my hand and say 'Come here'. A asks 'Did you mean me?' I say 'No, B'. – What went on when I meant B (since my pointing left it in no doubt which I meant)? – I said those words, made that gesture. Must still more have taken place, in order for the language-game to take place? But didn't I already know, while I was pointing, whom I meant? Know? Of course – going by the usual criteria of knowledge. (*Zettel*, §22)

The confusion here is the desire to follow "He meant B" with the question, "How does he mean B?," expecting an answer in terms of a process or power which somehow accompanies the words, or in terms of some inherent power in the act of pointing. Understanding lies in seeing that meaning here depends on the shared application that the words and the gestures have in this context. A similar confusion may arise in rituals in thinking that the power lies in the words or in the gestures: the curse is spoken, the wizard points, the man falls.

To see how the ritual speaks one must take account of its application in human life. Compare the following:

For how can it be explained what 'expressive playing is'? Certainly not by anything that accompanies the playing – What is needed for the explanation? One might say: a culture. – If someone is brought up in a particular culture – and then reacts to music in such-and-such a way, you can teach him the use of the phrase, 'expressive playing'. (*Zettel*, §164)

What we need to bring in to show how a ritual says something is its role in a culture. That role in magic and religion has much to do with the formal character of the ritual. Certain features of everyday life are formalized, set apart, celebrated at set times, solstices, equinoxes, phases of the moon, birth, death, harvest: the exact words are to be repeated in the exact order, surrounded by sanctions and responses of distinctive kinds.

It is this application in human life which is important, but which, as in the case of the gesture, "Come here" or expressive playing, may be distorted if it is thought that the power is an inherent property of the words, something accompanying them, as it were. The temptation to think this is particularly strong if the ritual does contain gestures and words which, in non-ritualistic circumstances, *would* be instances of ways of attaining certain ends. Wittgenstein warns us of this as follows:

The way music speaks. Do not forget that a poem even though it is composed in the language of information is not used in the language-game of giving information. (*Zettel*, § 160)

What underlies the temptation to think otherwise in these examples may be akin to what underlies the temptation towards the metaphysical conclusion about the connection between words and meanings. This is *one* way in which a connection might be established between magic and metaphysics.[13]

Consider another example. Apparently, in an earlier manuscript than his "Remarks on Frazer", Wittgenstein says that he finds the role of the scapegoat in rituals an inappropriate symbolism. It is not too difficult to understand the common enough conception in tribal societies of one man taking on himself the sins of another. The misdeeds of the fathers are visited on their children and on their children's children. Neither is it difficult to understand acts of self-immolation by which a priest may take on himself the sins and the guilt of his people. Neither is it hard to understand a longing on the part of people, through a ritual or sacrament, to be freed of the burden of their sins so that they may walk again with God. The difficulty is in seeing how any of this can be achieved through an animal. What does it mean to speak of an animal feeling remorse for his own misdeeds, let alone being able to remove the sins of a people? Consider the following comment which, to some extent, though not entirely, recognizes the difficulty:

On the ritual of the scapegoat, Matthew Henry observes that it 'had been a jest, nay an affront to God, if he himself had not ordained it' . . . But in these days can we any longer say that God ordained it? Ritual may be a substitute for true religion, or it may be its natural and spontaneous expression . . . Men may take a magical view of the sacraments, as of such rites as the scapegoat . . . It is obvious that sins could not really be transferred to a goat. But can sins be transferred at all? . . . Christ, as identified with man in his shame and sin, rejected by men and driven away bearing their sins and done to death for their forgiveness, is symbolically depicted, crudely and inadequately yet really, in the scapegoat.[14]

Notice that here one has the possibility of criticism within a tradition. The ritual concerning the scapegoat is called crude and inadequate. Wittgenstein might say that this crudity – and inadequacy – is partly connected, at least, with the confusion in the role attributed to an animal in the ritual. Thinking that the scapegoat can take away sins serves to obscure the perfectly legitimate longings of a people to be freed from the burdens of their sins; the sense which can be made of such longings changes, or what such longings amount to changes. Of course, the prophets criticized such magical conceptions of rituals. It might be instructive to compare how the belief, that one's sins are washed away connected with the practice of bathing in a holy river, may develop in diverse directions, some religious, others superstitious. A mechanistic view of what it is to lose one's sins may go hand in hand with conferring quasi-causal properties on the river. The power of baptism, let us say, in the river, for the remission of sins, may be partly confused in much the same way as the idea that the efficacy of a phrase resides in its inherent power: a baptism of meaning. In saying that the symbolism of the scapegoat jars, Wittgenstein is showing how reflection and criticism within religion may have affinities with the discussion of philosophical confusions.[15]

In the light of these considerations of how Wittgenstein shows that confusions of various kinds may enter into religions and rituals we can see that Coplestone's misgivings about a lack of fruitful dialogue between religious belief and critical philosophy are seen to be unfounded. Similarly we can see how Passmore's reaction to the distinction between modes of discourse is misplaced when he says that it "has recently attracted a good many admirers, particularly amongst those who desire to be uncritically religious without ceasing to be critically philosophical".[16] We have seen that Wittgenstein's views do not rule out criticism and that its possibility comes, not from distinguishing between language-games on the one hand, and modes of discourse and practices on the other, but from considering what may happen to certain language-games in the course of their application in human life.[17]

The Non-Derivability of Language-Games and the Desire for Explanation

In the previous section we saw how certain misunderstandings could arise from Wittgenstein's claim that language-games are complete in themselves. Yet, despite these misunderstandings which brought out certain limits in the analogy between language and games, this still does not affect the positive element in the analogy which was Wittgenstein's main purpose in using it; it does not affect his insistence on the non-derivability of language-games. Acknowledging the limitations in the analogy does not lead to the view put forward by Hepburn, Hick and Nielsen, namely, that distinctive language-games in rituals or religion require a further justification, foundation, or even verification. It is tempting to assume that since some practices may be confused, those which are not must be so by virtue of being well-founded. This temptation must be resisted. To say that the force of a religious or ritualistic response. cannot be appreciated in isolation from the form of life of which that response is a part, is not to say that there must be a further justification of the response; the response need not be related to that which surrounds it as a hypothesis is related to the evidence for it, a conclusion is related to its premises, or a belief to its reasons.[18] Once the response is elucidated one may say no more from within philosophy than, "Human life is like that." Our task is a descriptive one. In this task the big question about language will keep coming up, since there will always be the temptation to think that what we have before us are incomplete forms of expression awaiting completion in a wider system.

In his "Remarks on Frazer", Wittgenstein was simply examining one form which the urge to regard expressions in ritual as incomplete may take. There are important connections between Wittgenstein's remarks on Frazer and his remarks on Schlick's *Ethics*. Although in 1930 he still speaks of ethics as thrusting against the limits of language, he also says that he regards it "as very important to put an end to all the chatter about ethics". What he meant by this principally was the various attempts to give values a foundation, an explanation. Speaking of such explanations he says, "Whatever one said to me I would reject it; not indeed because the explanation is false, but because it is an *explanation*."[19]

Similarly, Wittgenstein's reason for rejecting Frazer's explanations is not that they are false, but that they are explanations and as such take us away from the philosophically arresting features of the rituals he is discussing. In the earlier set of remarks on Frazer, written about 1931,

Wittgenstein speaks as though we had in our possession, in the language, a principle by which all the different ritualistic practices could be ordered. But as Rhees points out in his introductory note, by the time he comes to the second set of remarks, at least five years later, this is not so. Here, to imagine a ritual is to imagine it in a form of life. Rhees says,

> It will in fact be helpful if we *do* hold on to the kinship between ritual and language here, not because ritual is a form of language, but because in order to understand *language* it is *also* necessary to look to the lives of the people who take part in it. What we call language, or what we call *'saying something'* is not determined by some 'knowledge of the language' which each of us carries 'within his own mind'. What *I* would call 'saying something', perhaps because it is correctly formed or constructed on every count, would *not* be 'saying something' unless it had what Wittgenstein called 'an application in our life'.[20]

When this application is considered, it should put an end to the chatter about rituals, just as it should put an end to the chatter about ethics. And when this is seen, philosophical clarity is achieved. Drury brings out the matter well:

> Frazer thinks he can make *clear* the origin of the rites and ceremonies he describes by regarding them as primitive and erroneous scientific beliefs. The words he uses are, 'We shall do well to look with leniency upon the errors as inevitable slips made in the search for truth.' Now Wittgenstein made it clear to me that on the contrary the people who practised these rites already possessed a considerable scientific achievement, agriculture, metalworking, building, etc., etc.; and the ceremonies existed alongside these sober techniques. They are not mistaken beliefs that produced the rites but the need to express something; the ceremonies were a form of language, a form of life. Thus today if we are introduced to someone we shake hands; if we enter a church we take off our hats and speak in a low voice; at Christmas perhaps we decorate a tree. These are expressions of friendliness, reverence, and of celebration. We do not believe that shaking hands has any mysterious efficacy, or that to keep one's hat on in church is dangerous! Now this I regard as a good illustration of how I understand clarity as something to be desired as a goal, as distinct from clarity as something to serve a further elaboration. For seeing these rites as a form of language immediately puts an end to all the elaborate theorising concerning 'primitive mentality'. The clarity prevents a condescending misunderstanding, and puts a full-stop to a lot of idle speculation.[21]

The urge for explanation is, however, deep-rooted. Having perhaps rid ourselves of the view of rites and rituals as theories or erroneous scientific beliefs, we can easily come to look for psychological explanations of the same phenomena. In Drury's remarks, for example, we find him talking of certain forms of behaviour as expressions of friendliness, reverence and celebration. But he also speaks of rites as the result of a need to express something. This too savours of an explanation. It makes it look as though the rites are the means by which something is expressed, as though there were a distinction between means and ends involved. Speaking of burning an effigy Wittgenstein says,

Burning an effigy. Kissing the picture of a loved one. This is obviously *not* based on a belief that it will have a definite effect on the object which the picture represents. It aims at some satisfaction and it achieves it. Or rather, it does not *aim* at anything; we act in this way and then feel satisfied. (RF, p. 31)

A man does not smash the portrait of his beloeved *in order* to express his anger. This is the form his anger takes. Whether the rites are regarded as erroneous scientific beliefs or as psychologically instrumental, these explanations take us away from the philosophically important features of the rites. G. K. Chesterton comments as follows:

even where the fables are inferior as art, they cannot be properly judged by science; still less properly judged as science. Some myths are very crude and queer like the early drawings of children; but the child is trying to draw. It is none the less an error to treat his drawing as if it were a diagram, or intended to be a diagram. The student cannot make a scientific statement about the savage, because the savage is not making a scientific statement about the world. He is saying something quite different; what might be called the gossip of the gods. We may say, if we like, that it is believed before there is time to examine it. It would be truer to say that it is accepted before there is time to believe it.[22]

Chesterton is bringing out the naturalness of religious responses, a naturalness which explanations obscure from us. But this naturalness is naturalness within a culture. To ignore this is to invite confusion. Thus, having said that "The weeping-willow, taken by the Elizabethans as a symbol of unhappy love, does resemble in its lines the drooping and hanging hands,"[23] Edwyn Bevan goes on to say that "if convention had once made a holly-bush instead of a weeping-willow the symbol of unhappy love, an association would in time be created in the mind between them, so that the sight of holly would immediately suggest the other".[24] This makes it look as though the significance of the weeping-willow were a function of a rule of association consisting in no more than a constant conjunction decreed by convention. What this obscures completely is the naturalness of seeing a connection between the weeping-willow and the drooping gait. A failure to see this is not failure of knowledge of an associative rule, but a failure of imagination.

The misunderstandings in the urge for explanations of religious responses are well illustrated in Bevan's chapter on 'Height'. He tries to give various explanations of why divinity has often been expressed in terms of height. He speculates, for example, that since commanders needed to get on high land to see the sweep of the land, those in authority became associated with height, they were to be looked up to. The association between height and authority could have developed from these facts. It may be temping to say that authority becomes connected with height because kings and thrones are placed on high. This simply postpones the issue. Why are they placed on *high*? Again, the explanation takes us away from the naturalness of the expression in a culture, a naturalness shown in the vision of the Divine Being which the prophet Isaiah expresses as "sitting on a throne high and lifted up". Here we have the language of exaltation. Bevan approaches a recognition of the naturalness of this way of talking when he says that "the idea of height, as an essential characteristic of supreme worth, was so interwoven in the very texture of all human languages that it is impossible for us even today to give in words a rendering of what was meant by the metaphor. We are inevitably forced, if we try to explain the metaphor, to bring in the very metaphor to be explained."[25] He is not content to rest with the expression as a natural response in a culture and proceeds, in some ways, absurdly, to try to explain it:

Of those symbols which are taken from the outside material world the significance of height seems to have come to men everywhere immediately and instinctively. We may feel it today so obvious as not to call for any explanation. And yet if one fixes the attention on what height literally is, the reason for this universal instinct seems problematic. For height literally is nothing but the distance from the earth's surface or extension of something on the earth's surface in a direction at right angles outwards. The proposition: Moral and spiritual worth is greater or less in ratio to the distance outwards from the earth's surface, would certainly seem to be, if stated nakedly like that, an odd proposition. And yet that is the premiss which seems implied in this universal association of height with worth and with the Divine.[26]

Bevan does not realize the import of his own remarks when he speaks of the expressive uses of height in connection with divinity not calling for explanation. For Bevan these uses are problematic, whereas in fact what is problematic is his own insistence that one must fix one's attention on what height literally is. He was ignoring what Wittgenstein calls the mythology in our language. To be aware of this mythology and to see the naturalness of its connection with religious beliefs and rituals is to give up asking why these things happen, why they are believed, or whether these expressions in language correspond to reality. Such enquiries are brought to a full stop.

I hope we are now in a position to see why what I have called Wittgenstein's full stop has nothing to do with any attempt, subtle or otherwise, to shield religion from criticism. Not only have we seen how philosophical criticism may draw attention to confusion in rituals but criticism of another kind is left precisely where it is. Seeing what religious belief or rituals come to, someone may still wish to make moral criticisms of them. Nothing Wittgenstein says prohibits such criticism. Neither do Wittgenstein's remarks imply that one should or should not want to see these practices flourish or decline and work to that end. When he says that he would not call the consulting of oracles wrong, in the sense of mistaken, he would not deny that people may want to combat that practice. On the contrary, he says that that is what they do when they oppose it. He asks us to think of what happens when missionaries convert natives.[27] He is not denying the fact of conversion from one view or belief to another. He is asking us to reflect on what that comes to. In particular he is asking us to see that it does not necessitate the postulation of a wider system in which the warring beliefs are contradictories. Think of the temptation to assume that when Callicles accused Socrates of passing off on his audience a low popular conception of what is fine, there must be a wider ethical system in which the views of Callicles and Socrates are contradictories. When Wittgenstein says that the language-games are complete he is resisting the postulation of a wider system of which they are the parts.

Similarly, nothing Wittgenstein says means that religious beliefs or rituals could not lose their sense for an individual or in a culture. Wittgenstein says that "new language-games . . . come into existence, and others become obsolete and get forgotten" (PI, I, 23). But what loss of sense amounts to involves many things.[28] A man may lose his faith, fail to see the sense in it, because it proves too hard for him. Other things win his allegiance. He finds he cannot serve God and Mammon. The more Mammon interests him, the less sense he sees in serving God. Such loss of faith may become a pervasive feature of a society as the result of the things held to be prestigious within it. Nothing Wittgenstein has said denies these possibilities. Neither would he deny that bad philosophy may bring about a loss of faith. A man may lose the sense of his faith because he comes to believe the stipulations of philosophers about the sense it must have. On the other hand, in other circumstances, shielding belief from intellectual enquiry may itself be a sign of religious, as well as intellectual, insecurity.

But, it may be said, there is one kind of criticism of religious beliefs and practices which Wittgenstein will not allow, namely, the kind of criticism one finds in Frazer. He would also reject the kind of request for foundations and verifications found in Nielsen, Hick and others. Neither could he regard religious belief as an ideology or illusion awaiting explanation in the styles of Marx or Freud. Therefore, it may be said, he does not leave all criticism where it is. Even if this were true, it would not be because it is *criticism*, but because it is bad philosophy, bad philosophy concerning logic. But the charge is not even true, since it cannot be said that Wittgenstein rules out *any* genuine form of criticism. What he does not allow is something which purports to be criticism, but which is itself a species of philosophical confusion.[29] A philosopher can hardly be expected to leave bad philosophy where it is. What Wittgenstein does not leave where it is are certain forms of rationalism and scientism and the criticism, justification and explanation of religion emanating from them. But he does so by an appeal to what already lies before us.

Examples in Philosophy

Wittgenstein, we say, appeals to what already is before us. The role of examples is crucial in the philosophy of religion as elsewhere in philosophy. If we want to show that there are a multiplicity of language-games which must be regarded as complete, and not as the in-complete parts of a wider system, the force of the example is essential. How else can the grammatical distinctions and the grammatical con-fusions be brought out? Yet, many, in face of Wittgenstein's examples, refuse to take them in the ways he wants us to, or cannot appreciate these ways. There have been similar reactions to Winch's discussion of witchcraft[30] and to the examples I gave in *The Concept of Prayer*. In another article Winch has discussed further the difficulty of trying to un-derstand a practice in another culture which has no parallel in one's own.[31] He has in mind the consultation of the poison oracle among the

Azande. We cannot assume that the English language is capable, without extension, of translating this concept. We have already seen that it will not do to say with Wittgenstein, in the first set of remarks on Frazer, that we already have in our minds a whole language by means of which these possibilities can be ordered. Neither will it do to say with Chesterton that all a student of folk-lore has to do in face of these examples is "to look at them from the inside, and ask himself how he would begin a story",[32] for why should the way *he* would order such a story be the principle which governs all possibilities? Chesterton, on the other hand, does bring out how, in some respects, the strangeness of an example can be an advantage (*pace* Winch) whereas its cultural proximity may be a disadvantage. "Things that may well be familiar as long as familiarity breeds affection," he argues, "had much better become unfamiliar when familiarity breeds contempt."[33] Speaking as a Catholic, Chesterton says that "the next best thing to being really inside Christendom is to be really outside it".[34] In this latter context there is still the possibility of approaching the beliefs with the wonder and strangeness of a child. What is fatal, Chesterton claims, is a kind of half-way position characterized by rationalism and scientism: "They suggest everywhere the grey gradations of twilight, because they believe it is the twilight of the gods. I propose to maintain that whether or no it is the twilight of the gods, it is not the daylight of men."[35]

There is no doubt that Wittgenstein thought that the grey gradations of twilight in Frazer stood in the way of seeing what is in rituals. And so he produced his examples. But, as I have said, there may be difficulties in discussion of getting people to take them in a certain way.[36] The obstacles may be partly aesthetic, akin to the difficulty of getting someone to see why one development of a theme is more appropriate than another. The obstacles may be moral or psychological – a person may be unable to bring himself to think in a certain way. The obstacles may be philosophical – a person may not see the implications of the language he himself uses quite naturally when not philosophizing. In all these cases an offered example will prove unacceptable; it will not be taken in the way one intended it to be taken. Speaking of the immortality of the soul, Wittgenstein says that

It might seem as though, if we asked such a question as 'Does Lewy *really* mean what so and so means when he says so and so is alive?' – it might seem as though there were two sharply divided cases, one in which he would say he didn't mean it literally. I want to say this is not so. There will be cases where we will differ, and where it won't be a question at all of more or less knowledge, so that we can come together.[37]

Examples will be offered in discussion, but they will not hit the mark. At this point, discussion itself may well come to a full stop. But, then, if the arguments in this paper have anything in them, that this is so should not be altogether surprising.

Nevertheless, that this is so has interesting consequences for Wittgenstein's conception of philosophy as purely descriptive. Kenny, in his book on Wittgenstein, says that,

In saying that in philosophy there are no deductions Wittgenstein set himself against the type of philosophy which offers proofs, e.g. of the existence of God or immortality of the soul . . . Throughout his life he remained sceptical of and hostile to philosophy of that kind. 'We must do away with all explanations' he wrote 'and description alone must take its place'. The point of the description is the solution of philosophical problems: they are solved not by the amassing of new empirical knowledge, but by the rearrangement of what we already know (*PI*, I, 109).[38]

But do we all know the same things? O. K. Bouwsma has brought out the difficulty as follows:

In the works of Wittgenstein there is ordinary language we understand. That ordinary language is related to words or expressions that give us trouble. In ordinary language we discover the corrective of the language which expresses the confusion. In the work of Kierkegaard there corresponds to ordinary language in Wittgenstein the language of scriptures, which Kierkegaard understands. Without this latter assumption Kierkegaard cannot be effective. And this is not how it is in Wittgenstein. There ordinary language is taken to be language which we all understand. Here there is agreement. But Kierkegaard's task is in that way more formidable. He has first to teach us the language of scripture.[39]

One might add that Kierkegaard's reflections often constitute a contribution to the language of religion, whereas Wittgenstein's do not.[40] Yet, in discussing Wittgenstein's remarks on Frazer and his lectures and conversations on belief, Bouwsma's sharp distinction between Kierkegaard and Wittgenstein cannot be maintained. Nevertheless, with regard to distinctively religious language-games, further difficulties have been indicated, difficulties which help us to see why, when one man sees that his spade is turned and a natural full stop has been reached, another wants to go on searching for proofs, foundations, explanations, justifications and verifications. So it is in contemporary philosophy of religion.

Notes

1. Anthony Kenny, "In Defence of God", *Times Literary Supplement*, 7 Feb. 1975, p. 145.
2. See Ronald Hepburn, "From World to God", *Mind*, LXXII (1963), 41, and John Hick, "Sceptics and Believers" in *Faith and the Philosophers*, ed. J. Hick (London: Routledge & Kegan Paul, 1964), p. 238.
3. F. C. Coplestone, *Religion and Philosophy* (Dublin: Gill & Macmillan, 1974), p. viii.
4. See Kai Nielsen, "Wittgensteinian Fideism", *Philosophy*, vol. 42 (1967).
5. H. O. Mounce, "Understanding a Primitive Society", *Philosophy*, vol. 48 (1973), p. 349.
6. Richard H. Bell, "Wittgenstein and Descriptive Theory", *Religious Studies*, vol. 5 (1969).
7. "Wittgenstein's Lecture on Ethics", *Philosophical Review*, vol. 74 (1965).
8. Mounce, pp. 350–1.
9. *ibid.*, p. 350.
10. D. Z. Phillips, *The Concept of Prayer* (London: Routledge & Kegan Paul, 1965; in paperback, Oxford: Basil Blackwell, 1981).
11. For a perceptive statement and treatment of these problems, see Rush Rhees, "Wittgenstein's Builders", *Proceedings of the Aristotelian Society*, 1959–60, reprinted in Rush Rhees, *Discussions of Wittgenstein* (London: Routledge & Kegan Paul, 1970).
     I have also benefited from a discussion with Norman Malcolm on questions concerning these issues.
12. I am indebted in the remainder of this section to a discussion with Rush Rhees.
13. Rhees put this forward simply as a suggestion of how Wittgenstein *might* have made the connection. On the other hand, he insisted that one could not rule out the possibility of this being rejected out of hand by Wittgenstein. In *Religion without Explanation* (Oxford: Blackwell, 1976), Chapter 7, I was puzzled by the analogy between magic and metaphysics. There, however, I am attacking an attempt to identify them in general as part of a strategy to show that religion is the product of confusion.
14. *The Interpreter's Bible*, vol. II (New York, 1953), pp. 82–4.
15. Again, this is simply a suggestion as to how Wittgenstein might have developed the analogy.
16. John Passmore, *A Hundred Years of Philosophy* (London: Pelican Books, 1968), Chapter 18, "Wittgenstein and Ordinary Language", pp. 450ff.
17. This is my disagreement with Mounce's paper which nevertheless does stress that religious beliefs though not mistakes may be confused, since not all confusion, including metaphysical confusion, can be called mistakes. Also Mounce would assign to the realm of confusion, I believe, too many examples of religious and magical practices which, I would argue, express various kinds of possibilities of meaning.
18. For a more detailed discussion see "Religious Beliefs and Language-games" in *Faith and Philosophical Enquiry* (London: Routledge & Kegan Paul, 1970).
19. "Lecture on Ethics", *Philosophical Review*, LXXIV, no. 1 (1965), pp. 15–16.
20. "Remarks on Frazer's *Golden Bough*", pp. 27–8. By 'earlier' and 'later' I simply mean to refer to the division in the published set of the work indicated by Rhees in his Introductory Note.
21. M. O'C. Drury, *The Danger of Words* (London: Routledge & Kegan Paul, 1973), pp. x–xi.
22. G. K. Chesterton, *The Everlasting Man* (New York: Dodd, Mead & Co), pp. 110–11.

23. Edwyn Bevan, *Symbolism and Belief* (London: Fontana/Collins, 1962), p. 11.

24. *ibid.*, p. 11.

25. *ibid.*, p. 25.

26. *ibid.*, pp. 26–7.

27. Cf. *On Certainty*, p. 612.

28. See J. R. Jones and D. Z. Phillips, "Belief and Loss of Belief" in *Faith and Philosophical Enquiry*, and the final chapter of D. Z. Phillips, *Religion without Explanation*.

29. This stronger way of expressing the matter was suggested to me by Gordon Graham in a discussion of this study at the University of St Andrews Philosophical Club.

30. Peter Winch, "Understanding a Primitive Society" in *Ethics and Action* (London: Routledge & Kegan Paul, 1972).

31. Peter Winch, "Language, Belief and Relativism" in *Contemporary British Philosophy*, fourth series, ed. H. D. Lewis (London: Allen & Unwin, 1977).

32. Chesterton, p. 112.

33. *ibid.*, p. xviii.

34. *ibid.*, pp. xi–xii.

35. *ibid.*, p. xvii.

36. These difficulties do not depend on whether or not the person one is arguing with is a religious believer. I say this because of the view attributed to myself and others, that one has to be a religious believer in order to understand religious belief. Despite the frequency of this claim it has little textual foundation. In my own work, for example, it has been denied explicitly. The most I have said is that "religious understanding" is a term which has application (but to understand *that* is not to be a religious believer), that some things are likely to be understood better by a worshipper or by a rebel against religion, and that in certain contexts philosophical and religious understanding may go hand in hand. There are no grounds here for the comprehensive thesis that only those who play the language-games involved in religious belief understand their character. Yet, this set response seems to be here to say and I am sceptical whether mere evidence will shift it.

37. L. Wittgenstein, *Lectures and Conversations on Aesthetics, Psychology and Religious Belief*, ed. Cyril Barrett (Oxford: Blackwell, 1966).

38. A. Kenny, *Wittgenstein* (London: Allen Lane The Penguin Press, 1973), pp. 229–30. Whether they are confused or not it is clear that those whom Kenny criticizes indirectly in his review are reflecting Wittgenstein's style of thought more than he is doing himself in his review article, "In Defence of God". The charge that they are imposing alien features on Wittgenstein's philosophy becomes even more implausible.

   Cf. "Some theologians regard religion as a way of life which can only be understood by participation and therefore cannot be justified to an outsider on neutral rational grounds. Such people must consider any attempt at a philosophical proof of God's existence to be wrong-headed, and must find it inconceivable that such matters as whether everything in motion has a mover could have any relevance to religion . . . To me it seems that if belief in the existence of God cannot be rationally justified, there can be no good grounds for adopting any of the traditional monotheistic religions", Anthony Kenny, *The Five Ways* (London: Routledge & Kegan Paul, 1969), p. 4.

39. O. K. Bouwsma, "Notes on 'The Monstrous Illusion'", *The Perkins School of Theology Journal*, XXIV (Spring 1971), 12.

40. I owe this observation to Ilham Dilman.

Quote: Judgments from our Brain

PAUL ZIFF

In 1938 Wittgenstein gave some lectures on aesthetics. Notes were taken by students and these notes have been published.[1] I shall comment on some aspects of the lectures as indicated by the notes.

There is a matter of style. Wittgenstein said:

How much we are doing is changing the style of thinking and how much I'm doing is changing the style of thinking and how much I'm doing is persuading people to change their style of thinking. (p. 28)

The style is romantic. He said:

The subject (Aesthetics) is very big and entirely misunderstood as far as I can see. The use of such a word as 'beautiful' is even more apt to be misunderstood if you look at the linguistic form of sentences in which it occurs than most other words. (p. 1)

Is the subject of aesthetics "very big and entirely misunderstood"? The words of Unmon are available: A monk asked Unmon "What is Buddha?" Unmon answered "A dung-wiping stick".[2] But the use of the word "beautiful" has little role to play nowadays.

Wittgenstein was a romantic. The author of the *Tractatus Logico-Philosophicus* was a stylistic descendant of Hegel: the lectures on aesthetics evoke images out of Rousseau:

There are lots of people, well-offish, who have been to good schools, who can afford to travel about and see the Louvre, etc., and who know a lot about and can talk fluently about dozens of painters. There is another person who has seen very few paintings, but who looks intensely at one or two paintings which make a profound impression on him.[3] [3. Someone who has not travelled much but who makes certain observations which show that he 'really does appreciate' . . . an appreciation which concentrates on one thing and is very deep – so that you would give your last penny for it.] (p. 9)

Another koan: what would you do with your last penny? And then there is the Tolstoian echo: "but change the picture ever so slightly and you won't want to look at it any more" (p. 36). What picture? Who won't? Compare: a towering stone construction delicately balanced so that if a single stone is moved the whole will come crashing down: a cantilevered pile immune to earthquakes. The latter supplies the more plausible model of (good) paintings. What "slight" change could spoil *Guernica*? Does the slight strabismus undo Da Vinci's *Ginevra de' Benci*? And what's a "slight" change and what's a big one?

Being a romantic in the 1930s, he saw science and the scientist as emblems of idolatry. This perspective is displayed in a comment on Jeans:

Jeans has written a book called *The Mysterious Universe* and I loathe it and call it misleading. Take the title. This alone I would call misleading. Cf. Is the thumb-catcher deluded or not. Was Jeans deluded when he said it was mysterious? I might say the title *The Mysterious Universe* includes a kind of idol worship, the idol being Science and the Scientist. (p. 28)

The reference to the "thumb-catcher" is explained in a footnote:

I have been talking about the game of 'thumb-catching'. What's wrong with that? 'Thumb-catching': holding the right thumb, say, in the left hand, then trying to grasp it with the right hand. The thumb 'mysteriously' disappears before it can be grasped. (p. 27)

A recent issue of *Science News* reports a mystery:

This is another to add to the menagerie of pulsed signals, but it is an extremely weird one. The bursts rise to maximum in about half a second and take ten seconds to die down. They occur on the average of every 15,718 seconds, but the repetition is not exactly precise. There is a 'phase jitter' of about 500 seconds one way or the other, the longest recorded discrepancy being about 1000 seconds. Such a difference between pulse length and repetition time is unique in pulsed X-ray phenomena. Normally, pulsed signals are attributed to pulsing or rotating bodies, but the difference in the numbers and the jitter make it hard to imagine what kind of body could produce these. If the source is indeed in the globular cluster in Sagittarius from the direction of which the bursts come, the intensity of a burst is a million times the intensity of all radiation from the sun.[3]

Some astrophysical aspects of our universe are mysterious. What kind of body can be such a weirdly jittery X-ray source? Is that like asking in the "game" of thumb-catching "Where has the thumb gone?"?

Scientific responses are not what Wittgenstein wanted to answer the questions he was concerned with:

Supposing it was found that all our judgements proceeded from our brain. We discovered particular kinds of mechanism in the brain, formulated general laws, etc. One could show that this sequence of notes produces this particular kind of reaction; makes a man smile and say: 'Oh, how wonderful.'[1] [1. If you knew the mechanism of molecules there, and then knew the sequence of notes in the music, we could show that . . . – R.] (Mechanism for English language, etc.)[2] [2. That he says it in English and not in French would also be explained by the fact that something is embodied in his brain: we could see the differences. – R.] Suppose this were done, it might enable us to predict what a particular person would like and dislike. We could calculate these things. The question is whether this is the sort of explanation we should like to have when we are puzzled about aesthetic impressions, e.g. there is a puzzle – 'Why do these bars give me such a peculiar impression?' Obviously it isn't this, i.e. a calculation, an account of reactions, etc., we want – apart from the obvious impossibility of the thing. (p. 20)

Is it impossible! Couldn't we discover particular kinds of brain mechanisms formulate general laws so that one could then show that a certain sequence of notes produces a particular kind of reaction makes a man smile and say "Oh how wonderful"? Nothing of the sort is known today. But there's no good reason to suppose that nothing of the sort will ever be discovered. Some effective method of scanning brain structure may be developed something comparable to the scan now possible with grosser features of the body: an X-ray delta scanner can nowadays supply a computer display a picture of the body discriminating between points a centimeter apart and allowing for the different densities of the tissues scanned. Possibly in time some new types of scanner will scan a particular person's brain supply a computerized analysis of the brain structure and allow us to make the predictions in question. Wittgenstein spoke of the obvious impossibility of the thing the impossibility of discovering such mechanisms of formulating general laws. He said:

[The] paradigm of the sciences is mechanics. If people imagine a psychology, their ideal is a mechanics of the soul.[1] [1. I suppose the paradigm of all science is mechanics, e.g. Newtonian mechanics. Psychology: Three laws for the soul. – S.] If we look at what actually corresponds to that, we find that there are physical experiments and there are psychological experiments. There are laws of physics and there are laws – if you wish to be polite – of psychology. But in physics there are almost too many laws; in psychology there are hardly any. So, to talk about a mechanics of the soul is slightly funny. (pp. 28–9)

The time was 1938 B.C. – before the computer. What is in question is not a "mechanics of the soul" but a precise detailed explict computerized analysis of human neurophysiological functions. And if by some amazing combination of circumstances the race manages to survive such an analysis will soon be forthcoming.

Wittgenstein was concerned with what he called "puzzles" about "aesthetic impressions". A puzzle is supposed to be a question an answer to which is hard to come by for some special sort of reason. At any rate it's not just any question an answer to which is not readily available. For example "What's the exact height of Old East dorm on the U.N.C. campus?" is a question I can't answer at the moment but I don't think that question is supposed to express a "puzzlement". Would that question serve to express a "puzzlement" for some primitive innocent of geometry and without access to records? Wittgenstein didn't discuss the matter.

Wittgenstein was concerned with puzzles about "aesthetic impressions". "There is" he said "a puzzle, why do these bars give me such a peculiar impression" (p. 20). The puzzle comes I shall suppose in various forms. So one might ask: why do these lines (of a poem) give that man such a peculiar impression? Or: why does this face in the painting give her such a peculiar impression? And so forth. The question the "puzzle" "why do these bars give me such a peculiar impression?" would seem to be a question about the effect of a work or of a part of a work on a person. And that is what Wittgenstein said: "Aesthetic puzzles – puzzles about the effects the arts have on us" (p. 28).

Consider a case: the line "A garden is a lovesome thing, God wot" gives George a peculiar impression: a feeling of delight of escape and release. The puzzle is: why does this line give him such a peculiar impression? It is discovered that George has been the victim of a psychological experiment: he has been subjected to an operant conditioning schedule supplied by ardent Skinnerians. The line "A garden is a lovesome thing, God wot" had been associated with positive reinforcement throughout the period of conditioning: it served to signalize release from unpleasant stimuli. Would this serve to explain why the line gave George this peculiar impression? Wittgenstein said:

One of the curious things about psychological experiments is that they have to be made on a number of subjects. It is the agreements of Smith, Jones and Robinson which allows you to give an explanation – in this sense of explanation, e.g. you can try out a piece of music in a psychological laboratory and get the result that the music acts in such and such a way under such and such a drug. This is not what one means or what one is driving at by an investigation into aesthetics. (p. 21)

But if we found that George had been subjected to this sort of operant conditioning wouldn't that serve to explain why the line "A garden is a lovesome thing, God wot" made such a peculiar impression on George? But aesthetic impressions are what are in question. George's feeling of delight of escape and release was occasioned by his hearing the line and for altogether explicable reasons. But it is not the sort of feeling or impression one is concerned with (that Wittgenstein was concerned with) in an investigation of aesthetics. Because it's not an aesthetic impression created by the line. But since to say this is not likely to make things much clearer let's turn to another case.

Some paintings make some people feel dizzy: a work of op art can have such an effect. Suppose then someone asks what it is about such a painting that makes him dizzy. The answer might be: the blurred edges blurred in the way that op artists know how to blur edges to make people dizzy. Wittgenstein said:

The sort of explanation one is looking for when one is puzzled by an aesthetic impression is not a causal explanation, not one corroborated by experience or by statistics about how people react. (p. 21)

That people are made dizzy by certain works of op art seems to be a fact and op artists seem to know what there is about a work of op art that makes a person dizzy. The explanation that an op artist could supply could be corroborated by experience or by statistics about how people react. The question "Why does this work of op art make me dizzy?" seems to admit of a straightforward answer of the type that Wittgenstein rejected.

Looking at a work of op art someone says "It makes me dizzy" and it does: is dizziness an aesthetically relevant reaction on viewing a work of art? A work of op art yes of course depending on the work. Maybe that isn't the way it was in 1938 but that's the way it is today. Art changes. Nausea boredom indifference any reaction whatever can be aesthetically relevant. If one can lend oneself to the catharsis of tragedy what could require one to avoid the purgation of nausea or boredom or indifference? Nausea can be difficult to account for. Some years ago Meret Oppenheim exhibited a tea cup and saucer covered with rat's fur or mouse fur. The work evoked nausea. Why? I don't know. The matter is I think a question for a psychologist. Did Wittgenstein deny this? I think so.

To stand back for a moment to survey: his conception of art is what is antiquated. "What belongs to a language-game" he said "is a whole culture" (p. 8). But his culture is alien to me: "What does a person who knows a good suit say when trying on a suit at the tailor's?" (p. 5) What does he say? "Who can beat Connors in Vegas?" Or:

If you say he appreciates it [Negro Art], I don't yet know what this means. He may fill his room with objects of Negro Art. Does he just say: "Ah!"? Or does he do what the best Negro musicians do? (p. 9)

What do the best "Negro" musicians do? Sniff horse or just smoke pot? And there is this other "person who has seen very few paintings, but who looks intensively at one or two paintings which make a profound impression on him": I don't want the peasant peering over my shoulder looking at my paintings.

Suppose one asks why one of Graham Sutherland's paintings of a thorn creates the peculiar impression it does. What impression does it create? Looking at the painting one says "It has a feeling of closeness of oppression of a brooding presence." One can say that this Sutherland painting creates this feeling has this feeling. But this is not to say that in looking at this Sutherland painting one has such a feeling. To say that a work creates a certain feeling is not to say that in looking at the work an observer has the feeling created. In this respect the feeling of closeness created by the Sutherland painting is in sharp contrast with the feeling of dizziness created by some work of op art. One could express this difference by saying that the Sutherland work "has a feeling of closeness" whereas the work of op art "makes one feel dizzy".

But (if I read him right) according to Wittgenstein the difference between these two cases is not as great as this way of expressing it can make it seem. For though in looking at the work of op art one may feel dizzy whereas in looking at the Sutherland one is not likely to feel oppressed in each case one does have a certain reaction to the work though a different reaction and one expresses these reactions by saying in one case "It makes me feel dizzy" and in the other "It has a feeling of closeness of oppression of a brooding presence."

On viewing the Sutherland work one may say "It has a feeling of closeness" etc. What impression is in question? Wittgenstein said:

. . . the audience easily distinguishes between the face of the actor and the face of Lloyd George. All have learnt the use of '='. And suddenly they use it in a peculiar way. They say: "This is Lloyd George," although in another sense there is no similarity. An equality which we could call the 'equality of expression'. We have learnt the use of 'the same'. Suddenly we automatically use 'the same' when there is not similarity of length, weight or anything of the sort. . . . The most exact description of my feelings here would be that I say: "Oh, that's Lloyd George!"[1] [1. Important thing is I say: 'Yes, this is Drury.' If you wish to describe feelings, the best way is to describe reactions. Saying 'This is Drury' is the most exact description of feelings I can give at all. Idea that most exact way of describing is by feelings in the stomach. –S.] Suppose the most exact description of a feeling is 'stomach-ache'. But why isn't the most important description of feeling that you say: "Oh, this is the same as that!"? (32–3)

The aesthetic impression Wittgenstein would have been concerned with here I suppose is that "impression" expressed in uttering the words "It has a feeling of closeness" etc. in reaction to and on viewing the Sutherland painting of a thorn. The "puzzle" for him would have been why this work gives the viewer this peculiar "impression".

Wittgenstein's use (or the use attributed to him in the lecture notes) of the word "feeling" was odd. If it dawns on me that an actor is playing the role of Lloyd George and I say "Oh that's Lloyd George" I am not expressing my feelings not if you reported my utterance would you be describing them. But given this odd use it appears that an odd question would on Wittgenstein's view then occasion the "puzzle" about the "impression" someone might receive from the Sutherland work. For the "puzzle" would be to explain why someone reacts to the work by uttering the utterance "It has a feeling of closeness" etc.

Wittgenstein said:

. . . we can dream of predicting the reactions of human beings, say to works of art. If we imagine the dream realized, we'd not thereby have solved what we feel to be aesthetic puzzlements, although we may be able to predict that a certain line of poetry will, on a certain person, act in such and such a way. What we really want, to solve aesthetic puzzlements, is certain comparisons – grouping together of certain cases. (p. 29)

Wittgenstein said the sort of explanation one is looking for is not a causal explanation. And he said this is connected with the difference between cause and motive:

In a lawcourt you are asked the motive of your action and you are supposed to know it. Unless you lie you are supposed to be able to tell the motive of your action. You are not supposed to know the laws by which your body and mind are governed. (p. 21)

Is that like saying that although someone may not know why the furry cup and saucer makes him nauseous he is supposed to know why he reacts to the Sutherland work by saying "It has a feeling of closeness" etc.? Wittgenstein is then surely right in suggesting that a causal answer is not wanted in answer to such a question as "Why does the Sutherland work give me that peculiar impression?" if the impression in question is taken to be the uttering of the utterance "It has a feeling of closeness" etc. on viewing the work. To give a causal answer to such a question one would have to know what causes him to utter precisely that English utterance in the given situation: but a mechanics of English is likely to be of little interest to one concerned with the aesthetic aspects of the Sutherland painting.

Why then does the Sutherland painting give one the peculiar impression it does? If that is to ask why one reacts to the work by uttering the utterance "It has a feeling of closeness" etc. the answer seems simple enough: someone may say "It has a feeling of closeness" etc. because it does and perhaps because she thinks someone else might like to know or perhaps just because she likes to say things out loud. Then why does the Sutherland painting have that feeling of closeness?

"What we really want" said Wittgenstein "to solve aesthetic puzzlements, is certain comparisons – grouping together of certain cases" (p. 29). There is a footnote to this remark:

A picture, 'Creation of Adam' by Michelangelo, comes to mind. I have a queer idea which could be expressed by: 'There is a tremendous *philosophy* behind this picture.' –S. (p. 29)

Elsewhere Wittgenstein remarked:

As far as one can see the puzzlement I am talking about can be cured only by peculiar kinds of comparisons, e.g. by an arrangement of certain musical figures, comparing their effect on us.[3] [3. When the written notes or the played notes are spread out, then you say . . . T]. "If we put in this chord it does not have that effect; if we put in this chord it does." (p. 20)

Why does the Sutherland painting of a thorn have that feeling of closeness of oppression of a brooding presence? There's no need to look for different versions of the work: comparisons would be otiose. An answer to our "puzzle" is readily to be found in the technical features of the work. That the work in question (which is to be found in the permanent collection of the New York Museum of Modern Art) has the feeling it has is directly attributable to various factors. First the section of the painting representing sky is a cadmium orange. Cadmium orange being a strongly advancing color deprives the painting of any airy or open spatial quality. Secondly the purplish greys of the areas in front of the cadmium orange areas are forced into a forward position by virtue of placement and general features of the drawing and this despite the tendency of such colors to recede. The upshot is a general feeling of closeness of oppression. Of course if it were not for other features of the painting e.g. the movement of the main mass and so forth the feeling in question perhaps would not have been created. But given the presence of the other features the salient feature accounting for the oppressiveness of the work is the cadmium orange sky.

Wittgenstein had much to say about aesthetic "puzzles" about the effects the arts have on us. But what he had to say doesn't fit any of the cases we have considered: not that of George's reaction to the line "A garden is a lovesome thing, God wot" not one's reaction to a work of op art or to Oppenheim's cup and saucer and not one's finding the Sutherland work to have the feeling it has. I think the reason for this lack of fit is that Wittgenstein was concerned with radically different kinds of "puzzles". He said:

You can sometimes find the similarity between the style of a musician and the style of a poet who lived at the same time, or a painter. Take Brahms and Keller. I often found that certain themes of Brahms were extremely Kellerian. This was extraordinarily striking. (p. 32)

And then there is his reference to Michelangelo's *Creation of Adam*: "I have a queer idea which could be expressed by: 'There is a tremendous *philosophy* behind this picture.'" The "puzzle" is: why did certain themes of Brahms strike him as Kellerian? And the "puzzle" is: why did Michelangelo's *Creation of Adam* give him the feeling that there is a tremendous philosophy behind the work? Are these in fact the sort of "puzzles" Wittgenstein was concerned with? I don't really know. How can one know? He didn't cite any real cases. But they seem to be. And how are these different kinds of "puzzles" from the ones we have been considering? Only in being vague and indefinite.

Why did certain themes of Brahms strike him as Kellerian? Which themes of Brahms? When did they give him that impression? Did he read Keller before he heard the themes or after? Which works of Keller struck him as Kellerian? All equally or some more than others? Not knowing the answer to any of these questions I have not the slightest idea why certain themes of Brahms struck him as Kellerian. I do not feel mystified by the matter. Or do vagueness and indefiniteness suffice to give rise to a "puzzle"? Wittgenstein said:

Here you actually have a case different from that of faces. With faces you can generally soon find something which makes you say: "Yes that's what made them so similar." Whereas I couldn't say now what it is that made Brahms similar to Keller. Nevertheless, I find that utterance of mine interesting. (p. 32)

That he could not say why certain themes of Brahms struck him as Kellerian may be owing simply to the fact that he failed to investigate the matter carefully. Or at all. Faces are easier to compare than words with music. And why did Michelangelo's *Creation of Adam* give him the feeling that there is a tremendous philosophy behind the work? Probably the answer has something to do with Wittgenstein's own views of philosophy what he took to be the subject matter of the painting his attitude towards matters of creation his feelings about Darwin and so forth. Most likely the solution to these "puzzles" would be of no aesthetic interest.

To ask why a work gives a certain impression to a certain person is to be concerned with the specific relation that obtains between the work and the person. But this relation may be of no aesthetic interest despite the fact that the work in question may be a work of art. Suppose attending to a certain work gives someone a certain impression. Why does it do that? Maybe primarily because of him: as in the case of George cited previously. In which case the impression can hardly be said to be an aesthetic impression created by the work. In contrast the impression may be primarily owing to the work in that it would give that impression to any reasonably sensitive discerning sort: as in the case of the Sutherland thorn.

Are there no "puzzles" of the kind Wittgenstein was concerned with that are of genuine aesthetic significance? There are questions without answers that are likely to remain without answers for some time. Looking at an unsigned drawing I say "That strikes me as a Klee." Why does it give me that impression? I say "Look at the lines!" But what about the lines? I can't say. What is in question is a visual analogy. Von Neumann concerned with such matters said:

About one fifth of the brain is a visual brain, which, as far as we know, does nothing except make decisions about visual analogies. So, using the figures we have, which are not very good, but which are probably all right for an orientation, we conclude that apparently a network of about 2 billion relays does nothing but determine how to organize a visual picture. It is absolutely not clear a priori that there is any simpler description of what constitutes a visual analogy than a description of the visual brain. [4]

Notes

1. L. Wittgenstein, *Lectures and Conversations* (Oxford: Blackwell, 1966).
2. Gyomay M. Kubose, *Zen Koans* (Chicago: Henry Regnery, 1973), p. 75.
3. *Science News*, February 14, 1976, Vol. 109, no. 7, p. 101.
4. John Von Neumann, *Theory of Self-Reproducing Automata* (Urbana and London: University of Illinois Press, 1966), p. 47.

Wittgenstein and the Fire-festivals

FRANK CIOFFI

I

In his notes on "Wittgenstein's Lectures (1930–33)" G. E. Moore reports that one of the chief points which Wittgenstein wished to make in connection with Frazer's *Golden Bough*[1] was that "it was a mistake to suppose that . . . the account of the Beltane Festival 'impresses us so much' . . . because it has 'developed from a festival in which a real man was burnt'.[2]

The following remarks will give an idea of the sort of thing Frazer says about Fire-festivals:

All over Europe the peasants have been accustomed from time immemorial to kindle bonfires on certain days of the year, and to dance round or leap over them. Not uncommonly effigies are burned in these fires, or a pretence is made of burning a living person in them. And there are grounds for believing that anciently human beings were actually burned on these occasions.[3]

In another chapter he writes:

The pretence of throwing the victim chosen by lot into the Beltane fire, and the similar treatment of the man at the Midsummer bonfire in Normandy, may naturally be interpreted as traces of an older custom of actually burning human beings on these occasions.[4]

In another, he says:

In the popular customs connected with the Fire-festivals of Europe there are certain features which appear to point to a form of practice of human sacrifice . . . the pretence of burning people is sometimes carried so far that it seems reasonable to regard it as a mitigated survival of an older custom of actually burning them. Thus in Aachen, as we saw, the man clad in pea-straw acts so cleverly that the children really believe he is being burned. At Jumieges in Normandy, the man clad all in green . . . was pursued by his comrades, and when they caught him they feigned to fling him upon the midsummer bonfire. Similarly, at the Beltane fires in Scotland the pretended victim was seized, and a show made of throwing him into the flames, and for some time afterwards the people affected to speak of him as dead.[5]

Frazer then goes on to describe human sacrifice by fire as practised by the Celts in ancient times and concludes that

it seems reasonable to suppose that . . . from these annual festivals are lineally descended some at least of the Fire-festivals which, with their traces of human sacrifices, are still celebrated year by year in many parts of Europe.[6]

What is there to object to in all this? For example, what is objectionable about invoking an ancient practice in which a man was burnt to explain a contemporary practice in which an effigy is burnt?

In the light of the "Remarks on Frazer's *Golden Bough*"[7] Wittgenstein seems to mean two (at least) distinct things by his claim that it was a mistake for Frazer to see the phenomenon of the Fire-festivals as calling for an historical reconstruction of the original sacrificial rituals of which they were mitigated survivals. He means that many of the Fire-festivals are intelligible as they stand, that in their details, or in the demeanour of their participants, they directly manifest their "inner character", their relation to the idea of the sacrificial burning of a man. They strike us as commemorations or dramatizations of this idea independently of any empirical evidence that they originated in such an event. But Wittgenstein has another more radical objection to Frazer's dealings with the Fire-festivals than his failure to see that the festivals themselves evince a sacrificial significance independently of empirical evidence as to their origins. It is his failure to see that what was called for by the "deep and sinister" character of the festivals was an account of "the experience in ourselves from which we impute" this "deep and sinister character" and of "what it is which brings this picture into connection with our own feelings and thoughts".

This view emerges unmistakably in the following:

But why should it not really be (partly, anyway) just the *thought* (of the Festival's sacrificial origin) that makes the impression on me? Aren't ideas frightening? . . . Hasn't the *thought* something terrible? – Yes, but that which I see in those stories is something they acquire, after all, from the evidence, including such evidence as does not seem directly connected with them – from the thought of man and his past, from the strangeness of what I see and what I have seen and heard in myself and others. (p. 251)

Here the antithesis to our thoughts of the sacrificial origin of the ritual is not our thoughts as to "its inner character" but "our thoughts of man and his past and the strangeness of what we have (noticed) in ourselves and in others".

I am not sure how aware Wittgenstein is of the distinctiveness of these theses, for he does not signal the transition from one to the other. (But these are notes meant for his own use.) The following remarks on the rule of succession to the priesthood of the Temple of Diana at Nemi, according to which the priest succeeded to office by slaying his predecessor and retained it till he himself was slain, also illustrate the duality of Wittgenstein's objections to Frazer:

> When Frazer begins by telling the story of the King of the Wood at Nemi, he does this in a tone which shows that something strange and terrible is happening here. And that is the answer to the question 'Why is this happening?': Because it is terrible. In other words, what strikes us in this course of events as terrible, impressive, horrible, tragic, etc., anything but trivial and insignificant, *that* is what gave birth to them.
>
> Here we can only *describe* and say, human life is like that.
>
> Compared with the impression that what is described makes on us, the explanation is too uncertain.
>
> Every explanation is an hypothesis.
>
> But for someone worried by love an explanatory hypothesis will not help much – it will not bring peace.
>
> The crush of thoughts that do not get out because they all try to push forward and are wedged in the door. (pp. 235–6)

The last three remarks do more than merely claim that the rule of succession does not require to be traced to its origins for us to see its point. They suggest the inappropriateness of *any* hypothesizing for enlightening us as to our relation to the Fire-festivals and that it is rather our "crush of thoughts" with respect to them which need clarification. But that "what strikes us . . . as terrible, impressive, horrible, tragic, etc., . . . is what gave birth to them" is no less an explanatory hypothesis than Frazer's account of their remote origins. And so knowledge of the inner character of the eighteenth-century festival, what it meant to its celebrants, can no more resolve "our puzzlement as to why they impress us" than can knowledge of its origins. But I will postpone discussion of this issue until I have dealt with Wittgenstein's first objection to Frazer – that Frazer gives an historical reconstruction of the origin of the festival when what is called for is an account of its 'inner character'.

II

According to Wittgenstein Frazer was mistaken in thinking that the impression produced on us by the Beltane Festival called for an effort of historical reconstruction which would trace it to its beginnings. The speculative wonder which colours our impression of the festival is not concerned with the origin of the festival, but with its expressive significance. And though the idea of the burning of a man enters into these speculations it is not as a causal antecedent of the festival but as its meaning. The ritual is *about* the burning of a man.

The question is: Is what we may call the sinister character of the Beltane Fire Festival as it was practised a hundred years ago – is this a character of the practice in itself, or only if the hypothesis regarding its origin is confirmed? I think it is clear that what gives us a sinister impression is the inner nature of the practice as performed in recent times. (p. 247)

The authors of a paper on "Wittgenstein's Implied Anthropology" (Rudich and Stassen) seem to have misunderstood Wittgenstein's point on this issue: "Wittgenstein's attack on Frazer's work is really an attack on the very idea of historical understanding, or more exactly on any causal account of history."[8] This is a mistake. What Wittgenstein denies is not the possibility of historical explanation but its appropriateness where what is at issue is "the inner nature of the practice" – the expressive significance a people's ritual practices have for them.

Rudich and Stassen say that Wittgenstein is denying that "a given set of practices can be explained by uncovering their origins and causes in the earlier experiences of a society". But what Wittgenstein says is: "even if its ancient origins and its descent from an earlier practice is established by history it is still possible that there is nothing sinister at all about the practice today . . ." And if it *is* sinister today we don't require the historical account to confirm that this is so. The historicity of the hypothetical explanation is of no account in such cases, not because

Wittgenstein thinks there can be no knowledge of historical causation, as Rudich and Stassen say, but because the practice need not have the significance for those whose behaviour impressed us and for which the historical explanation purports to account that it had for its originators, and can have this significance irrespective of how it originated.

If the impression that the practice is deep, sinister and age-old does not arise out of independent knowledge of its antiquity, etc., how then does it arise? Wittgenstein thinks the impression arises directly from the details of the ritual and the demeanour of the celebrants, who behave as if they were commemorating a remote, long past, horrific event. This may create the illusion that "it is the hypothesis (of antiquity) that gives the matter depth", whereas this springs from the aspect presented by the eighteenth-century ritual itself. Wittgenstein not only holds that what gives the Beltane Festivals their distinctiveness is our sense of their meaning rather than their origins, he also has a subsidiary thesis as to how genetic hypotheses contribute to our sense of this significance. Remarks on p. 241 and p. 251, together with allusions to "the spirit of the Festival" and to its "infusion" with a mood or atmosphere which mere play or a theatrical performance does not have (p. 242), constitute a subsidiary thesis as to how Frazer's stories of sacrificial origins (and genetic accounts in general) may contribute to clarifying our sense of the character of a phenomenon even when there is no genetic connection between them and what they purport to explain. On p. 241 he speaks of cases where an hypothetical link is not meant to do anything "except to draw attention to the similarity, the connexion, between the *facts*. As one might illustrate the internal relation of a circle to an ellipse by gradually transforming an ellipse into a circle but not in order to assert that a given ellipse, in fact, historically, originated from a circle (Theory of Development) but only to sharpen our eye for a formal connexion." And on p. 252 he says, "What is correct and interesting is not to say: this proceeded from that, but: it could have thus proceeded."

After remarking that it only "seems as if it is the hypothesis (of its origins) that gives the Festival depth" Wittgenstein says, "And we may remember the explanation of the strange relationship between Siegfried and Brunhilde in our Niebelungenlied. Namely that Siegfried seems to have seen Brunhilde before. It is now clear that what gives this practice depth is its *connexion* with the burning of a man . . ."

Wittgenstein's remark reminds us how often we express ourselves in a genetic–historical mode to evince our sense of the distinctiveness of an experience. Michelangelo describes his love for Vittoria Colonna (*La dove io t'amai prima*) and Goethe his for Frau von Stein (*Ach! du warst in abgelebten zeiten/Meine Schwester oder meine Frau* — in time long past and in another life/You must have been my sister or my wife) in terms similar to Siegfried's. This is how Theophile Gautier accounts for the deep impression made by the smiling faces of Leonardo's portraits: "We have seen these faces before, but not upon this earth; in some previous existence, perhaps, which they recall vaguely to us. How else explain the strange, almost magic charm which the portrait of the Mona Lisa has?" Henry Adams was so struck by his first sight of Chartres Cathedral that he had the absurd fancy that he had participated in its construction.

Frazer conjectures the "the King of the Wood was formerly burned, dead or alive, at the midsummer fire festival which was annually celebrated in the Arician grove". This fact (assuming it to be one) stands in quite a different relation to the rule of succession and the way of life it enforced on the Nemi priest than the original sacrificial burnings do to the Beltane Fire-festival. In spite of the causal warrantability of the connection it could not be said of the life of the Nemi priest, as Wittgenstein says of the Beltane Festival, "what gives this practice depth is its connection with the burning of a man". For it is not by way of historical evidence that the burning of a man enters into our impression of the Beltane Festival.

The Beltane Festival as it has come down to us is the performance of a play, something like children playing at robbers. But then again it is not like this. For even though it is prearranged so that the side which saves the victim wins, there is still the infusion of a mood or state of mind in what is happening which a theatrical production does not have. (p. 250)

We see more readily the work that Frazer's human sacrifice story does in the case of the Beltane Fire by looking at the Baldur Bale Fires, which he also traces to a defunct tradition of human sacrifice, this time Scandinavian rather than Druidical. In the Baldur Bale Fires no effigy is burned, and the theme of human sacrifice is entirely a product of Frazer's reconstructive ingenuity ("the burning of an effigy is a feature which might easily drop out after its meaning was forgotten"). It has been said that the Baldur Bale Fires "have as much to do with the Midsummer Fires as the crematorium at Golders Green".[9] But even if we put aside all doubts of this kind Frazer's account does not illuminate the Baldur Bale Fires as it does the Beltane Fires, for the idea of a burning a man, even if historical, is not expressed in the demeanour of the celebrants. The

Baldur Bale Fires are not *about* the burning of a man, even if they are causally related to ancient burnings in a way that makes it correct to speak of them as mitigated survivals of such burnings.

This point can be further illustrated by these remarks from an essay on "Mythological Forms of Bakers' Cakes":

The various shapes of bakers' cakes, handed down to us by former generations, are quite worthy of a little consideration. What is the real significance of these queer, mysterious forms, and why are they so time-honoured and so unchangeable? . . .

The gingerbread man can be traced back to the sacrifice of prisoners, knights and footsoldiers. Human sacrifices, however, even in the most ancient times, were sacred to the gods alone, and were not eaten by the worshippers themselves, but only their baked and painted effigies. These figures were originally painted with the blood of the victims. It is for this reason that these gingerbread figures are still ornamented with red . . .

In still more remote times according to the Edda, men not only drank the blood of their enemies slain in battle, but also ate their hearts. This was also done at the execution of prisoners of war. Later on, heart shaped cakes took the place of these hearts, and our gingerbread hearts are the lineal descendants of these hearts once offered in sacrifice.[10]

The effect on our thoughts of the knowledge, for example, that the red colouring on the gingerbread man once stood for the victim's blood tells us nothing about the place of gingerbread men in our lives. The sacrifice story gets no purchase. It has nothing to latch on to. "No trace of that ancient horror is left on it. . . . the depth lies merely in the thought of its descent". This is not the case with the Beltane Festival. The account of the different forms of bakers' cakes illustrates the difference between a practice possessing a physiognomy of terror, or depth, and these lying "merely in the thought of its descent".

("Madam Homais was very fond of those small, heavy loaves, shaped like a turban, which are eaten with salt butter during Lent: a last survival of Gothic fare, perhaps going back to the time of the Crusades, with which the sturdy Normans used once to gorge themselves, fancying that they saw in the yellow torchlight on the table, between the jugs of mead and the huge joints of pork, Saracens' heads to devour." I have seen those loaves again since being struck by this passage in *Madame Bovary* but they remained just loaves.)

Wittgenstein's objection to Frazer's supposing that "the Beltane

Festival impresses us so much because it developed from a festival in which a real man was burnt" has a parallel in the criticism Santayana makes of a certain kind of explanation of the impression made by the night sky. Paul Valéry speaks of "the mysterious effect that a clear night and the presence of stars has on men". Santayana once addressed himself to the question why the sight of a starry sky should have this mysterious effect:

To most people I fancy, the stars are beautiful; but if you ask why, they would be at a loss to reply, until they remembered what they had heard about astronomy and the great size and distance and possible habitation of those orbs. The vague and allusive ideas thus aroused fall in so well with the dumb emotion we were already feeling, that we attribute this emotion to those ideas, and persuade ourselves that the power of the starry heavens lies in the suggestion of astronomical facts.

Santayana argues against this view:

Before the days of Kepler, the heavens declared the glory of the Lord; and we needed no calculation of stellar distances, no fancies about a plurality of worlds, no image of infinite space to make the stars sublime.[11]

Santayana's "dumb emotion we were already feeling" is akin to Wittgenstein's "crush of thoughts that could not get out". The sinister aspect of the Fire-festivals is to the prehistoric burning of a real man as the power of the starry heavens to the suggestion of astronomical facts. In both cases the enlightening, perplexity-dissipating power of a hypothesis has been misattributed.

Wittgenstein's remark that a "hypothesis of development" may be "a disguise for a formal connection" alerts us to the ubiquity of ostensibly genetic explanations (*Entwicklungshypothese*) whose point lies in evincing a sense of the character of a phenomenon. What attention to the strictly formal features of genetic remarks overlooks is how often we implicitly translate them into a form other than that which they reveal to simple inspection. Genetic accounts are, on many occasions, taken as claims as to the 'inner nature" of the practice of which they purport to give the genealogy or as evocations or elucidations of the impression these make on us.

The view once found in rationalist polemic that the institution of female religious celibacy is the end product of a development which began with temple prostitution is not relished or resented as a hypothesis but as an articulation either of our own suspicions or of a vaguely familiar presumption as to the relation of religiosity to sexuality. It is taken as a claim as to its inner character rather than merely as a hypothesis as to its temporal development. The hypothesis puts the practice against a background which may alter its aspect for us. Similar considerations apply to the theory that the sacrament of the Eucharist was evolved from the totem feast. The real objection to the development hypothesis is not that it is empirically false but that it draws the terms sexuality and religiosity, or sacrament and primitive ritual (e.g. Holy Communion and ritual cannibalism) unjustifiably close together. Our rejection of the "formal connection" may take a misleading form as scepticism about the genetic hypothesis when it is really what Wittgenstein refers to as "the similarity between the facts" to which "one's eyes have been sharpened" by the "hypothetical connecting link" that one wishes to contest.[12]

The proposal of a genealogical relation between dynamically inert items, though it may invite scepticism, arouses no vehement repudiation because it involves no aspect change and thus no claim as to the "inner character" of a phenomenon. An effect similar to that of the developmental hypothesis may be produced by juxtaposition, arrangements of the data, which make no historical claims as to the unfolding of one practice from another or of both from a common prototype – for example, by introducing Bernini's *St Theresa* as an intermediate term between overtly orgiastic religiosity and the mystical transports of the female celibate, or the southern Italian practice of swallowing boluses on which the pictures of sacred personages have been pasted as a term between ritual cannibalism and the sacrament of the Eucharist.[13]

If one person assigns a genetic origin to a phenomenon, another person (or even the same person) is likely to find it redolent of that from which it supposedly originates. If someone says that a phenomenon has a sexual origin, someone else is likely to feel that it is redolent of sexuality. That is, it is those who bring mysticism and sex together for other reasons for whom there will seem point in bringing sexuality into phylo- or onto-genetic relationship with mysticism. The evolution of the genital apparatus from the cloaca is particularly striking for those whom the thought that love has pitched his mansion in the place of excrement has already struck. If the impulse to bite did not play a role in our erotic lives the hunger-into-sexuality theory would have a different kind of interest for us (if it retained any at all).

III

I have said that Wittgenstein has a more radical thesis according to which even the "inner nature of the practice as performed in recent times" is irrelevant to the question why the Beltane Festival impresses us. On this view the task set us by our impression of the Fire-festivals was rather to elicit, articulate and lay open to view "the crush of thoughts that do not get out because they all try to push forward and are wedged in the door".

The following remarks seem to support this construction:

Above all: whence the certainty that a practice of this kind must be age-old (what are the data, what is the verification)? But *have* we any certainty, may we not have been led into a mistake because we were over-impressed by historical considerations? Certainly, but that still leaves something of which we are sure . . . It is our *evidence* for it, that holds what is deep in this assumption. And this evidence is again non-hypothetical, psychological . . . What I want to say is. What is sinister, deep, does not lie in the fact that that is how the history of this practice went, for perhaps it did not go that way . . . but in what it is that gives me reason to assume it. (p. 248)

What makes human sacrifice deep and sinister anyway? . . . this deep and sinister aspect is not obvious just from learning the history of the external action, but we impute it from an experience in ourselves. (p. 249)

But it is not just the idea of the possible origin of the Beltane Festival that makes it impressive, but what we may call the overwhelming probability of this idea. What we get from the material. (p. 250)

. . . that which I see in those stories is something they acquire, after all, from the evidence, including such evidence as does not seem directly connected with them – from the thought of man and his past, from the strangeness of what I see and what I have seen and have heard in myself and others. (p. 251)

Moreover one element of (Frazer's) account is lacking and that is the one which brings this picture into connexion with our own feelings and thoughts. This element gives the account its depth. (p. 246)

These remarks seem to me to commit Wittgenstein to a stronger thesis than merely that the question to be asked concerning the Fire-festivals is not of what primitive practices they are "mitigated survivals", but rather of what features of human life they are emblematic and to what feelings about these features they give expression.

Preoccupation with the origins of the Fire-festivals is mistaken, not because it is impertinent to "the inner character of the ritual" but because it is impertinent to the impressions it engenders.

The following remark implies that the impression of depth produced by a practice may be a function not of the mien of the performers, or of any of its details but of the background we bring to it.

If it were the custom at some festival for men to ride on one another (as in horse-and-rider games), we would see nothing more in this than a way of carrying someone which reminds us of men riding horses. But if we know that among many peoples it had been the custom, say, to use slaves as mounts and to celebrate certain festivals mounted in this way, we should then see in the harmless practice of our time something deeper and less harmless. (p. 247)

But it now seems that, given "our thoughts of man and his past and the strangeness of what we have noticed in ourselves and in others", the fact that men pretend to burn men is sufficient to account for our impression that the practice is deep and sinister irrespective of the celebrants' conception of it.

"What makes human sacrifice something deep and sinister" is not to be determined by historical investigation into either the origin *or* the contemporary significance of the Fire-festivals. That men should pretend to burn men gets its "depth" from our prior knowledge that men have burned men, not from our conviction that in this particular ritual men were once burned. The worries provoked by accounts of the Fire-festivals are not historicity worries. The natural direction of enquiry in a case like this is towards "my thoughts of man and his past and the strangeness of what I have (noticed) in myself and in others". It is these which "make what is so uncertain into something to worry about".

If it is "the overwhelming probability of the idea" that men were once burned that makes the Beltane Festival impressive, then it is to an understanding of the source of this overwhelming probability that we must look to for "the satisfaction that comes from explaining". If "it is what connects this picture with our feelings and thoughts that gives the contemplation of its depth", then "it is what connects this picture with our feelings and thoughts" that is the proper subject of our enquiries and reflections. If "it is our evidence for it that holds what is deep in this assumption" then "it is our evidence for it" that requires investigation. (And, says Wittgenstein, "this evidence is non-hypothetical, psychological".) If ". . . what we see in these stories is something they acquire from the evidence, even from such evidence as does not seem directly connected with them", then what is called for is a garnering of this evidence. Facts like Pip's readiness (in *Great Expectations*) to credit Orlick's story that it was necessary to stoke the forge fire with a live boy every seven years ought to find a place in such an account.

The inner character of the festival (by which Wittgenstein says he means "All those circumstances in which it is carried out that are not included in the accounts of the festival") is just as conjectural as its origins and cannot be determined, as the question "Why does this impress us?" can, by merely bethinking ourselves. All that can be so determined is the relation in which we ourselves stand to the idea of the ceremonial burning of a man. And it is Frazer's failure to address himself to *this* question which is finally the basis of Wittgenstein's criticism of his dealing with the Fire-festivals.

Although whether any particular practice does symbolize what it seems to is a hypothetical question, i.e. an historical one, the relation between what it seems to mean and those features in virtue of which it seems to mean it is not hypothetical and so is not to be determined by historical research – for example, why the use of a cake for the drawing of lots seems especially terrible. On p. 249 Wittgenstein says: "The fact that for the lots they use a cake has something especially terrible to us is of central importance in our investigation of practices like these." Our response, our impression of the inner character of the festival, rests on the assumption that cakes play the same role in their lives as in ours. If we learned that the only purpose to which they put cakes was for choosing the Beltane victim and that they were considered inedible for normal purposes, this detail of the ritual would look very different to us. And to this extent historicity plays a role in our enquiries. But, historicity apart, "there is still something of which we are sure". The use of the cakes for drawing lots is just the kind of thing which Wittgenstein says we could invent for ourselves (pp. 238, 251). What Wittgenstein may be calling attention to here is the way in which the eruption of the demonic into the quotidian, or reminders of the domestic in the midst of the tragic and terrifying, confers a distinctive cast on phenomena. The principle is the same as that of the knocking at the gate in *Macbeth*, or Auden's lines about "the dreadful martyrdom" running its course while "the torturer's horse scratches its innocent behind on a tree", or the drowning boy and the oblivious ploughman in Breughel's *Fall of Icarus* which inspired them, or "the terrible blood sacrifice" in Hans Castorp's dream and the sunny Mediterranean seascape and tokens of "man's courteous and enlightened social state" against which it is consummated. It is as if the use of the cakes for picking victims was a deliberate attempt to make the ritual emblematic of this feature of life. But even if this were not the allusion intended the cakes would nevertheless be no less appropriate a means of making it. It is this which is "non-hypothetical, psychological" and "of which we are sure".

That this is happening "because it is terrible", that "what strikes us in this course of events as terrible, impressive, horrible, tragic, etc., . . . is what gave birth to them" is *not* "something of which we can be sure". What we can be sure of is that if *we* wished to give expression to the sentiments we feel to lie behind these practices then these practices would serve.

Wittgenstein says of Frazer's theory of sacrificial origins:

> . . . this ancestry may be very uncertain and one feels like saying: 'Why make what is so uncertain into something to worry about?' (like a backward-looking Clever Elsa). But worries of that kind are not involved here. (p. 248)

If ritual slaughter on the scale the Aztecs practised it strikes us as an appropriate way of dramatizing how things are, then even if Frazer is right, and they only did it from "a mistaken theory of the solar system", "there is still something of which we are sure", and it is this "which makes what is so uncertain into something to worry about".

In these remarks Wittgenstein seems to be approaching a conception of the kind of interest the stories of human sacrifice have for us which has been noted by the sociologist Simmel.

> For Simmel, our interest in histories is a product of two different kinds of interest. Certain 'events' – a very noble or very horrible deed, a peculiarly complicated personality, a strange fate of an individual or group – we find *interesting*, whether the events in question are known to have occurred or whether they are frankly fictional . . . (Simmel) is concerned with affirming that . . . 'the feelings attached to pure contents constitute a domain for itself, that they come to the fore and persist after the disappearance of those feelings produced by the existence (Sein) of the contents . . .'[14]

Jorge Luis Borges illustrates the distinction Simmel had in mind. "Among Paul Valéry's jottings, André Maurois observed the following: Ideas for a frightening story: it is discovered that the only remedy for cancer is living human flesh. Consequences."[15] Imagine someone momentarily taken in by Borges's anecdote, then realizing it was invention. The difference this would fail to make is the difference Simmel and Wittgenstein are calling attention to.

A phrase comes to mind from a discussion of poetry by the critic Hazlitt – "unravelling the web of associations wound round a subject by nature and the unavoidable conditions of humanity". I take Wittgenstein to be saying that our perplexity with respect to certain phenomena calls for this effort at unravelling rather than any search for further empirical knowledge.[16]

IV

The most interesting question to arise out of Wittgenstein's remarks on the Fire-festivals is why Frazer should be criticized for failing to answer a question he never posed. Wittgenstein makes it an objection to Frazer's empirical method that someone troubled by love will not be helped by a hypothesis. "It will not bring peace." (In other words – "Someone troubled by the thought of human sacrifice will not be helped by a hypothesis. It will not bring peace.") But Frazer never promised to bring peace, never even said he was addressing himself to "why human sacrifice impresses us". So Wittgenstein's objection must be that he ought to have. Now what kind of claim is this?

Why should accounts of the Fire-festivals be made the occasion of reflection on "what makes human sacrifice deep and sinister" rather than of enquiry into the origin and development of the Fire-festivals? The issue is one of deciding when an interest, or a felt perplexity with respect to a topic (in Wittgenstein's words "Why does this impress me?") calls for further empirical information for its resolution, and when this is an illusion.

There are two different kinds of situation in which this question arises. In one the problem is already sufficiently defined for us to be able to point out the error in expecting an empirical resolution of it. This is so with some of the aesthetic questions which Wittgenstein discusses in the lectures on Aesthetics – e.g. "Why do these bars give me such a peculiar impression?"[17] But there is another kind of situation, one in which the questions raised are empirical as formulated, and there is no lack of fit between them and the answers proposed, and where criticism takes the form of claiming that the wrong question has been posed. This is the case with respect to Wittgenstein's criticism of Frazer's account of the Fire-festivals. Unwedging our crush of thoughts with respect to a subject and allowing them to file through singly is an activity which can profitably be distinguished from empirical research, but how is it to be determined when it is to be pursued in its stead?

In 1906 William James was visiting Stanford University and found himself caught up in the San Francisco earthquake, of which experience he has left us an account.

I personified the earthquake as a permanent individual entity . . . It came moreover, directly to *me*. It stole in behind my back, and once inside the room, had me all to itself, and could manifest itself convincingly. Animus and intent were never more present in any human action, nor did any human activity ever more definitely point back to a living agent as its source and origin.

All whom I consulted on the point agreed as to this feature in their experience. "it expressed intention," "It was vicious," "It was bent on destruction," "It wanted to show its power," or what not . . . For science when the tensions in the earth's crust reach the breaking-point, and strata fall into an altered equilibrium, earthquake is simply the collective name of all the cracks and shakings and disturbances that happen. They *are* the earthquake. But for me *the* earthquake was the *cause* of the disturbances, and the perception of it as a living agent was irresistible. It had an overpowering dramatic convincingness.[18]

The sort of mistake Wittgenstein is charging Frazer with is the mistake James would have made had he felt that what his experience of the San Francisco earthquake called for was an account of the San Andreas Fault. For there would have been no 'formal' relation between the San Andreas Fault and James's "crush of thoughts".

But it is one thing to say that talk of the San Andreas Fault would not tell us anything as to James's experience of the San Francisco earthquake, and quite another to say that someone who undertakes a seismological study of the San Andreas Fault ought rather to address himself, in the manner of James, to the question of what it is like to get caught up in an earthquake. Though it is possible that someone whose interest in seismology was the sequel to his experience of an earthquake might come to agree that he had misunderstood himself, if he did not agree we would have to withdraw (failing behavioural tokens that he was mistaken). Whereas in the other kind of case we have hard philosophical arguments that his problems and his methods pass one another by. Someone who want to know what is going on in his brain when he listens to Brahms may be making a mistake, but it is not the same kind of mistake as that of someone who thinks his research into the brain is going to resolve his aesthetic puzzlement as to why he finds Brahms 'extremely Kellerian' or, generally, why certain bars make such a peculiar impression on him; what the 'tremendous philosophy' is which he senses behind *The Creation of Adam*; why Beethoven reminds him of Michelangelo.

The sight of a decaying carcass might provoke us to an investigation of the chemistry of putrefaction or it might take us to reflections of the kind which Rilke expressed apropos Baudelaire's poem "Une Charogne": "What was he to do when this presented itself to him? . . . It was his task to perceive, in this horrible, this apparently only repulsive, thing that existence which is valid throughout all existence. Selection and rejection are not possible."[19] It is as plain that the chemistry of putrefaction would be irrelevant to someone on whom the task that the sight of a decaying carcass imposed was to "perceive that existence which is valid throughout all existence" as that this achievement would be of no interest to someone whom the same sight provoked to biochemical speculation. What isn't plain is what it would be to show that one of these enterprises was undertaken in mistake for the other.

Argument on such an issue can only take the form of reminders that our perplexity with respect to certain topics is not always a matter of factual ignorance, and that the interest certain phenomena have for us does not invariably find its natural consummation in further empirical knowledge ("the stupid superstition of our time", p. 239), and of citing occasions on which we mistakenly overlooked this.

In an essay, "Hymns in a Man's Life", D. H. Lawrence says ". . . the miracle of the loaves and fishes is just as good to me now as when I was a child. I don't care whether it is historically a fact or not. What does it matter?" He quotes:

> O Galilee, sweet Galilee,
> Come sing thy songs again to me!

and comments "to me the word Galilee has a wonderful sound. The Lake of Galilee! I don't need to know where it is. I never want to go to Palestine."[20] No one would quarrel with Lawrence's feeling that a geographical or historical enquiry would not be an appropriate response to the wonder produced in him by the hymns of his childhood.

But are there general criteria for determining when such enquiries are inappropriate?

If someone searches for further information to relieve him of the oppression of his perplexity with respect to some impression, we cannot prove that this is a mistake. But if such a one were later to tell us that he had been under an illusion as to what more information could do for him we would understand him.[21]

An analogous kind of disillusionment is expressed by the Irish playwright John Millingron Synge over aspects of his sojourn on the Island of Aran. His enthusiasm for Gaelic culture led him to live, from time to time, among the Aran islanders, about whom he complained that it was "only in the intonation of a few sentences or some old fragments of melody" that he caught "the real spirit of the island . . . For in general the men sit together and talk with endless iteration of the tides and fish and the price of kelp in Connemara."[22] There are impressions which call for enquiry with respect to them to be undertaken in the spirit in which Synge visited Aran – to sit by a turf fire listening to Irish songs, poems and stories, avoiding as he could the talk of tides and fish and the price of kelp in Connemara.

What Synge was after were further manifestations of "the real spirit of the island" and perhaps a clearer sense of the unity of these manifestations. The contemplation of such cases may help us to avert a misunderstanding of the role which further experience plays in such enquiries. It is the formal relation in which it stands to the orginal impression ('the crush of thoughts') that gives new information its point.[23]

The same distinction can be illustrated by the predicament of someone infatuated with the idea of China, which he pictures as "A land of poetry and graciousness . . . where the most serious business of life is to drink tea in a latticed pavilion, beside a silent lake, beneath a weeping willow" (Hugh Honour, Chinoiserie), and who feels a lack of closure, a compulsion to find out or do something with respect to this picture. One conception of his problem would take him to Granet, Needham or Wittvogel, to hydraulic civilizations, patrimonial bureaucracy and the asiatic mode of production; the other to reminiscences of Arthur Waley's Hundred and Seventy Chinese Poems, willow-pattern plates, snatches of gnomic wisdom from Explaining Conjunctions or King Mu of Chou, even, perhaps, to The Wallet of Kai Lung and Terry and the Pirates, with all their multitudinous reverberations and interrelations, in search of the secret of their power over him. What such a Sinophile really wants is not further knowledge but something like Spengler's prime symbol or Goethe's "Urphenomen". Reflecting on the source and character of his infatuation with China is quite another enterprise from attempting to explain the sources and conditions of the distinctiveness of Chinese culture. We overlook the difference between these two enquiries because one so often contributes to the other. Proust says of his account of Chardin's life, "I have shown what the work of a great artist could mean to us by showing all that it meant to him." It is somewhat in this way that our Sinophile might profit from his Sinological researches.

A correct historical reconstruction of the role of human sacrifice in the development of culture, up to and including the survivals themselves, might well be as irrelevant and unilluminating as to the impression made on us by the Fire-festivals as Sinology to Chinoiserie, optics to the beauty of the rainbow, the topography of Palestine to 'Galilee, sweet Galilee' or sidereal astronomy to 'the frosty glories of Orion'. But why is this an objection to Frazer? Why should he not ignore the question "Why does this impress us?" for the question "How did this originate?"

It may sharpen our sense of the distinctiveness of the relation in which we stand to the theme of human sacrifice if we contrast this with the explanatory problem posed us by the outrigger canoe, say. A reconstruction of the origins of the outrigger canoe, tracing it to a raft, the centre log of which was hollowed out while the outer planks were retained as floats, may put me in mind that the sight of an outrigger canoe always makes me obscurely aware of its likeness to a raft, the central log of which had been hollowed out. But this reconstruction would diminish greatly in interest should it prove that the outrigger had evolved rather from a double canoe, the smaller of which had dwindled to a float. The fact that the mistaken reconstruction successfully evoked the impression made on me by the sight of an outrigger canoe would not redeem it. We do not stand to the accounts of human sacrifice as to the outrigger canoe. The impression produced by an outrigger canoe has no "depth".

There is a suggestion as to what Wittgenstein means by depth on p. 249:

What makes human sacrifice something deep and sinister anyway? Is it only the suffering of the victim that impresses us in this way? All manner of diseases bring just as much suffering and do *not* make this impression.

The contrast between the suffering of disease and that of sacrifice is not quite the contrast Wittgenstein means to make. He doesn't mean to contrast our impression of inflicted with that of non-inflicted suffering (though this too raises questions worth pondering). He means to contrast *ritually* inflicted suffering with suffering inflicted for some other purpose. We see what Wittgenstein is getting at if we compare any of the burnings Foxe recounts in his *Book of Martyrs* (which also make an impression in their way) with the impression made by the Beltane Festival. There is no "queer pointlessness" about the burnings Foxe describes, i.e. no rituality and thus, on Wittgenstein's anti-utilitarian view of rituality, no symbolic purport.

The remark continues: "No, this deep and sinister aspect is not obvious just from learning the history of the external action, but we impute it from an experience in ourselves." It is not just our conviction that "the festival is connected with the burning of a man" that confers depth on the practice, but our obscure sense of that in virtue of which he was burnt.

Rituality is often employed to mark the special relation in which we stand to a contingency. Therefore, contemplating such rituals differs from direct meditation on the contingency itself; e.g. the difference between thinking of those who fell in the world wars, say, and reflecting on, rather than joining in, the two minute silence. Ritual death and suffering may have natural death and suffering for its subject. So reflection on the Fire-festivals has features which distinguish it from the straightforward contemplation of atrocity. That to which it stands in some trophic, figurative relation is what gives the ritual its depth. And the task it sets us is to articulate this.

V

What then would be the kind of thing it would be appropriate to produce for the purpose of unperplexing someone who asked why an account of men celebrating a festival by pretending to throw one of their number into a fire should make such a deep impression on him? Something like this:

At all times and in all places men have been fascinated and appalled by the notion of divinity . . . This violent and deleterious aspect of divinity was generally manifested in sacrificial rites. Often moreover the rites were extravagantly cruel: children were offered to monsters of red-hot metal, gigantic wicker figures crammed with human beings were set alight, priests flayed living women and clad themselves in the streaming bloody spoils. Acts as horrifying as these were rare; they were not essential to the sacrifice but they underlined its significance . . . the frightfulness of the divine, (which) will only protect us once its basic need to consume and ruin has been satisfied.[24]

What makes Bataille's account more appropriate than Frazer's is that Bataille's is less likely to encourage the illusion that its assessment requires an effort of historical scholarship. It is more patent that what we are called on to do is to seek for what makes human sacrifice "deep and sinister" among our crush of thoughts about man and his past, to see whether "the frightfulness of the divine" is among the "experiences in ourselves from which we impute" this deep and sinister character. Someone who found Bataille's account acceptable would stand to it, not as he stands to a hypothesis, but as Wittgenstein says someone who was impressed by Frazer's account of the life of the King of the Wood at Nemi stood to the phrase "the majesty of death" (p. 236).

A common temptation with respect to troubling accounts like those of human sacrifice is the sceptical question "Did this really happen?"; but your troubled response need be no less appropriate if it had not really happened. It is the failure to see this which earns Wittgenstein's reproof "like a backward-looking Clever Elsa" (p. 248). (Clever Elsa, the eponymous heroine of a Grimm *märchen*, was sent to the cellar to fetch some beer with which to toast her betrothal, but having spied an axe on the wall above the barrel fell to brooding about the possibility that it might fall on her as yet unconceived child's head when in the course of time he was sent to the cellar to fetch beer.)

Suppose that on learning that in Africa, in times past, men were used as mounts you were caused to think, in a troubled way, of Marlowe's Tambourlaine harnessing his defeated enemies to his carriage, or of the Old Man of the Sea in Sinbad's fifth voyage, and other similar episodes. You might then experience relief on discovering that this African practice was due to the prevalence of the Tsetse fly, which precluded the use of animals as burden beasts, and thus sprang from a utilitarian motive and not any relish for degrading their fellows. But there are occasions on which the relief afforded you by this kind of discovery would be an illusory one. You would have failed to penetrate to the root of the matter, as Wittgenstein thinks Frazer did.

Dr Johnson observed that confronted with accounts of horror the mind takes refuge in incredulity. Sometimes it takes refuge in empirical research. I understand that there is an institute pursuing an enquiry into the history of the persecution and extermination of racial and religious minorities in Europe. Whatever the value of such an enquiry, it often generates illusions as to what its successful prosecution could achieve (and is in part fed from such illusions). There is an ingredient in the dismay occasioned by reminders of the theme of *homo homini daemon* with which even the most lucid narrative is incommensurate.[25]

There are several ways in which empirical enquiry, though fundamentally irrelevant, nevertheless ministers to the disturbance occasioned by certain phenomena. One of these is suggested by Proust in his dealings with jealousy. Swann tells Odette that providing him with details of her Lesbian affairs would relieve his torment: "If I were able to form an idea of the person that would prevent me from ever thinking of her again . . . It's so soothing to be able to form a clear picture of things in one's mind. What is really terrible is what one cannot imagine." What Proust says of Swann — "He was seeking information to dispel suffering" — has a more general application and helps explain our behaviour in these matters.[26]

Sometimes a different principle is at work — the psychic distance which certain modes of presentation are able to introduce between the facts and our troubled response to them. For example, this appreciation of a Frazerian scholar's treatment of cannibalism: "It is a welcome relief to pass sometimes from factual reports of head-hunting expeditions and the various grizly practices that follow such expeditions . . . to the deliberate and measured commentary of a man of E. O. James's calibre."[27] The relief afforded to some minds by "deliberate and measured" commentaries is derived by others from scientistic dealings with the "tragic" and the "terrible". There are people for whom an account which allows them to translate concentration camp guards herding men, women and children towards gas ovens into Lewinian topological vectors is as consoling as Sophocles or Job.

I am saying: we sometimes fail to see the irrelevance of our epistemic activities with respect to a certain phenomenon because we are more anxious to alter its aspect in a congenial direction than to understand that aspect in its relation to us. We are less likely to see fear in a handful of dust of which we know the chemical formula.

Nevertheless someone who has been moved by human sacrifice to devote himself to an historical reconstruction of the development and atrophy of the institution might find his conclusions, however warranted, disappointing in some obscure way. And if he chanced to read Hans Castorp's rhapsodizing on the lesson of his dream of the blood sacrifice — two hags in a temple dismembering and eating a child — ("Well and truly dreamt. I have taken stock. I will remember.") might feel, "that is what I really wanted."[28]

As an illustration of the ubiquity of the error with which Wittgenstein taxes Frazer, consider the following account of the state of Napoleon's Grand Army after crossing the Berezina in its retreat:

the temperature sank to $-13°$. To warm themselves for a few minutes, the soldiers would set whole houses on fire. Some of the details given by Segur seem scarcely credible: 'The light of these conflagrations', he writes, 'attracted some poor wretches whom the intensity of the cold and suffering had made delirious. They dashed forward in a fury, and with gnashing teeth and demoniacal laughter threw themselves into these raging furnaces, where they perished in dreadful convulsions. Their starving companions watched them die without apparent horror. There were even some who laid hold of the bodies disfigured and roasted by the flames, and – incredible as it may seem – ventured to carry this loathsome food to their mouths.' (One hopes that here Segur's sense of drama carried him somewhat beyond the literal truth).[29]

Why should we find comfort in the thought that Segur may have been exaggerating? Is this not reacting like a backward-looking Clever Elsa? The dismay Segur's story occasions us is not to be assuaged by casting doubts on its historicity. "Worries of that kind are not involved here." "There is still something of which we are sure." Segur's anecdote takes us to thoughts of human demoralization and the collapse of solidarity; and the question of what makes these virtualities so disturbing, what gives them their depth, remains to be dealt with even if Segur was exaggerating. We can extend to these contingencies what Wittgenstein says about ritual practices: "We could invent them for ourselves and it would only be an accident if they were not found somewhere or other."[30]

It is the space which the story finds already prepared for it that has to be scrutinized and understood, and not the space which the events themselves may occupy. If I am right about this, perhaps Wittgenstein's oft-quoted remark as to the existence of experimental psychology making us "think we have the means of solving the problems which trouble us; though problem and method pass one another by", is open to a supplementary construction. We begin in envious wonder at the blue-eyed ones, Yeats' "completed arcs", and this wonder takes the form of speculation as to how they got that way, but in the time we come to understand that we really want something other than, or at least more than, what differential psychology can tell us. What we really need is to understand how we stand to those images of daily beauty that make us ugly, how they enter our lives and our feelings about ourselves.

We must construe Wittgenstein's remarks not as attacks on historical or empirical enquiry, but as attempts to make us more clear-headed as to our purposes in undertaking such enquiries and as to the kind of satisfaction they can and cannot yield.

There is such a thing as disinterested curiosity about the past and it can be successfully prosecuted, but it sometimes happens that historical research presents itself as the appropriate response to the impression made by certain objects or events when this is as much an illusion, though one more insidious and less easily exposed, than the comparable illusion of thinking that learning what goes on in the brain when we listen to music is going to illuminate our feelings for music.

The main burden of my argument has been that on many occasions we mistake the nature of the problem involved in accounting for the impressions which perplex, preoccupy or trouble us, or in assessing the discourse in which this is attempted, thinking that what we want with respect to them are historical reconstructions or causal explanations, and that it is a merit of Wittgenstein's reflections on Fire-festivals to have forced this fact on our attention. Wittgenstein's most fundamental objection to Frazer is one which Frazer could not have met, either by attempting to do justice to the expressive–cathartic aspect of ritual, or by addressing himself to the "inner nature" of survivals themselves rather than to their origins. He would have had to concede that his entire programme had been misconceived; that what was called for by the notion of human sacrifice was neither an historical nor a causal enquiry, but rather an attempt to unravel the web of associations wound round the subject by nature and the unavoidable conditions of humanity.

Notes

1. Wittgenstein was using the one-volume abridged edition published in 1925 and it is to this edition that the page references in *Synthese* correspond. My quotations are also from the abridged edition.
2. G. E. Moore, *Philosophical Papers* (London, 1962), p. 309.
3. *ibid.*, first paragraph of Chapter 62, "The Fire-festivals of Europe".
4. *ibid.*, Chapter 65, "Balder and the Mistletoe".
5. *ibid.*, Chapter 64, "The Burning of Human Beings in the Fires".
6. *ibid.*
7. "Bemerkungen über Frazer's *The Golden Bough*", *Synthese*, XVIIX (1967), 223–53.

     All page references unless otherwise indicated are to *Synthese*. I have made use of three translations: an unpublished one by A. M. Miles; that by A. M. Miles and Rush Rhees published in *The Human World*, no. 3, May 1971, but with the omission of some twenty remarks which Rhees came to feel did not belong with the others; and an unpublished version by Professor A. E. Manser of the University of Southampton.

The bulk of Wittgenstein's remarks are not addressed to Fire-festivals or to human sacrifice, but to the general character of ritual.

The Fire-festivals are discussed in a sequence of remarks which begins on page 246 and end on page 252.

8. N. Rudich and M. Stassen, "Wittgenstein's Implied Anthropology" in *History and Theory*, vol. x, no. 1 (1971), pp. 84–9.

9. Sir William Ridgeway, "The Methods of Mannhardt and Frazer as Illustrated by the Writings of the Mistress of Girton", Cambridge Philosophical Society, 1923.

10. "Mythological Forms of Bakers' Cakes", *Current Literature*, 1898.

11. George Santayana, *The Sense of Beauty* (New York, 1961), p. 80.

12. The phrases in quotes are from p. 241. On this page Wittgenstein says: "'And so the Chorus hints at a hidden law' is what we feel like saying of Frazer's collection of facts." The quotation ("*Und so deutet das Chor auf ein geheimes Gesetz*") is from Goethe's poem to Christine Vulpius on the metamorphosis of plants. The reference to the schema of a plant which follows is an allusion to Goethe's notion of primal phenomena. Here is a gloss on Goethe's views which brings out their affinity to those I find in Wittgenstein. The expositor (Owen Barfield) says Goethe wants to distinguish "an arbitrary surmise not based on anything inherent in the phenomena but brought to them from outside from Goethe's *Ur-phänomen* which was more in the nature of a thought to be found in the phenomena themselves."

The capacity of practices to illuminate each other does not depend on the lineal descent of one from another or of both from a common ancestry. The "hidden law" proclaimed by Frazer's "collection of facts" is that of their association, not of their generation.

13. Frazer, Chapter 50, "Eating the God".

14. R. Weingartner, *Experience and Culture* (Middletown, 1962), pp. 136–7.

15. As quoted by William Gass.

16. An illustration of "the web of associations wound round a subject by nature and the unavoidable conditions of humanity" is given by Wittgenstein on p. 251 where he objects to Frazer's speaking of the primitive view that fire is purificatory or that it has some intimate connection with the sun, as theories.

> That fire was used for purification is clear. But nothing can be more probable than that the cleansing ceremonies of thinking people . . . were brought into connection with the sun. If one thought (fire-cleansing) is forced on one person, and another (Fire-sun) on another people, what can be more probable than both thoughts being forced on a people . . .
>
> The *complete* destruction through fire, or else through smashing to pieces, tearing apart, etc. must have struck man.
>
> But even if one knew nothing of such a connection in thought between purification and the sun, one could accept that it would appear in some place.

17. Cf. Wittgenstein, *Lectures on Aesthetics, Psychology and Religious Belief* (Oxford, 1966), p. 20.

> In the lectures Moore attended, the example Wittgenstein gave of aesthetic questions which he thought like "Why does the Beltane festival impress us?" were "Why is this beautiful?" and "Why will this bass not do?"

18. William James, "On Some Mental Effects of the Earthquake", *Memories and Studies* (New York, 1911), pp. 212–13.

19. R. M. Rilke, *Malte Laurids Brigge*.

20. D. H. Lawrence, "Hymns in a Man's Life", *Phoenix II* (London, 1968), p. 597.

21. Someone who mistakenly thinks that astronomical investigation is the appropriate response to the feelings produced in him by the stars at night might nevertheless fail to discover that

he has moved off in the wrong direction because the empirical enquiry prolongs his trafficking with the objects of his impression and so is the occasion of experiences continuous with those that initiated his interest. Suppose that Bradley, the eighteenth-century astronomer who discovered 3,000 new stars, owed his sense of vocation to the experience described by Valéry – the mysterious impression made on him by the night sky. Though he would be no wiser as to this mystery at the end of his professional life than he was at its beginning, he would at least have spent a considerable part of it looking at stars. And this might cause him to overlook the discrepancy between the questions with which he began and the answers with which he emerged.

If a modern star-fancier decided to make astronomy his vocation and, after arduous study, found himself indoors monitoring bleeps he might come to feel that he had misunderstood himself. John Cowper Powys said of the stars, "My tendency has been . . . to accept them with what Spengler calls the 'physiognomic eye'; in other words, to wonder at them *in their precise visible appearance*, eliminating from my consciousness all those bewildeɩing astronomical and mathematical calculations with regard to their size and distance, their origin and destination. What has always arrested me are the actual configurations of the stars; so many astounding twists and twirls and spirals up there in the Boundless (*Autobiography* (London, 1934), p. 171). If Powys had been less clear-headed as to the source of the fascination the night sky held for him and gone in for radio-astronomy we would have an example of the kind of disillusionment I am talking about.

22. John Millington Synge, *The Aran Islands* (Dublin, 1911), pp. 49–50.
23. William Empson illustrates the operation of this principle in the practice of criticism:
    Continually, in order to paraphrase a piece of verse, it is necessary to drag in some quite irrelevant conceptions; thus I have often been puzzled by finding it necessary to go and look things up in order to find machinery to express distinctions that were already in my mind; indeed, this is involved in the very notion of the activity, for how else would one know what to look up? So that many of my explanations may be demonstrably wrong and yet efficient for their purpose and vice-versa. (*Seven Types of Ambiguity*, 2nd edn (London, 1949), p. 253)
24. Georges Bataille, *Death and Sensuality* (New York, 1969), pp. 176–7.
25. Rush Rhees has discussed this sort of incommensurability in another area of our lives, that of sexuality, in "The Tree of Nebuchadnezer", *The Human World*, August 1971.
26. Edmund Leach, raising the question of "How is it that some thousands of people will spend their ten shillings on a paperback version of *The Golden Bough*?", answered in terms of the "fascination with the brute sadism of primitive sacrifice", and added "it is an odd thought but I can find no other" ("Golden Bough or Gilded Twig?", *Daedalus* 90 (Spring 1961), pp. 383–4). I don't know about the sales of *The Golden Bough* but I suggest that pursuits which seem to manifest "a fascination with brute sadism" are often undertaken not from relish but in the hope of making it less disturbing.
    What is gained by the journey which Dante forced his reader to make amid hideous detail, through depth beyond depth of horror? . . . The contemplation of all this scenery of torment has for its purpose the conquest of pain. (Maud Bodkin, *Archetypal Patterns in Poetry*, London, 1934)
27. Garry Hogg, *Cannibalism and Human Sacrifice* (London, 1958), pp. 135–6.
28. Hans Castorp's epiphany on "the horrible blood sacrifice" (in the chapter "Snow", *The Magic Mountain*) may seem to go further than Wittgenstein's desideratum – the provision of "a perspicuous presentation" which will leave us clearer as to the source of our impression

("arranging the factual material so that we can easily pass from one part to another and have a clear view of it. – Showing it in a perspicuous way." p. 241) But this account may over-intellectualize Wittgenstein's view as to the problem set us by the phenomenon of human sacrifice. Someone "troubled by love" is not likely to be untroubled by statements which address themselves to his condition just because they are non-hypothetical and confine themselves to sorting out his crush of thoughts.

Wittgenstein's analogy with someone troubled by love is better adapted to bring out the irrelevance of empirical hypotheses than to illustrate that what is wanted is "an arrangement of factual material", "putting together what we already know". What would this come to in such a case? A synoptic view of thraldom which took in Catullus, the Chevalier des Grieux, Quasimodo, King Kong and the love-troubled one among others? Would this bring peace?

The crush of thoughts formula may fail to do justice to what is at issue here, unless we construe it to encompass recognition of the need for some satisfactory mental attitude towards that which makes us uneasy as well as the purely intellectual relief of discovering what it is. (Rilke's turn of phrase can serve us here. The predicament of someone troubled by the Fire-festivals is better rendered: "What was he to do when this thing presented itself to him? What was it his task to see in it?" than as "what makes human sacrifice deep and sinister?").

29. Christopher Herold, *The Age of Napoleon* (New York, 1964), p. 323.
30. Wittgenstein, *Philosophical Investigations*, p. 232.

Wittgenstein on Rules and Private Language: An Elementary Exposition*

SAUL A. KRIPKE

I Introductory

Wittgenstein's celebrated argument against 'private language' has been discussed so often that the utility of yet another exposition is certainly open to question. Most of the exposition which follows occurred to the present writer some time ago, in the academic year 1962–3. At that time this approach to Wittgenstein's views struck the present writer with the force of a revelation: what had previously seemed to me to be a

* Various people, including at least Rogers Albritton, G. E. M. Anscombe, Irving Block, Michael Dummett, Margaret Gilbert, Barbara Humphries, Thomas Nagel, Robert Nozick, Michael Slote, and Barry Stroud, influenced this essay. In addition to the Wittgenstein Conference in London, Ontario, I gave various versions of this material as Howison Lectures, the University of California, Berkeley, 1977; as a series of lectures in a special colloquium held in Banff, Alberta, 1977; and at a Wittgenstein Conference held at Trinity College, Cambridge, England, 1978. Versions were also given in seminars at Princeton University, the first being in the Spring Term of 1964–5. No doubt I was influenced by the discussion of my argument at these conferences and seminars. I should especially thank Steven Patten and Ron Yoshida for their beautifully prepared transcripts of the Banff version, and Irving Block both for his help as editor of the present volume, and for inviting me to make this exposition more public at the London Conference. *Samizdat* transcripts of the version given at the London Conference have been circulated widely in Oxford and elsewhere. Work on the present version was partially supported by a Guggenheim Fellowship, by a Visiting Fellowship at All Souls College, Oxford, by a sabbatical from Princeton University, and by the National Science Foundation (USA).

I feel conscious of various imperfections of the present version that had to be let stand in order to publish the essay in the present volume. I hope that some of these may be improved in a later version.

somewhat loose argument for a fundamentally implausible conclusion based on dubious and controversial premises now appeared to me to be a powerful argument, even if the conclusions seemed even more radical and, in a sense, more implausible, than before. I thought at that time that I had seen Wittgenstein's argument from an angle and emphasis very different from the approach which dominated standard expositions. Over the years I came to have doubts. First of all, at times I became unsure that I could formulate Wittgenstein's elusive position as a clear argument. Second, the elusive nature of the subject made it possible to interpret some of the standard literature as perhaps seeing the argument in the same way after all. More important, conversations over the years showed that, increasingly, others were seeing the argument with the emphases I preferred. Nevertheless, recent expositions by very able interpreters differ enough from the following to make me think that a new exposition may still be of use.[1]

A common view of the 'private language argument' in *Philosophical Investigations* assumes that it begins with section 243, and that it continues in the sections immediately following.[2] This view takes the argument to deal primarily with a problem about 'sensation language'. Further discussion of the argument in this tradition, both in support and in criticism, emphasizes such questions as whether the argument invokes a form of the verification principle, whether the form in question is justified, whether it is applied correctly to sensation language, whether the argument rests on an exaggerated scepticism about memory, and so on. Some crucial passages in the discussion following §243 – for example, such celebrated sections as §258 and §265 – have been notoriously obscure to commentators, and it has been thought that their proper interpretation would provide the key to the 'private language argument'.

In my view, the real 'private language argument' is to be found in the sections *preceding* §243. Indeed, in §202 *the conclusion is already stated explicitly*: "Hence it is not possible to obey a rule 'privately': otherwise thinking one was obeying a rule would be the same thing as obeying it." I do not think that Wittgenstein here thought of himself as *anticipating* an argument he was to give in greater detail later. On the contrary, the crucial considerations are all contained in the discussion leading up to the conclusion stated in §202. The sections following §243 are meant to be read in the light of the preceding discussion; difficult as they are in any case, they are much less likely to be understood if they are read in isolation. The 'private language argument' as applied to *sensations* is only a special case of much more general considerations about language previously argued; sensations have a crucial role as an (apparently) convincing *counterexample* to the general considerations previously stated. Wittgenstein therefore goes over the ground again in this special case, marshalling new specific considerations appropriate to it. It should be borne in mind that *Philosophical Investigations* is not a systematic philosophical work where conclusions, once definitely established, need not be reargued. Rather the *Investigations* is written as a perpetual dialectic, where persisting worries, expressed by the voice of the imaginary interlocutor, are never definitively silenced. Since the work is not presented in the form of a deductive argument with definitive theses as conclusions, the same ground is covered repeatedly, from the point of view of various special cases and from different angles, with the hope that the entire process will help the reader see the problems rightly.

The basic structure of Wittgenstein's approach can be presented briefly as follows: A certain problem, or in Humean terminology, a 'sceptical paradox', is presented concerning the notion of a rule. Following this, what Hume would have called a 'sceptical solution' to the problem is presented. There are two areas in which the force, both of the paradox and of its solution, are most likely to be ignored, and with respect to which Wittgenstein's basic approach is most likely to seem incredible. One such area is the notion of a mathematical rule, such as the rule for addition. The other is our talk of our own inner experience, of sensations and other inner states. In treating both these cases, we should bear in mind the basic considerations about rules and language. Although Wittgenstein has already discussed these basic considerations in considerable generality, the structure of Wittgenstein's work is such that the special cases of mathematics and psychology are not simply discussed by citing a general 'result' already established, but by going over these special cases in detail, in the light of the previous treatment of the general case. By such a discussion, it is hoped that both mathematics and the mind can be seen rightly: since the temptations to see them wrongly arise from the neglect of the same basic considerations about rules and language, the problems which arise can be expected to be analogous in the two cases. In my opinion, Wittgenstein did not view his dual interests in the philosophy of mind and the philosophy of mathematics as interests in two separate, at best loosely related, subjects, as someone might be interested both in music and in economics. Wittgenstein thinks of the two subjects as involving the same basic considerations. For this reason, he calls his investigation of the foundations of mathematics "analogous to our investigation of psychology"[1] (*PI*, p. 232). It is no accident that essentially the same basic material on rules is included in both *Philosophical Investigations* and in *Remarks on the Foundation of Mathematics*,[3] both times as the basis of the discussions of the philosophies of mind and of mathematics, respectively, which follow.

In the following, I am largely trying to present Wittgenstein's argument, or, more accurately, that set of problems and arguments which I personally have gotten out of reading of Wittgenstein. With few exceptions, I am *not* trying to present views of my own; neither am I trying to endorse or to criticize Wittgenstein's approach. In some cases, I have found a precise statement of the problems and conclusions to be elusive. Although one has a strong sense that there is a problem, a rigorous statement of it is difficult. I am inclined to think that Wittgenstein's later philosophical style, and the difficulty he found (see his Preface) in welding his thought into a conventional work presented with organized arguments and conclusions, is not simply a stylistic and literary preference, coupled with a *penchant* for a certain degree of obscurity,[4] but stems in part from the nature of his subject.[5]

I suspect – for reasons that will become clearer later – that to attempt to present Wittgenstein's argument precisely is to some extent to falsify it. Probably many of my formulations and recastings of the argument are done in a way Wittgenstein would not himself approve.[6] So the present paper should be thought of as expounding neither 'Wittgenstein's' argument nor 'Kripke's': rather Wittgenstein's argument as it struck Kripke, as it presented a problem for him.

As I have said, I think the basic 'private language argument' *precedes* section 243, though the sections following 243 are no doubt of fundamental importance as well. I propose to discuss the problem of 'private language' initially without mentioning these latter sections *at all*. Since these sections are often thought to *be* the 'private language argument', to some such a procedure may seem to be a presentation of Hamlet without the prince. Even if this is so, there are many other interesting characters in the play.[7]

2 The Wittgensteinian Paradox

In *PI*, §201, Wittgenstein says, "this was our paradox: no course of action could be determined by a rule, because every course of action can be made to accord with the rule." In this section of the present paper, in my own way I will attempt to develop the 'paradox' in question. The 'paradox' is perhaps the central problem of *Philosophical Investigations*. Even someone who disputes the conslusions regarding 'private language', and the philosophies of mind, mathematics, and logic, that Wittgenstein draws from his problem, might well regard the problem itself as an important contribution to philosophy. It may be regarded as a new form of philosophical scepticism.

Following Wittgenstein, I will develop the problem initially with respect to a mathematical example, though the relevant sceptical problem applies to all meaningful uses of language. I, like almost all English speakers, use the word 'plus' and the symbol '+' to denote a well-known mathematical function, addition. The function is defined for all pairs of positive integers. By means of my external symbolic representation and my internal mental representation, I 'grasp' the rule for addition. One point is crucial to my 'grasp' of this rule. Although I myself have computed only finitely many sums in the past, the rule determines my answer for indefinitely many new sums that I have never previously considered. This is the whole point of the notion that in learning to add I grasped a rule: my past intentions regarding addition determine a unique answer for indefinitely many new cases in the future.

Let me suppose, for example, that '68 + 57' is a computation that I have never performed before. Since I have performed – even silently to myself, let alone in my publicly observable behavior – only finitely many computations in the past, such an example surely exists. In fact, the same finitude guarantees that there is an example exceeding, in both its arguments, all previous computations. I shall assume in what follows that '68 + 57' serves for this purpose as well.

I perform the computation, obtaining, of course, the answer '125'. I am confident, perhaps after checking my work, that '125' is the correct answer. It is correct both in the arithmetical sense that 125 is the sum of 68 and 57, and in the metalinguistic sense that 'plus', as I intended to use that word in the past, denoted a function which, when applied to the numbers I called '68' and '57', yields the value 125.

Now suppose I encounter a bizarre sceptic. This sceptic questions my certainty about my answer, in what I just called the 'metalinguistic' sense. Perhaps, he suggests, as I used the term 'plus' in the past, the answer I intended for '68 + 57' should have been '5'! Of course the sceptic's suggestion is obviously insane. My initial response to such a suggestion might be that the challenger should go back to school and learn to add. Let the challenger, however, continue. After all, he says, if I am now so confident that, as I used the symbol '+', my intention was that

'68 + 57' should turn out to denote 125, this cannot be because I explicitly gave myself instructions that 125 is the result of performing the addition in this particular instance. By hypothesis, I did no such thing. But of course the idea is that, in this new instance, I should apply the very same function or rule that I applied so many times in the past. But who is to say what function this was? In the past I gave myself only a finite number of examples instantiating this function. All, we have supposed, involved numbers smaller than 57. So perhaps in the past I used 'plus' and ' + ' to denote a function which I will call 'quus' and symbolize by ' ⊕ '. It is defined by:

$$x \oplus y = x + y, \text{ if } x, y < 57$$
$$= 5 \quad \text{otherwise.}$$

Who is to say that this is not the function I previously meant by ' + '?

The sceptic claims (or feigns to claim) that I am now misinterpreting my own previous usage. By 'plus', he says, I *always meant* quus;[8] now, under the influence of some insane frenzy, or a bout of LSD, I have come to misinterpret my own previous usage.

Ridiculous and fantastic though it is, the sceptic's hypothesis is not logically impossible. To see this, assume the common sense hypothesis that by ' + ' I *did* mean addition. Then it would be *possible*, though surprising, that under the influence of a momentary 'high', I should misinterpret all my past uses of the plus sign as symbolizing the quus function, and proceed, in conflict with my previous linguistic intentions, to compute 68 plus 57 as 5. (I would have made a mistake, not in mathematics, but in the supposition that I had accorded with my previous linguistic intentions.) The sceptic is proposing that I have made a mistake precisely of this kind, but with plus and quus reversed.

Now if the sceptic proposes his hypothesis sincerely, he is crazy; such a bizarre hypothesis as the proposal that I always meant quus is absolutely wild. Wild it indubitably is, no doubt it is false; but if it is false, there must be some fact about my past usage that can be cited to refute it. For although the hypothesis is wild, it does not seem to be *a priori* impossible.

Of course this bizarre hypothesis, and the references to LSD, or to an insane frenzy, are in a sense merely a dramatic device. The basic point is this. Ordinarily, I suppose that, in computing '68 + 57' as I do, I do not simply make an unjustified leap in the dark. I follow directions I previously gave myself that uniquely determine that in this new instance I should say '125'. What are these directions? By hypothesis, I never explicitly told myself that I should say '125' in this very instance. Nor can I say that I should simply 'do the same thing I always did,' if this means 'compute according to the rule exhibited by my previous examples.' That rule could just as well have been the rule for quaddition (the quus function) as for addition. The idea that in fact quaddition *is* what I meant, that in a sudden frenzy I have changed my previous usage, dramatizes the problem.

The ground rules of our formulation of the problem should be made clear. For the sceptic to converse with me at all, we must have a common language. So I am supposing that the sceptic, provisionally, is not questioning my *present* use of the word 'plus'; he agrees that, according to my *present* usage, '68 plus 57' denotes 125. Not only does he agree with me on this, he conducts the entire debate with me in my language as I *presently* use it. He merely questions whether my present usage agrees with my past usage, whether I am *presently* conforming to my *previous* linguistic intentions. The problem is not "How do I know that 68 plus 57 is 125?", which should be answered by giving an arithmetical computation, but rather "How do I know that '68 plus 57', as I *meant* 'plus' in the *past*, should denote 125?" If the word 'plus' as I used it in the past, denoted the quus function, not the plus function (say 'quaddition' rather than addition), then my *past* intention was such that, asked for the value of '68 plus 57', I should have replied '5'.

I put the problem in this way so as to avoid confusing questions about whether the discussion is taking place 'both inside and outside language' in some illegitimate sense.[9] If we are querying the meaning of the word 'plus', how can we use it (and variants, like 'quus') at the same time? So I suppose that the sceptic assumes that he and I agree in our *present* uses of the word 'plus': we both use it to denote addition. He does *not* – at least initially – deny or doubt that addition is a genuine function, defined on all pairs of integers, not does he deny that we can speak of it. Rather he asks why I now believe that by 'plus' in the *past*, I meant addition rather than quaddition. If I meant the former, then to accord with my previous usage I should say '125' when asked to give the result of calculating '68 plus 57'. If I meant the latter, I should say '5'.

The present exposition tends thus to differ from Wittgenstein's original formulations in taking somewhat greater care to make explicit a distinction between use and mention, and between questions about present and past usage. About the present example Wittgenstein might simply ask, "How do I know that I should respond '125' to the query '68 + 57'?" or "How do I know that '68 + 57' comes out 125?" I have found that when the problem is formulated this way, some listeners hear it as a sceptical problem about *arithmetic*: "How do I know that 68 + 57 is 125?" (Why not answer this question with a mathematical proof?) At least at this stage, scepticism about arithmetic should not be taken to be in question: we may assume, if we wish, that 68 + 57 *is* 125. Even if the question is reformulated 'metalinguistically' as "How do I know that 'plus', as I use it, denotes a function that, when applied to 68 and 57, yields 125?", one may answer, "Surely I know that 'plus' denotes the plus function and accordingly that '68 plus 57' denotes 68 plus 57. But if I know arithmetic, I know that 68 plus 57 is 125. So I know that '68 plus 57' denotes 125!" And surely, if I use language at all, I cannot doubt coherently that 'plus', as I now use it, denotes plus! Perhaps I cannot (at least at this stage) doubt this about my *present* usage. But I can doubt that my *past* usage of 'plus' denoted plus. The previous remarks – about a frenzy and LSD – should make this quite clear.

Let me repeat the problem. The sceptic doubts whether any instructions I gave myself in the past compel (or justify) the answer '125' rather than '5'. He puts the challenge in terms of a sceptical hypothesis about a change in my usage. Perhaps when I used the term 'plus' in the *past*, I always meant quus: by hypothesis I never gave myself any explicit directions that were incompatible with such a supposition.

Of course, ultimately, if the sceptic is right, the concepts of meaning and of intending one function rather than another will make no sense. For the sceptic holds that no fact about my past history – nothing that was ever in my mind, or in my external behavior – establishes that I meant plus rather than quus. (Nor, of course, does any fact establish that I meant quus!) But if this is correct, there can of course be no fact about which function I meant, and if there can be no fact about which particular function I meant in the *past*, there can be none in the *present* either. But before we pull the rug out from under our own feet, we begin by speaking as if the notion that at present we mean a certain function by 'plus' is unquestioned and unquestionable. Only *past* usages are to be questioned. Otherwise, we will be unable to *formulate* our problem.

Another important rule of the game is that there are no limitations, in particular, no *behaviorist* limitations, on the facts that may be cited to answer the sceptic. The evidence is not to be confined to that available to an external observer, who can observe my overt behavior but not my internal mental state. It would be interesting if nothing in my external behavior could show whether I meant plus or quus, but something about my inner state could. But the problem here is more radical. Wittgenstein's philosophy of mind has often been viewed as behavioristic, but to the extent that Wittgenstein may (or may not) be hostile to the 'inner', no such hostility is to be assumed as a premise; it is to be argued as a conclusion. So whatever 'looking into my mind' may be, the sceptic asserts that even if God were to do it, he still could not determine that I meant addition by 'plus'.

This feature of Wittgenstein contrasts, for example, with Quine's discussion of the 'indeterminacy of translation'.[10] There are many points of contact between Quine's discussion and Wittgenstein's. Quine, however, is more than content to assume that only behavioral evidence is to be admitted into his discussion. Wittgenstein, by contrast, undertakes an extensive introspective[11] investigation, and the results of the investigation, as we shall see, form a key feature of his argument.

To return to the sceptic. The sceptic argues that when I answered '125' to the problem '68 + 57', my answer was an unjustified leap in the dark; my past mental history is equally compatible with the hypothesis that I mean quus, and therefore should have said '5'. We can put the problem this way: When asked for the answer to 68 + 57, I unhesitatingly and automatically produced '125', but it would seem that if previously I never performed this computation explicitly I might just as well have answered '5'. Nothing justifies a brute inclination to answer one way rather than another.

Many readers, I should suppose, have long been impatient to protest that our problem arises only because of a ridiculous model of the instruction I gave myself regarding 'addition'. Surely I did not merely give myself some finite number of examples, from which I am supposed to extrapolate the whole table ('Let '+' be the function instantiated by the following examples: . . .''). No doubt infinitely many functions are compatible with *that*. Rather I learned – and internalized instructions for – a *rule* which determines how addition is to be continued. What was the rule? Well, say, to take it in its most primitive form: suppose we wish to add x and y. Take a huge bunch of marbles. First count out x marbles in one heap. Then count out y marbles in another. Put the two heaps together and count out the number of marbles in the union thus formed. The result is $x + y$. This set of directions, I may suppose, I explicitly gave myself at some earlier time. It is engraved on my mind as on a slate. It is incompatible with the hypothesis that I meant quus. It is this set of directions, not a finite list of particular additions I performed in the past, that justifies and determines my present response. This consideration is, after all, reinforced when we think what I really *do* when I add 68 and 57. I do not reply automatically with the answer '125', nor do I consult some non-existent past instructions that I should answer '125' in this case. Rather I proceed according to an *algorithm* for addition that I previously learned. The algorithm is more sophisticated and practically applicable than the primitive one just described, but there is no difference in principle.

Despite the initial plausibility of this objection, the sceptic's response is all too obvious. True, if 'count', as I used the word in the past, referred to the act of counting (and my other past words are correctly interpreted in the standard way), then 'plus' must have stood for addition. But I applied 'count', like 'plus', to only finitely many past cases. Thus the sceptic can question my present interpretation of my past usage of 'count' as he did with 'plus'. In particular, he can claim that by 'count' I formerly meant *quount*, where to 'quount' a heap is to count it in the ordinary sense, unless the heap was formed as the union of two heaps, one of which has 57 or more items, in which case one must automatically give the answer '5'. It is clear that if in the past 'counting' meant quounting, and if I follow the rule for 'plus' that was quoted so triumphantly to the sceptic, I must admit that '68 + 57' must yield the answer '5'. Here I have supposed that previously 'count' was never applied to heaps formed as the union of sub-heaps either of which has 57 or more elements, but if this particular upper bound does not work, another will do. For the point is perfectly general: if 'plus' is explained in terms of 'counting', a non-standard interpretation of the latter will yield a non-standard interpretation of the former.[12]

It is pointless of course to protest that I intended the result of counting a heap to be *independent* of its composition in terms of sub-heaps. Let me have said this to myself as explicitly as possible: the sceptic will smilingly reply that once again I am misinterpreting my past usage, that actually 'independent' formerly meant *quindependent*, where 'quindependent' means . . .

Here of course I am expanding Wittgenstein's well-known remarks about "a rule for interpreting a rule". It is tempting to answer the sceptic by appealing from one rule to another more 'basic' rule. But the sceptical move can be repeated at the more 'basic' level also. Eventually the process must stop — "justifications come to an end somewhere" — and I am left with a rule which is completely unreduced to any other. How can I justify my present application of such a rule, when a sceptic could easily interpret it so as to yield any of an indefinite number of other results? It seems that my application of it is an unjustified stab in the dark. I apply the rule *blindly*.

Normally, when we consider a mathematical rule such as addition, we think of ourselves as *guided* in our application of it to each new instance. Just this is the difference between someone who computes new values of a function and someone who calls out numbers at random. Given my past intentions regarding the symbol '+', one and only one answer is dictated as the one appropriate to '68 + 57'. On the other hand, although an intelligence tester may suppose that there is only one possible continuation to the sequence 2, 4, 6, 8, . . ., mathematical and philosophical sophisticates know that an indefinite number of rules (even rules stated in terms of mathematical functions as conventional as ordinary polynomials) are compatible with any such finite initial segment. So if the tester urges me to respond, after 2, 4, 6, 8, . . ., with *the* unique appropriate next number, the proper response is that no such unique number exists, nor is there any unique (rule determined) infinite sequence that continues the given one. The problem can then be put this way: Did I myself, in the directions for the future that I gave myself regarding '+', really differ from the intelligence tester? True, I may not merely stipulate that '+' is to be a function instantiated by a finite number of computations. In addition, I may give myself directions for the further computation of '+', stated in terms of other functions and rules. In turn, I may give myself directions for the further computation of these functions and rules, and so on. Eventually, however, the process must stop, with 'ultimate' functions and rules that I have stipulated for myself only by a *finite* number of examples, just as in the intelligence test. If so, is not my procedure as arbitrary as that of the man who guesses the continuation of the intelligence test? In what sense is my actual computation procedure, following an algorithm that yields '125', more justified by my past instructions than an alternative procedure that would have resulted in '5'? Am I not simply following an unjustifiable impulse?[13]

Of course, these problems apply throughout language and are not confined to mathematical examples, though it is with mathematical examples that they can be most smoothly brought out. I think that I have learned the term 'table' in such a way that it will apply to indefinitely many future items. So I can apply the term to a new situation, say when I enter the Eiffel Tower for the first time and see a table at the base. Can I answer a sceptic who supposes that by 'table' in the past I meant *tabair*, where a 'tabair' is anything that is a table not found at the base of the Eiffel Tower, or a chair found there? Did I think explicitly of the Eiffel Tower when I first 'grasped the concept of' a table, gave myself directions for what I meant by 'table'? And even if I did think of the Tower, cannot any directions I gave myself mentioning it be reinterpreted compatibly with the sceptic's hypothesis? Most importantly for the 'private language' argument, the point of course applies to predicates of sensations, visual impressions, and the like, as well: "*How do I know* that in working out the series + 2 I must write "20 004, 20 006" and not "20 004, 20 008"? (The question: "How do I know that this color is 'red'?" is similar [*Remarks on the Foundations of Mathematics*, I, §3].) The passage strikingly illustrates a central thesis of this paper: that Wittgenstein regards the fundamental problems of the philosophy of mathematics and of the 'private language argument' – the problem of sensation language – as at root identical, stemming from his paradox. The whole of §3 is a succinct and beautiful statement of the Wittgensteinian paradox; indeed the whole initial section of part I of *Remarks on the Foundations of Mathematics* is a development of the problem with special reference to mathematics and logical inference. It has been supposed that all I need to do to determine my use of the word 'green' is to have an image, a sample, of green that I bring to mind whenever I apply the word in the future. When I use this to justify my application of 'green' to a new object, should not the sceptical problem be obvious to any reader of Goodman?[14] Perhaps by 'green', in the past I meant *grue*,[15] and the color image, which indeed was grue, was meant to direct me to apply the word 'green' to *grue* objects always. If the *blue* object before me now is grue, then it falls in the extension of 'green', as I meant it in the past. It is no help to suppose that in the past I stipulated 'green' was to apply to all and only those things 'of the same color as' the sample. The sceptic can reinterpret 'same color' as same *schmolor*,[16] where things have the same schmolor if . . .

Let us return to the example of 'plus' and 'quus'. We have just summarized the problem in terms of the basis of my present particular response: what tells me that I should say '125' and not '5'? Of course the problem can be put equivalently in terms of the sceptical query regarding my present intent: nothing in my mental history establishes whether I meant plus or quus. So formulated, the problem may appear to be epistemological – how can anyone know which of these I meant? Given, however, that everything in my mental history is compatible both with the conclusion that I meant plus and with the conclusion that I meant quus, it is clear that the sceptical challenge is not really an epistemological one. It purports to show that nothing in my mental history or past behavior – not even what an omniscient God would know – could establish whether I meant plus or quus. But then it appears to follow that there was no *fact* about me that constituted my having meant plus rather than quus. How could there be, if nothing in my internal mental history or external behavior will answer the sceptic who supposes that in fact I meant quus? If there was no such thing as my meaning plus rather than quus in the past, neither can there be any such thing in the present. When we initially presented the paradox, we per force used language, taking present meanings for granted. Now we see, as we expected, that this provisional concession was indeed fictive. There can be no fact as to what I mean by 'plus', or any other word at any time. The ladder must finally be kicked away.

This, then, is the sceptical paradox. When I respond in one way rather than another to such a problem as '68 + 57', I can have no justification for one response rather than another. Since the sceptic who supposes that I meant quus cannot be answered, there is no fact about me that distinguishes between my meaning plus and my meaning quus. Indeed, there is no fact about me that distinguishes between my meaning a definite function by 'plus' (which determines my responses in new cases) and my meaning nothing at all.

Can we escape these incredible conclusions? Let me first discuss a response that I have heard more than once in conversation on this topic. According to this response, the fallacy in the argument that no fact about me constitutes my meaning plus lies in the assumption that such a fact must consist in an *occurent* mental state. Indeed the sceptical argument shows that my entire occurent past mental history might have been the same whether I meant plus or quus, but all this shows is the fact that I meant plus (rather than quus) is to be analyzed *dispositionally*, rather than in terms of occurent mental states. Since Ryle's *The Concept of Mind*, dispositional analyses have been influential; Wittgenstein's own later work is of course one of the inspirations for such analyses, and some may think that he himself wishes to suggest a dispositional solution to his paradox.

The dispositional analysis I have heard proposed is simple. To mean addition by ' + ' is to be disposed, when asked for any sum '$x + y$', to give the sum of x and y as the answer (in particular, to say '125' when queried about '68 + 57'); to mean quus is to be disposed when queried about any arguments, to respond with their *quum* (in particular to answer '5' when queried about '68 + 57'). True, my actual thoughts and responses in the past do not differentiate between the plus and the quus hypotheses; but, even in the past, there were dispositional facts about me that did make such a differentiation. To say that in fact I meant plus in the past is to say

— as surely was the case! — that had I been queried about '68 + 57', I *would* have answered '125'. By hypothesis I was not in fact asked, but the disposition was present none the less.

To a good extent this reply immediately ought to appear to be misdirected, off target. For the sceptic created an air of puzzlement as to my *justification* for responding '125' rather than '5' to the addition problem as queried. He thinks my response is no better than a stab in the dark. Does the suggested reply advance matters? How does it *justify* my choice of '125'? What it says is: "'125' is the response you are disposed to give, and (perhaps) it would also have been your response in the past?" Well and good, I know that '125' is the response I am disposed to give (I am actually giving it!), and maybe it is helpful to be told — as a matter of brute fact — that I would have given the same response in the past. How does any of this indicate that — now or in the past — '125' was an answer *justified* in terms of instructions I gave myself, rather than a mere jack-in-the-box unjustified and arbitrary response? Am I supposed to justify my present belief that I meant addition, not quaddition, and hence should answer '125', in terms of a *hypothesis* about my *past* dispositions? (Do I record and investigate the past physiology of my brain?) Why am I so sure that one particular hypothesis of this kind is correct, when all my past thoughts can be construed either so that I meant plus or so that I meant quus?

Intuitively, then, it seems highly questionable whether a dispositional account gets us anywhere towards answering the sceptic's suggestion that nothing *justifies* my present response. Nevertheless, it straightforwardly attempts to rebut the final sceptical conclusion that there is no *fact* about me that constitutes my meaning addition, not quaddition, by 'plus'; it gives a putative candidate for such a fact. If the dispositional view answers this aspect of the sceptical challenge, it defuses what perhaps is the most disturbing aspect of the problem. So let us examine the dispositional view as it touches this aspect. Ultimately, its weaknesses as an analysis of what it is to mean addition by a certain sign will be related to its failure to answer the questions mentioned in the preceding paragraph, but for the moment let us suspend these questions and consider the dispositional theory purely as a putative analysis of the fact that I meant plus.

As I said, probably some have read Wittgenstein himself as favoring a dispositional analysis. I think that on the contrary, although Wittgenstein's views have dispositional elements, any such analysis is inconsistent with Wittgenstein's view.[17] Let me mention some objections.

First, we must state the simple dispositional analysis. It gives a criterion that will tell me what number theoretic function φ I mean by a binary function symbol 'f', namely: The referent φ of 'f' is that unique binary function φ such that I am disposed, if queried about '$f(m, n)$', where 'm' and 'n' are numerals denoting particular numbers m and n, to reply 'p', where 'p' is a numberal denoting $\varphi(m, n)$. The criterion is meant to enable us to 'read off' which function I mean by a given function symbol from my disposition. The cases of addition and quaddition above would simply be special cases of such a scheme of definition.

The dispositional theory attempts to avoid the problem of the finiteness of my actual past performance by appealing to a disposition. But in doing so, it ignores an obvious fact: not only my actual performance, but also the totality of my dispositions, is finite. It is not true, for example, that if queried about the sum of any two numbers, no matter how large, I will reply with their actual sum, for some pairs of numbers are simply too large for my mind – or my brain – to grasp. When given such sums, I may shrug my shoulders for lack of comprehension; I may even, if the numbers involved are large enough, die of old age before the questioner completes his question. Let 'quaddition' be redefined so as to be a function which agrees with addition for all pairs of numbers small enough for me to have any disposition to add them, and let it diverge from addition thereafter (say, it is 5). Then, just as the sceptic previously proposed the hypothesis that I meant quaddition in the old sense, now he proposes the hypothesis that I meant quaddition in the new sense. A dispositional account will be impotent to refute him. As before, there are infinitely many candidates the sceptic can propose for the role of quaddition.

I have heard it suggested that the trouble arises solely from too crude a notion of disposition: *ceteris paribus*, I surely will respond with the sum of any two numbers when queried. And *ceteris paribus* notions of dispositions, not crude and literal notions, are the ones standardly used in philosophy and in science. Perhaps, but how should we flush out the *ceteris paribus* clause? Perhaps as something like: if my brain had been stuffed with sufficient extra matter to grasp large enough numbers, and if it were given enough capacity to perform such a large addition, and if my life (in a healthy state) were prolonged enough, then given an addition problem involving two large numbers, m and n, I would respond with their sum, and not with the result according to some quus-like rule. But how can we have any confidence of this? How in the world can I tell what would happen if my brain were stuffed with extra brain matter, or if my life were prolonged by some magic elixir? Surely such speculation should be left to science fiction writers and futurologists. We have no idea what the results of such experiments would be. They might lead me to go insane, even to behave according to a quus-like rule. The outcome really is obviously indeterminate. Failing further specification of these magic mind-expanding processes, and even with such specifications, it is highly speculative. But of course what the *ceteris paribus* clause really means is something like this: If I somehow were to be given the means to carry out my intentions with respect to numbers that presently are too long for me to add (or to grasp), and if I were to carry out these intentions, then if queried about '$m + n$' for some big m and n, I will respond with their sum (and not with their quum). Such a counterfactual conditional is true enough, but it is of no help against the sceptic. It presupposes a prior notion of my having an intention to mean one function rather than another by '$+$'. It is in virtue of a fact of this kind about me that the conditional is true. But of course the sceptic is challenging the existence of just such a fact; his challenge must be met by specifying its nature. Granted that I mean addition by '$+$', then of course if I were to act in accordance with my intentions, I would respond, given any pair of numbers to be combined by '$+$', with their sum; but equally, granted that I mean quaddition, if I were to act in accordance with my intentions, I would respond with the quum. One cannot favor one conditional rather than another without circularity.

Recapitulating briefly: if the dispositionalist attempts to define which function I meant as the function determined by the answer I am supposed to give for arbitrarily large arguments, he ignores the fact that my dispositions extend to only finitely many cases. If he tries to appeal to my responses under idealized conditions that overcome this finiteness, he will succeed only if the idealization includes a specification that I will still respond, under these idealized conditions, according to the infinite table of the function I actually meant. But then the circularity of the procedure is evident. The idealized dispositions are determinate only because it is already settled which function I meant.

The dispositionalist labors under another, equally potent, difficulty. Most of us have dispositions to make mistakes. For example, when asked to add certain numbers some people forget to 'carry'. They are thus disposed, for these numbers, to give an answer differing from the usual addition table. Normally, we say that such people have made a *mistake*. That means, that for them as for us, '$+$' means addition, but for certain numbers they are not disposed to give the answer they *should* give, if they are to accord with the table of the function they actually *meant*. But the dispositionalist cannot say this. According to him, the function someone means is to be *read off* from his dispositions; it cannot be presupposed in advance which function is meant. In the present instance a certain unique function (call it 'skaddition') corresponds in its table exactly to the subject's dispositions including his dispositions to make mistakes. (Waive the difficulty that the subject's dispositions are finite: suppose he has a disposition to respond to any pair of arguments.) So, where common sense holds that the subject means the same addition function as everyone else but systematically makes computational mistakes, the dispositionalist seems forced to hold that the subject makes no computational mistakes, but means a non-standard function ('skaddition') by ' + '. Recall that the dispositionalist held that we would detect someone who meant quus by ' + ' *via* his disposition to respond with '5' for arguments ⩾ 57. In the same way, he will 'detect' that a quite ordinary, though fallible, subject means some non-standard function by ' + '.

Once again, the difficulty cannot be surmounted by a *ceteris paribus* clause, by a clause excluding 'noise', or by a distinction between 'competence' and 'performance'. No doubt a disposition to give the true sum in response to each addition problem is part of my 'competence', if by this we mean simply that such an answer accords with the rule I intended, or if we mean that, if all my dispositions to make mistakes were removed, I would give the correct answer. (Again I waive the finiteness of my capacity.) But a disposition to make a mistake is simply a disposition to *give an answer other than the one that accords with the function I meant.* To presuppose this concept in the present discussion is of course viciously circular. If I meant addition, my 'erroneous' actual disposition is to be ignored; if I meant skaddition, it should not be. Nothing in the notion of my 'competence' as thus defined can possibly tell me which alternative to adopt.[17a] Alternatively, we might try to specify the 'noise' to be ignored without presupposing a prior notion of which function is meant. A little experimentation will reveal the futility of such an effort. Recall that the subject has a *systematic* disposition to forget to carry in certain circumstances: he tends to give a uniformly erroneous answer when well rested, in a pleasant environment free of clutter, etc. One cannot repair matters by urging that the subject would eventually respond with the right answer after correction by others. First, there are uneducable subjects who will persist in their error even after persistent correction. Second, what is meant by 'correction by others'? If it means rejection by others of 'wrong' answers (answers that do not accord with the rule the speaker means) and suggestion of the right answer (the answer that does accord), then again the account is circular. If random intervention is allowed (that is, the 'corrections' may be arbitrary, whether they are 'right' or 'wrong'), then, although educable subjects may be induced to correct their wrong answers, suggestible subjects may also be induced to replace their correct answers with erroneous ones. The amended dispositional statement will, then, provide no criterion for the function that is really meant.

The dispositional theory, as stated, assumes that which function I meant is determined by my dispositions to compute its values in particular cases. In fact, this is not so. Since dispositions cover only a finite segment of the total function and since they may deviate from its true values, two individuals may agree on their computations in particular cases even though they are actually computing different functions. Hence the dispositional view is not correct.

In discussions, I have sometimes heard a variant of the dispositional account. The argument goes as follows: the sceptic argues, in essence, that I am free to give any new answer to an addition problem, since I can always interpret my previous intentions appropriately. But how can this be? As Dummett put the objection: "A machine can follow this rule; whence does a human being gain a freedom of choice in this matter which a machine does not possess?"[17b] The objection is really a form of the dispositional account, for that account can be viewed as if it interpreted us as machines, whose output mechanically yields the correct result.

We can interpret the object as arguing that the rule can be *embodied* in a machine that computes the relevant function. If I build such a machine, it will simply grind out the right answer, in any particular case, to any particular addition problem. The answer that the machine would give is, then, the answer that I intended.

The term 'machine' is here, as often elsewhere in philosophy, ambiguous. Few of us are in a position to build a machine or draw up a program to embody our intentions; and if a technician performs the task for me, the sceptic can ask legitimately whether the technician has performed his task correctly. Suppose, however, that I am fortunate enough to be such an expert that I have the technical facility required to embody my own intentions in a computing machine, and I state that the machine is *definitive* of my own intentions. Now the word 'machine' here may refer to any one of various things. It may refer to a machine *program* that I draw up, embodying my intentions as to the operation of the machine. Then exactly the same problems arise for the program as for the original symbol '+': the sceptic can feign to believe that the program, too, ought to be interpreted in a quus-like manner. To say that a program is not something that I wrote down on paper, but an abstract mathematical object, gets us no further. The problem then simply takes the form of the question: what program (in the sense of abstract mathematical object) corresponds to the 'program' I have written on paper (in accordance with the way I meant it)? ('Machine' often seems to mean a program in one of these senses: a Turing 'machine', for example, would be better called a 'Turing program'.) Finally, however, I may build a concrete machine, made of metal and gears (or transistors and wires), and declare that it embodies the function I intend by '+': the values that it gives are the values of the function I intend. However, there are several problems with this. First, even if I say that the machine embodies the function in this sense, I must do so in terms of instructions (machine 'language', coding devices) that tell me how to interpret the machine; further, I must declare explicitly that the function always takes values as given, in accordance with the chosen code, by the machine. But then the sceptic is free to interpret all these instructions in a non-standard, 'quus-like' way. Waiving this problem, there are two others – here is where previous discussion of the dispositional view comes in. I cannot really insist that the values of the function are given by the machine. First, the machine is a finite object, accepting only finitely many numbers as input and yielding only finitely many as output – others are simply too big. Indefinitely many programs extend the actual finite behavior of the machine. Usually this is ignored because the designer of the machine intended it to fulfill just one program, but in the present context such an approach to the intentions of the designer simply gives the sceptic his wedge to interpret in a non-standard way. (Indeed, the appeal to the designer's program makes the physical machine superfluous; only the program is really relevant. The machine as physical object is of value only if the intended function can somehow be read off from the physical object alone.) Second, in practice it hardly is likely that I really intend to entrust the values of a function to the operation of a physical machine, even for that finite portion of the function for which the machine can operate. Actual machines can *malfunction*: through melting wires or slipping gears they may give the wrong answer. How is it determined when a malfunction occurs? By reference to the program of the machine, as intended by its designer, not simply by reference to the machine itself. Depending on the intent of the designer, any particular phenomenon may or may not count as a machine 'malfunction'. A programmer with suitable intentions might even have intended to make use of the fact that wires melt or gears slip, so that a machine that is 'malfunctioning' for me is behaving perfectly for him. Whether a machine ever malfunctions and, if so, when, is not a property of the machine itself as a physical object but is well defined only in terms of its program, as stipulated by its designer. Given the program, once again the physical object is superfluous for the purpose of determining what function is meant. Then, as before, the sceptic can concentrate his objections on the program. The last two criticisms of the use of the physical machine as a way out of scepticism — its finitude and the possibility of malfunction — obviously parallel two corresponding objections to the dispositional account.[18]

The moral of the present discussion of the dispositional account may be relevant to other areas of concern to philosophers beyond the immediate point at issue. Suppose I do mean addition by '+'. What is the relation of this supposition to the question how I will respond to the problem '68 + 57'? The dispositionalist gives a *descriptive* account of this relation: if '+' meant addition, then I will answer '125'. But this is not the proper account of the relation, which is *normative*, not descriptive. The point is *not* that, if I meant addition by '+', I *will* answer '125', but that, if I intend to accord with my past meaning of '+', I *should* answer '125'. Computational error, finiteness of my capacity, and other disturbing factors may lead me not to be *disposed* to respond as I *should*, but if so, I have not acted in accordance with my intentions. The relation of meaning and intention to future action is *normative, not descriptive*.

In the beginning of our discussion of the dispositional analysis, we suggested that it had a certain air of irrelevance with respect to a significant aspect of the sceptical problem — that the fact that the sceptic can maintain the hypothesis that I meant quus shows that I had no *justification* for answering '125' rather than '5'. How does the dispositional analysis even appear to touch this problem? Our conclusion in the previous paragraph shows that in some sense, after giving a number of more specific criticisms of the dispositional theory, we have returned full circle to our original intuition. Precisely the fact that our answer to the question of which function I meant is *justificatory* of my present response is ignored in the dispositional account and leads to all its difficulties.

I shall leave the dispositional view. Perhaps I have already belabored it too much. Let us repudiate briefly another suggestion. Let no one —

under the influence of too much philosophy of science – suggest that the hypothesis that I meant plus is to be preferred as the *simplest* hypothesis. I will not here argue that simplicity is relative, or that it is hard to define, or that a Martian might find the quus function simpler than the plus function. Such replies may have considerable merit, but the real trouble with the appeal to simplicity is more basic. Such an appeal must be based either on a misunderstanding of the sceptical problem, or of the role of simplicity considerations, or both. Recall that the sceptical problem was not merely epistemic. The sceptic argues that there is no fact as to what I meant, whether plus or quus. Now simplicity considerations can help us decide between competing hypotheses, but they obviously can never tell us what the competing hypotheses are. If the two competing hypotheses are not genuine hypotheses, not assertions of genuine matters of fact, no 'simplicity' considerations will make them so.

Suppose there are two conflicting hypotheses about electrons, both confirmed by the experimental data. If our own view of statements about electrons is 'realist' and not 'instrumentalist', we will view these assertions as making factual assertions about some 'reality' about electrons. God, or some appropriate being who could 'see' the facts about electrons directly, would have no need for experimental evidence or simplicity considerations to decide between hypotheses. We, who lack such capacities, must rely on indirect evidence, from the effects of the electrons on the behavior of gross objects, to decide between the hypotheses. If two competing hypotheses are indistinguishable as far as their effects on gross objects are concerned, then *we* must fall back on simplicity considerations to decide between them. A being – not ourselves – who could 'see' the facts about electrons 'directly' would have no need to invoke simplicity considerations, nor to rely on indirect evidence to decide between the hypotheses; he would 'directly perceive' the relevant facts that make one hypothesis true rather than another. To say this is simply to repeat, in colorful terminology, the assertion that the two hypotheses do state genuinely different matters of fact.

Now Wittgenstein's sceptic argues that he knows of no fact about an individual that could constitute his state of meaning plus rather than quus. Against *this* claim simplicity considerations are irrelevant. Simplicity considerations would have been relevant against a sceptic who argued that the indirectness of our access to the facts of meaning and intention *prevents us ever from knowing* whether we mean plus or quus. But such merely epistemological scepticism is *not* in question. The sceptic does not argue that our own limitations of access to the facts prevent us from knowing something hidden. He claims that an omniscient being, with access to *all* available facts, still would not find any fact that differentiates between the plus and the quus hypotheses. Such an omniscient being would have neither need nor use for simplicity considerations.[19]

The idea that we lack 'direct' access to the facts whether we mean plus or quus is bizarre in any case. Do I not know, directly, and with a fair degree of certainty, that I mean plus? There may be some facts about me to which my access is indirect, and about which I must form tentative hypotheses: but surely the fact as to what I mean by 'plus' is not one of them! To say that it is, is already to take a big step in the direction of scepticism.

Now the reference, in our exposition, to what an omniscient being could or would know is merely a dramatic device. When the sceptic denies that even God, who knows all the facts, could know whether I meant plus or quus, he is simply giving colorful expression to his denial that there is any fact of the matter as to which I meant. Perhaps if we remove the metaphor we may do better. The metaphor, perhaps, may seduce us towards scepticism by encouraging us to look for a reduction of the notions of meaning and intention to something else. Why not argue that "meaning addition by 'plus'" denotes an irreducible experience, with its own special *quale*, known directly to each of us by introspection? (Headaches, tickles, nausea are examples of inner states with such *qualia*.)[19a] Perhaps the "decisive move in the conjuring trick" has been made when the sceptic notes that I have performed only finitely many additions and challenges me, in the light of *this* fact, to adduce some fact that 'shows' that I did not mean quus. Maybe I appear to be unable to reply just because the experience of meaning addition by 'plus' is as unique and irreducible as that of seeing yellow or feeling a headache, while the sceptic's challenge invites me to look for another fact or experience to which this can be reduced.

I referred to an *introspectible* experience because, since each of us knows immediately and with fair certainty that he means addition by 'plus', presumably the view in question assumes we know this in the same way we know that we have headaches — by attending to the 'qualitative' character of our own experiences. Presumably the experience of *meaning addition* has its own irreducible quality, as does that of feeling a headache. The fact that I mean addition by 'plus' is to be identified with my possession of an experience of this quality.

Throughout *Philosophical Investigations* Wittgenstein engages in an extensive polemic against the view of meaning as an introspectible experience. His investigation here is an introspective one, designed to show that the supposed unique experience is a chimera. Of all the replies to the sceptic he combats, this one is probably the most natural and fundamental. But for the present day audience I dealt with it neither first nor at greatest length, for, though the Humean picture of an irreducible 'impression' corresponding to each psychological state or event has tempted many in the past, it tempts relatively few today. In fact, if in the past it was too readily and simplistically assumed, at present its force is – at least in my personal opinion – probably too *little* felt. There are several reasons for this. One is that, in this instance, Wittgenstein's critique of alternative views has been relatively well received and absorbed. And related writers – such as Ryle – have reinforced the critique of the Cartesian and Humean pictures. Another reason – unattractive to the present writer – has been the popularity of materialistic-behavioristic views that ignore the problem of felt qualities of mental states altogether, or at least attempt to analyze all such states away in broadly behavioristic terms.[20]

It is important to repeat in the present connection what I have said above: Wittgenstein does not base his considerations on any behavioristic *premise* that dismisses the 'inner'. On the contrary, much of his argumentation consists in detailed introspective considerations. Careful consideration of our inner lives, he argues, will show that there is no special inner experience of 'meaning' of the kind supposed by his opponent. The case is specifically in *contrast* with feeling a pain, seeing red, and the like.

It takes relatively little introspective acuteness to realize the dubiousness of the attribution of a special qualitative character to the 'experience' of meaning addition by 'plus'. Attend to what happened when I first learned to add. First, there may or may not have been a specifiable time, probably in my childhood, at which I suddenly felt (*Eureka!*) that I had grasped the rule for addition. If there was not, it is very hard to see in what the suppositious special experience of my learning to add consisted. Even if there was a particular time at which I could have shouted "*Eureka!*" – surely the exceptional case – in what did the attendant experience consist? Probably consideration of a few particular cases and a thought – "Now I've got it!" – or the like. Could just *this* be the content of an experience of 'meaning addition'? How would it have been different if I had meant quus? Suppose I perform a particular addition now, say '5 + 7'. Is there any special quality to the experience? Would it have been different if I had been trained in, and performed, the corresponding quaddition? How different indeed would the *experience* have been if I had performed the corresponding multiplication ('5 × 7'), other than that I would have responded automatically with a different answer? (Try the experiment yourself.)

Wittgenstein returns to points like these repeatedly throughout *Philosophical Investigations*. In the sections where he discusses his sceptical paradox (§§137–242), after a general consideration of the alleged introspectible process of understanding, he considers the issue in connection with the special case of *reading* (§§156–78). By 'reading' Wittgenstein means reading out loud what is written or printed and similar activities: he is not concerned with understanding what is written. I myself, like many of my coreligionists, first learned to 'read' Hebrew in this sense before I could understand more than a few words of the language. Reading in this sense is a simple case of 'following a rule'. Wittgenstein points out that a beginner, who reads by laboriously spelling words out, may have an introspectible experience when he really reads, as opposed to pretending to 'read' a passage he has actually memorized in advance; but an experienced reader simply calls the words out and is aware of no special conscious experience of 'deriving' the words from the page. The experienced reader may 'feel' nothing different when he reads from what the beginner feels, or does not feel, when he pretends. And suppose a teacher is teaching a number of beginners to read. Some pretend, other occasionally get it right by accident, others have already learned to read. When has someone passed into the latter class? In general, there will not be an identifiable moment when this has happened: the teacher will judge of a given pupil that he has 'learned to read' if he passes tests for reading often enough. There may or may not be an identifiable moment when the pupil first *felt*, "Now I am reading!" but the presence of such an experience is neither a necessary nor a sufficient condition for the teacher to judge of him that he is reading.

Again, (*PI*, §166), someone may, under the influence of a drug, or in a dream, be presented with a made-up 'alphabet' and utters certain words, with all the characteristic 'feeling' of reading, to the extent that such a 'feeling' exists at all. If, after the drug wears off (or he wakes up), he himself thinks he was uttering words at random with no real connection with the script, should we really say he was reading? Or, on the other hand, what if the drug leads him to read fluently from a genuine text, but with the 'sensation' of reciting something learned by heart? Wasn't he still reading?

It is by examples like these — *Philosophical Investigations* contains a wealth of examples and mental thought experiments beyond what I have summarized — that Wittgenstein argues that the supposed special 'experiences' associated with rule following are chimerical. As I said, my own discussion can be brief because this particular Wittgensteinian lesson has been relatively well learned, perhaps too well learned. But some points should be noted. First, to repeat, the method of the investigation, and of the thought-experiments is deeply introspective: it is exactly the kind of investigation a strict psychological behaviorist would *prohibit*. Second, although Wittgenstein does conclude that behavior, and dispositions to behavior, lead us to *say* of a person that he is reading, or adding, or whatever, this should not, in my opinion, be misconstrued as an endorsement of the dispositional theory: he does not say that reading or adding *is* a certain disposition to behavior.[21]

Wittgenstein's conviction of the contrast between states of understanding, reading and the like, and 'genuine', introspectible mental states or processes is so strong that it leads him — who is often regarded as a (or the) father of 'ordinary language philosophy', and who emphasizes the importance of respect for the way language is actually used — into some curious remarks about ordinary usage. Consider *PI*, §154: "In the sense in which there are processes (including mental processes) which are characteristic of understanding, understanding is not a mental process. (A pain's growing more and less; the hearing of a tune or sentence: these are mental processes.)" Or again, at the bottom of *PI*, p. 59, "'Understanding a word': a state. But a *mental* state? — Depression, excitement, pain, are called mental states. Carry out a grammatical investigation . . ." In the same ordinary sense, coming to understand, or learning, is a mental process *par excellence*. A pain's growing more and less, and especially the hearing of a tune or sentence, are probably not ordinarily thought of a 'mental' processes at all. Although depression and anxiety would ordinarily be called 'mental' states: pain (if genuine physical pain is meant) is probably *not* a 'mental' state. ("It's all in your mind" means that no genuine physical pain is present.) But Wittgenstein's concern is not really with usage but with a philosophical terminology. 'Mental states' and 'mental processes' are those introspectible 'inner' contents that I can find in my mind, or that God could find if he looked into my mind. Such phenomena, inasmuch as they are introspectible, 'qualitative' states of the mind, are not subject to immediate sceptical challenge of the present type. Understanding is not one of these.

Of course the falsity of the 'unique introspectible state' view of meaning plus must have been implicit from the start of the problem. If there really were an introspectible state, like a headache, of meaning addition by 'plus', it would have stared one in the face and would have robbed the sceptic's challenge of any appeal. But given the force of this challenge, the need philosophers have felt to posit such a state and the loss we incur when we are robbed of it should be apparent. Perhaps we may try to recoup, by arguing that meaning addition by 'plus' is a state even more *sui generis* than we have argued before. Perhaps it is simply a primitive state, not to be assimilated to sensations or headaches or any 'qualitative' states, nor to be assimilated to dispositions, but a state of a unique kind of its own.

Such a move may in a sense be irrefutable, and taken in an appropriate way Wittgenstein may even accept it. But it seems desperate: it leaves the nature of this postulated primitive state – the primitive state of 'meaning addition by "plus"' – completely mysterious. It is not supposed to be an introspectible state, yet we supposedly are aware of it with some fair degree of certainty whenever it occurs. For how else can each of us be confident that he *does*, at present, mean addition by 'plus'? Even more important is the logical difficulty implicit in Wittgenstein's sceptical argument. I think that Wittgenstein argues, not merely as we have said hitherto, that introspection shows that the alleged primitive state of understanding is a chimera, but also that it is logically impossible (or at least that there is a considerable logical difficulty) for there to be a state of 'meaning addition by "plus"' at all.

Such a state would have to be a finite object, contained in our finite minds. It does not consist in my explicitly thinking of each case of the addition table, nor even of my encoding each separate case in the brain: we lack the capacity for that. Yet (*PI*, §195) "in a *queer* way" each such case already is "in some sense present". (Before we hear Wittgenstein's sceptical argument, we surely suppose – unreflectively – that something like this is indeed the case. Even now I have a strong inclination to think this somehow must be right.) What can that sense be? Can we conceive of a finite state which *could* not be interpreted in a quus-like way? How could that be? The proposal I am now discussing brushes such questions under the rug, since the nature of the supposed 'state' is left mysterious. "But" – to quote the protest in *PI*, §195 more fully – "I don't mean that what I do now (in grasping a sense) determines the future use *causally* and as a matter of experience, but that in a *queer* way, the use itself is in some sense present." A causal determination is the kind of analysis supposed by the dispositional theorist, and we have already seen that that is to be rejected. Presumably the relation now in question grounds some entailment roughly like: "If I now mean addition by 'plus'; then, if I remember this intention in the future and wish to accord with it, and make no mistake, when asked for '68 + 57', I will respond '125'." If Hume is right, of course no past state of my mind can entail that I will give any particular response in the future. But that I meant 125 in the past does not itself entail this; I must remember my intention, and so on. Nevertheless, the nature of these conditions, and of the relations that support them, remain mysterious.

Mathematical realists, or 'Platonists', have emphasized the non-mental nature of mathematical entities. The addition function is not in any particular mind, nor is it the common property of all minds. It has an independent, 'objective', existence. There is then no problem – as far as the present considerations go – as to how the addition function (taken, say, as a set of triples)[22] contains within it all its instances, such as the triple (68, 57, 125). This simply is in the nature of the mathematical object in question, and it may well be an infinite object. The proof that the addition function contains such a triple as (68, 57, 125) belongs to mathematics and has nothing to do with meaning or intention.

Frege's analysis of the usage of the plus sign by an individual posits the following four elements: (a) the addition function, an 'objective' mathematical entity; (b) the addition sign '+' a linguistic entity; (c) the 'sense' of this sign, an 'objective' abstract entity like the function; (d) an idea in the individual's mind associated with the sign. The idea is a 'subjective' mental entity, private to each individual and different in different minds. The 'sense', in contrast, is the same for all individuals who use '+' in the standard way. Each such individual grasps this sense by virtue of having an appropriate idea in his mind. The 'sense' in turn *determines* the addition function as the *referent* of the '+' sign.

There is again no special problem, for this position, as to the relation between the sense and the referent it determines. It simply is in the nature of a sense to determine a referent. But ultimately the sceptical problem cannot be evaded, and it arises precisely in the question how the existence in my mind of any mental entity or idea can *constitute* 'grasping' any particular sense rather than another. The idea in my mind is a finite object: can it not be interpreted as determining a quus function, rather than a plus function? Of course there may be another idea in my mind, which is supposed to constitute its act of *assigning* a particular interpretation to the first idea; but then the problem obviously arises again at this new level. (A rule for interpreting a rule again.) And so on. For Wittgenstein, Platonism is largely an unhelpful evasion of the problem of how our finite minds can give rules that are supposed to apply to an infinity of cases. Platonic objects may be self-interpreting, or rather, they may need no interpretation; but ultimately there must be some mental entity involved that raises the sceptical problem. (This brief discussion of Platonism is meant for those interested in the issue. If it is so brief that you find it obscure, ignore it.)

3 The Solution and the 'Private Language' Argument

The sceptical argument, then, remains unanswered. There can be no such thing as meaning anything by any word. Each new application we make is a leap in the dark; any present intention could be interpreted so as to accord with anything we may choose to do. So there can be neither accord, nor conflict. This is what Wittgenstein said in *PI*, §202.

Wittgenstein's sceptical problem is related to some work of two other recent writers who show little direct influence from Wittgenstein. Both have already been mentioned above. The first is W. V. Quine,[23] whose well-known theses of the indeterminacy of translation and the inscrutability of reference also question whether there are any objective facts as to what we mean. If I may anticipate matters that the present exposition has not yet introduced, Quine's emphasis on agreement is obviously congenial to Wittgenstein's view.[24] So is his rejection of any notion that inner 'ideas' or 'meanings' guide our linguistic behavior. However, there are differences. As I have remarked above, Quine bases his argument from the outset on behavioristic premises. He would never emphasize introspective thought experiments in the way Wittgenstein does, and he does not think of views that permit a private inner world as in need of elaborate repetition. For Quine, the untenability of any such views should be obvious to anyone who accepts a modern scientific outlook. Further, since Quine sees the philosophy of language within a hypothetical framework of behavioristic psychology, he thinks of problems about meaning as problems of disposition to behavior. This orientation seems to have consequences for the form of Quine's problem as opposed to Wittgenstein's. The important problem for Wittgenstein is that my present mental state does not appear to determine what I *ought* to do in the future. Although I may *feel* (now) that something in my head corresponding to the word 'plus' mandates a determinate response to any new pair of arguments, in fact nothing in my head does so. Alluding to one of Wittgenstein's earliest examples, 'ostensive' learning of the color word 'sepia' (*PI*, §§28–30),[25] Quine protests against Wittgenstein that, given our 'inborn propensity to find one stimulation qualitatively more akin to a second stimulation than to a third' and sufficient conditioning 'to eliminate wrong generalizations', eventually the term will be learnt: "... in principle nothing more is needed in learning 'sepia' than in any conditioning or induction."[26] By "learning 'sepia'," Quine means developing the right disposition to apply 'sepia' in particular cases. It should be clear from Wittgenstein's text that he too is aware, indeed emphasizes, that in practice there need be no difficulty in this sense about the learning of 'sepia'. The fundamental problem, as I have stated it earlier, is different: whether my actual dispositions are 'right' or not, is there anything that mandates what they *ought* to be? Since Quine formulates the issues dispositionally, this problem cannot be stated within his framework. For Quine, since any question as to whether I mean plus or quus will show up in my behavior, there is no question, given my disposition, as to what I mean.

It has already been argued above that such a formulation of the issues seems inadequate. My actual dispositions are not infallible, nor do they cover all of the infinitely many cases of the addition table. However, since Quine does see the issues in terms of dispositions, he is concerned to show that even if dispositions were ideally seen as infallible and covering all cases, there are still questions of interpretation that are left undermined. First, he argues roughly that the interpretation of sufficiently 'theoretical' utterances, not direct observation reports, is undetermined even by all my ideal dispositions. Further, he seeks to show by examples such as 'rabbit' and 'rabbit-stage' that, even given fixed interpretation of our sentences as wholes and certainly given all our ideal dispositions to behavior, the interpretation (reference) of various lexical items is still not fixed.[27] These are interesting claims, distinct from Wittgenstein's. For those of us who are not as behavioristically inclined as Quine, Wittgenstein's problem may lead to a new look at Quine's theses. Given Quine's formulation of his theses, it appears open to a non-behaviorist to regard his arguments, *if* he accepts them, as demonstrations that any behavioristic account of meaning must be inadequate – it cannot even distinguish between a word meaning rabbit and one meaning rabbit-stage. But if Wittgenstein is right, and no amount of access to my mind can reveal whether I meant plus or quus, may the same not hold for rabbit and rabbit-stage? So perhaps Quine's problem arises even for non-behaviorists. This is not the place to explore the matter.

Nelson Goodman's discussion of the 'new riddle of induction' also deserves comparison with Wittgenstein's work.[28] Although our paradigm of Wittgenstein's problem was formulated for a mathematical problem, it was emphasized that it is completely general and can be applied to any rule or word. In particular, if it were formulated to the language of color impressions, as Wittgenstein himself suggests, Goodman's 'grue', or something similar, would play the role of 'quus'. But the problem would not be Goodman's about induction — "Why not predict that grass, which has been grue in the past, will be grue in the future?" — but Wittgenstein's about meaning: "Who is to say that in the past I didn't mean grue by 'green', so that now I should call the sky, not the grass, 'green'?" Although Goodman concentrates on the problem about induction and largely ignores the problem about meaning,[29] his discussions are occasionally suggestive for Wittgenstein's problem as well.[30] In fact, I personally suspect that serious consideration of Goodman's problem, as he formulates it, may prove impossible without consideration of Wittgenstein's.[31]

Wittgenstein has invented a new form of scepticism. Of course he does not wish to leave us with his problem, but to solve it: the sceptical conclusion is insane and intolerable. It is his solution, I will argue, that contains the argument against 'private language'; for allegedly, the solution will not admit such a language. But it is important to see that his achievement in posing this problem stands on its own, independently of the value of his own solution of it and the resultant argument against private language. For, if we see Wittgenstein's problem as a real one, it is clear that he has often been read from the wrong perspective. Readers, my previous self certainly included, have often been inclined to wonder: "How can he prove private language impossible? How can I possibly have any difficulty identifying my own sensations? And if there were a difficulty, how could 'public' criteria help me? I must be in pretty bad shape if I need external *help* to identify my own sensations!" But if I am right, a proper orientation would be the opposite. The main problem is *not*, "How can we show private language — or some other special form of language — to be *impossible?*"; rather it is, "How can we show *any language* at all (public, private, or what-have-you) to be *possible?*"[32] It is not that calling a sensation 'pain' is easy, and Wittgenstein must invent a difficulty.[33] On the contrary, Wittgenstein's main problem is that it appears that he has shown *all* language, *all* concept formation, to be impossible, indeed unintelligible.

It is important and illuminating to compare Wittgenstein's new form of scepticism with the classical scepticism of Hume; there are important analogies between the two. Both develop a sceptical paradox, based on questioning a certain *nexus* from past to future. Wittgenstein questions the nexus between past 'intention' or 'meanings' and present practice: for example, between my past 'intentions' with regard to 'plus' and my present computation '$68 + 57 = 125$'. Hume questions two other nexuses, related to each other: the causal nexus whereby a past event necessitates a future one, and the inductive inferential nexus from the past to the future.

The analogy is obvious. It has been obscured for several reasons. First, the Humean and the Wittgensteinian problems are of course distinct and independent, though analogous. Second, Wittgenstein shows little interest in or sympathy with Hume: he has been quoted as saying that he could not read Hume because he found it "a torture".[34] Furthermore, Hume is the prime source of some ideas on the nature of mental states that Wittgenstein is most concerned to attack.[35] Finally (and probably most important), Wittgenstein never avows, and almost surely would not avow, the label 'sceptic', as Hume explicitly did. Indeed, he has often appeared to be a 'common-sense' philosopher, anxious to defend our ordinary conceptions and dissolve traditional philosophical doubts. Is it not Wittgenstein who held that philosophy only states what everyone admits?

Yet even here the difference between Wittgenstein and Hume should not be exaggerated. Even Hume has an important strain, dominant in some of his moods, that the philosopher never questions ordinary beliefs. Asked whether he "be really one of those sceptics, who hold that all is uncertain", Hume replies "that this question is entirely superfluous, and that neither I, nor any other person, was ever sincerely and constantly of that opinion".[36] Even more forcefully, discussing the problem of the external world: "We may well ask, *What causes induce us to believe in the existence of body?* but it is vain to ask, *Whether there be body or not?* That is a point, which we must take for granted in all our reasonings."[37] Yet this oath of fealty to common sense begins a section that otherwise looks like an argument that the common conception of material objects is irreparably incoherent!

When Hume is in a mood to respect his professed determination never to deny or doubt our common beliefs, in what does his 'scepticism' consist? First, in a sceptical *account* of the causes of these beliefs; and second, in sceptical analyses of our common notions. In some ways Berkeley, who did not regard his own views as sceptical, may offer an even better analogy to Wittgenstein. At first blush, Berkeley, with his denial of matter, and of any objects 'outside the mind' seems to be *denying* our common beliefs; and for many of us the impression persists through later blushes. But not for Berkeley. For him, the impression that the common man is committed to matter and to objects outside the mind derives from an erroneous metaphysical interpretation of common talk. When the common man speaks of an 'external material object' he does not really mean (as we might say *sotto voce*) an *external material object* but rather he means something like 'an idea produced in me independently of my will'.[38]

Berkeley's stance is not uncommon in philosophy. The philosopher advocates a view apparently in patent contradiction to common sense. Rather than repudiating common sense, he asserts that the conflict comes from a philosophical misinterpretation of common language – sometimes he adds that the misinterpretation is encouraged by the 'superficial form' of ordinary speech. He offers his own analysis of the relevant common assertions, one that shows that they do not really say what they seem to say. For Berkeley this philosophical strategy is central to his work. To the extent that Hume claims that he merely analyses common sense and does not oppose it, he invokes the same strategy as well. The practice can hardly be said to have ceased today.[39]

Personally I think such philosophical claims are almost invariably suspect. What the claimant calls a 'misleading philosophical misconstrual' of the ordinary statement is probably the natural and correct understanding. The real misconstrual comes when the claimant continues, "All the ordinary man really means is . . ." and gives a sophisticated analysis compatible with his own philosophy. Be this as it may, the important point for present purposes is that Wittgenstein makes a Berkeleyan claim of this kind. For – as we shall see – his solution to his own sceptical problem begins by agreeing with the sceptics that there is no 'superlative fact' (*PI*, §192) about my mind that constitutes my meaning addition by 'plus' and determines in advance what I should do to accord with this meaning. But, he claims (in §§183–93), the appearance that our ordinary concept of meaning demands such a fact is based on a philosophical misconstrual – albeit a natural one – of such ordinary expressions as 'he meant such-and-such', 'the steps are determined by the formula', and the like. How Wittgenstein construes these expressions we shall see presently. For the moment let us only remark that Wittgenstein thinks that any construal that looks for something in my present mental state to differentiate between my meaning addition or quaddition, or that will consequently show that in the future I should say '125' when asked about '68 + 57', *is* a misconstrual and attributes to the ordinary man a notion of meaning that *is* refuted by the sceptical argument. "We are," he says in §194 – note that Berkeley could have said just the same thing! – "like savages, primitive people, who hear the expressions of civilized men, put a false interpretation on them, and then draw the queerest conclusions from it." Maybe so. Personally I can only report that, in spite of Wittgenstein's assurances, the 'primitive' interpretation often sounds rather good to me . . .

In his *Enquiry*, after he has developed his "Sceptical Doubts Concerning the Operations of the Understanding", Hume gives his "Sceptical Solution of These Doubts". What is a 'sceptical' solution? Call a proposed solution to sceptical philosophical problems a *straight* solution if it shows that on closer examination the scepticism proves to be unwarranted; an elusive or complex argument proves the thesis the sceptic doubted. Descartes gave a 'straight' solution in this sense to his own philosophical doubts. An *a priori* justification of inductive reasoning, and an analysis of the causal relation as a genuine necessary connection or nexus between pairs of events, would be straight solutions of Hume's problems of induction and causation, respectively. A *sceptical* solution of a sceptical philosophical problem begins on the contrary by conceding that the sceptic's negative assertions are unanswerable. Nevertheless our ordinary practice or belief is justified because – contrary appearances notwithstanding – it need not require the justification the sceptic has shown to be untenable. And much of the value of the sceptical argument consists precisely in the fact that he has shown that an ordinary practice, if it is to be defended at all, cannot be defended in a certain way. A sceptical solution may also involve – in the manner suggested above – a sceptical analysis or account of ordinary beliefs to rebut their *prima facie* reference to a metaphysical absurdity.

The rough outlines of Hume's sceptical solution to his problem are well known.[40] Not an *a priori* argument, but custom is the source of our inductive inferences. If A and B are two types of events which we have seen constantly conjoined, then we are conditioned – Hume is a grandfather of this modern psychological notion – to expect an event of type B on being presented with one of type A. To say of a particular event a that it caused another event b is to place these two events under two types, A and B, which we expect to be constantly conjoined in the future as they were in the past. The idea of necessary connection comes from the 'feeling of customary transition' between our ideas of these events.

The philosophical merits of the Humean solution are not our present concern. Our purpose is to use the analogy with the Humean solution to illuminate Wittgenstein's solution to his own problem. For comparative purposes one further consequence of Hume's sceptical solution should be noted. Naively, one might suppose that whether a particular event a causes another particular event b, is an issue solely involving the events a and b alone (and their relations), and involves no other events. If Hume is right, this is not so. Even if God were to look at the events, he would discern nothing relating them other than that one succeeds the other. Only when the particular events a and b are thought of as subsumed under two respective event types, A and B, which are related by a generalization that *all* events of type A are followed by events of type B, can a be said to 'cause' b. When the events a and b are considered by themselves alone, no causal notions are applicable. This Humean conclusion might be called: the impossibility of private causation.

Can one reasonably protest: surely there is nothing the event a can do with the *help* of other events of the same type that it cannot do by itself! Indeed, to say that a, by itself, is a sufficient cause of b is to say that, had the rest of the universe been removed, a still would have produced b! Intuitively this may well be so, but the intuitive objection ignores Hume's sceptical argument. The whole point of the sceptical argument is that the common notion of one event 'producing' another, on which the objection relies, is in jeopardy. It appears that there is no such relation as 'production' at all, that the causal relation fictive. After the sceptical argument has been seen to be unanswerable on its own terms, a sceptical solution is offered, containing all we can salvage of the notion of causation. It just is a feature of this analysis that causation makes no sense when applied to two isolated events, with the rest of the universe removed. Only inasmuch as these events are thought of as instances of event types related by a regularity can they be thought of as causally connected. If two particular events were somehow so *sui generis* that it was logically excluded that they be placed under any (plausibly natural) event types, causal notions would not be applicable to them.

Of course I am suggesting that Wittgenstein's argument against private language has a structure similar to Hume's argument against private causation. Wittgenstein also states a sceptical paradox. Like Hume, he accepts his own sceptical argument and offers a 'sceptical solution' to overcome the appearance of paradox. His solution involves a sceptical interpretation of what is involved in such ordinary assertions as "Jones means addition by '+'." The impossibility of private language emerges as a corollary of his sceptical solution of his own paradox, as does the impossibility of 'private causation' in Hume. It turns out that the sceptical solution does not allow us to speak of a single individual, considered by himself and in isolation, as ever meaning anything. Once again an objection based on an intuitive feeling that no one else can affect what I mean by a given symbol ignores the sceptical argument that undermines any such naive intuition about meaning.

I have said that Wittgenstein's solution to his problem is a sceptical one. He does not give a 'straight' solution, pointing out to the silly sceptic a hidden fact he overlooked, a condition in the world which constitutes my meaning addition by 'plus'. In fact, he agrees with his own hypothetical sceptic that there is no such fact, no such condition in either the 'internal' or the 'external' world. Admittedly, I am expressing Wittgenstein's view more straightforwardly than he would ordinarily allow himself to do. For in denying that there is any such fact, might we not be expressing a philosophical thesis that doubts or denies something everyone admits? We do not wish to doubt or deny that when people speak of themselves and others as meaning something by their words, as following rules, they do so with perfect right. We do not even wish to deny the propriety of an ordinary use of the phrase 'the fact that Jones meant addition by such-and-such a symbol', and indeed such expressions do have perfectly ordinary uses. We merely wish to deny the existence of the 'superlative fact' that philosophers misleadingly attach to such ordinary forms of words, not the propriety of the forms of words themselves.

It is for this reason that I conjectured above (p. 241) that Wittgenstein's professed inability to write a work with conventionally organized arguments and conclusions stems at least in part, not from personal and stylistic proclivities, but from the nature of his work. Had Wittgenstein – contrary to his notorious and cryptic maxim in *PI*, § 128 – stated the outcomes of his conclusions in the form of definite theses, it would have been very difficult to avoid formulating his doctrines in a form that consists in apparent sceptical denials of our ordinary assertions. Berkeley runs into similar difficulties. Partly he avoids them by stating his thesis as the denial of the existence of 'matter', and claiming that 'matter' is a bit of philosophical jargon, not expressive of our common sense view. Nevertheless he is forced at one point to say – apparently contrary to his usual official doctrine – that he denies a doctrine 'strangely prevailing amongst men'.[41] If, on the other hand, we do not state our conclusions in the form of broad philosophical theses, it is easier to avoid the danger of a denial of any ordinary belief, even if our imaginary interlocutor (e.g. *PI*, §189; see also §195)[42] accuses us of doing so. Whenever our opponent insists on the perfect propriety of an ordinary form of expression (e.g. that 'the steps are determined by the formula', 'the future application is already present'), we can insist that if these expressions are properly understood, we agree. The danger comes when we try to formulate what we deny, the erroneous interpretation we place on ordinary means of expression.

So Wittgenstein, perhaps cagily, might well disapprove of the straightforward formulation given here. Nevertheless I choose to be so bold as to say: Wittgenstein holds, with the sceptic, that there is no fact as to whether I mean plus or quus. But if this is to be conceded to the sceptic, is this not the end of the matter? What *can* be said on behalf of our ordinary attributions of meaningful language to ourselves and to others? Has not the incredible and self-defeating conclusion, that all language is meaningless, already been drawn?

In reply we must say something about the change in Wittgenstein's philosophy of language from the *Tractatus* to the *Investigations*. Although in detail the *Tractatus* is among the most difficult of philosophical works, its rough outlines are well known. To each sentence there corresponds a (possible) fact. If such a fact obtains, the sentence is true; if not, false. For atomic sentences, the relation between a sentence and the fact it alleges is one of a simple correspondence or isomorphism. The sentence contains names, corresponding to objects. An atomic sentence is itself a fact, putting the names in a certain relation; and it says that (there is a corresponding fact that) the corresponding objects are in the same relation. Other sentences are (finite or infinite) truth-functions of these. Even though the details of this theory have struck some as an implausible attempt to give natural language a chimerical *a priori* structure based on logical analysis alone, similar ideas, often advanced without any specific influence from the *Tractatus*, are much alive today.[43]

The simplest, most basic idea of the *Tractatus* can hardly be dismissed: a declarative sentence gets its meaning by virtue of its *truth conditions*, by virtue of its correspondence to facts that must obtain if it is true. For example, "the cat is on the mat" is understood by those speakers who realize that it is true if and only if a certain cat is on a certain mat; it is false otherwise. The presence of the cat on the mat is a fact or condition-in-the-world that would make the sentence true (express a truth) if it obtained.

So stated, the *Tractatus* picture of the meaning of declarative sentences may seem not only natural but even tautological. None the less, as Dummett says, "the *Investigations* contains implicitly a rejection of the classical (realist) Frege—*Tractatus* view that the general form of explanation of meaning is a statement of the truth conditions".[44] In place of this view, Wittgenstein proposes an alternative rough general picture. (To call it an alternative *theory* probably goes too far. Wittgenstein disclaims (*PI*, §65) any intent of offering a general account of language to rival that of the *Tractatus*. Rather we have different activities related to each other in various ways.) Wittgenstein replaces the question, "What must be the case for this sentence to be true?" by two others: first, "Under what conditions may this form of words be appropriately asserted (or denied)?"; second, given an answer to the first question, "What is the role, and the utility in our lives of our practice of asserting (or denying) the form of words under these conditions?"

Of course Wittgenstein does not confine himself to declarative sentences, and hence to assertion and denial, as I have just done. On the contrary, any reader of the earlier parts of *Philosophical Investigations* will be aware that he is strongly concerned to deny any special primacy to assertion, or to sentences in the indicative mood. (See his early examples "Slab!", "Pillar!", etc.) This in itself plays an important role in his repudiation of the classical realist picture. Since the indicative mood is not taken as in any sense primary or basic, it becomes more plausible that the linguistic role even of utterances in the indicative mood that superficially look like assertions need not be one of 'stating facts'.[45] Thus, if we speak properly, we should not speak of conditions of 'assertion', but rather, more generally, of the conditions when a move (a form of linguistic expression) is to be made in the 'language game'. If, however, we allow ourselves to adopt an oversimplified terminology more appropriate to a special range of cases, we can say that Wittgenstein proposes a picture of language based, not on *truth conditions*, but on *assertability conditions* or *justification conditions*:[46] under what circumstances are we allowed to make a given assertion? Pictures, indeed explicit theories, of this kind are hardly unknown before Wittgenstein and probably influenced him. The positivist verification theory of meaning is one of this kind. So, in a more special context, is the intuitionist account of mathematical statements. (The classical mathematician's emphasis on truth conditions is replaced by an emphasis on provability conditions.)

But of course Wittgenstein's rough picture should not be identified with either of these. Its second component is distinct: granted that our language game permits a certain 'move' (assertion) under certain specifiable conditions, what is the role in our lives of such permission? Such a role must exist if this aspect of the language game is not to be idle.

Wittgenstein's alternative picture of language is already clearly suggested in the very first section of *Philosophical Investigations*. Many philosophers of mathematics — in agreement with the Augustinian conception of 'object and name' — ask such questions as, "What entities ('numbers') are denoted by numerals? What relations among these entities ('facts') correspond to numerical statements?" (Nominalistically inclined philosophers would counter, sceptically, "Can we really believe that there are such entities?") As against such a 'Platonist' conception of the problem, Wittgenstein asks that we discard any *a priori* conceptions and *look* ("Don't think, look!") at the circumstances under which numerical assertions are actually uttered, and at what roles such assertions play in our lives.[47] Suppose I go to the grocer with a slip marked 'five red apples', and he hands over apples, reciting by heart the numerals up to five and handing over an apple as each numeral is intoned. It is under circumstances such as these that we are licensed to make utterances using numerals; the role and utility of such a license is obvious. In *PI*, §§8–10, Wittgenstein imagines the letters of the alphabet, recited in alphabetical order, used in a minature language game, just as the numbers are in this example. We have little inclination to wonder about the nature of the entities 'denoted' by the letters of the alphabet. Nevertheless, if they are used in the way described, they can properly be said to 'stand for numbers'. Indeed, to say words stand for (natural) numbers *is* to say that they are used as numerals, that is, used in the way described. Nevertheless the legitimacy, in its own way, of the expression 'stand for numbers' should not lead us to think of numerals as similar to expressions such as 'slab', 'pillar', and the like, except that the entities 'denoted' are not spatio-temporal. If the use of the expression 'stands for numbers' misleads in this way, it would be best to think in terms of another terminology, say, that an expression 'plays the role of a numeral'. This role, as Wittgenstein describes it, is plainly in strong *contrast* with the role of such expressions as 'slab', 'pillar', 'block', in the language games he describes in his early sections. (See § 10.)

The case is a fine example of various aspects of Wittgenstein's technique in the *Investigations*. An important view in the philosophy of mathematics is suggested briefly almost *en passant*, almost hidden in a general discussion of the nature of language and 'language games'.[48] In the style discussed above, Wittgenstein suggests that such an expression as 'stands for a number' is in order, but is dangerous if it is taken to make a certain metaphysical suggestion. In the sense this is intended by 'Platonists', one suspects him of *denying* that numerals stand for entities called 'numbers'. Most important for the present purpose, the case exemplifies the central questions he wishes to ask about the use of language. Do not look for 'entities' and 'facts' corresponding to numerical assertions, but look at the circumstances under which utterances involving numerals are made, and the utility of making them under these circumstances.

Now the replacement of truth conditions by justification conditions has a dual role in the *Investigations*. First, it offers a new approach to the problems of how language has meaning, contrasted with that of the *Tractatus*. But second, it can be applied to give an account of assertions about meaning themselves, regarded as assertions *within* our language. Recall Wittgenstein's sceptical conclusion: no facts, no truth conditions, correspond to statements such as "Jones means addition by '+'." (The present remarks about meaning and use do not in themselves provide such truth conditions. According to them, Jones now means addition by '+' if he presently intends to use the '+' sign in one way, quaddition if he intends to use it in another way. But nothing is said to illuminate the question as to the nature of such an intention.)

Now if we suppose that facts, or truth conditions, are of the essence of meaningful assertion, it will follow from the sceptical conclusion that assertions that anyone ever means anything are meaningless. On the other hand, if we apply to these assertions the tests suggested in *Philosophical Investigations*, no such conclusion follows. All that is needed to legitimize assertions that someone means something is that there be roughly specifiable circumstances under which they are legitimately assertable, and that the game of asserting them under such conditions has a role in our lives. No supposition that 'facts correspond' to those assertions is needed.

I would therefore give the following rough structure to *Philosophical Investigations* (but the breaks between parts are not sharp and to an extent are arbitrary). §§1–137 give Wittgenstein's preliminary refutation of the *Tractatus* theory of language, and suggest the rough picture he intends to put in its place. These sections come first for more than one reason. First, Wittgenstein himself once found the *Tractatus* theory natural and inevitable – Malcolm[48a] says he regarded it as the *only* alternative to his later work – and sometimes he writes as if the reader will naturally be inclined to the *Tractatus* theory unless he personally intervenes to prevent it. Thus the initial sections contain a refutation, not only of the most basic and apparently inevitable theories of the *Tractatus* (such as meaning as stating facts), but also of many of its more special doctrines (such as that of a special realm of 'simples').[49] Wittgenstein's contrast in these initial sections between his new way of looking at matters and his old way of thinking ranges from such special views of the *Tractatus* to the nature of philosophy. This first aspect of the initial sections has, I think, been clear to most readers. Less obvious is a second aspect. The sceptical paradox is the fundamental problem of *Philosophical Investigations*. If Wittgenstein is right, we cannot begin to solve it if we remain in the grip of the natural presupposition that meaningful declarative sentences must purport to correspond to facts; if this is our framework, we can only conclude that sentences attributing meaning and intention are themselves meaningless. Whether or not Wittgenstein is right in thinking that the entire *Tractatus* view is a consequence of natural and apparently inevitable presuppositions, he is surely right about this fundamental part of it. The picture of correspondence-to-facts must be cleared away before we can begin with the sceptical problem.

Sections 138–242 deal with the sceptical problem and its solution. These sections – the central sections of *Philosophical Investigations* – have been the primary concern of this essay. We have not yet looked at the solution of the problem, but the astute reader will already have guessed that Wittgenstein finds a useful role in our lives for a 'language game' that licences, under certain conditions, assertions that someone 'means such-and-such' and that his present application of a word 'accords' with what he 'meant' in the past. It turns out that this role, and these conditions, involve reference to a community. They are inapplicable to a single person considered in isolation. Thus, as we have said, Wittgenstein rejects 'private language' as early as §202.

The sections following §243 – the sections usually called 'the private language argument' – deal with the *application* of the general conclusions about language drawn in §§138–242 to the problem of sensations. The sceptical conclusion about rules, and the attendant rejection of private rules, is hard enough to swallow in general, but it seems especially unnatural in two areas. The first is mathematics, the subject of most of the preceding discussion in the present essay (and of much of Wittgenstein's in §§138–242). Do I not, in elementary mathematics, grasp rules such as that for addition, which determine all future applications? Is it not in the very nature of such rules that, once I have grasped one, I have no future choice in its application? Is not any questioning of these assertions a questioning of mathematical proof itself? And is not the grasping of a mathematical rule the solitary achievement of each mathematician independent of any interaction with a wider community? True, others may have taught me the concept of addition, but they acted only as heuristic aids to an achievement – the 'grasping of the concept' of addition – that puts me in a special relation to the addition function. Platonists have compared the grasping of a concept to a special sense, analogous to our ordinary sensory apparatus but percipient of higher entities. But the picture does not require a special Platonic theory of mathematical objects. It depends on the observation – apparently obvious on any view – that in grasping a mathematical rule I have achieved something that depends only on my own inner state, and that is immune to Cartesian doubt about the entire external material world.[50]

Now another case that seems to be an obvious counterexample to Wittgenstein's conclusion is that of a sensation, or mental image. Surely I can identify these after I have felt them, and any participation in a community is irrelevant! Because these two cases, mathematics and inner experience, seem so obviously to be counterexamples to Wittgenstein's view of rules, Wittgenstein treats each in detail. The latter case is treated in the sections following §243. The former case is treated in remarks that Wittgenstein never prepared for publication, but which are excerpted in *Remarks on the Foundations of Mathematics* and elsewhere. He thinks that only if we overcome our strong inclination to ignore his general conclusions about rules can we see these two areas rightly. For this reason, the conclusions about rules are of crucial importance both to the philosophy of mathematics and to the philosophy of mind. Although in his study of sensations in §243 onward he does not simply *cite* his general conclusions but argues this special case afresh (he does the same for mathematics elsewhere), we will only increase our difficulties in understanding an already difficult argument if we call §243 onward 'the private language argument' and study it in isolation from the preceding material. Wittgenstein had a definite plan of organization when he placed this discussion where it is.

Of course the division is not sharp. The initial 'anti-*Tractatus*' sections contain several anticipations of the 'paradox' of §§138–242,[51] and even of its solution. Sections 28–36 and sections 84–9 are examples. Even the very first section of the *Investigations* can be read, with hindsight, as anticipating the problem.[52] Nevertheless these anticipations, being cryptic allusions to the problem in the context of the problems of earlier discussions, do not fully develop the paradox and often elide the main point into other subsidiary ones.

Consider first the anticipation in sections 84–9, especially section 86, where Wittgenstein introduces the ambiguity of rules and the possibility of an infinite regress of 'rules to interpret rules'. Knowing the central problem of *Philosophical Investigations*, it is easy to see that in these sections Wittgenstein is concerned to bring out this problem, and even to allude to part of his approach to a solution (end of §87: "The sign post is in order if, in normal circumstances, it serves its purpose"). In the context, however, Wittgenstein shades his deep paradox into a much more straightforward point – that typically uses of language do not give a precise determination of their application in all cases. (See the discussion of names in §79 – "I use the name . . . without a *fixed* meaning"; of the 'chair'(?) in §80; of 'Stand roughly here' in §88.) It is true, as Wittgenstein says, that his paradox shows, among other things, that every explanation of a rule could conceivably be misunderstood, and that in this respect the most apparently precise use of language does not differ from 'rough' or 'inexact', or 'open-textured' uses. Nevertheless, surely the real point of Wittgenstein's paradox is not that the rule of addition is somehow *vague*, or leaves some cases of its application undetermined. On the contrary, the word 'plus' denotes a function whose determination is *completely* precise – in this respect it does *not* resemble the vague notions expressed by 'large', 'green', and the like. The point is the sceptical problem, outlined above, that anything in my head leaves it undetermined *what* function 'plus' (as I use it) denotes (plus or quus), what 'green' denotes (green or grue), and so on. The ordinary observation, made in abstraction from any scepticism about the meaning of 'green', that the property of greenness is itself only vaguely defined for some cases, is at best distantly related. In my opinion, Wittgenstein's sceptical arguments in no way show, in this sense, that the addition function is only vaguely defined. The addition function – as Frege would emphasize – yields one precise value for each pair of numerical arguments. This much is a theorem of arithmetic. The sceptical problem indicates no vagueness in the *concept* of addition (in the way there *is* vagueness in the concept of greenness), or in the word 'plus', *granting* it its usual meaning (in the way the word 'green' *is* vague). The sceptical point is something else.[53]

In the sections under discussion, Wittgenstein is arguing that *any* explanation *may* fail of its purpose: if it does not in fact fail, it may work perfectly, even if the concepts involved violate the Fregean requirement of 'sharp boundaries' (§71). See §88: "If I tell someone "Stand roughly here" may not this explanation work perfectly? And cannot every other one fail too?" At least two issues are involved here: the propriety of vagueness, of violations of the Fregean requirement (actually Wittgenstein questions whether this requirement, in an absolute sense, is well-defined); and an adumbration of the sceptical paradox of the second portion (§§138–242) of the *Investigations*. In its present context, the paradox, briefly foreshadowed, is not clearly distinguished from the other considerations about vagueness and sharp boundaries. The real development of the problem is yet to come.

Similar remarks apply to the discussion of ostensive definition in §§28–36, which is part of a larger discussion of naming, one of the important topics for the first portion (§§1–137) of the *Investigations*. Wittgenstein emphasizes that ostensive definitions are always in principle capable of being misunderstood, even the ostensive definition of a color word such as 'sepia'. How someone understands the word is exhibited in the way someone goes on, "the use that he makes of the word defined". One may go in the right way given a purely minimal explanation, while on the other hand one may go on no matter how many clarifications are added, since these too can be misunderstood (a rule for interpreting a rule again; see especially §§28–9).

Much of Wittgenstein's argument is directed against the view of a special, qualitatively unique experience of understanding the ostensive definition in the right way (§§33–6). Once again Wittgenstein's real point, here in the context of naming and ostensive definition, is the sceptical paradox. The case of ostensive definition of a color ('sepia') has a special connection with the so-called 'private language argument', as developed for sensations in §§243ff. Here too, however, the argument is adumbrated so briefly, and is so much embedded in a context of other issues, that at this stage of the argument the point can easily be lost.[54]

Yet another feature of the situation indicates how the ideas can be connected in a way that cuts across the indicated divisions of *Philosophical Investigations*. The first part (up to §137), as we have said, criticizes Wittgenstein's earlier picture of the nature of language and attempts to suggest another. Since Wittgenstein's sceptical solution of his paradox is possible only given his later conception of language and is ruled out by the earlier one, the discussion in the second part (§§138–242) is dependent on that of the first. The point to be made here is that, at the same time, the second part is important for an ultimate understanding of the first. Wittgenstein's earlier work had taken for granted a natural relation of interpretation between a thought in someone's mind and the 'fact' it 'depicts'. The relation was supposed to consist in an isomorphism between one fact (the fact that mental elements are arranged in a certain way) and another (the fact-in-the-world 'depicted'). Some of Wittgenstein's attack on this earlier idea is developed in the first part through a criticism of the notion, crucial to the *Tractatus* theory of isomorphism, of a unique decomposition of a complex into its 'ultimate' elements (see, for example, §§47–8). Clearly, however, the paradox of the second part of the *Investigations* constitutes a powerful critique of any idea that 'mental representations' uniquely correspond to 'facts', since it alleges that the components of such 'mental representations' do not have interpretations that can be 'read off' from them in a unique manner. So *a fortiori* there is no such unique interpretation of the mental 'sentences' containing them as 'depicting' one 'fact' or another.[55] In this way the relationship between the first and the second portions of the *Investigations* is reciprocal. In order for Wittgenstein's sceptical solution of his paradox to be intelligible, the 'realistic' or 'representational' picture of language must be undermined by another picture (in the first part). On the other hand, the paradox developed in the second part, antecedently to its solution, drives an important final nail (perhaps the crucial one) into the coffin of the representational picture.[56] No doubt this is one reason Wittgenstein introduces foreshadowings of the paradox already in the sections of the first part. But it also illustrates that the structural divisions I have indicated in *Philosophical Investigations* are not sharp. The investigation goes 'criss cross in every direction' (*PI*, preface).

Wittgenstein's sceptical solution concedes to the sceptic that no 'truth conditions' or 'corresponding facts' in the world exist that make a statement like "Jones, like many of us, means addition by '+'" true. Rather we should look at how such assertions are *used*. Can this be adequate? Do we not call assertions like the one just quoted 'true' or 'false'? Can we not with propriety precede such assertions with 'It is a fact that' or 'It is not a fact that'? Wittgenstein's way with such objections is short. Like many others, Wittgenstein accepts the 'redundancy' theory of truth: to affirm that a statement is true (or presumably, to precede it with 'It is a fact that . . .') is simply to affirm the statement itself, and to say it is not true is to deny it: ('*p*' is true$=p$). However, one might object: (a) that only utterances of certain forms are called 'true' or 'false' – questions, for example, are not – and these are so called precisely because they purport to state facts; (b) that precisely the sentences that 'state facts' can occur as components of truth-functional compounds and their meaning in such compounds is hard to explain in terms of assertability conditions alone. Wittgenstein's way with this is also short. We *call* something a proposition, and hence true or false, when in our language we apply the calculus of truth functions to it. That is, it is just a primitive part of our language game, not susceptible of deeper explanation, that truth functions are applied to certain sentences. For the present expository purpose it is worth nothing that the sections in which he discusses the concept of truth (*PI*, §§134–7) *conclude* the preliminary sections on the *Tractatus* and immediately *precede* the discussion of the sceptical paradox. They lay the final groundwork needed for that discussion.

Finally, we can turn to Wittgenstein's sceptical solution and to the consequent argument against 'private' rules. We have to see under what circumstances attributions of meaning are made and what role these attributions play in our lives. Following Wittgenstein's exhortation not to think but to look, we will not reason *a priori* about the role such statements *ought* to play; rather we will find out what circumstances *actually* license such assertions and what role this license *actually* plays. It is important to realize that we are *not* looking for necessary and sufficient conditions (truth conditions) for following a rule, or an analysis of what such rule-following 'consists in'. Indeed such conditions would constitute a 'straight' solution to the sceptical problem, and have been rejected.

First, consider what is true of one person considered in isolation. The most obvious fact is one that might have escaped us after long contemplation of the sceptical paradox. It holds no terrors in our daily lives; no one actually hesitates when asked to produce an answer to an addition problem! Almost all of us unhesitatingly produce the answer '125' when asked for the sum of 68 and 57, without any thought to the theoretical possibility that a quus-like rule might have been appropriate! And we do so without justification. Of course, if asked why we said '125', most of us will say that we added 8 and 7 to get 15, that we put down 5 and carried 1 and so on. But then, what will we say if asked why we 'carried' as we do? Might our past intention not have been that 'carry' meant *quarry*; where to 'quarry' is . . .? The entire point of the sceptical argument is that ultimately we reach a level where we act without any reason in terms of which we can justify our action. We act unhesitatingly but *blindly*.

This then is an important case of what Wittgenstein calls speaking without 'justification' ('*Rechtfertigung*'), but not 'wrongfully' ('*zu Unrecht*').[57] It is part of our language game of speaking of rules that a speaker may, without ultimately giving any justification, follow his own confident inclination that this way (say, responding '125') is the *right* way to respond, rather than another way (e.g. responding '5'). That is, the 'assertability conditions' that license an individual to say that, on a given occasion, he ought to follow his rule this way rather than that, are, ultimately, that he does what he is inclined to do.

The important thing about this case is that, if we confine ourselves to looking at one person alone, his psychological states and his external behavior, this is as far as we can go. We can say that he acts confidently at each application of a rule; that he says – without further justification – that the way he acts, rather than some quus-like alternative, is *the* way to respond. There are no circumstances under which we can say that, even if he inclines to say '125', he *should* have said '5', or *vice versa*. By definition, *he* is licensed to give, without further justification, the answer that strikes him as natural and inevitable. Under what circumstances can he be wrong, say, following the wrong rule? No one else by looking at his mind and behavior alone can say something like, "He is wrong if he does not accord with his own past intentions"; the whole point of the sceptical argument was that there can be no facts about him in virtue of which he accords with his intentions or not. All we can say, if we consider a single person in isolation, is that our ordinary practice licenses him to apply the rule in the way it strikes him.

But of course this is *not* our usual concept of following a rule. It is by no means the case that, just because someone thinks he is following a rule, there is no room for a judgement that he is not really doing so. Someone – a child, an individual muddled by a drug – may think he is following a rule even though he is actually acting at random, in accordance with no rule at all. Alternatively, he may, under the influence of a drug, suddenly act in accordance with a quus-like rule changing from his first intentions. If there could be no justification for anyone to say of a person of the first type that his confidence that he is following some rule is misplaced, or of a person of the second type that he is no longer in accord with the rule that he previously followed, there would be little content to our idea that a rule, or past intention, *binds* future choices. We are inclined to accept conditionals of such a rough type as, "If someone means addition by '+', then, if he remembers his past intention and wishes to conform to it, when he is queried about '68 + 57', he will answer '125'." The question is what substantive content such conditionals can have.

If our considerations so far are correct, the answer is that, if one person is considered in isolation, the notion of a rule as guiding the person who adopts it can have *no* substantive content. There are, we have seen, no truth conditions or facts in virtue of which it can be the case that he accords with his past intentions or not. As long as we regard him as following a rule 'privately', so that we pay attention to *his* justification conditions alone, all we can say is that he is licensed to follow the rule as it strikes him. This is why Wittgenstein says, "To think one is obeying a rule is not to obey a rule. Hence it is not possible to obey a rule 'privately'; otherwise thinking one was obeying a rule would be the same thing as obeying it." (*PI*, §202)

The situation is very different if we widen our gaze from consideration of the rule follower alone and allow ourselves to consider him as interacting with a wider community. Others will then have justification conditions for attributing correct or incorrect rule following to the subject, and these will *not* be simply that the subject's own authority is unconditionally to be accepted. Consider the example of a small child learning addition. It is obvious that his teacher will not accept just any response from the child. On the contrary, the child must fulfill various conditions if the teacher is to ascribe to him mastery of the concept of addition. First, for small enough examples, the child must produce, almost all the time, the 'right' answer. If a child insists on the answer '7' to the query '2 + 3', and a '3' to '2 + 2', and makes various other elementary mistakes, the teacher will say to him, "You are not adding. Either you are computing another function" – I suppose he would not really talk quite this way to a child! – "or, more probably, you are as yet following no rule at all, but only giving whatever random answer enters your head." Suppose, however, the child gets almost all 'small' addition problems right. For larger computations, the child can make more mistakes than for 'small' problems, but it must get a certain number right and, when it is wrong, it must recognizably be 'trying to follow' the proper procedure, not a quus-like procedure, even though it makes mistakes. (Remember, the teacher is not judging how accurate or *adept* the child is as an adder, but whether he can be said to be following the rule for adding.) Now, what do I mean when I say that the teacher judges that, for certain cases, the pupil must give the 'right' answer? I mean that the teacher judges that the child has given the same answer that he himself would give. Similarly, when I said that the teacher, in order to judge that the child is adding, must judge that, for a problem with larger numbers, he is applying the 'right' procedure even if he comes out with a mistaken result, I mean that he judges that the child is applying the procedure he himself is inclined to apply.

Something similar is true for adults. If someone whom I judge to have been computing a normal addition function (that is, someone whom I judge to give, when he adds, the same answer I would give), suddenly gives answers according to procedures that differ bizarrely from my own, then I will judge that something must have happened to him, and that he is no longer following the rule he previously followed. If this happens to him generally, and his responses seem to me to display little discernible pattern, I will judge him probably to have gone insane.

From this we can discern rough assertability conditions for such a sentence as "Jones means addition by 'plus'." *Jones* is entitled, subject to correction by others, provisionally to say, "I mean addition by 'plus'," whenever he has the feeling of confidence – "now I can go on!" – that he can give 'correct' responses in new cases; and *he* is entitled, again provisionally and subject to correction by others, to judge a new response to be 'correct' simply because it is the response he is inclined to give. These inclinations (both Jones's general inclination that he has 'got it' and his particular inclination to give particular answers in particular addition problems) are to be regarded as primitive. They are not to be justified in terms of Jones's ability to interpret his own intentions or anything else. But Smith need *not* accept Jones's authority on these matters: *Smith* will judge Jones to mean addition by 'plus' only if he judges that Jones's answers to particular addition problems agree with those *he* is inclined to give, or, if they occasionally disagree, he can interpret Jones as at least following the proper procedure. (If Jones gives answers for very small problems disagreeing with those Smith is inclined to give, it will be difficult or impossible for Smith to interpret Jones as following the proper procedure. The same will hold if Jones's responses to larger problems are too bizarre to be errors in addition in the normal sense: for example, if he answers '5' to '68 + 57'.) If Jones consistently fails to give responses in agreement (in this broad sense) with Smith's, Smith will judge that he does not mean addition by 'plus'. Even if Jones did mean it in the past, the present deviation will justify Smith in judging that he has lapsed.

Sometimes Smith, by substituting some alternative interpretation for Jones's word 'plus', will be able to bring Jones's responses in line with his own. More often, he will be unable to do so and will be inclined to judge that Jones is not really following any rule at all. In all this, Smith's inclinations are regarded as just as primitive as Jones's. In no way does Smith test directly whether Jones may have in his head some rule agreeing with the one in Smith's head. Rather the point is that if, in enough concrete cases, Jones's inclinations agree with Smith's, Smith will judge that Jones is indeed following the rule for addition.

Of course if we were reduced to a babble of disagreement, with Smith and Jones asserting of each other that they are following the rule wrongly, while others disagreed with both, and with each other, there would be little point to the practice just described. In fact, our actual community is (roughly) uniform in its practices with respect to addition. Any individual who claims to have mastered the concept of addition will be judged by the community to have done so if his particular responses agree with those of the community in enough cases, especially the simple ones (and if his 'wrong' answers are not often *bizarrely* wrong, as in '5' for '68 + 57', but seem to agree with ours in *procedure*, even when he makes a 'computational mistake'). An individual who passes such tests is admitted into the community as an adder; an individual who passes such tests in enough other cases is admitted as a normal speaker of the language and member of the community. Those who deviate are corrected and told (usually as children) that they have not grasped the concept of addition. One who is an incorrigible deviant in enough respects simply cannot participate in the life of the community, and in communication.

Now Wittgenstein's general picture of language, as sketched above, requires for an account of a type of utterance not merely that we say under what conditions an utterance of that type can be made, but also what role and utility in our lives can be ascribed to the practice of making this type of utterance under such conditions. We say of someone else that he follows a certain rule when his responses agree with our own and deny it when they do not; but what is the utility of this practice? The utility is evident and can be brought out by considering again a man who buys something at the grocer's. The customer, when he deals with the grocer and asks for five apples, expects the grocer to count as he does, not according to some bizarre non-standard rule and so, if his dealings with the grocer involve a computation, such as '68 + 57', he expects the grocer's responses to agree with his own. Indeed, he may entrust the computation to the grocer. Of course the grocer may make mistakes in addition: he may even make dishonest computations. But as long as the customer attributes to him a grasp of the concept of addition, he expects that at least the grocer will not behave bizarrely, as he would if he were to follow a quus-like rule; and one can even expect that, in many cases, he will come up with the same answer the customer would have given himself. When we pronounce that a child has mastered the rule of addition, we mean that we can entrust him to react as we do in interactions such as that just mentioned between the grocer and the customer. Our entire lives depend on countless such interactions, and on the 'game' of attributing to others the master of certain concepts or rules, thereby showing that we expect them to behave as we do.

This expectation is *not* infallibly fulfilled. It places a substantive restriction on the behavior of each individual, and is *not* compatible with just any behavior he may choose. (Contrast this with the case where we considered one person alone.) A deviant individual whose responses do not accord with those of the community in enough cases will not be judged, by the community, to be following its rules; he may even be judged to be a madman, following no coherent rule at all. When the community denies of someone that he is following certain rules, it excludes him from various transactions such as the one between the grocer and the customer. It indicates that it cannot rely on his behavior in such transactions.

We can restate this in terms of a device that has been common in philosophy, *inversion* of a conditional.[58] For example, it is important to our concept of causation that we accept some such conditional as: "If evens of type A cause events of type B, and if an event e of type A occurs, then an event e' of type B must follow." So put, it appears that acceptance of the conditional commits us to a belief in a nexus so that, given that the causal connection between even types obtains, the occurrence of the first event e necessitates (by fulfilling the antecedent of the conditional), that an event e' of type B must obtain. Humeans, of course, deny the existence of such a nexus; how do they read the conditional? Essentially they concentrate on the assertability conditions of a contrapositive form of the conditional. It is not that any antecedent conditions necessitate that some event e' must take place; rather the conditional commits us, whenever we know that an event e of type A occurs and is not followed by an event of type B, to deny that there is a causal connection between the two event types. If we did make such a claim, we must now withdraw it. Although a conditional is equivalent to its contrapositive, concentration on the contrapositive reverses our priorities. Instead of seeing causal connections as primary, from which observed regularities 'flow', the Humean instead sees the regularity as primary, and – looking at the matter contrapositively – observes that we withdraw a causal hypothesis when the corresponding regularity has a definite counterinstance.

A similar inversion is used in the present instance. It is essential to our concept of a rule that we maintain some such conditional as "If Jones means addition by '+', then if he is asked for '68 + 57', he will reply '125'." (Actually many clauses should be added to the antecedent to make it strictly correct, but for present purposes let us leave it in this rough form.) As in the causal case, the conditional as stated makes it appear that some mental state obtains in Jones that guarantees his performance of particular additions such as '68 + 57' – just what the sceptical argument denies. Wittgenstein's picture of the true situation concentrates on the contrapositive, and on justification conditions. If Jones does *not* come out with '125' when asked about '68 + 57', we cannot assert that he means addition by '+'. Actually, of course, this is not strictly true, because our formulation of the conditional is overly loose; other conditions must be added to the antecedent to make it true. As the conditional is stated, not even the possibility of computational error is taken into account, and there are many complications not easily spelled out. The fact remains that if we ascribe to Jones the conventional concept of addition, we do not expect him to exhibit a pattern of bizarre, quus-like behavior. By such a conditional we do not mean, on the Wittgensteinian view, that any state of Jones guarantees his correct behavior. Rather by asserting such a conditional we commit ourselves, if in the future Jones behaves bizarrely enough (and on enough occasions), no longer to persist in our assertion that he is following the conventional rule of addition.

The rough conditional thus expresses a restriction on the community's game of attributing to one of its members the grasping of a certain concept: if the individual in question no longer conforms to what the community would do in these circumstances, the community can no longer attribute the concept to him. Even though, when we play this game and attribute concepts to individuals, we depict no special 'state' of their minds, we do something of importance. We take them provisionally into the community, as long as further deviant behavior does not exclude them. In practice, such deviant behavior rarely occurs.

It is, then, in such a description of the game of concept attribution that Wittgenstein's sceptical solution consists. It provides both conditions under which we are justified in attributing concepts to others and an account of the utility of this game in our lives. In terms of this account we can discuss briefly three of Wittgenstein's key concepts.

First, *agreement*. The entire 'game' we have described – that the community attributes a concept to an individual so long as he exhibits sufficient conformity, under test circumstances, to the behavior of the community – would lose its point outside a community that generally agrees in its practices. If one person, when asked to compute '68 + 57' answered '125', another '5', and another '13', if there was no general agreement in the community responses, the game of attributing concepts to individuals – as we have described it – could not exist. In fact of course there is considerable agreement, and deviant quus-like behavior occurs rarely. Mistakes and disagreements do occur, but these are another matter. The fact is that, extreme cases of uneducability or insanity aside, almost all of us, after a sufficient training, respond with roughly the same procedures to concrete addition problems. We respond unhesitatingly to such problems as '68 + 57', regarding our procedure as the only comprehensible one (see, e.g., *PI*, §§219, 231, 238), and we *agree* in the unhesitating responses we make. On Wittgenstein's conception, such agreement is essential for our game of describing rules and concepts to each other (see §240).

The set of responses in which we agree, and the way they interweave with our activities, is our *form of life*. Beings who agreed in consistently giving bizarre quus-like responses would share in another form of life. By definition, such another form of life would be bizarre and incomprehensible to us. ("If a lion could talk, we could not understand him" (*PI*, p. 223).) However, if we can imagine the abstract possibility of another form of life (and no *a priori* argument would seem to exclude it), the members of a community sharing such a quus-like form of life could play the game of attributing rules and concepts to each other as we do. Someone would be said, in such a community, to follow a rule, as long as he agrees in his responses with the (*quus*-like) responses produced by the members of *that* community. Wittgenstein stresses the importance of agreement, and of a shared form of life, for his solution to his sceptical problem in the concluding paragraphs of the central section of *Philosophical Investigations* (§§240–2; see also the discussion of agreement in *PI*, pp. 225–7).

On Wittgenstein's conception, a certain type of traditional – and overwhelmingly natural – explanation of our shared form of life is excluded. We cannot say that we all respond as we do to '68 + 57' *because* we all grasp the concept of addition in the same way, that we share common responses to particular addition problems *because* we share a common concept of addition. (Frege, for example, would have endorsed such an explanation, but one hardly needs to be a philosopher to find it obvious and natural.) For Wittgenstein, an 'explanation' of this kind ignores his treatment of the sceptical paradox and its solution. There is no objective fact – that we all mean addition by '+', or even that a given individual does – that explains our agreement in particular cases. Rather our license to say of each other that we mean addition by '+' is part of a 'language game' that sustains itself only because of the brute fact that we generally agree. (Nothing about 'grasping concepts' guarantees that it will not break down tomorrow.) The rough uniformities in our arithmetical behavior may or may not some day be given an explanation on the neurophysiological level, but such an explanation is not here in question. Note again the analogy with the Humean case. Naively, we may wish to explain the observed concomitance of fire and heat by a causal, heat-producing, 'power' in the fire. The Humean alleges that any such use of causal powers to explain the regularity is meaningless. Rather we play a language game that allows us to attribute such a causal power to the fire as long as the regularity holds up. The regularity must be taken as a brute fact. So too for Wittgenstein (*PI*, p. 226): "What has to be accepted, the given, is . . . *forms of life.*"[59]

Finally, *criteria*. The exact interpretation and exegesis of Wittgenstein's concept of a criterion has been the subject of much discussion among students of Wittgenstein's later work. Criteria play a fundamental role in Wittgenstein's philosophy of mind: "An 'inner process' stands in need of outward criteria" (*PI*, §580). Often the necessity for criteria for mental concepts has been taken, both by advocates and critics of Wittgenstein's philosophy of mind, as a fundamental *premise* of his private language argument. Critics have sometimes argued that it constitutes an undefended and indefensible verificationist assumption. Some advocates respond that if it is a verificationist premise of some sort, that form of verificationism is clearly correct.

It is not my present purpose to enter into the finer exegetical points involved in Wittgenstein's notion of a criterion,[60] but rather to sketch the role of the notion in the picture we have been developing. Wittgenstein's sceptical solution to his problem depends on agreement, and on checkability – on one person's ability to test whether another uses a term as he does. In our own form of life, how does this agreement come about? In the case of a term like 'table', the situation, at least in elementary cases, is simple. A child who says "table" or "That's a table" when adults see a table in the area (and does not do so otherwise) is said to have mastered the term 'table': he says "That's a table", based on his observation, in agreement with the usage of adults, based on their observation. That is, they say, "That's a table" under like circumstances, and confirm the correctness of the child's utterances.

How does agreement emerge in the case of a term for a sensation, say 'pain'? It is not as simple as the case of 'table'. When will adults attribute to a child mastery of the avowal "I am in pain"?[61] The child, if he learns the avowal correctly, will utter it when he feels pain and not otherwise. By analogy with the case of 'table', it would appear that the adult should endorse this utterance if he, the adult, feels (his own? the child's?) pain. Of course we know that this is not the case. Rather the adult will endorse the child's avowal if the child's behavior (crying, agitated motion, *etc.*) and, perhaps, the external circumstances surrounding the child, indicate that he is in pain. If a child generally avows pain under such appropriate behavioral and external circumstances and generally does not do so otherwise, the adult will say of him that he has mastered the avowal, "I am in pain."

Since, in the case of discourse on pain and other sensations, the adult's confirmation whether he agrees with the child's avowal is based on the adult's observation of the child's behavior and circumstances, the fact that such behavior and circumstances characteristic of pain exist is essential in this case to the working of Wittgenstein's sceptical solution. This, then, is what is meant by the remark, "An 'inner process' stands in need of outward criteria." Roughly speaking, outward criteria for an inner process are circumstances, observable in the behavior of an individual, which, when present, would lead others to agree with his avowals. If the individual generally makes his avowals under the right such circumstances, others will say of him that he has mastered the appropriate expression ("I am in pain," "I feel itchy," etc.). We have seen that it is part of Wittgenstein's *general* view of the workings of *all* our expressions attributing concepts that others can confirm whether a subject's responses agree with their own. The present considerations simply spell out the form this confirmation and agreement take in the case of avowals.

It should then be clear that the demand for 'outward criteria' is no verificationist or behaviorist *premise* that Wittgenstein takes for granted in his 'private language argument'. If anything, it is *deduced*, in a sense of deduction akin to Kant's. A sceptical problem is posed, and a sceptical solution to that problem is given. The solution turns on the idea that each person who claims to be following a rule can be checked by others. Others in the community can check whether the putative rule follower is or is not giving particular responses that they endorse, that agree with their own. The way they check this is, in general, a primitive part of the language game;[62] it need not operate the way it does in the case of 'table'. 'Outward criteria' for sensations such as pain are simply the way this general requirement of our game of attributing concepts to others works out in the special case of sensations.[63]

It is not my purpose here to enter in detail into the exegesis of Wittgenstein's attack on an 'object and designation' model for sensation language (*PI*, §293). I am not, in fact, sure that I fully understand it. But it seems likely that it relates to one aspect of our present considerations. The model of the way agreement operates with respect to a word like 'table' (perhaps a paradigm of 'object and designation') is a very simple one: the child says "Table!" when he sees that a table is present and the adult agrees if he also sees that a table is present. It is tempting to suppose that this model ought to be a general one, and that if it does not apply to the case of 'pain' we must conclude that in some sense the adult can never really confirm the correctness of the child's use of "I am in pain." Wittgenstein's suggestion is that there cannot and need not be such a demand based on generalizing the use of 'table'. No *a priori* paradigm of the way concepts ought to be applied governs all forms of life, or even our own form of life. Our game of attributing concepts to others depends on agreement. It so happens that in the case of ascribing sensation language, this agreement operates in part through 'outward criteria' for first person avowals. No further 'justification' or 'explanation' for this procedure is required; this simply is *given* as how we achieve agreement here. The important role played in our lives by the practice of attributing sensation concepts to others is evident. If I attribute mastery of the term 'pain' to someone, his sincere utterance of "I am in pain," even without other signs of pain, is sufficient to induce me to feel pity for him, attempt to aid him, and the like (or, if I am a sadist, for the opposite); and similarly in other cases.

Compare the case of mathematics. Mathematical statements are generally not about palpable entities: if they are indeed to be regarded as about 'entities', these 'entities' are generally suprasensible, eternal objects. And often mathematical statements are about the infinite. Even such an elementary mathematical truth as that any two integers have a unique sum (perhaps implicitly accepted by everyone who has mastered the concept of addition, and, in any case, explicitly accepted by people with elementary sophistication as a basic property of that concept) is an assertion about infinitely many instances. All the more so is this true of the 'commutative' law, that $x + y = y + x$ for all x and y. Yet how does agreement operate in the case of mathematics? How do we judge of someone else that he has mastered various mathematical concepts? Our judgement, as usual, stems from the fact that he agrees with us in enough particular cases of mathematical judgements (and that, even if he disagrees, we are operating with a common procedure). We do not compare his mind with some suprasensible, infinite reality: we have seen through the sceptical paradox that this is of no help if we ask, say, whether he has mastered the concept of addition. Rather we check his observable responses to particular addition problems to see if his responses agree with ours. In more sophisticated mathematical areas, he and we accept various mathematical statements on the basis of proof; and among the conditions we require for attributing to him the mastery of our mathematical concepts is his general agreement with us on what he regards as proof. Here 'proofs' are not abstract objects laid up in a mathematical heaven (say, lengthy proofs in a formal system such as *Principia*). It refers to visible (or audible or palpable), concrete phenomena – marks or diagrams on paper, intelligible utterances. Proofs in this sense are not only finite objects; they are also small and clear enough to be able to judge of another man's proof whether I too would regard it as proof. This is why Wittgenstein emphasizes that proof must be *surveyable*. It must be surveyable if it is to be usable as a basis for agreement in judgements.

   This parallel illuminates Wittgenstein's remark that "Finitism and behaviorism are quite similar trends. Both say, but surely all we have here is . . . Both deny the existence of something, both with a view to escaping from a confusion." (*RFM*, p. 63) How are the two trends 'quite similar'? The finitist realizes that although mathematical statements and concepts may be about the infinite (e.g. to grasp the '+' fraction is to grasp an infinite table), the criteria for attributing such functions to others must be 'finite', indeed 'surveyable' – for example, we attribute mastery of the concept of addition to a child on the basis of his agreement with us on a finite number of instances of the addition table. Similarly, though sensation language may be about 'inner' states, the behaviorist correctly affirms that attribution to others of sensation concepts rests on publicly observable (and thus on behavioral) criteria. Further, the finitist and the behaviorist are right when they deny that the relation of the infinitary mathematical or inner psychological language to its 'finite' or 'outward' criteria is an adventitious product of human frailty, one that an account of the 'essence' of mathematical or sensation language would dispense with. Mathematical finitists and psychological behaviorists, however, make parallel unnecessary moves when they deny the legitimacy of talk of infinite mathematical objects or inner states. Behaviorists either condemn talk of mental states as meaningless or illegitimate, or attempt to define it in terms of behavior. Finitists similarly regard the infinistic part of mathematics as meaningless. Such opinions are misguided: they are attempts to repudiate our ordinary language game. In this game we are allowed, for certain purposes, to assert statements about 'inner' states or mathematical functions under certain circumstances. Although the criteria for judging that such statements are legitimately introduced are indeed behavioral (or finite), finite or behavioral statements cannot replace their role in our language as we use it.

Let me, then, summarize the 'private language argument' as it is presented in this paper. (1) We all suppose that our language expresses concepts — 'pain', 'plus', 'red' — in such a way that, once I 'grasp' the concept, all future applications of it are determined (in the sense of being uniquely *justified* by the concept grasped). In fact, it seems that no matter what is in my mind at a given time, I am free in the future to interpret it in different ways — for example, I could follow the sceptic and interpret 'plus' as 'quus'. In particular, this point applies if I direct my attention to a sensation and name it; nothing I have done determines future applications (in the justificatory sense above). Wittgenstein's scepticism about the determination of future usage by the past contents of my mind is analogous to Hume's scepticism about the determination of the future by the past (causally and inferentially). (2) The paradox can be resolved only by a 'sceptical solution of these doubts', in Hume's classic sense. This means that we must give up the attempt to find any fact about me in virtue of which I mean 'plus' rather than 'quus', and must then go on in a certain way. Instead we must consider how we actually use: (i) the categorical assertion that an individual is following a given rule (that he means addition by 'plus'); (ii) the conditional assertion that "if an individual follows such-and-such a rule, he must do so-and-so on a given occasion" (e.g., "if he means addition by '+', his answer to '68 + 57' should be '125'"). That is to say, we must look at the circumstances under which these assertions are introduced into discourse, and their role and utility in our lives. (3) As long as we consider a single individual in isolation, all we can say is this: An individual often does have the experience of being confident that he has 'got' a certain rule (sometimes that he has grasped it 'in a flash'). It is an empirical fact that, after that experience, individuals often are disposed to give responses in concrete cases with complete confidence that proceeding this way is 'what was intended'. We cannot, however, get any further in explaining on this basis the use of the conditionals in (ii) above. Of course, dispositionally speaking, the subject is indeed determined to respond in a certain way, say, to a given addition problem. Such a disposition, together with the appropriate 'feeling of confidence' could be present, however, even if he were not really following a rule at all, or even if he were doing the 'wrong' thing. The justificatory element of our use of conditionals such as (ii) is unexplained. (4) If we take into account the fact that the individual is in a community, the picture changes and the role of (i) and (ii) above becomes apparent. When the community accepts a particular conditional (ii), it accepts its *contraposed* form: the failure of an individual to come up with the particular responses the community regards as right leads the community to suppose that he is not following the rule. On the other hand, if an individual passes enough tests, the community (endorsing assertions of the form (i)) accepts him as a rule follower, thus enabling him to engage in certain types of interactions with them that depend on their reliance on his responses. Note that this solution explains how the assertions in (i) and (ii) are introduced into language; it does *not* give truth conditions for these statements to be true. (4) The success of the practices in (3) depends on the brute empirical fact that we agree with each other in our responses. Given the sceptical argument in (1), this success cannot be explained by 'the fact that we all grasp the same concepts'. (5) Just as Hume thought he had demonstrated that the causal relation between two events is unintelligible unless they are subsumed under a regularity, so Wittgenstein thought that the considerations in (2) and (3) above showed that all talk of an individual following rules has reference to him as a member of a community, as in (3). In particular, for the conditionals of type (ii) to make sense, the community must be able to judge whether an individual is indeed following a given rule in particular applications, i.e. whether his responses agree with their own. In the case of avowals of sensations, the way the community makes this judgement is by observing the individual's behavior and surrounding circumstances.

A few concluding points regarding the argument ought to be noted. First, following *PI*, §243, a 'private language' is usually defined as a language that it is logically impossible for anyone else to understand. The private language argument is taken to argue against the possibility of a private language in this sense. This conception is not in error, but it seems to me that the emphasis is somewhat misplaced. What is really denied is what might be called the 'private model' of rule following, that the notion of a person following a given rule is to be analyzed simply in terms of facts about the rule follower and the rule follower alone, without reference to his membership in a wider community. (In the same way, what Hume denies is the private model of causation: that whether one event causes another is a matter of the relation between these two events alone, without reference to their subsumption under larger event types.) The impossibility of a private language in the sense just defined does indeed follow from the incorrectness of the private model for language and rules, since the rule following in a 'private language' could only be analyzed by a private model, but the incorrectness of the private model is more basic, since it applies to all rules. I take all this to be the point of *PI*, §202.

Does this mean that Robinson Crusoe, isolated on an island, cannot be said to follow any rules, no matter what he does?[64] I do not see that this follows. What does follow is that *if* we think of Crusoe as following rules, we are taking him into our community and applying our criteria for rule following to him.[65] The falsity of the private model need not mean that a *physically isolated* individual cannot be said to follow rules; rather that an individual, *considered in isolation* (whether or not he is physically isolated), cannot be said to do so. Remember that Wittgenstein's theory is one of assertability conditions. Our community can assert of any individual that he follows a rule if he passes the tests for rule following applied to any member of the community.

Finally, the point just made in the last paragraph, that Wittgenstein's theory is one of assertability conditions, deserves emphasis. Wittgenstein's theory should not be confused with a theory that, for any *m* and *n*, the value of the function we mean by 'plus', *is* (by definition) the value that (nearly) all the linguistic community would give as the answer. Such a theory would be a theory of the *truth* conditions of such assertions as "By 'plus' we mean such-and-such function," or "By 'plus' we mean a function, which, when applied to 68 and 57 as arguments, yields 125 as value." (An infinite, exhaustive totality of specific conditions of the second form would determine which function was meant, and hence would determine a condition of the first form.) The theory would assert that 125 is the value of the function meant for given arguments, if and only if '125' is the response nearly everyone would give, given these arguments. Thus the theory would be a social, or community-wide, version of the dispositional theory, and would be open to at least some of the same criticisms as the original form. I take Wittgenstein to deny that he holds such a view, for example, in *Remarks on the Foundations of Mathematics*, V, 33 (p. 184): "Does this mean, e.g., that the definition of same would be this: same is what all or most human beings take for the same? – Of course not."[66] (See also *Philosophical Investigations*, p. 226, "Certainly the propositions, "Human beings believe that twice two is four" and "Twice two is four" do not mean the same"; and see also §§240–1.) One must bear firmly in mind that Wittgenstein has no theory of truth conditions – necessary and sufficient conditions – for the correctness of one response rather than another to a new addition problem. Rather he simply points out that each of us *automatically* calculates new addition problems (without feeling the need to check with the community whether our procedure is proper); that the community feels entitled to correct a deviant calculation; that in practice such deviation is rare, and so on. Wittgenstein thinks that these observations about sufficient conditions for justified assertion are enough to illuminate the role and utility in our lives of assertion about meaning and determination of new answers. What follows from these assertability conditions is *not* that the answer everyone gives to an addition problem is, by definition, the correct one, but rather the platitude that, if everyone agrees upon a certain answer, then no one will feel justified in calling that answer wrong.[67]

Obviously, there are countless relevant aspects of Wittgenstein's philosophy of mind that I have not discussed. About some aspects I am not clear, and others have been left untouched because of the limits of this essay.[68] In particular, I have not discussed numerous issues arising out of the paragraphs *following PI*, §243 that are usually called the 'private language argument', nor have I really discussed Wittgenstein's attendant positive account of the nature of sensation language and of the attribution of the psychological states. Nevertheless, I do think that the basic 'private language argument' precedes these passages, and that only with an understanding of this argument can we begin to comprehend or consider what follows. That was the task undertaken in this essay.

Notes

1. Looking through some of the most distinguished commentaries on Wittgenstein of the last ten or fifteen years, I find some that still treat the discussion of rules cursorily, virtually not at all, as if it were a minor topic. Others treat the discussion of rules as if it were important for Wittgenstein's views on mathematics and logical necessity but separate it from 'the private language argument'. Since Wittgenstein has more than *one* way of arguing for a given conclusion, and even of presenting a single argument, to defend the present exegesis I need not necessarily argue that these other commentaries are in error. Indeed, they may give important and illuminating' expositions of facets of the *Investigations* and its argument deemphasized or omitted in this essay. Nevertheless, in emphasis they certainly differ considerably from the present exposition.

2. Hereafter the abbreviation *PI* is used. The small numbered units of *Philosophical Investigations* are termed 'sections' (or 'paragraphs'). Page references are used only if a section reference is not possible. I quote G. E. M. Anscombe's English translation. *Philosophical Investigations* (x + 232 pp., in German and English translation) has undergone many editions. All have the same pagination and paragraphs. The publishers are Basil Blackwell in Britain and Macmillan in the United States.

   This essay does not proceed by giving detailed exegesis of Wittgenstein's text but rather develops the argument in its own way. I recommend that the reader reread the *Investigations* in the light of the present exegesis and see whether it illuminates the text.

3. Basil Blackwell, Oxford, 1956, xix + 204 pp. The editors of *Remarks on the Foundations of Mathematics* (*RFM*) assert (p. vi) that Wittgenstein appears originally to have intended to include some of the material on mathematics in *Philosophical Investigations*.

   The latest (third) edition (1978) includes more material than earlier editions, and rearranges some of the sections and divisions of earlier editions. When I wrote the present work, I did not know that an expanded edition had appeared and used my copy of the original edition. *All references here are to the original edition.*

4. Personally I feel, however, that the role of stylistic considerations here cannot be denied. It is clear that purely stylistic and literary considerations meant a great deal to Wittgenstein. His own stylistic preference obviously contributes to the difficulty of his work as well as to its beauty.

5. See the discussion of this point on page 272 below.

6. See again the same discussion on page 272.

7. Looking over what I have written below, I find myself worried that the reader may lose the main thread of Wittgenstein's argument in the extensive treatment of finer points. In particular, the treatment of dispositional theory below became so extensive because I heard it urged more than once as an answer to the sceptical paradox. That discussion may contain somewhat more of Kripke's argumentation in support of Wittgenstein rather than exposition of Wittgenstein's own argument than does most of the rest of this essay. (See notes 17 and 18 for *some* of the connections. The argument is, however, inspired by Wittgenstein's original text.) I urge the reader to concentrate, on a first reading, on understanding the intuitive force of Wittgenstein's sceptical problem and to regard byways such as these as secondary.

8. Perhaps I should make a remark about such expressions as "By 'plus' I meant quus (or plus)," "By 'green' I meant green," etc. I am not familiar with an accepted felicitous convention to indicate the object of the verb 'to mean'. There are two problems. First, if one says, "By 'the woman who discovered radium' I meant the woman who discovered radium," the object

can be interpreted in two ways. It may stand for a woman (Marie Curie), in which case the assertion is true only if 'meant' is used to mean referred to (as it can be used); or it may be used to denote the *meaning* of the quoted expression, not a woman, in which case the assertion is true with 'meant' used in the ordinary sense. Second, as is illustrated by 'referred to', 'green', 'quus', etc. above, as objects of 'meant', one must use various expressions as objects in an awkward manner contrary to normal grammar. (Frege's difficulties concerning unsaturatedness are related.) Both problems tempt one to put the object in quotation marks, like the subject; but such a usage conflicts with the convention of philosophical logic that a quotation denotes the expression quoted. Some special 'meaning marks', as proposed for example by David Kaplan, could be useful here. If one is content to ignore the first difficulty and always use 'mean' to mean denote (for most purposes of the present paper, such a reading would suit at least as well as an intensional one; often I speak as if it is a *numerical function* that is meant by plus), the second problem might lead one to nominalize the objects – 'plus' denotes the plus function, 'green' denotes greenness, etc. I contemplated using italics ("'plus' means *plus*"; "'mean' may mean *denote*"). The convention reads awkwardly in the written language but sounds rather reasonable in the spoken language.

Since use–mention distinctions are significant for the argument as I give it, I try to remember to use quotation marks when an expression is mentioned. However, quotation marks are also used for other purposes where they might be invoked in normal non-philosophical English writing (for example, in the case of "'meaning marks'" in the previous paragraph, or "'quasi-quotation'" in the next sentence). Readers familiar with Quine's 'quasi quotation' will be aware that in some cases I use ordinary quotation where logical purity would require that I use quasi quotation or some similar device. I have not tried to be careful about this matter, since I am confident that in practice readers will not be confused.

9. I believe I got the phrase "both inside and outside language" from a conversation with Rogers Albritton.

10. See W. V. Quine, *Word and Object* (MIT, The Technology Press, Cambridge, Massachusetts, 1960, xi + 294 pp.), especially Chapter 2, 'Translation and Meaning' (pp. 26–79). See also *Ontological Relativity and Other Essays* (Columbia University Press, New York and London, 1969, viii + 165 pp.), especially the first three chapters (pp. 1–90); and see also "On the Reasons for the Indeterminacy of Translation," *The Journal of Philosophy*, vol. 67 (1970), pp. 178–83.

11. I do not mean the term 'introspective' to be laden with philosophical doctrine. Of course much of the baggage that has accompanied this term would be objectionable to Wittgenstein in particular. I simply mean that he makes use, in his discussion, of our own memories and knowledge of our 'inner' experiences.

12. The same objection scotches a related suggestion. It might be urged that the quus function is ruled out as an interpretation of '+' because it fails to satisfy some of the laws I accept for '+' (for example, it is not associative; we could have defined it so as not even to be commutative). One might even observe that, on the natural numbers, addition is the only function that satisfies certain laws that I accept – the 'recursion equations' for +: $(x)(x+o=x)$ and $(x)(y)(x+y'=(x+y)')$ where the stroke or dash indicates successor; these equations are sometimes called a 'definition' of addition. The problem is that the other signs used in these laws (the universal quantifiers, the equality sign) have been applied in only a finite number of instances, and they can be given non-standard interpretations that will fit non-standard interpretations of '+'. Thus for example '(x)' might mean for every $x < h$, where h is some upper bound to the instances where universal instantiation has hitherto been applied, and similarly for equality.

In any event the objection is somewhat overly sophisticated. Many of us who are not mathematicians use the '+' sign perfectly well in ignorance of any explicitly formulated laws of the type cited.

13. Few readers, I suppose, will by this time be tempted to appeal a determination to "go on the same way" as before. Indeed, I mention it at this point primarily to remove a possible misunderstanding of the sceptical argument, not to counter a possible reply to it. Some followers of Wittgenstein – perhaps occasionally Wittgenstein himself – have thought that his point involves a rejection of 'absolute identity' (as opposed to some kind of 'relative' identity). I do not see that this is so, whether or not doctrines of 'relative' identity are correct on other grounds. Let identity be as 'absolute' as one pleases: it holds only between each thing and itself. Then the plus function is identical with itself, and the quus function is identical with itself. None of this will tell me whether I referred to the plus function or to the quus function in the past, nor therefore will it tell me which to use in order to apply the same function now.

In fairness to Peter Geach, the leading advocate of the 'relativity' of identity, I should mention (lest the reader assume I had him in mind) that he is *not* one of those I have heard expound Wittgenstein's doctrine as dependent on a denial of 'absolute' identity.

14. See Nelson Goodman, *Fact, Fiction, and Forecast* (3rd ed., Bobbs-Merrill, Indianapolis, 1973, xiv + 131 pp.).

15. The exact definition of 'grue' is unimportant. It is best to suppose that past objects were grue if and only if they were (then) green while present objects are grue if and only if they are (now) blue. Strictly speaking, this is not Goodman's original idea, but it is probably most convenient for present purposes. Sometimes Goodman writes this way as well.

16. 'Schmolor', with a slightly different spelling, appears in Joseph Ullian, "More on 'Grue' and Grue," *The Philosophical Review*, vol. 70 (1961), pp. 386–9.

17. Russell's *The Analysis of Mind* (George Allen and Unwin, London, in the Muirhead Library of Philosophy, 310 pp.) already gives dispositional analyses of certain mental concepts: see especially, Lecture III, "Desire and Feeling," pp. 58–76. It is explicitly influenced by Watsonian behaviorism; see the preface and the first chapter. I am inclined to conjecture that Wittgenstein's philosophical development was influenced considerably by this work, both in the respects in which he sympathizes with behavioristic and dispositional views, and to the extent that he opposes them. I take *Philosophical Remarks* (Basil Blackwell, Oxford, 1975, 357 pp., translated by R. Hargreaves and R. White), § §21ff., to express a rejection of Russell's theory of desire, as stated in Lecture III of *The Analysis of Mind*. The discussion of Russell's theory played, I think, an important role in Wittgenstein's development: the problem of the relation of a desire, expectation, etc., to its object ('intentionality') is one of the important forms Wittgenstein's problem about meaning and rules takes in the *Investigations*. I think that even in the *Investigations*, as in *Philosophical Remarks* (which stems from an earlier period), Wittgenstein still rejects Russell's dispositional theory because it makes the relation between a desire and its object an 'external' relation (*PR*, §21), even if he no longer holds the 'picture theory'. *PI*, § §429–65 discusses the fundamental problem of the *Investigations* in the form of 'intentionality'. I am inclined to take §440 and §460 to refer obliquely to Russell's theory and to reject it.

17a. None of this is intended to *repudiate* Chomsky's distinction between 'competence' and 'performance'. Rather the point is that the distinction itself shows that only 'performance', not 'competence', is a dispositional notion. The concept of 'competence' is intimately bound up with that of following a rule, and is 'normative', not 'descriptive' in the sense explained on page 257 below.

17b. M. A. E. Dummett, "Wittgenstein's Philosophy of Mathematics," *The Philosophical Review*, vol. 68 (1959), pp. 324–48, see p. 331, reprinted in George Pitcher (ed.), *Wittgenstein: The Philosophical Investigations* (Macmillan, 1966, pp. 420–47), see p. 428.

18. Wittgenstein discusses machines explicitly in *PI*, §§193–5. See the parallel discussion in *Remarks on the Foundations of Mathematics* (*RFM*), part I, §§118–30, especially §§119–25; see also, e.g., II, §87, and III, §§48–9, there. The criticisms in the text of the dispositional analysis and of the use of machines to solve the problem are inspired by these sections. In particular, Wittgenstein himself draws the distinction between the machine as an abstract program ("der Maschine, als Symbol" *PI*, §193) and the actual physical machine, which is subject to breakdown ("do we forget the possibility of their bending, breaking off, melting, and so on?" (§193)). The dispositional theory views the subject himself as a kind of machine, whose potential actions embody the function. So in this sense the dispositional theory and the idea of the machine-as-embodying-the-function are really one. Wittgenstein's attitude toward both is the same: they confuse the 'hardness of a rule' with the 'hardness of a material' (*RFM*, II, §87). On my interpretation, then, Wittgenstein agrees with his interlocutor (*PI*, §194 and §195) that the sense in which all the values of the function are already present is not simply causal, although he disagrees with the idea that the future use is already present in some mysterious non-causal way.

Although, in an attempt to follow Wittgenstein, I have emphasized the distinction between concrete physical machines and their abstract programs in what I have written above, it might be instructive to look at the outcome when the limitation of machines is idealized as in the modern theory of automata. A finite automaton, as usually defined, has only finitely many states, receives only finitely many distinct inputs, and has only finitely many outputs, but it is idealized in two respects: it has no problem of malfunction, and its lifetime (without any decay or wearing out of its parts) is infinite. Such a machine can, in a sense, perform computations on arbitrarily large whole numbers. If it understands the single digits from zero through nine, inclusive, it can receive arbitrarily large positive whole numbers as inputs simply by being given their digits one by one. (We cannot do this, since our effective lifetimes are finite, and there is a minimum time needed for us to understand any single digit.) Such an automaton can add according to the usual algorithm in decimal notation (the digits for the numbers being added should be fed into the machine starting from the last digits of both summands and going backwards, as in the usual algorithm). Any function computed by such a machine that purports to be multiplication will, for large enough arguments, exhibit 'quus-like' (or rather, 'quimes-like') properties at sufficiently large arguments. Even if we were idealized as finite automata, a dispositional theory would yield unacceptable results.

Suppose we idealized even further and considered a Turing machine which has a tape to use which is infinite in both directions. Such a machine has infinite extent at every moment, in addition to an infinite lifetime without malfunctions. Turing machines can multiply correctly, but it is well known that even here there are many functions we can define explicitly that can be computed by no such machine. A crude dispositional theory would attribute to us a non-standard interpretation (or no interpretation at all) for any such function.

I have found that both the crude dispositional theory and the function-as-embodied-in-a-machine come up frequently when Wittgenstein's paradox is discussed. For this reason, and their close relation to Wittgenstein's text, I have expounded these theories, though sometimes I have wondered whether the discussion of them is excessively long. On the other hand, I have resisted the temptation to discuss 'functionalism', even though various forms of it have been so attractive to so many of the best recent writers that it has almost become the received philosophy of mind in the USA. Especially I have feared that some readers of the discussion in the text will think that 'functionalism' is precisely the way to modify the crude dispositional theory so as to meet the criticisms (especially those that rely on the circularity of *ceteris paribus* clauses). (I report, howver, that thus far I have not run into such reactions in practice.) Since I have chosen not to discuss 'functionalism', I can offer only the briefest partial hints here. Functionalists are fond of comparing psychological states to the abstract states of a (Turing) machine, though some are cognizant of certain limitations of the comparison. But then the remarks of the text stand here as well: any concrete physical object can be viewed as an imperfect realization of many machine programs. Taking a human organism as a concrete object, what is to tell us *which* program he should be regarded as instantiating? In particular, does he compute 'plus' or 'quus'? If the remarks on machines in my own (and Wittgenstein's) text are understood, I think it will emerge that as far as the present problem is concerned, functionalism does not take us materially beyond the crude dispositional analysis.

I hope to elaborate on these remarks elsewhere.

19. A different use of 'simplicity', not that by which we evaluate competing theories, might suggest itself with respect to the discussion of machines above. There I remarked that a concrete physical machine, considered as an object without reference to a designer, may (approximately) instantiate any number of programs that (approximately, allowing for some 'malfunctioning') extend its actual finite behavior. If the physical machine was not designed but, so to speak, 'fell from the sky', there can be no fact of the matter as to which program it 'really' instantiates, hence no 'simplest hypothesis' about this non-existent fact.

Nevertheless, given a physical machine, one might ask what is the *simplest program* that the physical machine approximates. To do this one would have to find a measure of the simplicity of programs, a measure of the trade-off of the simplicity of the program with the degree to which the concrete machine fails to conform to it (malfunctions), and so on. I, who am no expert, nor even an amateur, am unaware that this problem has been considered by theoretical computer scientists. Whether or not it has been considered, intuition suggests that something might be made of it, though it would not be trivial to find simplicity measures that give intuitively satisfying results.

I doubt that any of this would illuminate Wittgenstein's sceptical paradox. One might try, say, to define the function I meant as the one that, according to the simplicity measure, followed the simplest program approximately compatible with my physical structure. Suppose brain physiologists found – to their surprise – that actually such a simplicity measure led to a program that did not compute addition for the '+' function, but some other function. Would this show that I did not mean addition by '+'? Yet, in the absence of detailed knowledge of the brain (and the hypothetical simplicity measure), the physiological discovery in question is by no means inconceivable. The justificatory aspect of the sceptic's problem is even more obviously remote from any such simplicity measure. I do not justify my choice of '125' rather than '5' as an answer to '68 + 57' by citing a hypothetical simplicity measure of the type mentioned. (I hope to elaborate on this in the projected work on functionalism mentioned in note 18 above.)

19a. It is well known that this type of view is characteristic of Hume's philosophy. See note 35 below.

20. Although there are clear classical senses of behaviorism in which such current philosophies of mind as 'functionalism' are not behaviorist, nevertheless, speaking for myself, I find much

contemporary 'functionalism' (especially those versions that attempt to give 'functional' *analyses* of mental terms) are far too behavioristic for my own taste. It would require an extensive digression to go into the matter further here.

21. I should not deny that Wittgenstein has important affinities to behaviorism (as to finitism – see pp. 293–4 below). Such a famous slogan as "My attitude toward him is an attitude towards a soul (*Seele*). I am not of the *opinion* that he has a soul," (*PI*, p. 178) sounds much too behavioristic for me. I personally would like to think that anyone who does not think of me as conscious is wrong about the facts, not simply 'unfortunate', or 'evil', or even 'monstrous' or 'inhuman', in his 'attitude' (whatever that might mean).

(If '*Seele*' is translated as 'soul', it might be thought that the 'attitude' ('*Einstellung*') to which Wittgenstein refers has special *religious* connotations. But it is clear from the entire passage that the issue relates simply to the difference between my 'attitude' toward a conscious being, and toward an automaton, even though one of the paragraphs refers specifically to the religious doctrine of the immortality of the soul ('*Seele*'). Perhaps in some respects 'mind' might be a less misleading translation of '*Seele*' in the sentence quoted above, since it is somewhat less loaded with special philosophical and religious connotations. Anscombe translates '*Seele*' and its derivatives sometimes as 'soul', sometimes as 'mind', depending on the context.)

22. Of course Frege would not accept the identification of a function with a set of triples. Such an identification violates his conception of function as 'unsaturated'. Although this complication is very important for Frege's philosophy, it can be ignored for the purposes of the present presentation.

23. See page 246 above, and note 10.

24. For 'agreement' and the related notion of 'form of life' in Wittgenstein, see pp. 288–90 below. Quine, *Word and Object*, p. 27, characterizes language as "the complex of present dispositions to verbal behavior, in which speakers of the same language have perforce come to resemble one another"; also, see *PI*, §2; *Word and Object*, pp. 5–8. Some of the concepts of *Word and Object*, such as that of 'observation sentence', depend on this uniformity in the community. Nevertheless, agreement seems to have a more crucial role in Wittgenstein's philosophy than in Quine's.

25. This example is discussed below. See p. 280 and note 54.

26. Quine, *Ontological Relativity and Other Essays*, p. 31.

27. Roughly, the first assertion is the 'indeterminacy of translation', while the second is the 'inscrutability of reference'.

28. See Goodman, *Fact, Fiction, and Forecast*, p. 13b, n. 1. See also the papers in part VII ("Induction") in *Problems and Projects* (Bobbs-Merrill, Indianapolis and New York, 1972, xii + 463 pp.).

29. In part Goodman's discussion of the problem seems to presuppose that the extension of each predicate ('green', 'grue'), etc., is known, and that this question does not itself get entangled in the 'new riddle of induction'. Sidney Shoemaker, "On Projecting the Unprojectible," *The Philosophical Review*, vol. 84 (1975), pp. 178–219, questions whether such a separation is possible (see his concluding paragraph). I have not yet made a careful study of Shoemaker's argument.

30. See especially his "Positionality and Pictures," *The Philosophical Review*, vol. 69 (1960), pp. 523–5, reprinted in *Problems and Projects*, pp. 402–4. See also Ullian, "More on 'Grue' and Grue", and *Problems and Projects*, pp. 408–9 (comments on Judith Thompson).

31. Briefly: Goodman insists that there is no sense that does not beg the question according to

which 'grue' is 'temporal', or 'positional', and 'green' is not; if either of the pairs 'blue-green' and 'grue-bleen' is taken as primitive, the predicates of the other pair are 'temporally' definable in terms of it (see *Fact, Fiction, and Forecast*, pp. 77–80). Nevertheless, intuitively it does seem clear that 'grue' is positional in a sense that 'green' is not. Perhaps that sense can be brought out by the fact that 'green', but not 'grue', is learned (learnable?) ostensively by a sufficient number of samples, without reference to time. It would seem that a reply to this argument should take the form, "Who is to say that it is not 'grue' that others (or even, myself in the past?) learned by such ostensive training?" But this leads directly to Wittgenstein's problem. The papers cited in the previous footnote are relevant. (It is true, however, that problems like Goodman's can arise for competing predicates that do not appear, intuitively, to be defined positionally.)

32. So put, the problem has an obvious Kantian flavor.

33. See especially the discussions of 'green' and 'grue' above, which plainly could carry over to pain (let 'pickle' apply to pains before *t*, and tickles thereafter!); but it is clear enough by now that the problem is completely general.

34. Karl Britton, "Portrait of a Philosopher," *The Listener*, LIII, no. 1372 (June 16, 1955), p. 1072, quoted by George Pitcher, *The Philosophy of Wittgenstein* (Prentice Hall, Englewood Cliffs, NJ, 1964, viii + 340 pp), p. 325.

35. Much of Wittgenstein's argument can be regarded as an attack on characteristically Humean (or classical empiricist) ideas. Hume posits an introspectible qualitative state for each of our psychological states (an 'impression'). Further, he thinks that an appropriate 'impression' or 'image' can constitute an 'idea', without realizing that an image in no way tells us how it is to be applied. (See the discussion of determining 'green' with an image on p. 249 above.) Of course the Wittgensteinian paradox is, among other things, a strong protest against such suppositions.

36. David Hume, *A Treatise of Human Nature* (ed. L. A. Selby-Bigge. Clarendon Press, Oxford, 1888), Book I, Part IV, Section I (p. 183 in the Selby-Bigge edition).

37. Hume, *ibid.*, Book I, Part II, Section II (p. 187 in the Selby-Bigge edition). Hume's occasional affinities to 'ordinary language' philosophy should not be overlooked. Consider the following: "Those philosophers, who have divided human reason into *knowledge and probability*, and have defined the first to be *that evidence, which arises from a comparison of ideas*, are obliged to comprehend all our arguments from causes or effects under the general term of probability. But tho' everyone be free to use his terms in what sense he pleases . . . 'tis however certain, that in common discourse we readily affirm, that many arguments from causation exceed probability, and may be received as a superior kind of evidence. One would appear ridiculous, who would say, that 'tis only probable the sun will rise tomorrow, or that all men must dye . . ." (*ibid.*, Book I, Part III, Section XI, p. 124 in the Selby-Bigge edition).

38. George Berkeley, *The Principles of Human Knowledge*, §§ 29–34. Of course the characterization may be oversimplified, but it suffices for present purposes.

39. It is almost 'analytic' that I cannot produce a common contemporary example that would not meet with vigorous opposition. Those who hold the cited view will argue that, in this case, their analyses of ordinary usage are really correct. I have no desire to enter into an irrelevant controversy here, but I myself find that many of the 'topic-neutral' analyses of discourse about the mind proposed by contemporary materialists are just the other side of the Berkeleyan coin.

40. Writing this sentence, I find myself prey to an appropriate fear that (some) experts in Hume and Berkeley will not approve of some particular thing that I say about these philosophers here. I have made no careful study of them for the purpose of this paper. Rather a crude and fairly conventional amount of the 'rough outlines' of their views is used for purposes of comparison with Wittgenstein.

41. Berkeley, *The Principles of Human Knowledge*, §4. Of course Berkeley might mean that the prevalence of the doctrine stems from the influence of philosophical theory rather than common sense, as indeed he asserts in the next section.

42. *PI*, §189: "But *are* the steps then *not* determined by the algebraic formula?" In spite of Wittgenstein's interpretation within his own philosophy of the ordinary phrase "the steps are determined by the formula," the impression persists that the interlocutor's characterization of his view is really correct. See §195: "But I don't mean that what I do now (in grasping a sense) determines the future use *causally* and as a matter of experience, but that in a *queer* way, the use itself is in some sense present," which are the words of the interlocutor, and the bland reply, "But of course it is, 'in *some* sense'! Really the only thing wrong with what you say is the expression "in a queer way". The rest is all right; and the sentence only seems queer when one imagines a different language-game for it from the one in which we actually use it."

43. Donald Davidson's influential and important theory of natural language has many features in common with the *Tractatus*, even if the underlying philosophy is different. Davidson argues that some simple, almost *a priori* considerations (not requiring detailed empirical investigation of specific natural languages) put strong constraints on the form of a theory of meaning for natural languages (it must be a finitely axiomatized Tarski-style theory of truth conditions). (Although the *form* of a theory is determined without detailed empirical investigation, for a particular language the specific theory adopted is supposed to require detailed empirical support.) The fact that a theory of meaning must have this form, it is argued, puts strong constraints on the logical form, or deep structure, of natural language – very probably that it ought to be close to classical extensional first order logic. All these ideas are close to the spirit of the *Tractatus*. In particular, like the *Tractatus*, Davidson holds (i) that truth conditions are a key element in a theory of language; (ii) that the uncovering of a hidden deep structure of language is crucial to a proper theory of interpretation; (iii) that the form of the deep structure is constrained in advance by theoretical, quasi-logical considerations; (iv) that in part the constraints show that the deep structure has a logical form close to that of a formal language of symbolic logic; (v) that in particular sentences are built up from 'atoms' by logical operators; (vi) that in particular the deep structure of natural language is extensional in spite of the misleading appearances of surface structure. All these ideas of the *Tractatus* are repudiated in the *Investigations*, which is hostile to any attempt to analyze language by uncovering a hidden deep structure. In this last respect, modern transformational linguistics, since Noam Chomsky, has been closer to the *Tractatus* than to the *Investigations*.

See also the programs of the generative semanticists and of Richard Montague. Of course many of the ideas of the *Tractatus*, or of 'logical atomism', have not been revived in any of these theories.

44. Dummett, "Wittgenstein's Philosophy of Mathematics," p. 348 in original; p. 427 as reprinted in Pitcher (ed.).

45. See, for example, *PI*, §304, where Wittgenstein is dealing with sensation language: "The

paradox disappears only if we make a radical break with the idea that language . . . always serves the same purpose: to convey thoughts – which may be about houses, pains, good and evil, or anything else you please."

46. Speaking of 'justification conditions' does not suggest the primacy of the indicative mood as much as 'assertibility conditions', but it has its own drawbacks. For Wittgenstein, there is an important class of cases where a use of language properly has no independent justification other than the speaker's inclination to speak thus on that occasion (e.g. saying that one is in pain). In such cases, Wittgenstein says (*PI*, §289), "To use a word without a justification (*Rechtfertigung*) does not mean to use it *zu Unrecht*." Anscombe's translation of '*zu Unrecht*' is not consistent. In her translation of *Philosophical Investigations*, §289, she translates it 'without right'. However, in her translation of *Remarks on the Foundations of Mathematics*, V, §33 (p. 184), where almost exactly the same German sentence occurs, she translates it as 'wrongfully'. The German dictionary I have at hand (Wildhagen-Heraucourt, Brandstetter Verlag, Wiesbaden, and Allen and Unwin, London), translates '*zu Unrecht*' as 'unjustly, unfairly'; '*Unrecht*' in general is an 'injustice' or a 'wrong'. All this is reasonably consistent with 'wrongfully' but gives little support to 'without right', even though the idea that we have a 'right' to use a word in certain circumstances without 'justification' ('*Rechtfertigung*') is obviously in harmony with the point Wittgenstein is trying to make. However, by '*zu Unrecht*' Wittgenstein seems to mean that the use of a word without independent justification need not be a 'wrongful' use of the word – one without proper epistemic or linguistic support. On the contrary, it is essential to the workings of our language that, in some cases, such a use of language is perfectly proper. When we use the terminology of 'justification conditions', we must construe them to include such cases (where Wittgenstein would say there is no 'justification'). (Simply 'incorrectly', or perhaps 'wrongly', might be a more idiomatic translation than 'wrongfully'. 'Without right' sounds to me too much as if a difficult new technical term is being introduced.) See also pp. 282–3 and note 57 below.

47. In some ways Frege can be taken to be the target here. It is he who insists on regarding numbers as *objects*, and on asking about the nature of these objects (even insisting that we can ask whether Julius Caesar is a number or not). On the other hand, the famous contextual principle of *Grundlagen der Arithmetik* (that one should ask for the signification of a sign only in the context of a sentence) and his emphasis in particular on asking how numerical expressions are actually applied is in the spirit of Wittgenstein's discussion. Perhaps the best conception of Wittgenstein's relation to Frege here is to say that Wittgenstein would regard the spirit of Frege's contextual principle as sound but would criticize Frege for using 'name of an object' as a catch-all for uses of language that are 'absolutely unlike' (*PI*, §10).

48. Paul Benacerraf, in "What Numbers Could Not Be", *The Philosophical Review*, vol. 74 (1963), pp. 47–73, see especially pp. 71–2, concludes with suggestions strikingly similar to Wittgenstein's, though much of the preceding argumentation has no direct parallel in Wittgenstein. It is possible that one reason the resemblance of the views to those of a fairly well-known portion of the *Investigations* was not noticed is the *en passant* way Wittgenstein introduces the issue in the philosophy of mathematics in the context of a more general discussion. (Although I do not take it upon myself to criticize Wittgenstein in this essay, it seems to me that a great deal of further work must be done if one wishes to defend Wittgenstein's position here, since mathematics involves much more by way of apparently treating numbers as entities than can be covered by the simple case of counting. Perhaps some later authors can be interpreted as attempting to carry out such a project, but it is not my task to discuss these issues here.)

48a. See Norman Malcolm, *Ludwig Wittgenstein: A Memoir*, with a biographical sketch by G. H. von Wright (Oxford University Press, London, 1958), p. 69.

49. Although Wittgenstein's concern in these initial sections is primarily with his own earlier way of thinking, of course he is concerned as well with related views (the 'object and name' model of language, the picture of sentences 'as corresponding to facts', etc.) in other writers, even though these writers may have views that differ in detail from those of the *Tractatus*. He wishes to relate the discussion to larger issues as well as to his own specific views.

50. Although Wittgenstein's views on mathematics were undoubtedly influenced by Brouwer, it is worth noting here that Brouwer's intuitionist philosophy of mathematics is, if anything, even more solipsistic than its traditional 'Platonist' rival. According to this conception, mathematics can be idealized as the isolated activity of a single mathematician ('creating subject') whose theorems are assertions about his own mental states. The fact that mathematicians form a community is irrelevant for theoretical purposes. (Indeed, Brouwer himself is said to have held mysterious 'solipsistic' views that communication is impossible. The point would remain even if we left these aside.)

51. Barry Stroud emphasized this fact to me, though the responsibility for the examples and exposition in the following paragraphs is my own.

52. See: "But how does he know where and how he is to look up the word 'red' and what he is to do with the word 'five'? – Well, I assume that he *acts* as I described. Explanations come to an end somewhere." (*PI*, §1) In hindsight, this is a statement of the basic point that I follow rules 'blindly', without any justification for the choice I make. The suggestion in the section that nothing is wrong with this situation, provided that my use of 'five', 'red', etc. fits into a proper system of activities in the community, anticipates Wittgenstein's sceptical solution, as expounded below.

53. Though perhaps vagueness, in the ordinary sense, enters into Wittgenstein's puzzle in this way: when a teacher *introduces* such a word as 'plus' to the learner, if he does not reduce it to more 'basic', previously learned concepts, he introduces it by a finite number of examples, plus the instructions: "Go on in the same way!" The last clause may indeed be regarded as vague, in the ordinary sense, though our grasp of the most precise concept depends on it. This type of vagueness *is* intimately connected with Wittgenstein's paradox.

54. In these sections, Wittgenstein does not cite examples like 'grue' or 'quus' but begins by emphasizing the ordinary possibilities for misunderstanding an ostensive definition. Many philosophers who have been influenced by Wittgenstein have happened also to be attracted to the idea that an act of ostension is ill defined unless it is accompanied by a sortal ('the entity I am pointing to' versus 'the color I am pointing to', 'the shape . . .', 'the table . . .', etc.). Then morals regarding naming and identity (as associated with 'sortal terms') are drawn from this fact. I have the impression that many of these philosophers would interpret Wittgenstein's *PI*, §§28–9 as making the same point; but it seems clear to me that the *main* point of these sections is almost the exact opposite. It should be clear from reading §29 that the idea of adding a sortal ("This *number* is called 'two'") is introduced by Wittgenstein's imaginary interlocutor. As against this, Wittgenstein replies that the point is in a sense correct, but that the original ostensive definition – without a sortal – is perfectly legitimate provided that it leads the learner to apply such a word as 'two' correctly in the future, while even if the sortal term is added, the possibility of future misapplication is not removed, since the sortal too may be interpreted incorrectly (and this problem cannot be removed by further explanations). Really there are two separable issues, as in the case of §§84–9. One issue is analogous to the one about vagueness in §§84–9: that an ostensive definition without

an accompanying sortal is vague. The other, which clearly is the main point, is Wittgenstein's sceptical problem, presented here in terms of the possibility of misunderstanding an ostensive definition.

55. The criticisms of the earlier ideas about 'isomorphism' are thus criticisms of a special alleged way of obtaining a unique interpretation of a mental representation. For Wittgenstein, given his earlier views, criticisms of the notion of isomorphism are thus of obvious special importance as a stage setting for his paradox. They are relatively less important as such a stage setting for someone who is not working his way out of this special *milieu*.

56. Michael Dummett emphasized this fact to me, though the responsibility for the present formulation is my own.

57. See note 46. Note that in *RFM*, V, 33 (p. 184), Wittgenstein develops this point with respect to his general problem about rules, agreement, and identity, while the parallel passage in *PI*, §289, is concerned with avowals of pain. This illustrates again the connection of Wittgenstein's ideas on sensation language with the general point about rules. Note also that the *RFM* passage is embedded in a context of the philosophy of mathematics. The connection of Wittgenstein's discussions of mathematics with his discussions of sensations is another theme of the present essay.

58. As will be seen immediately, inversion in this sense is a device for reversing priorities. William James summarized his famous theory of the emotions (*The Principles of Psychology*, Henry Holt & Co., New York, 1913, in 2 volumes; chapter 25 (vol. 2, 442–85), "The Emotions") by the assertion, ". . . the . . . rational statement is that we feel sorry because we cry . . . not that we cry . . . because we are sorry . . ." (p. 450). Many philosophies can be summed up crudely (no doubt, not really accurately) by slogans in similar form: "We do not condemn certain acts because they are immoral; they are immoral because we condemn them." "We do not accept the law of contradiction because it is a necessary truth; it is a necessary truth because we accept it (by convention)." "Fire and heat are not constantly conjoined because fire causes heat; fire causes heat because they are constantly conjoined." (Hume) "We do not all say 12 + 7 = 19 and the like because we all grasp the concept of addition; we say we all grasp the concept of addition because we all say 12 + 7 = 19 and the like" (Wittgenstein).

The device of inversion of a conditional in the text achieves the effect of reversing priorities in a way congenial to such slogans. Speaking for myself, I am suspicious of philosophical positions of the types illustrated by the slogans, whether or not they are so crudely put.

59. Can we imagine forms of life other than our own, that is, can we imagine creatures who follow rules in bizarre quus-like ways? It seems to me that there may be a certain tension in Wittgenstein's philosophy here. On the one hand, it would seem that Wittgenstein's paradox argues that there is no *a priori* reason why a creature could not follow a quus-like rule, and thus in this sense we ought to regard such creatures as conceivable. On the other hand, it is supposed to be part of our very form of life that we find it natural and, indeed, inevitable that we follow the rule for addition in the particular way that we do. (See *PI*, §231: " "But surely you can see . . .?" That is just the characteristic expression of someone who is under the compulsion of a rule.") But then it seems that we should be unable to understand 'from the inside' (cf. the notion of '*Verstehen*' in various German writers) how any creature could follow a quus-like rule. We could describe such behavior extensionally and behavioristically, but we would be unable to find it intelligible how the creature finds it

natural to behave in this way. This consequence does, indeed, seem to go with Wittgenstein's conception of the matter.

Of course we can define the quus function, introduce a symbol for it, and follow the appropriate rule for computing its values. I have done so in this very essay. What it seems may be unintelligible to us is how an intelligent creature could get the very training we have for the addition function, and yet grasp the appropriate function in a quus-like way. If such a possibility were really completely intelligible to us, would we find it so inevitable to apply the plus function as we do? Yet this inevitability is an essential part of Wittgenstein's own solution to his problem.

The point is even stronger with respect to a term like 'green'. Can we grasp how someone could be presented with a number of green objects, and be told to apply the term 'green' just to 'things like these', and yet apply the term learnt as if it meant 'grue'? It would seem that if we find our own continuation to be inevitable, in some sense we cannot.

60. One detailed attempt to enter into such issues is Rogers Albritton, "On Wittgenstein's Use of the Term 'Criterion'," in George Pitcher (ed.), *Wittgenstein: The Philosophical Investigations* (Macmillan, 1966, pp. 231–50), reprinted with a new postscript from *The Journal of Philosophy*, vol. 56 (1959), pp. 845–57.

61. Following recent (perhaps not wholly attractive) philosophical usage, I call a first person assertion that the speaker has a certain sensation (e.g. "I am in pain") an 'avowal'.

62. The criterion by which others judge whether a person is obeying a rule in a given instance cannot simply be his sincere inclination to say that he is, otherwise there would be no distinction between his thinking he is obeying the rule and his really obeying it (*PI*, §202), and whatever he thinks is right will be right (§258). However, *after* the community judges (based on the original criteria) that he has mastered the appropriate rule, the community may (for certain rules) take the subject's sincere claim to follow it in this instance as in itself a new criterion for the correctness of his claim, without applying the original criteria. According to Wittgenstein, we do this in the case of 'I am in pain.' In the case of 'I dreamt,' the terminology is originally taught to a subject who wakes up reporting certain experiences. We judge that he has mastered the rule for 'I dreamt' if he prefaces it to reports of experiences he says he had the night before. After we judge that he has mastered the language, we take 'I dreamt that such-and-such' as in itself a criterion for correctness. In both the cases of 'I am in pain' and 'I dreamt', the first person utterance is new behavior that replaces the behavior that constituted the old criterion.

Reports of after-images or hallucinations are similar. We judge that someone has mastered 'I see something red' if he ordinarily utters it only when something red is present. Once we judge, however, that he has mastered this bit of language, we will accept his utterance that he sees red even when we think nothing red is present. Then we will say that he is suffering from an illusion, a hallucination, an after-image, or the like.

63. One delicate point regarding sensations, and about 'criteria', ought to be noted. Wittgenstein often seems to be taken to suppose that for any type of sensation, there is an appropriate 'natural expression' of that sensation type ('pain behavior' for pain). The 'natural expression' is to be externally observable behavior 'expressing' the sensation other than, and prior to, the subject's verbal avowal that he has the sensation. If the theory of *PI*, §244 that first person sensation avowals are verbal replacements for a 'primitive natural expression' of a sensation has the generality it appears to have, it would follow that Wittgenstein holds that such a 'primitive natural expression' must always exist if the first person avowal is to be

meaningful. The impression is reinforced by other passages such as §§256–7. Further, the presentation of the private language argument in the present essay argues that for each rule I follow there must be a criterion – other than simply what I say – by which another will judge that I am following the rule correctly. Applied to sensations, this seems to mean that there must be some 'natural expression', or at any rate some external circumstances other than my mere inclination to say that this is the same sensation again, in virtue of which someone else can judge whether the sensation is present, and hence whether I have mastered the sensation term correctly. So the picture would be that to each statement of the form "I have sensation S" there must be an 'outward criterion' associated with S, other than the mere avowal itself, by which others recognize the presence or absence of S.

Not only professed followers of Wittgenstein but many who think of themselves as opponents (or, at least, not followers) of Wittgenstein, seem to think that something of this kind is true. That is to say, many philosophical programs seem to suppose that all sensation types are associated with some characteristic external phenomena (behavior, causes). In this essay I have largely suppressed my own views, which are by no means always in agreement with Wittgenstein's. However, I will permit myself to remark here that any view that supposes that, in this sense, an inner process always has 'outward criteria', seems to me probably to be *empirically* false. It seems to me that we have sensations or sensation *qualia* that we can perfectly well identify but that have no 'natural' external manifestations; an observer cannot tell in any way whether an individual has them unless that individual avows them. Perhaps a more liberal interpretation of the private language argument – which *may* be compatible with what Wittgenstein intended – would allow that a speaker might introduce some sensation terms with no 'outward criteria' for the associated sensations beyond his own sincere avowal of them. (Hence these avowals do not 'replace' any 'natural expressions' of the sensation(s), for there are none.) There will be no way anyone else will be in any position to check such a speaker, or to agree or disagree with him. (No matter what many Wittgensteinians – or Wittgenstein – would infer here, this need *not* imply that his avowals are regarded as infallible nor need it mean that there could not later come to be ways of checking on his avowals.) However, the language of the speaker, even his language of sensations, will not have the objectionable form of a 'private language', one in which anything he calls 'right' is right. The speaker can demonstrate, for many sensations that do have 'public criteria', that he has mastered the appropriate terminology for identifying these sensations. If we agree with his responses in enough cases of various sensations, we say of him that he has mastered 'sensation language'. All this, so far, is subject to external correction. But it is a primitive part of our language game of sensations that, if an individual has satisfied criteria for a mastery of sensation language in general, we then respect his claim to have identified a new type of sensation even if the sensation is correlated with nothing publicly observable. The the only 'public criterion' for such an avowal will be the sincere avowal itself.

How does the view sketched here liberalize the private language argument as developed in the text? In the text we argued that *for each particular rule*, if conditionals of the form "If Jones follows the rule, in this instance he will . . ." are to have any point, they must be contraposed. If the community finds that in this instance Jones is not doing . . . , he is not following the rule. Only in this 'inverted' way does the notion of my behavior as 'guided' by the rule make sense. Thus for each rule there must be an 'external check' on whether I am following it in a given instance. Perhaps *PI*, §202 should be taken to assert this. But this means the community must have a way of telling ('criterion') whether it is being followed in a given instance, which it uses to judge the speaker's mastery of the rule. This criterion cannot be simply the speaker's own sincere inclination to follow the rule a certain way – otherwise, the conditional has no content. This condition seems to be satisfied even in those cases where, *after* the community is satisfied that the speaker has mastered the language, it lets the speaker's sincere utterance be a (or *the*) criterion for their correctness. (See note 62.) In contrast, the liberal version allows that once a speaker, judged by criteria for mastery of various rules, is accepted into the community, there should be some rules where there is no way for others to check his mastery, but where that mastery is simply presumed on the basis of his membership in the community. This is simply a primitive feature of the language game. Why should Wittgenstein not allow language games like this?

I regret that I have discussed this matter so briefly in a note. I had thought at one time to expound the 'liberal' view sketched here as the 'official' Wittgensteinian doctrine, which would have facilitated an exposition at greater length in the text. Certainly it is the one Wittgenstein should adopt in accordance with the slogan "Don't think, look!", and it really is compatible with his attack on private language. On writing the final version of this essay, however, I came to worry that passages such as *PI*, §244 and §§256–7 are highly misleading unless Wittgenstein holds something stronger.

64. See the well-known exchange between A. J. Ayer and Rush Rhees under the title "Can there be a Private Language?", *Proceedings of the Aristotelian Society*, Supp. vol. 28 (1954), pp. 63–94, reprinted in George Pitcher (ed.), *Wittgenstein: The Philosophical Investigations* (Macmillan, 1966, pp. 251–85). Both participants in the exchange assume that the 'private language argument' excludes Crusoe from language. Ayer takes this alleged fact to be fatal to Wittgenstein's argument, while Rhees takes it to be fatal to Crusoe's language. Others, pointing out that a 'private language' is one that others *cannot* understand (see the preceding paragraph in the text), see no reason to think that the 'private language argument' has anything to do with Crusoe (as long as we could understand his language). My own view of the matter, as explained very briefly in the text, differs somewhat from all these opinions.

65. If Wittgenstein would have any problem with Crusoe, perhaps the problem would be whether we have any 'right' to take him into our community in this way, and attribute our rules to him. See Wittgenstein's discussion of a somewhat similar question in §§199–200, and his conclusion, "Should we still be inclined to say they were playing a game? What right would one have to say so?"

66. Although, in the passage in question, Wittgenstein is speaking of a particular language game of bringing something else and bringing the same, it is clear in context that it is meant to illustrate his general problem about rules. The entire passage is worth reading for the present issue.

67. I feel that some uneasiness may remain here. Considerations of time and space, as well as the fact that I might have to abandon the role of advocate in favor of that of critic, have prevented me from carrying out a more extensive discussion of this point.

68. I might mention that, in addition to the Humean analogy emphasized in this essay, it has struck me that there is perhaps a certain analogy between Wittgenstein's private language argument and Ludwig von Mises's celebrated argument concerning economic calculation under socialism. (See, e.g., his *Human Action*, 2nd edition (Yale University Press, New Haven, 1963, xix + 907 pp.), Chapter 26, pp. 698–715, for one statement.) According to Mises, a rational economic calculator (say, the manager of an industrial plant) who wishes to choose the most efficient means to achieve given ends must compare alternative courses of action for cost effectiveness. To do this, he needs an array of prices (e.g. of raw materials, or

machinery) set by *others*. If *one* agency set *all* prices, it could have no rational basis to choose between alternative courses of action. (Whatever seemed to it to be right would be right, so one cannot talk about right.) I do not know whether the fact bodes at all ill for the private language argument, but my impression is that although it is usually acknowledged that Mises's argument points to a real practical difficulty for centrally planned economies, it is now almost universally rejected as a theoretical proposition.

Index